THE MAMMOTH BOOK OF
the edge

D1471907

THE MAMMOTH BOOK OF
the edge

Edited by Jon E. Lewis

ROBINSON
London

Constable & Robinson Ltd
3 The Lanchesters
162 Fulham Palace Road
London W6 9ER
www.constablerobinson.com

First published in the UK by Robinson,
an imprint of Constable & Robinson Ltd 2001

A copy of the British Library Cataloguing in Publication Data is
available from the British Library.

ISBN 1-84119-264-3

Printed and bound in the EU

10 9 8 7 6 5 4 3

"Well, we knocked the bastard off"
Edmund Hillary, 1953

"Have we vanquished an enemy? None but ourselves"
George Mallory

Contents

Introduction   ix

Glossary   xi

LADDER DOWN THE SKY   1
Robert Bates

TRIUMPH AND TRAGEDY ON THE
MATTERHORN   16
Edward Whymper

THE STORM   27
Herbert Tichy

THE DEATH ZONE   35
Walter Bonatti

MIRROR, MIRROR   52
Ed Drummond

KING OF THE EQUATOR   67
Sebastian Snow

THIN AIR   104
Greg Child

THE DEVIL'S THUMB   116
Jon Krakauer

THE ASCENT OF NANDA DEVI   127
H.W. Tilman

THE LONG GRIND   158
Sir Edmund Hillary

ANNAPURNA, MON AMOUR   170
Maurice Herzog

AURORA   214
Jonathan Waterman

THE CLIMB   230
René Desmaison

ABOVE AND BEYOND   279
Reinhold Messner

THE LONELIEST PLACE ON EARTH   286
Hermann Buhl

THE GODS GIVETH, THE GODS TAKETH
AWAY   295
Kurt Diemberger

THE HARD WAY   303
Doug Scott and Dougal Haston

ATTACK ON KANGCHENJUNGA   323
F.S. Smythe

THE RIDGE   346
Tom Hornbein

THE UPPER TOWER   366
Peter Boardman

THE WHITE SPIDER   389
Heinrich Harrer

MISCHABEL   441
Geoffrey Winthrop Young

AVALANCHE   458
George Leigh Mallory

THE VOID   467
Kees Egeler

ACTS OF FOLLY   476
Christian Klucker

Afterword   488

THE PLEASURES AND PENALTIES OF
MOUNTAINEERING
A.F. Mummery

Acknowledgments and Sources   495

Introduction

There is, of course, nothing new about climbing mountains. Humankind has probably scrambled up slopes and along ridges since they took to two legs way back in the African dawn. Doubtless these early ventures were prompted by needs of warfare, of hunting, of exploration and colonisation, but it is tempting to think that some ancestral *homo sapiens sapiens* reached the top simply because the mountain 'was there'.

As an organised sport, however, mountaineering is an entirely modern phenomenon and owes much to de Saussure's reward, offered in 1760, to the first person to conquer Mont Blanc. This was not achieved until 1786, when Balmat and Paccard reached the top, followed by de Saussure himself a year later. Within a century, Mont Blanc and the Alps were crawling with advocates of the new sport of mountaineering, the Alpine Club had been formed, and Edward Whymper had become the pursuit's first bonafide star, a celestial ranking he ensured by his 1865 ascent of the Matterhorn. And like many a climber after him, Whymper was no mean hand with a pen as well as a piton. Mountaineering literature may not have begun with Whymper but his *Scrambles amongst the Alps*, 1871, defined and established the form like little else.

It was perhaps inevitable that climbers, having scaled the major peaks of the Alps, should turn their eyes ever higher, to the Andes, the Caucasus and most of all to the Himalayas, where taunted the giants, Kanchenjunga, Nanga Parbat, Annapurna, K2 and greatest of all, Everest (8848m/ 29,028 feet). The first serious attempt on Everest came in

1922 but it was the tragedy of Mallory and Irvine, who disappeared almost within grasp of the top, in 1934 that elevated that lofty peak into legend. Everest was finally summited in 1953 by Edmund Hillary and Tenzing Norgay. Summited but not beaten. Scores of climbers since have been thrown off Everest's white walls to their death. Nature is only subdued for the moment, never mastered. Which is part of the allure of mountaineering. If Nature wasn't dangerous, mountaineering wouldn't be exciting, neither for those that do it nor for those who like their dangers experienced vicariously from the safety of the armchair.

The world's biggest mountain may have been conquered in 1953, but mountaineering itself had far from peaked. There are always fresh challenges, new routes, even in some remote corners unclimbed summits. And new ways of doing things. Over the last half century, the fashion in mountaineering has been towards 'alpine style' lightly equipped fast assaults, exemplified by Reinhold Messner's solo, oxygenless assault on Everest in 1980. This singular achievement required athleticism of the highest order; there is little doubt that the late 20th century, early 21st century climber is pushing harder against the limits of the body than his or her predecessors. There is equally little doubt that mountaineering today takes what it has always taken: courage, the ability to endure. And the triumph of the mind.

It is a curious fact, I think, that the real beauty, drama and interest of mountaineering is not the mountains themselves, not even the physical aspect of their conquest but what goes on in the mind of the men and women who climb the far peaks.

No-one sees further, clearer, deeper than those whose life is hanging by finger tips on the edge of the abyss.

Thus the selections on the following pages, eyewitness accounts of epic exploits by some of the world's greatest climbers, make up a book of high adventure and of philosophy too. It only helps that the more epic and dangerous the recounted exploit, the better the writing, the more nerve-wracking the read, the bigger the illumination of the human soul.

What more could you want?

Glossary

A
abseil   descent of rock face by sliding down a rope
arete   sharp rock or ridge

B
bergschrund   the gap between a glacier and upper face

C
col   a pass
cornice   protuding mass of snow
couloir   open gully
crevasse   crack or gap
cwm   valley or rounded hollow in valley formed by
              glacial action

J
Jumar   friction device to aid climbers ascending
              fixed ropes

M
moraine   loose stone

N
neve   bed of frozen snow

S
serac   pinnacle of ice, usually unstable

Ladder Down the Sky

Robert Bates

Bates was a member of the 1953 American expedition to K2 (Trans-Himalaya), at 8,611 m (28,261 ft) the second highest mountain in the world. A ten day storm foiled the summit bid and when Art Gilkey developed thrombophlebitis his comrades determined to lower him down from Camp VIII on the Abruzzi Ridge. The weather not withstanding.

We all knew now that some of us might never get down the mountain alive. Each had long recognized the near impossibility of evacuating an injured man from the upper ledges of K2. We had told one another that "if somebody broke a leg, you never could get him down the mountain," but now that we were faced with Gilkey's helplessness, we realized that we *had* to get him down. We didn't know how, but we knew that we had to do it.

Schoening in particular, and also Bob Craig and Dec Molenaar, had done a lot of mountain rescue work, and the rest of us placed great confidence in their faith that somehow we could get our casualty to Base Camp. Gilkey's high morale and his confidence in us was a great boost to our spirits and we faced the job ahead with strong determination. When on the morning of August 10th Charlie Houston thrust his shoulders through the tunnel entrance of the tent where Schoening, Streather and I, shoulder rubbing shoulder, had tossed during the long night hours, we spoke almost in unison: "How is he?"

"We've got to take him down," said the doctor. "His other leg has a clot now and he can't last long *here*."

The wind was hammering the tent fabric so hard that we had to yell at one another. Drifts of fine powder snow were sifting in through a strained seam in the tent vestibule, though we had done our best to keep the shelter airtight, and we could feel the whole tent vibrate as gusts stretched the fabric to the utmost.

"What? Move in this storm?" said someone.

"We've got to," said Houston. "He'll soon be dead if we don't get him down."

Nothing needed saying after that, for we knew what this decision meant. All of us had fought mountain storms before, but we had never seen anything like the duration and violence of this furious wind and snow that was still battering us. We all knew the story of the storm on Nanga Parbat in 1934, when nine members of a German expedition had died of exhaustion while battling the wind and snow. Willy Merkl, Uli Wieland and Willi Welzenback had been famous mountaineers, but a storm had exhausted them and killed them one by one. Here on K2 we had not only the storm to fight but the steepest part of the mountain, and we were trying to bring down these precipitous slopes a crippled companion as well!

We all realized that our adventure had now become grim, for the odds against getting Art down were obvious, and our own position was getting more critical all the time. While Houston and Schoening were easing Art out of his tent into the storm, the rest of us began packing light loads to take down. We would need one tent in case of emergency, and we took the Gerry tent, our lightest one. We also might need a stove and pot, and some meat bars, chocolate, or quick-energy food that needed no cooking. Often the effects of altitude so weaken one's determination that doing nothing becomes a positive pleasure, but this was no time for lethargy, and as we moved purposefully out of the tents into the stinging blasts of snow, we knew that we had to move fast, while fingers and toes still had feeling. Little was spoken. Each of us realized that he was beginning the most dangerous day's work of his lifetime.

Gilkey seemed in no pain as we wrapped him in the smashed tent, put his feet in a rucksack, and tied nylon ropes to him in such a way that they cradled him. Four ropes, tied to this cradle, could be held by one man ahead, one man behind, and one on either side. We had already put on all our warm clothing – sweaters, wool jackets, down jackets and nylon parkas – and stripped our packs to the minimum. As we worked, the disabled man watched the preparations silently. He was an experienced mountaineer and realized what all of us were up against. But he knew also that we would never leave him, and that we would bring him down safely if it were humanly possible. Art's cap was pulled down over his face, which looked drawn and bluish-grey, but he gave a wan smile whenever someone asked, "How is it going?"

"Just fine," he would say. "Just fine." And his mouth would smile. He never showed a moment's fear or the slightest lack of confidence, but he realized of course that he had been stricken by something that was likely to be fatal, that his condition was getting worse, and that he was 9,000ft above Base Camp in a terrible monsoon storm. The nearest tent, at Camp VI, was 2,000 ft below. He knew that we could not carry him down the tricky route we had come up, and that we must go only where we could lower him. Even in perfect weather with all men in top physical condition, the task might prove impossible – yet Art Gilkey could smile, and his smile gave us strength.

While we were adjusting the tow ropes, Schoening and Molenaar strapped on their crampons and disappeared into the storm. They were to find the best route past the dangerous avalanche slope that had blocked us a few days before, and to go over to the Camp VII cache to get a climbing rope that was strung on the ice slope just above. It would be useful in the descent. After their departure Houston called Base Camp on the walkie-talkie and told Ata-Ullah our plans. "It's pretty desperate, Ata," he said grimly, "but we can't wait. We're starting down now. We'll call you at three o'clock."

Each man took his place on a rope tied to Gilkey and for a couple of hundred yards we lunged hard at the tow ropes to pull Art through the knee-deep drifts of powder snow; then gravity took over and we had to hold back just as strongly to keep our helpless 185-pound load from plunging into the abyss. The steep slope we were on disappeared below us into nothingness. Was there a cliff there, a jumping-off place? We strained our eyes peering into the storm, but we could not wait for clearing weather. Instead we had to depend on Schoening and Molenaar, who had gone ahead to scout out the way. As we descended, Craig and Bell pulled the front ropes, one on each side, and Houston directed operations from a point immediately behind Gilkey, while Streather and I anchored the rope higher up. Gradually we worked our way to a rock ridge, climbed down alongside it, and then began to lower Gilkey down a steep snow slope leading to a snow chute and an ice gully below. This route was not the one we would have taken had Gilkey been able to walk, but now we had no choice: we could go only where we could lower our companion, and we had faith that the two men ahead would find a route down. Once we were well started, return to Camp VIII would be impossible for any of us.

The wind and cold seeped insidiously through our layers of warm clothing so that by the end of the third hour none of us had feeling in his toes any longer, and grotesque icicles hung from our eyebrows, beards and moustaches. Goggles froze over and we continually raised them on our foreheads in order to see how to handle the rope. Moving the sick man was frightfully slow. We had to belay one another as well as Gilkey, and our numb fingers would not move quickly. Somehow, when we got to the steepest pitch, however, someone managed to tie two 120-foot nylon ropes together and we started to lower Gilkey down, down in the only direction the slope would permit. Houston and I, braced on the storm-swept ridge, backs to the wind, could feel the terrible gusts trying to hurl us off the rocks. We could not see where we were lowering Art, but we could hear faint shouts from Schoening and Molenaar, who were out of sight below. As we slowly paid out the coils of rope, thankful that they were of nylon and would not freeze in kinks, Bob Craig unroped from us and climbed down alongside the injured man to direct the descent. Soon he was completely obscured, too, but Streather climbed down to where he could see Craig's arm signals, yet still see us, and so we belayers had communication with Craig and Gilkey and knew whether to lower or to hold the rope. Alternatively we anchored and paid out line until we were nearly frozen, and our arms were strained when Tony Streather, whom we could barely see, turned and shouted, "Hold tight! They're being carried down in an avalanche!"

We held. Our anchorage was good and the rope stretched taut. For a moment snow flurries blotted out everything, and then we could hear a muffled shout from Streather. "They're still there!" The rope had broken loose a wind-slab avalanche of powder snow that had roared down over both men, blotting them from sight. Craig clung to the rope to Gilkey, and held on to it for his life. The pull of the hissing particles must have been terrible, but the avalanche was of unconsolidated snow. The falling powder slithered out of sight and down off the side of the mountain, where it must have kept falling long after we could hear it. When it was gone, Craig still clung to the rope, grey and very chilled. Both men were safe. The grim descent continued.

Schoening and Molenaar, who were not far from Camp VII, soon were able to reach Gilkey, but it seemed like hours to the four of us on the icy rocks of the wind-swept ridge before they shouted up that they had him strongly belayed "on the edge of a cliff," and we could climb down. Stiffly we shifted from our frozen positions, and climbed clumsily down the steep, crumbly rocks to the snow chute above the ice gully. Houston and I were on one rope, Bell and Streather on the other. All were so cold, so near exhaustion, that moving down over dangerous, snow covered ice stretched us to the limit. Through the murk of blowing snow we saw Schoening standing in front of a large, rounded rock that had become frozen on to a narrow ledge. His ice-axe was thrust deep into the snow above the rock and the rope with which he held Art Gilkey was looped tightly around the shaft of the axe. The sick man was at the edge of a 20-foot cliff, beneath which we could glimpse the ice gully dropping off steeply into the storm toward the

Godwin-Austen Glacier nearly two miles below.

Schoening looked like a man from another world. So much frost had formed on our beards that faces were unrecognizable, and we knew that we were fast reaching the breaking point. We could not continue much longer without shelter from the driving storm and food to renew our energy. Some 150 yards below us to the east was the tiny shelf, at 24,500 ft, nicked into the ice slope, where Schoening and Gilkey had spent the night of July 30th during their reconnaissance above Camp VI. We had called it Camp VII or Camp VII cache. None of us had expected anyone to spend another night there, but Bob Craig, whose struggle against the avalanche had so completely exhausted him temporarily that he could hardly tie a crampon strap, had been belayed over to this site to rest and clear some of the avalanche snow that had seeped under his parka. We yelled to him to try to enlarge the ledge. Meanwhile, with Schoening anchoring the rope, we lowered Gilkey slowly over the short rock cliff until he was resting against the forty-five degree ice slope. Streather, who was roped to Bell, climbed down to Gilkey. Schoening held Gilkey's rope firmly while Houston belayed me across a delicate pitch of steep, hard ice and then Houston climbed down to a point opposite the man suspended against the slope. The problem now was not to get Gilkey down, but to swing him across the steep ice slope to the ice shelf at Camp VII. Our plan was to get a firm anchorage and then pendulum him across, but unfortunately the ice near him was too hard for axes to be driven in and the slope was relentlessly steep.

Even during the best weather conditions the manoeuvre would have been dangerous, and our position at that moment I shall never forget. Schoening was belaying Gilkey, who hung 60 feet below him, suspended against the sharply angled ice. On the same level as Gilkey, and forty feet across from him, five of us, facing into the stinging, drifting snow, were searching for a place where we could stand and anchor the rope to Gilkey as we pulled him across the ice in the direction of Craig on the ice shelf. With our spiked crampons biting the hard ice, Streather, Houston, Molenaar and I stood close together. Bell and Streather were roped together, Houston and I were on a rope together – and Molenaar had just "tied in" to a loose rope to Gilkey. He had done this when Craig had unroped and gone over to the ice shelf to rest, and it was Molenaar's precaution that saved us all, for George Bell, who was some 60 feet above us, began to descend a delicate stretch of hard ice in order to help with Gilkey's ropes. At that moment, what we had all been dreading occurred. Something threw Bell off balance and he fell.

I never saw Bell fall, but to my horror I saw Streather being dragged off the slope and making desperate efforts to jam the pick of his axe into the ice and stop. Streather had been standing above the rope from Houston to me. In almost the same instant I saw Houston swept off, and though I turned and lunged at the hard ice with the point of my axe, a terrible jerk ripped me from my hold and threw me backward headfirst down the slope. *This is it!* I thought as I landed heavily on my pack. There was nothing I could do now. We had done our best, but our best wasn't good enough. This was the end. Since nobody was on the rope with Houston and me, there was no one else to hold us, and I knew that nothing could stop us now. On the slope below, no rock jutted on which the rope between us could catch. Only thousands of feet of empty space separated us from the glacier below. It was like falling off a slanting Empire State Building six times as high as the real one.

Thrown violently backward, with the hood of my down jacket jammed over my eyes, I had a feeling of unreality, of detachment. The future was beyond my control. All I knew was that I landed on my pack with great force, bouncing faster and faster, bumping over rocks in great thumps. The next bound I expected to take me over a cliff in a terrible drop that would finish it all, when, by a miracle, I stopped sliding.

I was on my back with my hood over my eyes and my head a yard below my feet. My arms, stretched over my head, were so completely tangled with the taut rope that I could not loosen them. I was helpless, and when I tried to move, I realized that I was balanced on the crest of some rocks and that a change of position might throw me off the

edge. The rope had apparently snagged on a projection –
though how and where I couldn't imagine – but it might not
be securely caught. Whether it was firmly held, whether
anyone else was alive, I did not know, but I didn't need to
wait. Almost immediately I heard a groan coming from
nearly on top of me. "Get me loose," I called, and immediately I felt the pressure of a leg braced against my
shoulder and the rope was pulled off my arms.

Grabbing a rock, I swung my head around. Dee Molenaar and I were clinging to a rocky outcrop at the side of a
steep ice slope, studded with rocks, about 150 to 200 ft
below the place where we had been working on the ropes to
Gilkey. Blood from Dee's nose trickled across his moustache and beard, and he looked badly shaken. My rope was
tight to someone or something above, and I heard a distant
yell, "Get your weight off that rope!" Fifty feet higher,
through a mist of blowing snow, I could see Tony Streather
staggering to his feet, a tangle of ropes still tight about his
waist. Below me I heard a cry, "My hands are freezing!"
and, looking down, to my amazement, I saw George Bell,
who seconds before had been sixty feet above me. Now
about sixty feet *below*, he was climbing up over the edge of
nothingness. He wore neither pack nor glasses and was
staggering up over the steep rocks, obviously dazed, with
his hands held out grotesquely in front of him. His mittens
had been ripped off in the fall, and already the colour of his
hands had turned an ugly fish-belly white. If his hands were
badly frozen, of course, we might never be able to get him
down off the mountain.

Turning to Molenaar, I thrust my pack into his arms.
Most of the lashing had ripped loose and the walkie-talkie
radio, which had been on rope, was gone; my sleeping bag
was half off, held by a single twist of line. Without sleeping
bags we were unlikely to survive the night, no matter how
we tried! Since Molenaar wore no pack, I imagined that his
sleeping bag also had been torn off in the fall. Whether or
not the tent someone had been carrying had survived the
fall, I didn't know. "For God's sake, hold this," I yelled
above the wind, placing my load in Molenaar's arms. (For
all I knew, mine was the only sleeping bag to survive the fall

and we must not lose it now.) The loose pack was awkward to hold securely while we were standing on such steep rock, but Molenaar grasped it and I unroped and started to climb shakily down to meet Bell. As I climbed down, I wondered about the ropes that had saved us. They were snagged to something up above, but the driving snow kept us from seeing what was holding them. Luckily I had a spare pair of dry, loosely woven Indian mitts in the pouch pocket of my parka, and when I reached Bell, whose face was grey and haggard, I helped him to put them on. Already his fingers were so stiff with cold that he couldn't move them, but balancing on projections of rock on the steep slope, we struggled to save his hands and finally forced the big white mittens past his stiff thumbs and down over his wrists.

Bell's fall had ended with him suspended over the edge of a ledge, below which the slope dropped away precipitously for thousands of feet. The weight of his pack pulled his head down, and he had lost it while trying to get right side up and back over the ledge. While Bell crouched down, working desperately to warm his hands under his parka, I left him, for Molenaar and I had seen a crumpled figure lying below a 30-foot cliff on a narrow shelf that seemed projecting over utter blankness below. It was Houston. Somehow a rope to him was snagged high above us, too. Climbing unsteadily but cautiously, for I was not roped and felt shaken by the fall, I worked my way down the steep rocks and across to the ledge. Houston was unconscious, but his eyes opened as I touched his shoulder. When he staggered to his feet, I felt relief it is impossible to describe.

"Where are we?" he asked. "What are we doing here?"

He was obviously hurt. His eyes did not focus and he appeared to be suffering from a concussion. Again and again I tried to persuade him to climb up the cliff, while Molenaar anchored the rope still attached to him from above. He didn't understand. "Where are we?" he kept saying, for my replies did not convey any meaning to him in his confused state.

The wind and blowing snow were searing our faces. We were all near exhaustion and in danger of crippling frostbite. If we were to survive, we had to get shelter at once, or we would be so numbed by exposure that we could not protect ourselves. What had happened in the Nanga Parbat storm which had taken so many men was a grim reminder. All of us working together did not now have strength enough to pull or carry Houston up the steep rock and snow to the ice ledge, 150 ft above, which we had called Camp VII.

"Charlie," I said with the greatest intensity, remembering the names of his wife and daughter, and looking directly into his eyes, "if you ever want to see Dorcas and Penny again, climb up there *right now*!"

Somehow this demand penetrated to his brain, for with a frightened look and without a word, he turned and, belayed by Molenaar, fairly swarmed up the snowy rocks of the cliff. Instinct and years of climbing helped him now in his confused condition, for he climbed brilliantly up to Molenaar. I followed more slowly because, being fully conscious, I had a good deal of respect for this steep rock wall, and with great care I pulled myself up over the snow covered slabs. When I reached Molenaar, he was looking puzzled and very unhappy as he tried to answer Houston's repeated question, "What are we doing here?"

When I reached Molenaar, I still did not know what had caused the near disaster or how all five of us who fell had been saved. Up above, through the murk of blinding snow, I caught glimpses of Art Gilkey, anchored where he had been before the fall, but now Bob Craig was near him. Tony Streather, in a direct line above me, seemed to be untangling himself from a confused snarl of nylon climbing ropes, one of which led down to me.

Much later I learned the sequence of events that had put us in this position and marvelled even more at our escape. When Bell fell, he pulled off Streather, who was hurled into the rope between Houston and me and became entangled with it. We were in turn knocked off by the impact, and all three of us – Streather, Houston and I – began tumbling in a blind, uncontrolled whirl toward the glacier far below. Nothing we could do could stop us now. But our time had not come. For Molenaar was standing below us on the slope, farther away from the sick man, and he had just tied one of the loose ropes from Art Gilkey about his waist. That circumstance saved us, for our wild fall sent us all into and across the rope from Gilkey to Molenaar, and somehow Streather fouled on to this rope too. But our impact had thrown Molenaar head-first down the slope, and we all bounded on unchecked until stopped by the tightening of the rope from Gilkey to Molenaar – a rope in which Streather was now completely tangled. Gilkey was not pulled loose, for he was anchored by Schoening, who stood on a rock ledge 60 feet above him, and the whole strain of the five falling men, plus Gilkey, was transmitted to Schoening, the youngest member of the party. Fortunately for us all, Schoening is an expert belayer, and his skill and quick thinking saved our lives. Later he told us how he did it.

By the time I returned to Molenaar and Houston, it was clear that through some miracle every climber was still able to move under his own power, but our exposure to the wind-driven snow was chilling us dangerously; we had to move fast to take shelter before we became too numb to set up a tent or became so crippled by frost-bite that we would never be able to continue the descent. Since Molenaar's leg hurt and he didn't feel like moving much, I took Charlie Houston's rope and began climbing slowly up toward the ice ledge at Camp VII. I couldn't hurry to save my life. Houston was obviously confused, but by instinct he climbed well and did what was asked. I hadn't climbed far when Tony Streather threw me a rope-end, and then Bob Craig returned from anchoring Art Gilkey and he and Streather took over the task of escorting Houston to the ledge. Craig had not seen the fall, but had looked up suddenly and been horrified to see the slope bare except for Schoening and Gilkey and a solitary ice-axe with its pick end jabbed into the ice. At that moment a cloud of snow had blown across the ice, blotting out everything. When it cleared, Schoening, whose tight grip on the rope was freezing his hands, called to Craig to help him to anchor Gilkey. The sick man had not fallen, and he lay suspended against the ice as he had been at the time of the accident. He was probably the warmest of us all, but we could not continue to move him until the injured were cared for and we had more manpower to help get him across the slope.

When Craig reached him, Art handed over his ice-axe, which he had retained for use in the descent. To make a secure anchorage was not easy, and Craig, still exhausted from his struggle against the avalanche, was not secured by anyone while he did it, but he skilfully found firm snow and drove in Art's ice-axe right up to the head. He told the sick man that we would return for him as soon as we had a tent up. Gilkey understood. Not until then, when Craig had an ice-axe firmly embedded, could Pete Schoening release his grip – which had held six men! – and begin to warm his freezing hands. Craig had not been involved in the accident, but all the rest of us owed our lives to Schoening's skill, courage and technique.

Fortunately the tent had not been in one of the lost packs, but as I started to unroll it, the wind threatened to sweep it off the mountain. Craig and I were trying to wrestle the corners of the tent into position when Streather, who had now anchored Gilkey with a second ice-axe, joined us to help pin the flapping edges under loose rocks till we could get anchorage for the guy ropes. The slope was so steep that the outer third of the tent was off the ledge and over-hanging, so that it was impossible to keep the wind from sucking under the tent and trying to tear it away.

We were fortunate that this was our smallest two-man tent, for it held the ledge better than a wider one. Actually, in Exeter before the expedition, we had thought it too small for two men and had almost failed to bring it. Pitching the tent was frustrating, for each time we would secure one corner, another corner would shudder loose. Finally we tied the front guy rope to a rock piton and lashed the inside corners as well as we could to projecting rocks. When Bob Craig later pounded in a Bernays ice-piton, we felt some-what safer, though the nylon shroud line attached to it didn't look too strong and the outer section of the tent bulged out over the slope. If someone inside forgot how precariously the tent was poised and leaned against the outer wall, we knew that the fabric would probably tear or the whole tent pull loose from the little ledge, and with everyone in it roll down the mountain into space.

The moment the tent was up, we moved Bell and Houston inside, where they would be under shelter and their weight would be useful in anchoring the tent. Molenaar at this point joined them to help take care of Houston, for Dee by now had lashed my loose pack together and carried it to the ledge. His left thigh hurt and he had a cracked rib.

While these men were trying to warm themselves in the tent, the rest of us began to hack out another platform in the ice for Schoening's bivouac tent, which had previously been cached on the ledge as a safeguard for Streather and me on the day when we climbed from Camp VI to Camp VIII. This tent was meant for one person or in any emergency two, but if we could get it up, we meant to use it for three men to huddle inside.

At this moment Peter Schoening climbed down to us and declared laconically, "My hands are freezing." He too crawled into the tent to try to save his hands. All of us were still too busy to find out how Schoening had held us, for it seemed as if we would never get a platform flat enough or wide enough to pitch the bivouac tent. All our strength and energy went into chipping out an ice platform, for we had to get shelter from the bitter blast for everyone; but when we did get an uneven floor carved out, the wind whipped the fabric violently. It was like working in the slipstream behind an airplane as it taxied across the snow, spraying stinging particles behind. Finally Pete crawled out to help us insert the poles and we fastened the tent insecurely to rócks and pitons near the shelf of ice. It, too, overhung in an alarming manner.

The moment the bivouac tent was up, three of us prepared to go back for Art Gilkey. He was only 150 ft away, but a low rib of rock hid from sight the ice gully where we had left him suspended from the two widely separated ice-axes, each firmly thrust into the snow. Gilkey had called to us a couple of times while we were desperately hacking at the slope to make a platform for the bivouac tents, but the severity of the storm and the position of the gully made it impossible to distinguish words. Gilkey sounded as if he were shouting encouragement, but the wind blurred his words, as it must have muffled our answering shouts to him. He knew that we were making a shelter and would come for him as soon as we could.

About ten minutes after Gilkey's last shout, Streather, Craig and I roped up and began to cross the slope to reach the injured man and move him somehow to the ice ledge where we now had two small tents. We knew that moving him even this short distance would take every bit of strength we had left, and we roped together carefully and braced ourselves for the effort.

Schoening would have come with us, but as he emerged from the tent, he began a fit of coughing so long and painful that it doubled him up and made us urge him to crawl back into the tent. Pete had gulped in deep draughts of frigid air while climbing up to collect the fixed rope above Camp VII earlier in the day, and apparently the cold had somehow temporarily affected his lungs. He coughed until he seemed exhausted. At the moment we were particularly dismayed by Schoening's near collapse, because he had always been strong and we were counting heavily on him to help in moving Gilkey and in getting the party down the mountain. We didn't know at the moment what his trouble was or how serious it might be, and in great distress we started out into the wind to traverse the slope to Art Gilkey. Streather and I had had our snow glasses off most of the day, because snow had frozen over the lenses, turning them almost to blinders. Apparently we had developed a touch of snow blindness, because we now seemed to be seeing everything through a very light mist. This mist was hard to distinguish from blowing snow, and we seemed to be moving in a dream. Fortunately, the wind had dropped as we reached the rock rib and looked into the gully where Art had been left suspended. What we saw there I shall never forget. The whole slope was bare of life. Art Gilkey had gone!

Our sick comrade, who had called to us a few minutes before, had disappeared. Even the two ice-axes used to anchor him safely had been torn loose. The white, wind-swept ice against which he had been resting showed no sign that anyone had ever been there. It was as if the hand of God had swept him away.

The shock stunned us. Blowing snow stung our faces as
we silently stared and stared, but the slope remained empty.
Something about it had changed, however, for there
seemed to be a groove on the lower part of the slope that
had not been there before. A snow or ice avalanche must
have swept the sick man away scant minutes before we came
to get him. As Craig and I belayed Streather out on to the
centre of the gully, he looked down past his cramponed feet
to where the slope disappeared into the storm below. We
called and shouted, but all of us knew that there would be
no answer. Nobody could slide off that slope out of sight
and remain alive. Dazed and incredulous, we turned and
plodded back to the tents.

Triumph and Tragedy
on the Matterhorn

Edward Whymper

*A London wood-engraver, Whymper first went to the
Alps as an illustrator for the publisher W. Longman.
Once there, however, he determined to become a climber
(he had no previous climbing experience) and ambitiously
concentrated on untrodden Alpine peaks. The most pres-
tigious of these was the Matterhorn at 4,477 m (14,782
ft) and from 1861 onwards Whymper made no less than
seven attempts on the mountain until it finally succumbed
to him in 1865 from the Swiss side.*

*Accompanying Whymper was Lord Francis Douglas
and the guide Young Peter Taugwalder. Through chance
meetings, the party had grown to include the guides Old
Peter Taugwalder and Michel-Auguste Croz, together
with the mountaineer Charles Hudson and his inexperienced companion Hadow. Whymper's account of the climb,
and its tragic denouement, begins with the party at 3,352 m
(11,000 ft), preparing to make their summit bid.*

We assembled together outside the tent before dawn on
the morning of July 14th, and started directly it was
light enough to move. Young Peter came on with us as a
guide, and his brother returned to Zermatt.[1] We followed
the route which had been taken on the previous day, and in

1 It was originally intended to leave both the young men behind. We found it
difficult to divide the food, and so the new arrangement was made.

a few minutes turned the rib which had intercepted the view of the eastern face from our tent platform. The whole of this great slope was now revealed, rising for 3,000 ft like a huge natural staircase. Some parts were more, and others were less, easy; but we were not once brought to a halt by any serious impediment, for when an obstruction was met in front it could always be turned to the right or to the left. For the greater part of the way there was, indeed, no occasion for the rope, and sometimes Hudson led, sometimes myself. At 6.20 we had attained a height of 12,800 ft, and halted for half an hour; we then continued the ascent without a break until 9.55, when we stopped for fifty minutes, at a height of 14,000 ft. Twice we struck the NE ridge, and followed it for some little distance – to no advantage, for it was usually more rotten and steep, and always more difficult, than the face.[2] Still, we kept near to it, lest stones perchance might fall.[3]

We had now arrived at the foot of that part which, from the Riffelberg or from Zermatt, seems perpendicular or overhanging, and could no longer continue upon the east-

2 There is very little to choose between in the arêtes leading from the summit towards the Hörnli (NE ridge) and towards the Col du Lion (SW ridge). Both are jagged, serrated ridges, which any experienced climber would willingly avoid if he could find another route. On the northern (Zermatt) side the eastern face affords another route, or any number of routes, since there is hardly a part of it which cannot be traversed! On the southern (Breil) side the ridge alone, generally speaking, can be followed; and when it becomes impracticable, and the climber is forced to bear down to the right or to the left, the work is of the most difficult character.

3 Very few stones fell during the two days I was on the mountain, and none came near us. Others who have followed the same route have not been so fortunate; they may not, perhaps, have taken the same precautions. It is a noteworthy fact that the lateral moraine of the left bank of the Furggengletscher is scarcely larger than that of the right bank, although the former receives all the debris that falls from the 4,000 ft of cliffs which form the eastern side of the Matterhorn, whilst the latter is fed by perfectly insignificant slopes. Neither of these moraines is large. This is strong evidence that stones do *not* fall to any great extent from the eastern face. The inward dip of the beds retains the detritus in place. Hence the eastern face appears, when one is upon it, to be undergoing more rapid disintegration than the other sides: in reality, the mantle of ruin spares the mountain from further waste. Upon the southern side, rocks fall as they are rent off; "each day's work is cleared away" every day; and hence the faces and ridges are left naked, and are exposed to fresh attacks.

ern side. For a little distance we ascended by snow upon the
arête – that is, the ridge – descending towards Zermatt, and
then, by common consent, turned over to the right, or to the
northern side. Before doing so, we made a change in the
order of ascent. Croz went first, I followed, Hudson came
third; Hadow and old Peter were last. "Now," said Croz, as
he led off, "now for something altogether different." The
work became difficult, and required caution. In some places
there was little to hold, and it was desirable that those
should be in front who were least likely to slip. The general
slope of the mountain at this part was *less* than forty
degrees, and snow had accumulated in, and had filled
up, the interstices of the rock-face, leaving only occasional
fragments projecting here and there. These were at times
covered with a thin film of ice, produced from the melting
and refreezing of the snow. It was the counterpart, on a
small scale, of the upper 700 ft of the Pointe des Ecrins –
only there was this material difference; the face of the
Ecrins was about, or exceeded, an angle of fifty degrees,
and the Matterhorn face was less than forty degrees.[4] It was
a place over which any fair mountaineer might pass in
safety, and Mr Hudson ascended this part, and, as far as
I know, the entire mountain, without having the slightest
assistance rendered to him upon any occasion. Sometimes,
after I had taken a hand from Croz, or received a pull, I
turned to offer the same to Hudson; but he invariably
declined, saying it was not necessary. Mr Hadow, however,
was not accustomed to this kind of work, and required
continual assistance. It is only fair to say that the difficulty
which he found at this part arose simply and entirely from
want of experience.

This solitary difficult part was of no great extent.[5] We
bore away over it at first, nearly horizontally, for a distance
of about 400 ft; then ascended directly towards the summit
for about 60 ft; and then doubled back to the ridge which
descends towards Zermatt. A long stride round a rather
awkward corner brought us to snow once more. The last

4 This part was less steeply inclined than the whole of the eastern face.
5 I have no memorandum of the time that it occupied. It must have taken about
   an hour and a half.

doubt vanished! The Matterhorn was ours! Nothing but 200 ft of easy snow remained to be surmounted!

You must now carry your thoughts back to the seven Italians who started from Breil on the 11th of July. Four days had passed since their departure, and we were tormented with anxiety lest they should arrive on the top before us. All the way up we had talked of them, and many false alarms of "men on the summit" had been raised. The higher we rose, the more intense became the excitement. What if we should be beaten at the last moment? The slope eased off, at length we could be detached, and Croz and I, dashing away, ran a neck-and-neck race, which ended in a dead heat. At 1.40 p.m. the world was at our feet, and the Matterhorn was conquered. Hurrah! Not a footstep could be seen.

It was not yet certain that we had not been beaten. The summit of the Matterhorn was formed of a rudely level ridge, about 350 ft long,[6] and the Italians might have been at its farther extremity. I hastened to the southern end, scanning the snow right and left eagerly. Hurrah! again; it was untrodden. "Where were the men?" I peered over the cliff, half doubting, half expectant. I saw them immediately – mere dots on the ridge, at an immense distance below. Up went my arms and my hat. "Croz! Croz! come here!" "Where are they, Monsieur?" "There, don't you see them, down there?" "Ah! the *coquins*, they are low down." "Croz, we must make those fellows hear us." We yelled until we were hoarse. The Italians seemed to regard us – we could not be certain. "Croz, we *must* make them hear us; they *shall* hear us!" I seized a block of rock and hurled it down, and called upon my companion, in the name of friendship, to do the same. We drove our sticks in, and prised away the crags, and soon a torrent of stones poured down the cliffs.

6 The highest points are towards the two ends. In 1865 the northern end was slightly higher than the southern one. In bygone years Carrel and I often suggested to each other that we might one day arrive upon the top, and find ourselves cut off from the very highest point by a notch in the summit-ridge which is seen from the Theodule and from Breil. This notch is very conspicuous from below, but when we were upon the summit it was hardly noticed, and it could be passed without the least difficulty.

There was no mistake about it this time. The Italians turned and fled.[7]

Still, I would that the leader of that party could have stood with us at that moment, for our victorious shouts conveyed to him the disappointment of the ambition of a lifetime. He was *the* man, of all those who attempted the ascent of the Matterhorn, who most deserved to be the first upon its summit. He was the first to doubt its inaccessibility, and he was the only man who persisted in believing that its ascent would be accomplished. It was the aim of his life to make the ascent from the side of Italy, for the honour of his native valley. For a time he had the game in his hands: he played it as he thought best; but he made a false move, and he lost it. Times have changed with Carrel. His supremacy is questioned in the Val Tournanche; new men have arisen; and he is no longer recognized as *the* chasseur above all others: though so long as he remains the man that he is today, it will not be easy to find his superior.

The others had arrived, so we went back to the northern end of the ridge. Croz now took the tent-pole,[8] and planted it in the highest snow. "Yes," we said, "there is the flag-staff, but where is the flag?" "Here it is," he answered, pulling off his blouse and fixing it to the stick. It made a poor flag, and there was no wind to float it out, yet it was seen all around. They saw it at Zermatt – at the Riffel – in the Val Tournanche. At Breil, the watchers cried, "Victory is ours!" They raised "bravos" for Carrel, and "vivas" for Italy, and hastened to put themselves *en fête*. On the morrow they were undeceived. "All was changed; the explorers returned sad – cast down – disheartened – confounded – gloomy." "It is true," said the men. "We saw them ourselves – they hurled stones at us! The old traditions *are* true – there are spirits on the top of the Matterhorn!"[9]

7 I have learnt since from J.-A. Carrel that they heard our first cries. They were then upon the south-west ridge, close to the "Cravate", and *twelve hundred and fifty* feet below us; or, as the crow flies, at a distance of about one-third of a mile.

8 At our departure the men were confident that the ascent would be made, and took one of the poles out of the tent. I protested that it was tempting Providence; they took the pole, nevertheless.

9 Signor Giordano was naturally disappointed at the result, and wished the men to start again. *They all refused to do so, with the exception of Jean-Antoine.* Upon

We returned to the southern end of the ridge to build a cairn, and then paid homage to the view.[10] The day was one of those superlatively calm and clear ones which usually precede bad weather. The atmosphere was perfectly still, and free from all clouds or vapours. Mountains fifty – nay a hundred – miles off looked sharp and near. All their details – ridge and crag, snow and glacier – stood out with faultless definition. Pleasant thoughts of happy days in bygone years came up unbidden, as we recognized the old, familiar forms. All were revealed – not one of the principal peaks of the Alps was hidden.[11] I see them clearly now – the great inner circles

the 16th of July he set out again with three others, and upon the 17th gained the summit by passing (at first) up the south-west ridge, and (afterwards) by turning over to the Z'Mutt, or north-western side. On the 18th he returned to Breil.

Whilst we were upon the southern end of the summit-ridge, we paid some attention to the portion of the mountain which intervened between ourselves and the Italian guides. It seemed as if there would not be the least chance for them if they should attempt to storm the final peak directly from the end of the "shoulder". In that direction cliffs fell sheer down from the summit, and we were unable to see beyond a certain distance. There remained the route about which Carrel and I had often talked, namely to ascend directly at first from the end of the "shoulder", and afterwards to swerve to the left – that is, to the Z'Mutt side – and to complete the ascent from the north-west. When we were upon the summit we laughed at this idea. The part of the mountain that I have described was not easy, although its inclination was moderate. If that slope was made only ten degrees steeper, its difficulty would be enormously increased. To double its inclination would be to make it impracticable. The slope at the southern end of the summit-ridge, falling towards the north-west, was *much* steeper than that over which we passed, and we ridiculed the idea that any person should attempt to ascend in that direction, when the northern route was so easy. Nevertheless, the summit was reached by that route by the undaunted Carrel. From knowing the final slope over which he passed, and from the account of Mr F. C. Grove – who is the only traveller by whom it has been traversed – I do not hesitate to term the ascent of Carrel and Bich in 1865 the most desperate piece of mountain-scrambling upon record. In 1869 I asked Carrel if he had ever done anything more difficult. His reply was, "Man cannot do anything much more difficult than that!"

10 The summit-ridge was much shattered, although not so extensively as the south-west and north-east ridges. The highest rock, in 1865, was a block of mica schist, and the fragment I broke off it not only possesses, in a remarkable degree, the *character* of the peak, but mimics, in an astonishing manner, the details of the form.

11 It is most unusual to see the southern half of the panorama unclouded. A hundred ascents may be made before this will be the case again.

of giants, backed by the ranges, chains and *massifs*. First came the Dent Blanche, hoary and grand; the Gabelhorn and pointed Rothhorn; and then the peerless Weisshorn: the towering Mischalbelhörner, flanked by the Allaleinhorn, Strahlhorn and Rimpfischhorn; then Monte Rosa – with its many Spitzes – the Lyskamm and the Breithorn. Behind was the Bernese Oberland governed by the Finsteraarhorn, and then the Simplon and St Gothard groups; the Disgrazia and the Orteler. Towards the south we looked down to Chivasso on the plain of Piedmont, and far beyond. The Viso – one hundred miles away – seemed close upon us; the Maritime Alps – one hundred and thirty miles distant – were free from haze. Then came my first love – the Pelvoux; the Ecrins and the Meije; the clusters of the Graians; and lastly, in the west, gorgeous in the full sunlight, rose the monarch of all – Mont Blanc. Ten thousand feet beneath us were the green fields of Zermatt, dotted with chalets, from which blue smoke rose lazily. Eight thousand feet below, on the other side, were the pastures of Breil. There were black and gloomy forests, bright and cheerful meadows; bounding waterfalls and tranquil lakes; fertile lands and savage wastes; sunny plains and frigid plateaux. There were the most rugged forms, and the most graceful outlines – bold, perpendicular cliffs, and gentle, undulating slopes; rocky mountains and snowy mountains, sombre and solemn, or glittering and white, with walls – turrets – pinnacles – pyramids – domes – cones – and spires! There was every combination that the world can give, and every contrast that the heart could desire.

We remained on the summit for one hour:

"One crowded hour of glorious life."

It passed away too quickly, and we began to prepare for the descent.

Hudson and I again consulted as to the best and safest arrangement of the party. We agreed that it would be best for Croz to go first,[12] and Hadow second; Hudson, who was

---

12 If the members of the party had been more equally efficient, Croz would have been placed *last*.

almost equal to a guide in sureness of foot, wished to be third; Lord F. Douglas was placed next, and old Peter, the strongest of the remainder, after him. I suggested to Hudson that we should attach a rope to the rocks on our arrival at the difficult bit, and hold it as we descended, as an additional protection. He approved the idea, but it was not definitely settled that it should be done. The party was being arranged in the above order whilst I was sketching the summit, and they had finished, and were waiting for me to be tied in line, when someone remembered that our names had not been left in a bottle. They requested me to write them down, and moved off while it was being done.

A few minutes afterwards I tied myself to young Peter, ran down after the others, and caught them just as they were commencing the descent of the difficult part. Great care was being taken. Only one man was moving at a time; when he was firmly planted the next advanced, and so on. They had not, however, attached the additional rope to rocks, and nothing was said about it. The suggestion was not made for my own sake, and I am not sure that it even occurred to me again. For some little distance we two followed the others, detached from them, and should have continued so had not Lord F. Douglas asked me, about 3 p.m., to tie on to old Peter, as he feared, he said, that Taugwalder would not be able to hold his ground if a slip occurred.

A few minutes later, a sharp-eyed lad ran into the Monte Rosa hotel, to Seiler, saying that he had seen an avalanche fall from the summit of the Matterhorn on to the Matterhorngletscher. The boy was reproved for telling idle stories; he was right, nevertheless, and this was what he saw.

Michel Croz had laid aside his axe, and in order to give Mr Hadow greater security, was absolutely taking hold of his legs, and putting his feet, one by one, into their proper positions.[13] As far as I know, no one was actually descending. I cannot speak with certainty, because the two leading

---

13 Not at all an unusual proceeding, even between born mountaineers. I wish to convey the impression that Croz was using all pains, rather than to indicate extreme inability on the part of Mr Hadow. The insertion of the word "absolutely" makes the passage, perhaps, rather ambiguous. I retain it now, in order to offer the above explanation.

men were partially hidden from my sight by an intervening mass of rock, but it is my belief, from the movements of their shoulders, that Croz, having done as I have said, was in the act of turning round to go down a step or two himself; at this moment Mr Hadow slipped, fell against him, and knocked him over. I heard one startled exclamation from Croz, then saw him and Mr Hadow flying downwards; in another moment Hudson was dragged from his steps, and Lord F. Douglas immediately after him.[14] All this was the work of a moment. Immediately we heard Croz's exclamation, old Peter and I planted ourselves as firmly as the rocks would permit:[15] the rope was taut between us, and the jerk came on us both as on one man. We held; but the rope broke midway between Taugwalder and Lord Francis Douglas. For a few seconds we saw our unfortunate companions sliding downwards on their backs, and spreading out their hands, endeavouring to save themselves. They passed from

14 At the moment of the accident, Croz, Hadow and Hudson were all close together. Between Hudson and Lord F. Douglas the rope was all but taut, and the same between all the others, who were *above*. Croz was standing by the side of a rock which afforded good hold, and if he had been aware, or had suspected, that anything was about to occur, he might and would have gripped it, and would have prevented any mischief. He was taken totally by surprise. Mr Hadow slipped off his feet on to his back, his feet struck Croz in the small of the back, and knocked him over, head first. Croz's axe was out of his reach, yet without it he managed to get his head uppermost before he disappeared from our sight. If it had been in his hand I have no doubt that he would have stopped himself and Mr Hadow.

Mr Hadow, at the moment of his slip, was not occupying a bad position. He could have moved either up or down, and could touch with his hand the rock of which I have spoken. Hudson was not so well placed, but he had liberty of motion. The rope was not taut from him to Hadow, and the two men fell ten or twelve feet before the jerk came upon him. Lord F. Douglas was not favourably placed, and could neither move up nor down. Old Peter was firmly planted, and stood just beneath a large rock which he hugged with both arms. I enter into these details to make it more apparent that the position occupied by the party at the moment of the accident was not by any means excessively trying. We were compelled to pass over the exact spot where the slip occurred, and we found – even with shaken nerves – that *it* was not a difficult place to pass. I have described the *slope generally* as difficult, and it is so undoubtedly to most persons; but it must be distinctly understood that Mr Hadow slipped at an easy part.

15 Or more correctly, we held on as tightly as possible. There was no time to change our position.

our sight uninjured, disappeared one by one, and fell from precipice to precipice on to the Matterhorngletscher below, a distance of nearly 4,000 ft in height. From the moment the rope broke it was impossible to help them.

So perished our comrades! For the space of half an hour we remained on the spot without moving a single step. The two men, paralyzed by terror, cried like infants, and trembled in such a manner as to threaten us with the fate of the others. Old Peter rent the air with exclamations of "Chamounix! Oh, what will Chamounix say?" He meant, Who would believe that Croz could fall? The young man did nothing but scream or sob, "We are lost! we are lost!" Fixed between the two, I could neither move up nor down. I begged young Peter to descend, but he dared not. Unless he did, we could not advance. Old Peter became alive to the danger, and swelled the cry, "We are lost! we are lost!" The father's fear was natural – he trembled for his son; the young man's fear was cowardly – he thought of self alone. At last old Peter summoned up courage, and changed his position to a rock to which he could fix the rope; the young man then descended, and we all stood together. Immediately we did so, I asked for the rope which had given way, and found, to my surprise – indeed, to my horror – that it was the weakest of the three ropes. It was not brought, and should not have been employed, for the purpose for which it was used. It was old rope, and, compared with the others, was feeble. It was intended as a reserve, in case we had to leave much rope behind, attached to rocks. I saw at once that a serious question was involved, and made him give me the end. It had broken in mid-air, and it did not appear to have sustained previous injury.

For more than two hours afterwards I thought almost every moment that the next would be my last; for the Taugwalders, utterly unnerved, were not only incapable of giving assistance, but were in such a state that a slip might have been expected from them at any moment. After a time we were able to do that which should have been done at first, and fixed ropes to firm rocks, in addition to being tied together. These ropes were cut from time to time, and

were left behind.[16] Even with this assurance the men were
sometimes afraid to proceed, and several times old Peter
turned with ashy face and faltering limbs, and said, with
terrible emphasis, "*I cannot!*"

About 6 p.m. we arrived at the snow upon the ridge
descending towards Zermatt, and all peril was over.

---

16 Those ends, I believe, are still attached to the rocks, and mark our line of
   ascent and descent. I saw one of them in 1873.

The Storm

Herbert Tichy

Tichy led the successful 1954 Austrian assault on Cho Oyu, an 8201 m (26,913 ft) peak in East Nepal. Success was preceded by near disaster, however, when Tichy was forced down the mountain by a hurricane.

It was not a comfortable evening, but you could not expect better at that altitude. No cause for worry. Once I was inside the tent I could not bring myself to creep out again and photograph Camp IV. Tomorrow, I decided, on our return from the summit. Then the two tents would be seen from above standing out like dark pearls against the white snow; the Nangpa La glacier, the grey mountain-ranges of Tibet and the evening sky would form the background.

Sleeplessness, the great problem at these heights, is a cause of bodily and nervous fatigue. If you take sleeping-pills there is the danger of falling asleep in the early morning just when you need all your energy. Lowe, the New Zealander, had that experience on Everest.

I was lucky. As I lay in my sleeping bag side by side with Pasang I felt the fatigue of the day overcoming me and had scarcely time to notice how at this altitude breathing is not automatic but a conscious effort. On many a night much lower down I had got up with a feeling of suffocation and fought for breath because I had forgotten in my sleep to breathe consciously as one does for a medical examination. I heard Pasang breathing regularly; probably he was already asleep.

I felt protected and safe in spite of the utter solitude of our bivouac and although I was perhaps sleeping at a point higher and more remote from the world than any other man alive. I had Pasang with me, and Adjiba, and Ang Nyima. I tried to explain to myself the intimacy and warmth of my feeling for them, but weariness carried my thoughts away as the current of a river floats the drift-wood away from its banks. The day was over; I fell asleep.

I did not dream that night, but waking was a nightmare and I clung to the hope that it was actually a bad dream. The sound of Pasang groaning convinced me that it was real. The side of the tent was being pressed down on my face by some invisible force, preventing me from breathing, and an uproar of rattling, whistling and screaming filled the air. It took me half a minute to realize what had occurred.

The wind had become a hurricane and had torn our tents from their moorings; the tent pegs had snapped. I put out my hand and felt for Pasang, who was groaning, in his sleep perhaps, or perhaps from a presentiment of disaster to come. Stare as I might, no chink of light was to be seen. It was still night.

There was no actual cause for anxiety. We two and our rucksacks were heavy enough to hold the tent down. We should not be blown away. I edged over to the outer side to deprive the wind of purchase, and after making a free space for my mouth fell into a doze. No, there was no cause for anxiety. Often a storm at night was followed by a clear, still day.

By the time daylight glimmered through the canvas, the wind had increased in violence. I can't say whether I had slept in the interval or lain awake, but it was now day and I had to come to some decision. I couldn't lie on in a twilight state between sleeping and waking, between life and death; that would be too easy.

The sun penetrated the yellow fabric. It seemed to promise life and warmth, in strange contrast to the icy hurricane which threatened to hurl us down the mountainside.

I nudged Pasang again.

"Wait? Go down?" he asked.

I didn't know which. I didn't even know whether it was morning or evening, whether we had passed a long day in our wretched tents, or whether the sun had just risen and we still had the day to endure.

"We'll see," I added.

We crept out from under the tent. It was not easy, for the wind kept the canvas tight down on us like a fisherman's net and hugged us. As soon as I was out I was surprised to see the sun in the east, and about two hours up. So the day was not behind us and we could not indulge in any illusion that the time for decision had passed by. If we had had the night in front of us we could have settled down to wait in resignation.

There was not a cloud in the sky. But we could not always see the sky; it was hidden by thick flurries of snow. A hurricane of a force I had never experienced scourged the snow-covered mountainside, and Helmut, who took observations from lower down with his instruments, estimated its speed at about eighty miles an hour. The temperature was thirty to thirty-five degrees below zero. The most horrible part of it was the cloudless blue sky.

I crouched down beside Pasang in the snow. We could not stand up. The wind would have thrown us down or lifted us from the ground.

The other tent was also wrecked. The huddled bodies of Ang Nyima and Adjiba were moulded by the flattened canvas. We gave them a prod. They were still alive and crept out to join us.

The four of us cowered together beside the flattened tents and stared into the vortex. We could only speak in shouts.

"Never known a storm like this," Pasang shouted. "All die."

He repeated it again and again.

I agreed with him. We should all die.

Adjiba and Ang Nyima said nothing. They sat huddled and dumb, their faces a bluish grey, marked by death – no, dead already. Their dark eyes were fixed on mine, asking no questions, hinting no reproach. They were gates to another world, at whose frontier we had now arrived.

I experienced a strange split in my ego.

Like Pasang and Adjiba and Ang Nyima, I was a poor wretch, tortured by cold and the fear of death, whose only comfort in face of the final and utter solitude was derived from the presence of my three companions. And at the same time the other part of me looked down without the least emotion, almost with irony, on the four of us. My fate was not at all terrible to this second me. "You've always played fast and loose a bit with this possibility; you can't complain if it has come true. But how can you answer to yourself for the death-stricken faces of these three Sherpas?"

This split personality persisted throughout the events that followed; one part acted instinctively and suffered in the flesh, and the other followed events without feeling or pity, merely as a critical observer, coldly making his own comments upon them.

We were still huddling together, overwhelmed by the violence of nature and incapable of coming to any decision, when suddenly the wind lifted the other tent and threatened to blow it right away. I threw myself on it without thinking and held it down, my body on the tent, my hands in the snow. I had had my mittens stripped off in creeping out of our own tent, but that did not matter very much as I had put my hands in my warm trouser pockets inside an outer windproof smock. While we sat cowering together, I never thought of my hands; they were well off compared with the rest of my shuddering body.

Now they were in contact with the snow, and in the next two or three minutes this is what happened:

The tent was rescued. The Sherpas salvaged it. But I felt a burning sensation in my hands. The pain got worse and throbbed through my whole body.

Probably their warmth melted the snow when they first touched it. The icy hurricane seized on and sucked at the moisture, a hurricane of eighty miles an hour at a temperature of thirty-five degrees below zero, and the circulation of the blood at that altitude is sluggish.

The pain got worse and worse. I chafed my hands, and beat them against my sides; it did not stop the pain. I thought of creeping into my tent, but it lay like a sail, flat on the snow. I got into a panic, as if I had been on fire – and actually the injuries caused by frost and fire are similar – and started shouting.

The Sherpas, who had been busy so far salvaging the tent, rushed up, and as soon as they realised my disaster, Pasang and Ang Nyima undid their trousers and my hands felt a little warmth between their thighs. It was the only place in our half-frozen bodies where any warmth lingered. Pasang knew that. Meanwhile, Adjiba was hunting under my tent for my mittens.

My watching, critical self showed up again. I saw it all before my eyes as a picture, Pasang and Ang Nyima with their backs pressed against the wind, and myself kneeling crucified between them, my hands outstretched and hidden within the remnants of warmth which might still be my salvation. My animal self relished these few seconds of warmth and shelter, but that other self thought: "What a subject for Kubin to paint! 'The Crucifixion' or 'Journey's End'."

I tried to think of a good title for this macabre scene, then went on inconsequently to wonder where Kubin lived now. Was he still at Linz, among those misty, sombre Danube landscapes which inspired his paintings?

Then my animal, life-loving self returned. Adjiba brought my mittens; I seized them. My hands were white and swollen. I felt they were done for, but *we* were not done for yet.

Panic returned.

"If we mean to live," I yelled, "we must go down, not sit here."

The Sherpas' grey death-masks did not come alive, but the three men acted promptly.

Values had altered. A wrap was worth more than a Rolleiflex. We snatched up any aid to warmth among the equipment and left everything else behind. The tents stayed where they were. The storm might destroy them completely or perhaps we might be able to recover them later, but now our lives were all we thought of.

I don't mean to suggest that it was my panic-stricken initiative that got us down. Our retreat was not the reward of my efforts or my fright, but the work of the three Sherpas. All the same, I feel that my will played the decisive part.

The Sherpas, owing perhaps to their religious faith or to their almost animal links with the earth, do not, as we do, regard death as the dark gateway to unknown dread. They die more simply and more harmoniously, and if I had said to Pasang, "There's no way down. We must die where we are," we should have stayed in Camp IV – for ever.

Yet it was nothing I did; it was just that un-asiatic tincture in my blood which made me shout: "We must get down unless we mean to die here."

The Sherpas took the brunt of the journey down. Their resource and energy returned as soon as the decision was made. We anchored the tents and left them where they were. It was not a retreat, but a rout.

My hands were useless. Pasang had to strap on my crampons for me, then we roped up and began the descent. I recall very little of the strenuous hours which ended in Camp III. I can only remember the violence of the storm, which drove us on over the snow, and the sight of the Sherpas throwing themselves down and creeping like cats when a sudden gust caught us. I could feel the throbbing agony in my hands and the wind cutting my face like a knife. I could see the clouds of driven snow, which showed us how vain our hopes and efforts were. It was hard going.

But I also remember the feeling of security and friend-ship. We were four on a rope, and I felt sure that all or none would get down. It was not conceivable that the strongest of us would unrope and leave the rest to their fate; it was equally inconceivable that we should abandon the weakest because he hindered the rest. Anything of the sort would have made nonsense of the life we led.

Perhaps memory idealises, but I doubt it. The rope was not just a rope to be tied and untied as desired. It was too strong a bond to be severed lightly.

As we got down the storm abated, but by now the Sherpas too had their finger-tips frost-bitten. When we reached the perpendicular step in the ice-fall we let each other down on the rope to Camp III, where we found Sepp.

He had got back his form and climbed up to Camp III, from where he had tried for several hours to come to our rescue, but he was blown again and again off the steps of the ice-fall. Once the wind carried him a hundred and seventy feet through the air and he landed in soft snow not far from a sheer drop.

He looked ghastly. His face was aged and furrowed, and ice and snow clung to his beard.

Later I asked him, when we were looking over our photographs, why he had not taken some shots of us then. He could have got some striking pictures.

"I didn't like to," he said. "You looked so frightful. Pasang was crying and talking about dying all the time."

I remember nothing of all that. I only remember how glad I was to see Sepp, and how it dawned on me for the first time that we had failed.

I showed him my hands. They were like tuberous growths by now.

"They're finished and the summit's finished."

The flight was resumed, Camp III vacated. The rope was no longer needed, we were at home on the ridge now, and at this height the storm was endurable. We had given death the slip. But the pain in my hands pulsated through my whole body. I knew my life was saved; I was sure my hands were done for.

Down to Camp II. I tottered down the ridge which we had ascended a few days before feeling so confident of success. Glorious, no doubt, to have been on such terms with death. But sad to be a cripple, I thought, as I tottered on.

Camp II. Late afternoon by now. Helmut was there. Although not yet well and although it was his job to organize the "lift", he had come up through the storm with the presentiment that we might need his help. He was not a doctor of medicine, but he was able to give me the first injection to stimulate my circulation.

Tents were not yet put up. I sat among the rocks in the wind and bared my arm. Pasang held me in his arms with motherly solicitude while Helmut gave the injection.

Flight was still our one thought. We wanted to get away from the mountain which had handled us so cruelly, down to Camp I, where we should be less exposed to the storm, but I was too weak and could go no farther. I was afraid of the long screes. I was tired and only wanted to forget.

Two tents were set up and four of us stayed there for the night, Sepp and I in one, Gyalsen and Da Nurbu in the other. All the rest went on down.

I was lying down when Pasang came to say goodbye. He was going to take my hand when he saw my hands, so he bent over me instead and kissed my cheek. I felt like a corpse to whom he was bidding farewell.

Never could I have dared to believe that we should kiss each other again two weeks later, again with tears in our eyes, tears not of pain this time but of happiness because we stood together on the summit.

But that night at Camp II I had no hope whatever. All I had was the ever-recurrent certainty that my hands were done for and the peak lost.

I was as helpless as a babe and Sepp looked after me with tender care. The same thoughts went round and round in my head like a never-resting wheel; again I asked the question mankind has always asked: Why had it to be? Why could the weather not have held up one day longer? Why had the wind to blow with that destructive fury? Where and when had I committed the crowning mistake? But no, the assault had been properly organized and there had not been any mistake. Where then was the hidden blight? Was it that arrogant self-confidence of the evening before? Or could we be so cruelly punished for no reason?

Despite the frost-bite injury to his fingers, Tichy summitted Cho Oyu just two weeks later. He was accompanied by J. Jochter and Pasang Dawa Lama.

The Death Zone

Walter Bonatti

*Walter Bonatti was an Italian alpinist, and his 1955 solo
ascent of the South-West Pillar of Petit Dru was one of
the outstanding achievements of European postwar climbing. Five years later, on the Central Pillar of Mont
Blanc, Bonatti was involved in one of its greatest
tragedies . . .*

We climbed quickly and reached the base of the last
pinnacle about noon instead of two o'clock as we had
expected. We had noticed mist trailing overhead, but it had
not worried us overmuch considering the altitude we had
now reached; we hoped to be able to reach the summit
before any brewing storm should break. However the storm
caught us just as Mazeaud and Kohlman were beginning to
climb the last pinnacle. We had only about 150 ft of overhanging monolith to climb to complete our climb on the
Pillar and to reach the ridge which led to the summit of
Mont Blanc.

We all gathered together on the few ledges there were.
The snowstorm was now raging furiously; it was thundering and the lightning flashed around us. The air was
saturated with electricity and the gusts of wind blew pow-
dered snow into our faces, blinding us. We were at a height
of nearly 15,000 ft on the Pillar, the lightning-conductor of
Mont Blanc. We three Italians were squatting on a little
ledge; the Frenchmen were in two groups. Then, without
warning, Kohlman's face was grazed by a flash of lightning.

He was blinded by the flash but Mazeaud with a leap caught hold of him and managed to support him. For some minutes Kohlman was almost paralyzed. We looked for the cora-mine and Mazeaud made him gulp some down. At last the Frenchman recovered and we were able to settle down.

At this moment, with the storm raging, we were as follows: I was on one narrow ledge, with Oggioni and Gallieni; Vielle, Mazeaud and Guillaume were on another ledge beside us while Kohlman was by himself on a third and slightly larger one farther down to give him a chance of stretching out. It was perhaps here that his psychological tragedy began, though we did not know it at the time.

The summit of Mont Blanc was not more than twelve hours' climb away from us. Beyond the summit, after we had conquered the Pillar, the Vallot hut was waiting, a sure shelter; after that, it was an easy descent to Chamonix. A break in the clouds for half a day would have been enough for us to achieve this, but in fact we never reached the summit.

It began to grow darker. The storm was more and more violent. We shut ourselves into our little tent and could judge the strength of the storm only by the intensity of the thunderclaps. Sometimes our spirits rose when we thought them to be very far off, sometimes we lost heart when we thought them close to us. The lightning flashes blinded us even through the opaque tent. We were there, alive, yet unable to do anything against the furious outpouring of the elements. Around us, secured to the same pitons that supported us in space, hung all our equipment for the climb: pitons, crampons and ice-axes; better bait for the lightning could not be imagined. We would have liked to throw them away, but how could we either ascend or descend without them? No one spoke; everyone was wrapped up in his own thoughts.

Just as we were thinking for the nth time that we were at the mercy of fate, we felt as if some force wanted to tear off our legs. We had all been grazed by the lightning. We yelled wildly. But we were alive, though now we knew that the storm could reduce us all to ashes at any time it chose. We called to one another to find out if everyone was still all right. Then there was a terrifying lull, which we knew heralded a last concentration of electricity which would inevitably break loose around us.

A few moments later a shock, similar to the one we had already experienced, but even more violent, nearly threw us off the face. Amid the commotion and shouts I could hear one voice clearly. I heard: "We must get away!" I don't know if it was Oggioni or Gallieni. The words were born of despair and mirrored our state of mind. I thought that we were lost and I believe that we all thought the same. I relived my whole life and in my mind's eye saw all those dear faces and places which I should certainly never see again. Though by now resigned to my fate, I felt sorry that during my life I had not been able to do all the things I had intended. These are sensations which last only for seconds, yet they are clear and seem incredibly long.

Miraculously, however, the storm seemed to be dying away in the distance. Now we could only hear the drumming of the frozen snow on the rubberised cloth which covered us. We remained inert and apathetic; we did not even look outside the tent, for outside it was already dark. No one spoke. We did not eat. We were indifferent to everything. The snow which was falling though it was a very serious matter for us, almost gave us a sense of relief. We had been saved from the lightning and were still alive. I had never before been on such a face in such a storm: there was no skill and no technique which could have saved us.

Our complete immobility and the long stay in the tent had stifled us. We tore away a piece of the cloth and breathed avidly. Our tent was now buried in the snow, and the warmth of our bodies had created inside it watery drops which were transformed, by the sudden changes in temperature, now into water and now into ice crystals. I did not want to look at my watch, so as not to be disappointed by the slow passage of time. We did not speak to one another. All that could be heard were moans due sometimes to the discomfort of our positions, sometimes to the cold and sometimes to the feeling of suffocation which tortured us. We knew nothing about the Frenchmen, but we could often hear similar noises from them.

The night passed and a milky radiance heralded Wednesday's dawn. Only then did we emerge from the tent and were amazed at the amount of snow which had fallen during the night. The Frenchmen beside us were quite buried in it. Kohlman, on the wider ledge, was already standing up and looked like a dark blotch against the incandescent horizon, which seemed to announce a splendid day. We were overcome by a feeling of joy; the enormous quantity of fallen snow and the terrible frost were harbingers of good weather. Soon all of us were out of the tent, ready to begin the last stretch. I took a few snaps and we dismantled the little tent. But just as we were packing it up we found ourselves – I still do not know where those mists could have come from – again enveloped in the snowstorm. The very strong wind made the fresh snow whirl around us; we could not tell if it were snowing or whether this was the work of the wind.

We once more took refuge in our tent and the Frenchmen did the same. This time we went farther down, to Kohlman's ledge, which was larger and where the three of us – Oggioni, Gallieni and myself – could be a little more comfortable. Kohlman climbed up a few feet to where we had passed the night. He took his own bivouac equipment with him, a down sleeping-bag covered with plastic cloth, which wrapped him like a mummy. We belayed ourselves to pitons and settled down to wait.

During a short break a little earlier I had noticed that the snow had fallen even at a low altitude. We could scarcely believe that after snowing so long, the storm could come back once more. The Frenchmen asked me what I intended to do. I replied that we would wait, always in the hope of being able to get to the summit, the shortest way to safety. We were not short of provisions or equipment and could stay where we were. At this time of year the bad weather could not last very much longer and the idea of so dangerous and complicated a descent in the midst of a snowstorm terrified us, since we could reach the summit in less than half a day.

Mazeaud and his companions were belayed to a piton about twenty feet above me. Kohlman was alongside them. Mazeaud, who had a certain leadership over his companions, exchanged a few words with me and proposed that we two should set out together as soon as a break in the weather made it possible. Our job would be to fix pitons and ropes up the last 250 ft of overhang, so that our five companions could come up after us. We agreed on this, but the break never came. We ate a little ham, some roast meat and jam, but we could not drink anything because the storm made it impossible to light a fire to make tea with melted snow.

It went on snowing, hour after monotonous hour. Amid the thoughts which jostled one another in my mind, I tried to remember other occasions, similar to this, when I had been trapped in the mountains by bad weather. I remembered that snowstorms had never lasted more than a day or two. So I said to myself: "One day has gone already. The snowstorm cannot last more than another twenty-four hours. It is only a question of lasting out one day longer and then we shall be able to start."

To remain in this very uncomfortable position squashed one against the other in a space which could hardly hold a single person, became more and more intolerable. We could not turn our heads, we could not lie on our sides and the constant slope made it seem that our spines would crack. In such conditions it is easy to fall prey to irritability. There were moments when we would have liked to tear off our covering, but woe to us had we done so! Oggioni, Gallieni and I talked; we talked of everything; memories, plans, hopes, friendships, happy and unhappy reminiscences, just to kill time and to keep ourselves occupied.

Oggioni said to me: "Do you remember when we said in Peru: Will the day ever come when we shall be together on the Pillar?" He said it sarcastically, since at that time we thought that everything on our home mountains would be easier. Yet now we were in conditions similar to those we had found on the Rondoy, when we had had to master that peak in the midst of a snowstorm and had been without shelter for two days and two nights. Gallieni was our vitamin man; he gave us pills, especially of vitamins C and A, to make up for our lack of food. He gave them to the Frenchmen by a primitive sort of pulley which we had made out of ropes and added some of our provisions. The Frenchmen were a little short of food.

The problem of passing water then arose. It was not possible to go out of the tent. I suggested to Gallieni that he should sacrifice his plastic cap and we each used it in turn. It was a terrifying experience; we had to make all sorts of contortions and hold fast to one another not to fall over. The whole operation took half an hour; our legs were hanging in space and our clothes hampered us.

It was now Wednesday evening. It was snowing harder than ever. I asked Gallieni, who was near the edge: "Where's the wind blowing from?" "Still from the west," he said. That meant a snowstorm. Mazeaud, full of vitality and initiative, shouted to me: "As soon as it gets better, you and I ought to go. If you think it would be better to start towards the left, then we will certainly go that way." Oggioni, who did not know French, asked me what Mazeaud had been saying and I explained. He agreed but asked: "Do you think it possible to get out by way of the summit even in this weather?" He knew that I could find the way down from the summit whatever the weather, as I had already done it several times before. I said: yes, but that we should have to stay where we were another night, since in my heart I felt almost certain that the snowstorm would end next day.

Our breath in the tent was transformed into watery vapour and we were wet through. I thought with terror about what might happen when the hard frost which always precedes good weather came and hoped I would be able to bear it. We would have to spend an hour or so warming ourselves in the sun before making the last assault. We could not sleep. Night came upon us almost unawares. We were all on edge. Gallieni began to speak of his young children. My thoughts were ten thousand feet farther down, with my loved ones, in the intimacy of my home. Oggioni talked of Portofino. He had never been there and said: "We mountaineers are really unlucky . . . with all the lovely things there are in the world, we get caught up in this sort of thing . . ." Gallieni said: "And to think that I have a cosy home in Milano Marittima and such a nice beach: you

can jump into the warm water and don't even have to take
the trouble to swim, it's so shallow . . . You can walk for
miles and miles . . ." Oggioni hid his apprehension with
jokes. To look at, he was the calmest of the lot of us. I was
sure that he, other than myself, was the only one to be fully
aware that our plight was desperate.

The night between Wednesday and Thursday passed. In
the fore-noon Mazeaud came into our tent, because the
plastic cloth over the Frenchmen's sleeping-bags had split
under the gusts of wind. We managed to arrange ourselves
after a thousand contortions and so passed the day. We tried
to keep up our spirits, telling ourselves that the next day –
Friday – would be fine, but we were not greatly convinced.
In my inmost self I was already considering which would be
the safest manner of retreating down the way we had come;
in my opinion it was now impossible to reach the summit of
the Pillar. I did not mention this to my companions so as
not to discourage them.

Mazeaud told me about the south-west pillar of the Petit
Dru which he had made the previous week. We spoke of our
pleasure at getting to know one another and in sharing this
adventure. We promised to meet again one day at Courmayeur or Chamonix and to talk over today's experiences.
Our thirst was intense and we had to quench it by eating
snow. We made pellets of snow and kept gnawing at them.
We thought longingly of a tap at home which would give us
all the water we wanted at a turn. It was paradoxical that in
the midst of so much snow we should have a burning thirst.
The frozen snow made our mouths burn and very sore.

Thursday passed and night came. During the long hours
of darkness Oggioni and I, who were farthest from the edge,
suffered particularly from lack of air. To him alone I
confided my intention of descending at all costs. He agreed,
but was terrified at the idea. Thursday night also passed.
We had to set the alarm for half-past three. When I heard it
ringing I shouted to everyone: "We must go down at all
costs. We cannot stay here any longer, otherwise it will be
too late and we will not have the strength."

When dawn began to break on the Friday morning the
storm had been ranging incessantly for more than sixty

hours. Mist and snow merged into an impenetrable curtain. We dismantled everything and left a certain amount of our equipment behind. I was without an ice-axe which one of my companions had let fall by mistake on the first day. We began the descent by double rope. We had decided that I must lead, preparing the rappels. Behind me came all the others: Mazeaud, whose task was to help anyone who needed it, then the others and finally Oggioni who, strong in his experience, would be last man and recover the ropes.

At exactly six I lowered myself into the grey and stormy void almost blindly, without knowing where I was going. I felt as if I were in a stormy sea. The snow flurries gave me a feeling of dizziness. I had to watch every detail and try to recognize every fold of the rock to find out where I was. The manoeuvre took a long time and waiting for the ropes and pitons to come down from above in order to make the next rappel took even longer. Sometimes we were all bunched together, belayed to a piton, four or five of us hanging in space. About half-way down the Pillar I was unable to find a place to stop when the double rope came to an end. With some difficulty because of the snow flurries I managed to make myself understood. I needed another rope to attach to the one I was holding on to. There were no holds; the snow had packed tight even under the overhangs. I tied the two ropes together with my bare hands and continued my descent into space. There was now a 400-ft rope down which I was sliding like a spider.

It was now no longer possible to talk with any of the others. I was completely suspended, looking for a hold which I could not find. I was worried, partly because I did not know where I could halt in my descent, partly because an enormous overhang cut off all possibility of communicating with my companions who, higher up, were waiting for my signal. At last, after some acrobatic swings in space, I managed to land on an outcrop of rock. I shouted repeatedly through the storm, hoping that my companions would understand that they could begin their descent. At one moment I saw the rope ascending and thought that one of them was on it and had begun to descend. Then, suddenly, the rope slipped away from me and disappeared from sight. I was left there, on an outcrop, secured by a cord to a piton, in the heart of the Pillar, without any means of continuing my descent and wondering if my companions would be able to find me or would descend in some other direction. I went on shouting at the top of my voice, hoping to be heard, so that, if nothing else, they could tell me where they were. Several moments of anxiety passed. At last a dark patch appeared near me; it was Mazeaud who had realised where I was and had come to join me.

Our rappels continued with the same rhythm. We were getting closer to the foot of the Pillar. We were frozen and soaked through. Then, hearing the dull thuds of some snowfalls, I realized that we had reached the base of the Pillar. But by now it was late in the afternoon and all we could do that night was to prepare a camp on the Col de Peuterey, which forms the base of the Pillar. We set foot on the level but the snow was extraordinarily deep; sometimes we sank into it up to our chests. I made Mazeaud take the lead for a bit, followed by all the others. I stayed where I was to give the direction. At one time the group seemed to have foundered in a very deep snowdrift. I joined them and then took the lead again, setting out by instinct towards the spot I thought suitable for a camp. Though I could not see it, it was imprinted on my mind. Behind me was Oggioni with whom I discussed whether it would be better to chance the protection which a crevasse could give us rather than build an igloo, since the snow was unstable. This was not so important for us who had our tent as for the four Frenchmen who hadn't one. We decided on the crevasse and told the Frenchmen, who accepted our advice.

We made arrangements for our camp before the night between Friday and Saturday fell. We had been making rappels for twelve hours. Kohlman seemed the most exhausted of all of us. We put him in our tent. With what was left of a butane gas cylinder Guillaume prepared some hot tea and gave it to him. The cold was atrocious. The wind was blowing continually and made the snow whirl around us. That was the worst night of all. We divided what was left of the provisions; prunes, chocolate, sugar and a little meat, now frozen. Oggioni refused the meat, preferring the sweetstuffs. All the others, however, nibbled at it. Kohlman showed me his fingers; they were livid. I thought it a good idea to massage them with cooking alcohol, of which we still had plenty. I passed him the alcohol flask, but he put it to his mouth and began to gulp it down. It was a most ill-advised action, but I thought he must have mistaken it for drinking alcohol. I took the flask away from him, but not before he had swallowed a couple of gulps. Were we already on the brink of madness?

It was pitch dark. We were in an inferno. Everyone was moaning and shivering with cold. The wind howled and the snow fell more and more heavily. Every now and then we would shake the snow off the tent, otherwise it would have smothered us. I tried to light the spirit-stove but had to give up for lack of air and, as in the last few days, we had to eat snow to quench our thirst. We were desperate, but no one said a word. Finally Oggioni said to me: "Let's make a vow: if we get out of this safely, let us forget that the Pillar even exists." I said, "Yes."

The night passed slowly and despairingly. At the same time as on the day before, at half-past three, at the sound of my little alarm, we rose from our uncomfortable resting-place. We wanted to save time and to get out of that terrifying situation which seemed as if it would never come to an end. The night had added another eighteen inches of snow to what had been there before. We set out in the midst of the storm. We all seemed to have endured that terrible camp well enough. Now I no longer had to take counsel with my companions; they left everything to me and I felt the heavy responsibility of a guide who must bring every-one back safely by the only possible route, the very danger-ous Roches Gruber. We had to get to the Gamba before evening, otherwise it would be all over for all of us.

Before starting, Robert Guillaume gave Kohlman a cor-amine injection. Meanwhile, I, followed by Oggioni and Gallieni, began to clear a burrow through the very deep snow in the direction of the route chosen for our descent. We were now on a single rope in this order: Bonatti, Oggioni, Gallieni, Mazeaud, Kohlman, Vielle and Guil-laume. The face which precedes the Roches Gruber was heavily laden with fresh snow which might avalanche at any moment. I told my companions to hurry up and join me and to get into shelter so that I could hold on to a rope if an avalanche should catch me while I was cutting the channel which would lead us to the Roches Gruber. I managed to do so and called to the others to pass, one by one, but when it came to Vielle's turn he could not do it. He kept falling and rising again, with every sign of exhaustion. Guillaume was beside him and encouraged him. He took Vielle's rucksack which he had thrown away on the slope, but Vielle seemed deaf to all our appeals which became rougher and rougher.

Meanwhile I went on to prepare the first of a very long series of rappels down the Roches Gruber. The sky had cleared for a moment, but the fine spell only lasted a short time. I could hear my companions inciting Vielle who had still not got across the couloir. I shouted to them to hurry up and begin the descent if we didn't want to die up there. I was the farthest down and was waiting for Kohlman who had followed me. Half an hour passed. Not understanding the delay, I again went up the rope for a few feet to see what was happening. Gallieni told me that Vielle was exhausted, that he was unable to cross the couloir by himself. He asked me if it would be possible to slide him along the snow to lighten the fatigue of walking. I agreed and told him to act quickly, adding that at this pace not only would we not get to the Gamba hut, but we would not even get down the Roches Gruber.

I went down again and rejoined Kohlman. I gathered from the excited voices of my companions that they were putting their plan into effect. I went on waiting for one of them to lower himself to me. Another half hour passed and not only did no one come down to join me, but their voices began little by little to die away. I didn't know what to do. Must every rappel take as long as this? Once again I shinned up the rope a few feet, far enough to be able to see my companions. I asked them: "Why don't you come down?" A voice, possibly Gallieni's, followed by that of Mazeaud, told me: "Vielle is dying!" I was petrified. I could see before me the little group of friends gathered around Vielle's body, which looked like a dark, inert bundle on the white snow. He was belayed to the rock and wrapped in our tent-cover to prevent the crows from getting at him.

I went back to Kohlman without telling him anything. Several more minutes, perhaps twenty, passed; now I knew it was all over with Vielle. There were no more voices to be heard, only the sound of the wind. It had begun to snow again. This agony unbroken by any human word was terrible. I went up the rope again and saw my companions busy securing to a piton Vielle's body and Gallieni's ruck-sack, full of superfluous things. There were no laments. It was then ten o'clock. I went back again to Kohlman and told him to hold fast. Then Mazeaud arrived, who told him in broken phrases what had happened. Kohlman was dee-ply affected, and wept.

We continued the rappel. Taking advantage of a moment when all six of us were hanging on the same piton, I advised the greatest possible speed if we did not want to share Vielle's fate. Oggioni, as always, was my right-hand man and took the rear. Like Mazeaud, Guillaume and myself, he was carrying a full rucksack. Mazeaud, the strongest and the acknowledged leader of the Frenchmen, had the job of keeping the others up to the mark.

Not quite an hour had passed when we heard voices. I was the farthest down the rope at the time and I thought they must be the voices of my companions above me. Soon, however, I was convinced that someone was searching for us on the glacier below. I shouted back and asked my companions to shout all together, so that they could hear us. From the cries which came from below I understood that they wanted to tell me something, but the gusts of wind prevented me from understanding. For my part, I was quite certain that down there they would not be able to under-stand what I was shouting, which was: where were they and could they hear us. We went on in better spirits. When we reached the end of the Roches Gruber; about half-past three, I calculated that from the morning before, when we had begun the descent, we had made at least fifty rappels.

A brief break in the storm allowed us to see the whole surface of the chaotic Freney glacier. What a lot of snow had fallen! There were no furrows in the snow, which meant that no rescue party had passed that way. Where had the voices come from? We could see no one and fell into a mood of the blackest despair. Perhaps it was all over for all of us. We had been sure that the voices had come from the foot of the Roches Gruber and that had given us strength to overcome the terrible difficulties and dangers of that exceedingly difficult passage. We were, however, alone at the foot of the rocks and we still had before us many unforeseeable dangers on our way to the Gamba hut.

The slow and exhausting descent of the glacier began. We refused to accept our bad luck. The snow was still very deep. Not even in winter climbs could I recall having met with so much. We left behind us not a trail but a burrow. Fortunately the mists were beginning to rise and visibility gradually improved. That made it possible for us to enter safely the labyrinth of crevasses which led to the Col de l'Innominata, the last serious difficulty on our way to safety. But the deep snow so slowed down our advances, that we despaired of being able to reach the base of the col while there was still daylight.

I felt faint with fatigue, physical suffering and cold, but refused to give up.

Our file grew longer. Oggioni was stumbling every few steps, at the end of his tether. He was without a rucksack, which he had handed over to Gallieni. Sometimes he was last man, sometimes last but one. We groped our way on to the glacier in complete disorder, drunk with fatigue. We were roped together, but each went his own way without heeding anything. I realized that in such conditions it would be very hard for us to reach the foot of the Col de l'Innominata in daylight. Gallieni, behind me, seemed the least exhausted. I decided to unrope myself and him in order to go ahead as quickly as we could and prepare the couloir of the Innominata, otherwise our companions would no longer be able to climb it. This task would have to be completed by nightfall.

Our companions followed in our tracks. Meanwhile I attacked the terrible ice which had encrusted the Col de l'Innominata. Guillaume had remained behind. Within half

an hour it would be dark and we were still struggling to
reach the col. Now we were again all roped together; myself,
Gallieni, Oggioni, Mazeaud and Kohlman. Our only hope
was to reach the rescue parties while we still had a little
strength left. They alone might be able to save those left
behind. It was pitch dark when I reached the Col de
l'Innominata. It was Saturday evening, after nine o'clock,
and we had been out for six days. The powdery snow driven
by the wind had begun again and in the west we could see
the flashes of an approaching thunderstorm. There was
nowhere to fix a piton to anchor the rope which supported
my four companions and I had to hold it on my shoulders. I
urged them to hurry. But the operation was very long and
desperate. Orders mingled with cries of pain and desperation. Behind Gallieni, Oggioni seemed unable to grip the
rock. Gallieni tried to help him in every way he could,
supported in his turn by the rope which I held on my
shoulders. The two Frenchmen down at the end of the rope
were shouting and raving.

It was chaos. Three hours passed and we were still at the
same point. I could not move. Every so often there were
tugs at the rope which nearly pulled me into space. The
pain of the rope and the cold made me feel faint. But if I
collapsed it meant the end for everyone. In all those three
hours Oggioni had not been able to move. All encouragement was in vain. Now and then he would reply with a wail;
he seemed to be in a sort of trance. He was attached by a
karabiner to a piton, and would have to free himself from it
to give us a chance of hauling him up. But he hadn't the
strength and he was so exhausted that perhaps he was
incapable of thinking. I would have liked to go down to
him but that was impossible since I had to keep the rope,
which was holding him as well as Gallieni, firmly on my
shoulders. At last, not being able to do anything else,
Gallieni made sure that Oggioni was firmly fixed to the
piton, undid the rope that bound him to Oggioni and the
Frenchmen and came up to join me and was thus able to
carry on rapidly towards the rescue parties. Oggioni remained roped to the strong Mazeaud, to whom I shouted to
wait and look after the others who would soon be rescued.

While we were doing this we saw Kohlman fumbling his way along the rope in the darkness on the ice-covered face. He was unroped. He came towards us and passed Mazeaud, Oggioni and Gallieni with an energy born of desperation which bordered on madness. Gallieni, guessing his state, managed to grasp him and tie him to the rope. Soon all three of us reached the col. Kohlman told us he was hungry and thirsty and then went on: "Where is the Gamba hut?" He was completely out of his senses, but we could not abandon him.

We roped him between us. Gallieni was the first to begin the descent, followed by Kohlman who seemed to have forgotten all the rules of prudence. The slope was very difficult, steep and covered with ice. For the first 150 ft we let ourselves slide along a fixed rope evidently left there by the rescue parties searching for two Swiss on the Pointe Gugliermina. Then we went on as best we could. But Kohlman became more and more dangerous. He let himself slide on his back, hanging on to the rope and without using his crampons. At the end of the rope he continued to hang there and I had to support him, which made it impossible for me to catch up with him. When at last the rope became lighter, after he had found some sort of foothold, an unexpected tug told me he had again broken away and exposed us all to the risk of falling.

Neither threats nor encouragements moved him. He shouted disconnected phrases, gesticulated, raved. We thought we should have managed to get down in an hour; with Kohlman, now delirious, that hour became three.

With God's help, we reached the bottom. We still had an hour before us to reach the Gamba hut over snowdrifts which presented neither dangers nor difficulties save for their depth. We began to recover our spirits and our only thought was how to reach the hut quickly when an unexpected incident delayed us. Gallieni had dropped one of his gloves. He bent down to recover it and tried to keep his hand warm by thrusting it into his jacket. Kohlman, who interpreted this movement as an attempt to draw a pistol, spread his arms and rushed on Gallieni, clasping him tightly and making him roll down the slope. Gallieni managed to break free and I tried to check their movements with the rope. Kohlman then hurled himself at me. I dodged and he fell and began to roll, writhing in delirium. He had completely lost his senses. Then he rose again and tried to rush at us. By pulling both ends of the rope, we managed to keep him at a distance. We were all three roped together and one of us could break free. We could not drag him with us and it was essential not to lose a minute.

To untie ourselves from him, we had first to undo the iced-up knots. We had no knife, yet we had to get away from our poor crazed companion. He was watching every movement, ready to launch himself at us. One at a time, keeping the rope taut with our teeth, we lowered our breeches so as to be able to slip the noose of rope about our waists over our hips. We succeeded in this without Kohlman realizing what we were doing. Then I shouted to Gallieni: "Let go and run!" and we rushed off, rolling on the snow. There was ony one thing to do: we must get to the hut in time to tell the rescue squads. Kohlman, up there, was in no danger of falling. But, as it happened, the first squad only arrived in time to see him draw his last breath.

In this way we covered the last 1,200 ft which still divided us from the Gamba hut. It was pitch dark. We only managed to find it because I knew this area as well as my own house. Gallieni followed me unhurt. We circled the hut, hammering on the windows with our fists. We had just reached the door when we heard heavy steps inside and a hand raised the latch. The door burst open; we saw the interior of the hut dimly lit by a small lamp. It was full of sleeping men. We stepped over several bodies without recognizing anyone. Then suddenly one of the men leapt to his feet and shouted: "Walter, is that you?" and there was a rush of people and we were suffocated by embraces.

"Be quick!" I shouted. "There's one man still out there! The others are on the Innominata! Be quick!" It was three o'clock on Sunday morning. The storm was still raging. We stretched out on the table in the middle of the hut and the others took the frozen crampons from our feet, undressed us and gave us dry clothes and warm drinks. I fell into a heavy stupor. When I awoke about three hours had gone by. The bodies of my companions had been found, except Vielle. They told me that Oggioni was dead and I was filled with uncontrollable grief. Dear Mazeaud, the only one of them to be found alive, embraced me and wept with me.

Mirror, Mirror

Ed Drummond

*In 1972 the American Ed Drummond made the first
ascent of Arch Wall on the North Face of Trollrygen in
Norway. The climb took twenty days.*

We reached Oslo in two days, nudging in under the
shrouds of cloud spreading a thin fine rain upon
toast-faced Norwegians and palefaces alike. It was the first
rain for a month. Burning up to Romsdal on the bike, I
found my cagoule was promiscuous in the rain, but Lindy,
at the back of me, kept dry and fed me on chocolate and
made me hum with her big hugs. I couldn't lean on her as I
could my cold companion of other years who pulled on my
neck: my rain-slimed haul bag, my meticulous Humpty
Dumpty. She was continually delighted at new waterfalls;
she flew oohs to my ears and near the end of the journey, my
goggles crying with rain, I raised a soggy arm at the alp of
cloud shearing up a white mile. "That's the wall," I roared.
She gripped her hand on my arm, and yelled about the
coming bend.

Where am I? I'm cold. Thin mists shift past, touching
me. Where is she? She must have got out of the bag. I shake
my head out, struggling to look. There is another near me,
raw-red in the white air. Hugh! A dream. I'm not on the
Romsdalhorn. That was a week ago. Lindy isn't here. This
is the wall.

So. Three nights. Almost 1,000 ft. Our second ledge,
Luckys. Seven pitches and a paper-dry cag. Hugh's still in

the bag, sleeping the sleep of the just, sound as a foetus, on his first wall. During the past three years I had, in three summers and a spring, snailed the mile-long approach scree twenty-three times and twenty times I came back. Not this time. "The Northern European Wall"; "The Mourning Wall"; "The Rurt Wall" (Realised Ultimate Reality Troll); "The Lord of the Walls"; "The Drummond Route" (if we said nothing they'd call it this); "The Royal Wall", naw, what has Robbins ever done for you? You'll never level with him.

On our first cralk up to the wall – the scree is so steep that it's like trying to ski uphill – we had climbed the first slabs, 200 ft or so, gritty, nasty, wobbling to extreme. There had been the snow pitch, cricket size, and the jokes about forgetting the ice-axes, using skyhooks and étriers as we had no crampons and the ice was marble. Then the 'schrund and my little leap; it was all fun. After three trips we'd brimmed the hauls and I'd climbed the third, a squirrelly free up a great crooked slab, funnelling to an upside-down squeeze chimney that made me squeak. Then we went down, Lindy, who'd come up to watch, and I, slowly, like two old people, while Hugh flew off to the river where he swam among the salmon; the fishermen had all gone home. We just promised us a swim when it was all over.

Returning, two days later, Hugh went first and the hauls went after, quite a while after. His first haul; his first artyfishyl; first hamouac; first air jumar (barring one from a tree in Mexico). Hugh was, slowly, going up the wall. So it was noon when I set out on the fourth pitch.

And it was seven in the evening when Hugh's jumars gritted their teeth to follow. What passed in those seven hours is unforgettable: my mouth, sock-hot; my larynx strangling for spit; a fine trembling as of a thin wind trembling through me. It began with a layback of twenty feet, wonderful but for the iron stone around my neck – it was a struggle, favourite uncle, was it not? Then the footholds faded away and I muttered on nuts under this thin roof until the only way up was up.

There was a crack, not a crack crack, but a line, a cra . . .;

the start of a crack say. At any rate the bolts were in the haul bag and this was the third pitch of the N.A. Wall as far as I was concerned. My rurps curled up when I banged their heads and refused to sit still. After five fingernail knife-blades I got out my hook and sat on that, about as secure as the last angel to make it on to that pin head. Then I struck dirt. Now dirt is okay if you can get dug in. I began and ended with a knifeblade which dangled sillily from my waist, and I was glad that it was not me that was holding the rope, for after four hours and forty feet I might have been caught napping. But Hugh wasn't and as it was I only went fifteen feet for the hook stuck and though it trembled it snapped not, O Dolt.

So then I had to free that bit, but after that it eased some. Nuts hammered in the dirt and at long last a ding dong bong. Hotheaded I'd reached a ledge, feeling a bit sorry for myself. "No Ledges" we called it and it all hung out. There we had a pantomime in hammocks by headtorch which was really not in the least bit funny. Hugh, as chattery as a parrot, floated above me in his one-point. He even said he was comfortable and had the cheek to take a shit. By a battery *son-et-lumiere* I watched his anus line an angry eye; no voyeur but it might look my way. However, he missed me, my arms full of ropes like some deeply confused spider.

"Ed! Come on, it's light."

Oh, God, awake already.

"Look at the sun."

Why don't you go back to sleep?

"Unh uh."

There and then I decided that if he was unable to lead the next pitch, then that was it. I'd led every pitch so far (didn't you want to?) and it was unthinkable that I'd lead all of them. Not bloody likely. I'd make that clear. I tortoised out. What are you smiling at? Rather him than me. I've had about bloody five minutes bloody sleep. "Right, coming."

It was strange to be there, sitting up in the hammock, feet stirring in the air over the side, opening the haul, fingers weaseling in the cold stuff bags, tramp-thankful for food in the hand. Eating quietly we heard the whipcrack of break-ing ice in the gloomy cwm below and I'd yell "hello" with a dervish fervour (wake up, Drummond, grow up, you can't go back). The echoes yodelled and I'd say to Hugh, "He's there."

"Who?" he'd ask.

"That bloke," I'd tell him. "Listen." And I'd do it again and we'd both cackle like kids with a home-made phone.

By 7 a.m. I was ready to belay him. I wasn't laughing now. One more pitch and there would be no retreat. I moled into the cold rope bag, my arms up to my elbows, fingers fiddling for the iron sling. I had a krab, empty, ready on the belay to receive it. My fingers curled in the sling; I moved my arm gracefully, slowly (I was cold), to clip it into the krab before passing it up to him. If I drop the iron sling we'll have to go back down. From the end of my arm my little family of fingers waved at me. And it went, there, no, once, twice, there, oh, down, out, there, and under and into the heart of the icefield, clinking like lost money.

I couldn't believe it. Hugh was silent. I kept saying I was sorry. I didn't mean it. Not this time (How do you know?). I couldn't believe it. Hugh said nothing.

"I've done it now."

Instantly, "How long will it take you to get back up?"

He's got you now.

I got back by noon, gasping. I'd come down to earth. A 600 ft abseil, my figure-of-eight sizzling my spits at it, and then a free jumar all the way back. I was furious. "Right, belay on."

His pitch was perfect after a bit. Dirty at first, then a cool, clean fist-lock crack. Iron out in the air like a bunch of weapons, he groped at the sky like something falling. All around a sea-sheer swell of wall, untouchable. Him the one sign of life.

Then the rain came. A dot in the eye. I heave for my cagoule, one eye on Hugh, an invisible drizzle blackening the rock. New noises fizz in. Twitters of water and Hugh is yelling for his cagoule, but I point out the time and that he's leaking already. Well, for a couple of hours I kept pushing boiled sweets in my mouth and Hugh kept on moaning and kept on. After 150 ft he had to stop and pin himself to the wall.

Early evening. There he hung, wringing himself like fresh washing. Thank God he had no cagoule, or we would both have been up there for the night, him perched above, if not on, my head like a great wet heron. The waterfalls would weep all night. "Why wait for Godot?" I yelled up. He said, "Eh?" so I said, "Come on down, let's piss off."

We stripped the ropes off the hauls, tied the lot together and down we went, happy as nuns in a car. A slalom down the scree and back before dark. Back in the camp hut we listened with Lindy, gladly, to the rain hissing outside while we kissed at a smug mug of tea and drooled on the food to come. That night I slept like a child.

Eight days later, well picked, we humped up the boulder-fields in epileptic sunshowers, snagged at by cold-cutting winds. The days were getting shorter.

The bergschrund had rotted back and we had to go down inside the mouth. Our ropes were twenty feet up the slabs, strung taut to a peg. I manteled up on this mica jug, massaging off the dust, feeling sick with this white pit under me, thirty feet deep, rocks in its dark, lurking.

When I had the end of the rope I dangled a bong on and looped it to him. Three times I threw and three times I missed; each time the bong tolled dolefully. "Hey, our funeral knell," I yelled, but he wasn't impressed.

Two and half jumehours later Hugh brooded on the haul eggs, sucking the sacred sweet, as I botched up the freeasy and awkwaid of the next pitch. When I warbled down about the ledge I'd found, he said he'd kiss me, but on arrival he didn't hold me to the treat. In fact, the first thing that he said was that the next pitch looked a bit steep for him and ordered me to do it. But since it was dark I could wait until tomorrow. Under the tube-tent, scarfed in cigar smoke, we crept to sleep like refugees.

Pitch 7 took me all the next day. It is 156 ft long; our ropes were 150 ft long, at a stretch. That last six feet to the belay cracks saw me lying flat on my face on the ledge, hammering like front-crawling. Hugh climbed up from his end, pulling the haul bags (one at a time, and there were three, each weighing over 50 lb) on to his shoulder and then weightlifting them up so that I could get them through the pulley. Hugh studied Law at university.

So. Three nights. Almost 1,000 ft. Lucky's Ledge is no longer important. A stab of butter, a jab of honey; the pumpernickel crumbling among your fingers, a steamy censer of tea, packing your bags, hurrying as a jostle of cumulus smudges out the sun and the stove starts to fizz the drizzle.

As I remember we made three pitches that day in a rain as insidious as gas. For two or three seconds, suddenly the valley would come like an answer, and we would stumble into conversation, then numb up, sullen with wet clothes and cold, clubbed feet. In the downpouring darkness I jumed up to Hugh, squatting on blocks, owl aloof. While he belayed me I hand-traversed down to a ledge on his left, where I backheeled and rubbled away for over half an hour, making the bed. We couldn't find pin placements for the tube tent, so we hung our bivi bags from the rope and crept into their red, wet dark.

Sneaking out the next day at noon like shell-less tortoises, I realized as we both emptied a gallon of fresh water from our bags, that it might be better to have the opening at the front rather than at the top of the bag. A point that had escaped me as I tried out the bag on the floor in front of the fire at home. Sneer not. Wasn't the first Whillans Box a plastic mac and a pram? The Drummond Cot would have its night in time. Well, we strung the tube tent as an awning, lit the stove, and wrung our pulpy feet out, sitting in the cloud, machine-gunned by water drops from the great roofs that crashed out over 200 ft wide, a thousand feet above our heads. We wriggled a little in the tent, slowly gulping lumpy salami, a bit stunned, stuttering with cold.

At about four we took the hood off our heads and saw the valley for the first time in twenty hours: the curve of the railway line, the thin black line of the road, pastures of grass, the glitter of the river, the big stacks of corn like yellow firs. The red tractor a slow blood drop. Then we heard yells, names, my name, and saw a spot of orange jump at the toe of the scree. It was Lindy calling, calling, and I called for my favourite team: "LindyLindy LindyLindy," and the wall called with me. Hugh even asked if I was going out that night.

Morning. The fifth day. Cornflower blue skies, fiord-cold in the shade, and above us brooded a huge wing of white granite, its edge a thin black slab about as long and steep as the spire of Salisbury Cathedral. I had seen this from the scree. We go that way.

Two skyhooks raised me off the rubble, and dash, wobbling, for ten feet without protection – a necessary enema after the 30-hour sit-in. Then I'm staring at a poor flare where I belt a nut. Little chains of sweat trickle down my back. I'm struggling to free climb and Hugh's not even looking. Jerkily I straggle to a ledge, not a word of wonder escaping his lips as I braille for holds and shake on to this ledge with a flurry of boots. With time against us I was doing all the leading. Hugh sat still on his stone throne while I squirmed about, greasing my palms with myself. Still, a cat may look, and he was the one rock, the one unshakeable, all the way there and back.

Abseiling down in the dying day, the bergschrund breaking its wave beneath my feet 1,500 ft below in the cold ammonia air, the tube tent was a rush of bright flesh, raw on the ledge, and Hugh, his back bent, peering, was a black bird feeding at it. After a soup supper, watched by the smouldery eye of Hugh's cigar, I blew my harmonica, and brought tears of laughter to our eyes. We were doing okay. Hugh even said he liked to hear me play.

Two days later we were barely 300 ft higher, and what I could see was not pretty. It looked as though, during the night, someone had pumped Hugh's foot up. His skin transparent as tracing paper, the foot was a mallet of flesh, the toes tiny buds; thalidomide. I didn't want to say too much. Perhaps the strain of his jumaring had done it, or the rotting wet when we were at Lucky's taking the waters. It was early yet; we had a long way to go. He said he just needed to rest it.

The ledge was lovely and I was glad to linger there. We spread ourselves around, Hugh blowing gently on his foot while I had a bath. A snip of cotton for a flannel, line for a towel, and a nip of antiseptic to give my spit a bit of bite. With behindsight I don't recommend the antiseptic neat, my dears. Let me tell you it wasn't a red face I had. The funny thing was it didn't hurt at the time I dabbed it, lovingly, my back turned while I blinked over the drop; but the day after, well, as they say, there hangs a tale.

A week later, his feet out like two heady cheeses in the dim pink light of the tent, Hugh has the mirror. He's checking on the stranger – the first time in twelve days, squeezing his pimples, humming some Neil Young song. For four days we've been in and out of this womb tube, harassed each time we go outside by the web of stuff bags breeding at the hole end. They are our other stomachs. We feel in them for our pots, our pottage, and our porter (although the porter is water since we've finished the orange). Cosmetics ended, we turn to draughts, drawing a board on the white insulating pad and inventing a set of signs for pieces and moves. So we pass an hour; doze, shift, fidget, sleep, talk, warn, fart, groan or cackle, plan, doze, and watch the light dissolve like a dye in the darkness. Snuggled together we are pre-eminently grateful that there is another here at the end of the day. We don't talk about failing and I hardly think about it now – we've been here so long it's a way of life. The pendulum's done now and the only sign I'm waiting for is a weather one. The valley in my mind is out of sight.

In raggy mists we moved quickly, leaving our hauls on the bivouac ledge. Hugh, some deflated astronaut, swam slowly up on jumars as though someone had taken the gravity away. Breezes whiffed up my cuffs and my icy cagoule etherised the back of my neck. After those two pitches, I frog-legged left, my numb hands bungling on the flat holds, to reach a little ledge from where I would go down to pendulum. After each pitch I was getting a bit desperate with the cold and I'd can-can to keep warm. Hugh, only forty feet away, was a white ghastly shadow.

Below us, Norway was at war. A volcanic pit of bursting water; the cwm boomed, a vat of slashed air. Stones howled around us and avalanching crashes trembled the wall. And I.

Nothing could be seen in the gassing mist. No pendulum today.

Going back to our home, Hugh passed out into the cloud first, using the haul lines as a back rope to the bivouac ledge, which would otherwise have been impossible to return to because of the overhanging wall. When I got down he'd a brew ready which lit a fire, briefly, inside me. My thanks that it wasn't snowing just about made it.

During the night it snowed.

In the morning it was still falling, so we rolled over; better sleep on it. In the fitful sleep of that day I had my dream! The editor of *Mountain* had arrived at the foot of the scree and, with a foghorn or some kind of voice, had managed to wake me, telling me that he had come all the way from England to let me know what a great job I was doing for British rock-climbing (he never mentioned Hugh), and also how we were contributing to better Anglo-Norwegian political relations.

By the time I awoke he was gone but Hugh hadn't; he was just vanishing down the hole at the other end. My watch told 4 a.m. the night had gone. I oozed out of my pit to find lard-pale Hugh with the blue black foot, sitting stinking in a skinful of sun. For half an hour we wallowed, exposing ourselves to the warm air. New creatures we were, able, if not to fly, at least to jumar, up there. And up there, today, I had to swing for it.

I try, flying, at thirty feet below Hugh, then fifty feet, then eighty feet, then at over a hundred feet and I'm a bit too low so I jume up to about ninety-five. "Ed Leadlegs," I tell him but only the wind hears me. I'm getting a bit tired; Hugh has given up asking me how I'm doing and he is just hanging, staring, his pipe alight – the wind brings a tang of it to me. No doubt he's thinking of his girl in Mexico.

The white wall is so steep here that I can barely keep hold of it when I crab myself right for the big swing. But my first swings wing me out into space away from the wall and I have to pirouette to miss smashing my back. This is ridiculous. Like a spider at puberty I toil but spin not. It's after 2 p.m. Lindy will be here soon.

When I've fingernailed back as far right as I can (and this time I manage about four feet more) I'm nearly eighty feet away from the groove that I'm trying to reach.

I'm off, the white rushing past; out, out, away from the wall, way past the groove, out – I tread air, the valley at my feet. Hugh moons down, he's yelling something – can't hear a word he's saying – rushing, coming back, crashing in, wall falling on top of me, I kick, jab, bounce my boot, bounce out, floating, an easy trapeze. Then the unknown groove is running into my open arms and I strike at a flake and stick. Fingers leeching its crack.

I hung a nut in (my jumars attaching me to the rope are pulling me up), then I get an et. and stand in it. The nut stays put. Jumars down. Now put a knife under that block. The press of the block keeps it in as I weigh in on it. Out flips the nut. Whoops. I know I'm going to get there. I can't see Hugh but I know he's there. A tiny nut like a coin in a slot. Watch me. The knifeblade tinkles out. Thank you. The nut gleams a gold tooth at me. There you go. To climb is to know the universe is All Right. Then I clink a good pin in at a stretch. Can't get the nut now (it's still there). And then I'm in the groove, appalled at the sheer, clean walls around and below me, baying for breath, my heart chopping through my chest.

We have lost 100 ft, but gained a narrow track of cracks that will, I believe, lead to the "Arch Roof", the huge, square-cut overhang that from the valley looks like an old press photo of the Loch Ness Monster. I saw a crack in 1970 through binoculars going out through the top of his head. "Loch Ness Monster sighted on Troll Wall." I'd out-yeti Whillans yet. Just before dark Hugh lands and goes on ahead to order dinner; we're eating out at the Traveller's Tube tonight, a farewell meal. The pendulum being done, our time was going and so must we.

But it snowed for two days.

On the thirteenth day the sun rubbed shoulders with us again, and Hugh jumared up at a snail sprint. He found that the yellow perlon he was on had rubbed through to half its core, so he tied that out with an overhand before I came up at a slow rush. Halfway up I worked loose a huge detached flake which had hung 100 ft above our tent; it took me five minutes so we had no need to worry. We watch it bounce, bomb-bursting down to the cwm, and the walls applaud.

The crack above the pendulum's end was a nice smile for standard angles except where a ladder of loose flakes is propped. Bloody visions slump at the belay below me. Silence. Care. The hauls zoom out well clear.

The next two pitches, up a bulging, near-blind groove, were ecstasy. I had to free climb. The hooks were only for luck, and I was quick in the blue fields. Above, suddenly, two swifts flashed past, thuds of white. "That's us," I yelled to myself. Lindy may not have been here, but there she was. I could hear her, naming my name, and I flew slowly up. Four fine patches of ledgeless pleasure that day. In the dark Hugh jumared up to the Arch, me guiding his feet with my head torch.

But that night the sky shone no stars. Packs of black cloud massed. Not enough food to eat. A sweet or two. No cigar. And too late to fish for hammocks. All night, four hours, I squirmed in my seat sling. I speculated on recommending to the makers that they rename it the Iron Maiden, but it was too suitable an epitaph to laugh about. My hip is still numb from damaged nerves.

Came the morning I was thrashed. The sun did not exist. The roof over my head was a weight on my mind. Suddenly, over Vengetind the weather mountain, clouds boiled, whipping and exploding in avalanching chaos. Over Lillejfel, a low shoulder on the other side of the valley cauldron, a dinosaur mass of white cloud was rat-arrowing toward us. We could hardly run away; we were so cold and hungry we could hardly move.

I was scared as I moved out under the Arch, a clown without props, all these things were real, there were no nets here, only dear patient Hugh blowing on his fingers.

No man walks on air was all my thought as I melted out of sight, upside down for forty feet, my haul line dissolving in the mist. I couldn't feel that I was connected to anything solid. Fly sized, I mimed away under three giant inverted steps, lips. Not a single foothold, not a toehold in a hundred feet. Just over the final lip, in a single strand of crack, I pinned myself to a wall of water and started to land the hauls.

They must have seen me coming. I couldn't believe it. Rain-drops ripped into me, making me wince. The cold rose an octave, catapulting hail into my face. The wind thrummed a hundred longbow cords. I could hardly see through my chinese eyes. Only while I hauled could I stop shaking. My fingers, cut deeply at the tips, were almost helpless. People at upstairs windows watching a road accident in the street below. My feet were dying. My silent white hands.

Hugh came up for air, grinning. He'd had no idea down there. Up here he had the thing itself. Murdering, washing out more than ears. I led off, hardly knowing where, except that we couldn't stay there. I could only just open my karabiners with two hands. Sleet had settled thickly on the bunches of tie-offs. Both of us were really worried. Hugh cried up after an hour that he was getting frostbite. What could I say? I had to find a place for the night.

If you ever go there and have it the way we did, you'll know why we called it "The Altar". I remember the rush in the drowning dark to hang the tent, the moss churning to slush beneath our feet. Back to back, our backs to the wall, we slumped on three feet of ledge for three days. We had nothing to drink for the first two of those days; our haul bags were jammed below us and we were diseased with fatigue. Lice trickles of wet get everywhere.

I remember Hugh drinking the brown water that had collected in his boots, instantly vomiting it out, and me silently mouthing the gluey water from my helmet. You didn't miss much. Hugh. He shared his food with me, some cheese and dates and a bag of sweets; rare fruits. After a day he had to piss and used quadrupled poly bags which I politely declined to use; I had no need. A day later my proud bladder was bursting. But sitting, propped in a wet bed of underwear, I was impotent. For over two hours I strained and grunted in scholastic passion. Hugh said it was trench penis. A sort of success went to my head, however, or rather on to and into my sleeping bag. After that I felt like some great baby, trapped in his wet cot, the air sickly with urine, and sleep would not come.

To get more room, both of us, we later confessed when there were witnesses present, developed strategies of delay while we shuffled the status quo. "Could you sit forward a minute?" Or, "Would you hold this for me?" At times I'd get Hugh to tuck my insulating pads around me to bluff off the cold stone. It was deeply satisfying to have someone do that. Grizzly, bristly Hugh: what a mother.

We wondered if this could continue for more than a week. But we didn't wonder what would happen if it did. We never talked about not finishing. (We were just over 1,000 ft below the summit.) It was no longer a new route to us. It was not possible to consider anything else as real. There were no echoes from the valley. There was no valley. There was no one to call your name. No wall now; unhappy little solipsists, all we had was each other.

We began to get ratty, like children locked in a bedroom. An elbow scuffled against a back once or twice as we humped back to stop the slow slide off the ledge. A ton of silence rested on us like a public monument, for hours on end. I felt that this was all sterile. I ate food, wore out my clothes, used up my warmth, but earned nothing, made nothing. The art was chrysalising into artifice. A grubby routine. Trying not to die. Millions have the disease and know it not. My sleep a continual dream of hammering: banging in pins, clipping in, moving up, then back down, banging, banging, taking them out. A bit like having fleas. Searching for an ultimate belay. Unable to stop: the Holy Nail. My Dad, my dad, why hast thou forsaken me? At times I was pretty far gone.

But it wasn't all self-pity. We talked about the plight of the Trolls and could clearly see a long bony hairy arm poking under the tent, handing us a steaming pan of hot troll tea, and although nothing appeared in our anaesthetic dark, the idea lit a brief candle.

Three days later we were released.

Lindy yelled us out. A giant marigold sun beamed at us. Everywhere up here – and we could see hundreds of miles – was white, perfect, appalling. Across the river I could clearly make out scores of tourists, a distant litter of colour in one of the camping fields opposite the wall. Cars flashed their headlamps and horns bugled as we struggled into view and flagged them with our tent.

Then, quickly, the charging roar of an avalanche. I flattened to the wall. And then I spotted it, a helicopter, gunning in a stone's throw from the wall, a military green with yellow emblems. A gun poked from the window. "Hugh, they're going to shoot us," then, tearing his head up he saw it: an arm waving. We waved arms, heads, legs; danced, jigged, yelled, while they circled in and away like something from another world. Later we learned that it was Norwegian television, but we fluttered no blushes on the wall. The spell of our selves was broken.

Five hours later, after a long lovely 130 ft of aid, intricate and out in space, I was on the final summit walls, the last roofs wiped with light, 700 ft above me.

All that night, while a white moon sailed over our shoulders, we perched on our haul bags and cut off the blood to our already damaged feet, too exhausted to know. Sharing our last cigar while the nerves in our feet were suffocating to death, we shone in our hunger and smiled a while.

As soon as I put my weight on my foot in the new dawn I knew I'd had it. Hugh's foot was an unspeakable image, and I had to tell him when his heel was grounded inside his boot. He could hardly have his laces tied at all and I was terrified that one of his boots might drop off.

All that day the feeling was of having my boots being filled with boiling water that would trickle in between my toes and flood my soles. Then a sensation of shards of glass being wriggled into the balls of my feet. And upon each of my feet a dentist was at work, pulling my nails and slowly filing my toes. Then nothing but a rat-tatting heart when I stopped climbing. I would tremble like water in a faint breeze. I knew it was hypothermia. We had had no food for three days. Maybe it was two.

All the last day we called, a little hysterically I think, for someone on the summit; they were coming to meet us. Sitting fifteen feet below the top, with Hugh whimpering up on jumars I heard whispers . . . "Keep quiet . . . wait until he comes over the top".

There was no one there. Only, thank God, the sun. It seemed right in a way to meet only each other there. At the summit cairn Hugh sucked on his pipe while my tongue nippled at a crushed sweet that he had found in his pocket. We dozed warm as new cakes, in a high white world, above impenetrable clouds which had shut out the valley all day. We were terribly glad to be there. After midnight we collapsed into a coma of sleep, half a mile down in the boulder-field.

We met them the next morning, quite near the road; it must have been about half-past eight. They were coming up to meet us. Lindy flew up the hill to hug me forever. I was Odysseus, with a small o, I was Ed, come back for the first time. Hugh grinned in his pain when I told the Norwegian journalists that his real name was Peer Gynt, and that he was an artist like Van Gogh, but that he had given a foot for the wall, instead of an ear to his girl.

On our last hobble, he had, before we met the others, found himself dreaming of the walks he used to have with his Dad, as a child, into the park to feed the ducks, and of the delights of playing marbles (we were both pocketing stones and rare bits from the summit on down). When we arrived in Andalsnes with our friends, I saw the apples burning on the boughs, glowy drops of gold and red (the green gargoyle buds, the little knuckle apples had lit while we were gone); and the postbox in its red skirt shouted to me as we turned the corner into town. Bodil washed Hugh's feet, sent for her doctor, and everyone in our house was alive and well. Only the Troll Wall gave me black looks, over the hill and far away at last. Black iceberg under eye-blue skies.

Back in England my feet were as irrefutable as war wounds. I was on my back for a month, and I had the cuttings from the Norwegian press, as precious as visas. But nowhere to get to.

King of the Equator

Sebastian Snow

*Snow was a British explorer. After discovering the source
and travelling the length of the Amazon river in 1952,
Snow determined that his next challenge was the scaling
of both Chimborazo, 6, 248 m (20,500 ft) and Cotopaxi
(the world's highest volcano, at 5,989 m – 19, 650 ft) in
Ecuador. He arrived in 1953, in typical Snow-style, with
little equipment and less preparation. And absolutely no
climbing experience.*
Snow died in 2001, aged 73.

I sailed for Ecuador in late June, arriving at Guayaquil,
sixty miles up the River Guayas, four weeks later. I
should have disembarked, instead I continued south down
the Peruvian coast to Lima with the general idea of obtaining mountain provisions and additional information on the
volcanoes.

I stayed ten days at the Grand Hotel Bolivar, named after
the famous Simon Bolivar, the liberator of the Andean
Republics. An adjoining night club is also called the Bolivar
Grill. There are only two first-class hotels in Lima; if you
are not at the one, then you *must* undoubtedly be at the
other.

The Bolivar, the older establishment, occupies a domi-
nant position overlooking the Central Plaza of San Martin;
in many ways commodious, it nevertheless contrives to
embody all the hectic atmosphere of a large terminal station
during the "rush hour" – people just leaving, people just

arriving, and just people. Three flights upstairs all is comparatively calm, and I was shown into a comfortable little room with all the "mod. cons." including one extra – one of those china things shaped like a keyhole. Raising an eyebrow, I was told, if I liked I could do my laundry in it!

On the ground-floor there is the Bolivar Bar, a room of dark panelling occupied by men with crew cuts, addicted to dice and beer, and dressed in tight blue jeans and open-necked shirts. Many of these were mining engineers down from "The Hill". This affectionate understatement is bestowed upon the topographical position of the mining communities run by the Cerro de Pasio Copper Corporation which spread over the high Andes, often to be found 14,000 feet above the sea. These men would come down for a week-end or a vacation.

During my ten days here I met Doctor Hans Spann, an eminent geologist, photographer, and mountaineer. Bavarian by birth, he had come to Peru in 1939 on disagreement with the shape of things within Germany, and since that time has been on no less than ten expeditions to various unexplored parts of Peruvian Sierras and Oriente. I do not remember the circumstance of our first encounter.

At that time he was interested in making an expedition to an unexplored region between the Rivers Apurimac and Urubamba at a point some 400–500 miles due east of the capital. Within this unknown country there were rumoured to be "ruins" of a lost civilization; possibly Inca. Unfortunately, these expeditions, including one under his own leadership, had failed to confirm this report. The attitude of the Indian tribes was most discouraging. Dr Spann wished to try again when the rains ceased in the following May. Was I interested? Yes, but first I must go and climb Chimborazo and Cotopaxi. At the end of ten days I had gained nothing materially. I could get no suitable mountain provisions and no-one seemed to know anything about Chimborazo – and, frankly, did not care. My position now was as follows:

1. I knew no-one in Ecuador.
2. I possessed a parrot's knowledge of commercial Spanish.

3. No mountain experience.
4. No provisions.
5. One brand-new .22 rifle had been confiscated by the Customs at Callao (part of Lima). I was strongly advised to leave it as a permit would have meant delay.

Having sorted myself out, I tied my haversack together and made ready for immediate departure for Ecuador by Pan-American Airways to Quito via Guayaquil. Then at the eleventh hour two things happened – one good, one bad. The first was an introduction given me by Dr Spann to a certain photographer named Bodo Wuth who had a business in Quito, the second was the irrevocable pronouncement at the Air Station that 44 lb of baggage was allowed per person, which meant I had to undo my rucksack, take out some warm clothes and leave them on Peruvian soil (I collected them a year later on the next expedition) and enter the aeroplane with less than the weight of a soldier's pack with which to ascend the twin giants of Chimborazo and Cotopaxi. Things did not look overwhelmingly bright – but I flew north with a great faith that things always work out in the end.

The flight north over the Peruvian coastal desert was smooth and even. Below, the brilliance of the early morning sun illuminated the high peaks of the Cordillera Blanca to the east and the milk-white surf of the otherwise leaden and tranquil Pacific to the west, while in between lay the sands of the marginal region – known as the Costa. This desert or littoral is on the average thirty miles wide and extends from northernmost Peru as far south as Central Chile. It consists in general of hard sand, burning in the noonday heat, where no shrub, bush or tree can find fertility; occasionally it is broken by an oasis of vegetation where a river, fed by the melting snows of the high Cordillera, breaks through and flows into the Pacific. Sometimes the rivers themselves get lost in these wastes.

The view to the east compensates of the desert as tier upon tier of foothills rise ever higher into the sky – like a gigantic wedding-cake – until they are finally capped by the great and beautiful peaks of the Cordillera Blanca which often rise more than 20,000 ft above the ocean. I had previously had a panoramic view of the White Range; it occurred during one moonlit night in November 1951 while driving a young donkey over a "pass" above the Marañyon Canyons. For a moment the moon was free of cloud and bathed the lone peaks in a roseate light of memorable beauty.

After about an hour and a half we touched down at an airport in the desert and then a little later crossed the Ecuadorian frontier, came low over the Rio Guayas, and landed at Guayaquil (250,000 population), where everything is green, tropical, and humid. In olden days in order to reach Quito, situated at 9,000 feet in the Sierras, one would be obliged to take a river-boat for a further six hours up the Guayas to Las Bodegas and from thence set out on the back of a mule for the weary journey to the capital. Later, at the turn of the century, a railway was built, but is now superseded by an air service that transports one from coast to capital in ninety minutes.

It is said to be possible to catch a glimpse of mighty Chimborazo's symmetrical dome from Guayaquil – and from the Pacific. W. H. Prescott in his famous *History of the Conquest of Peru* says, "it affords a magnificent prospect to the mariner on the Pacific Ocean". Undoubtedly this is true, but only recently have I met a person – an Ecuadorian sea-captain – who has actually seen it; I never did. However, as we fastened our seat-belts, after changing aeroplanes, the air-host said there would be another – and final – chance of seeing it within twenty minutes of the take-off. As we gained height, flying spiral fashion, into the Cordilleras I kept a sharp look-out for my quarry through the thick paned glass window on the starboard side. But after half an hour of constant straining I gave it up; the Monarch – El Rey de los Andes – was evidently unwilling to unveil her breath-taking attraction to anyone – least of all to a prospective candidate for her honour. I realized suddenly that Chimborazo has changed her sex but – like ships and Mt Everest, supported by Sir Edmund Hillary's baptismal words ("We've done the bitch") – I consider she should retain her femininity.

The last fifteen minutes, high in the Cordillera, was positively terrifying; we seemed never to rid ourselves of an interminable series of frustrating air-pockets that spun the aircraft around like a ball; to such an extent that a poor woman, next to me, opened her copious handbag in a moment green with apprehension; ten seconds later she snapped it shut with an air of smug approval. She had waited overlong, but went back to her knitting as if nothing had happened. I rushed aft.

Driving in the taxi for the few kilometres that separated the aerodrome from Quito I found that most of the back seat was taken up by a gigantic American; indeed our Chevrolet had not proceeded far before my companion, without either warning or introduction, thrust a huge face into mine and, fixing me with a choleric eye, said:

"You've, of course, come for the Humming Bird."

"Yes, yes – that's it," I replied, feeling for the sympathy of my ice-axe.

There was then a long pause while I waited to be enlightened, but my friend, who remained deep in thought, never spoke again. It was only after he got out that I realized that people do indeed journey to Ecuador for the Humming Bird just like others go to Japan for the blossom. Very stupid of me. Ecuador is the Mecca of the many varieties of Humming Birds.

Ecuador, one of South America's smallest Republics, is as its name suggests bisected laterally by the Equator and by the Andes vertically. To the north it is bounded by Colombia, to the east by the Amazon system from whence no less than five large tributaries of that river, the Santiago, Morona, Pastaza, Tigre and Napo – are given birth on the easternmost slopes of the most eastern Cordillera of the Andes. The Napo – the largest of these great affluents – rises at the very foot of El Cotopaxi and it was from thence, breaking away from Gonzalo Pizarro, brother of the great Francisco Pizarro, that another famous adventurer, Conquistador Orellana, started the first journey ever made across the Continent via the Amazon to the Atlantic Coast in the sixteenth century.

To the south of Ecuador lies Peru, and the forests of the

upper Marañyon within whose fastnesses live the notorious tribe of Indians known as Los Jivaros who are still *au fait* with the hereditary rites of shrinking heads. (This was country through which I was to pass in 1952.) To the west, the Republic is flanked by the calm waters of the Pacific and the volcanic Islands of Galapagos that rise out of the sea 600 miles west of the Gulf of Guayaquil, Ecuador's only external possession – famous for its giant tortoises.

Quito (population 223,000), situated 9,000 ft above the sea on a plateau between the western and eastern chains of the Andes, is overlooked, rather than dominated, by the extinct volcano, Pichincha, that rises for some 6,000 ft above the city – to the west. It would be hard to discover a more suitable base camp from which to start climbing expeditions – all the important volcanoes and mountains are within a hundred miles and most of them under fifty.

The climate is pleasant, warm and sunny – when it doesn't rain – and retains a more or less constant temperature throughout the year on account of its proximity to the Equator Line, which is in fact denoted a few kilometres to the north of the capital by a stone monument, where, of course, it is possible to be in both hemispheres simultaneously; indeed it is possible to unite the waters of the Pacific with those of the Atlantic on a knife-like watershed at the source of the Amazon in a similar kind of stance.

The town is picturesque, quiet and lovely; the many old buildings, convents, monasteries and churches of Spanish Colonial architecture somehow seem to blend with the modern unpretentious suburban villas. The streets in the old quarter are narrow, medieval and tortuous, and only intended for pedestrian or equestrian traffic, whereas in the New Quarter can be seen wide, straight avenues constructed for all the needs of the fastest motorist.

The little Indian policemen, dressed in light tropical khaki, are helpful, polite, and have a lovely time blowing shrilly, if a little incomprehensibly, on Christmas-cracker whistles, from the edge of the sidewalks, at everyone in general and no-one in particular. The significance is hard for the tourist to understand.

Among modern amenities there are some up-to-date

cinemas (the largest and grandest is the Ciné Bolivar); three presentable hotels – the "Cordillera", "Colon" and the "Embajador"; a little bevy of out-of-town night clubs, very friendly, with rather shoddy girls and orchestras – but with more capital and *clientèle* they could be amusing. All the cars were glitteringly American except for the elderly, sombre Humber belonging to the British Ambassador (a previous plenipotentiary rode a horse). Although the city has a population of nearly a quarter of a million, there were no more than six British residents within its limits in 1953. There are more in Guayaquil where there is a Consul and a Vice-Consul, and the officers of the Pacific Steam Navigation Company.

I arrived in Quito on Tuesday, 10 August, and immediately set to work to put my plans into action. I needed two reliable mountaineers before I could contemplate carrying out my mission. The first few days were very depressing in this respect, but they must be described as they in their turn heralded better ones that were to come.

The first thing I did on quitting my hotel the day after my arrival was to take Dr Spann's visiting card from my wallet and pay a call upon his friend – the photographer, Bodo Wuth, who occupied a studio in the Central Plaza, near the cathedral in the Old Quarter.

Bodo Wuth was sympathetic towards my ideas, but could not give any direct assistance beyond most considerately – being a busy man – inviting me to journey for the sake of photography and acclimatization to the regions of the crater lake of Quilotoa near Latacuniga at the week-end. I accepted. However I felt I was not on the right track, and was wondering how I could get upon it, when on emerging into the brilliant sunlight of the Plaza I gazed absently across at the House of Representatives and suddenly recollected that Jorge Espinoza, the ever co-operative Ecuadorian Chargé d'Affaires in London, had furnished me with a verbal introduction to ex-President Galoplaza. This excited me for I went on to remember that Jorge had told me that Galoplaza owned a hacienda at the very base of the world's highest volcano. Then I tried to formulate in my mind what help in the way of the acquisition of climbers I could possibly derive from this introduction, provided Galoplaza was good enough to see me at all.

Although I could not hope for mountaineers I considered that the ex-President might be able to assist with a first-hand knowledge of weather conditions upon Cotopaxi, and perhaps loan me a number of transport mules to carry provisions (which I had not purchased) and the equipment of companion climbers (which I had not found) to set up a base camp preparatory to an assault.

Although it was rather putting the proverbial cart before the horse, I decided as I stood in the sunlight within the Plaza that I'd seek out ex-President Galoplaza.

The location of his current whereabouts was not difficult to ascertain for his name is naturally very well known to most Ecuadorians. In fact I jumped into the first taxi and instructed, "*Hacienda Galoplaza, por Favour.*"

"*Si, señor*" – and off we went.

After about two and a half hours' drive along the main trunk-road I considered it was time I was catching a view of the unmistakable geographical features of the cone of Cotopaxi. There was no sign – nothing resembling the magnitude of the famous volcano. I became very worried as I knew that Cotopaxi was not more than forty miles in a straight line from Quito – then where could we be? I leant over and asked the driver:

"Where is the Volcano Cotopaxi, if you please?"

"South of Quito, *señor*."

"But this *is* south."

"No, *señor* – this is north!"

Then it dawned upon me, as we entered the very gates of the patio of the ex-President's hacienda that there were two Hacienda Galoplazas and this was the other one.

We pulled up in the patio, beside a light blue shooting-brake, as dusk was falling. The taxi-driver turned to me and said:

"There is *Señor* Galoplaza."

"Where?"

"In the car."

"Please go and tell him that you have a 'gringo' who wishes to see him."

The taxi-man hesitated for a moment, slightly awed, then opened the door of his car and walked bravely over to the beautiful blue shooting-brake. The window was misty, so the ex-President jerked it down and talked to the driver, who almost at once beckoned me over.

I told my sad story while Galoplaza listened. Having finished, he said:

"I'd like to put you up, but the house is full of guests, but my sister, who runs *the* Cotopaxi hacienda, will help you – go to the Oficina Galoplaza in Quito."

Thus I drove back on the long journey south to Quito and finally arrived at the Hotel Embajador late and exhausted. Next day I went early to the Oficina Galoplaza, but was told by the staff that the *señora* would not be coming until the morning. I therefore spent the remainder of the long day in a state of frustration until the following day I reported at the same hour, only to be told that the *señora* was not expected until the afternoon.

Later that Friday morning I met Paul Feret, a blue-suited, broad-shouldered, freckle-faced Frenchman, who kept chickens and went out of his way to help me. He had been in Ecuador eight years and had done some climbing himself, notably on the volcano of Altar, but now possessed neither the time nor the equipment to do more. Nevertheless he took the greatest trouble with me and together we drove down to the Old Quarter to the bottom of a narrow street on a hill not far from the Central Plaza, where we entered a windowless draper's store.

Feret shouted "Pépé", and glancing up to where he (Feret) was looking, I saw someone turning outwards towards us from the top of a step-ladder while in the act of bringing down a bale of gaudy yellow cotton.

A few seconds later Pépé Sandoval – the manager of the shop – came down and Feret introduced us.

"Monsieur Snow, here, wants to climb Cotopaxi, could you accompany him?"

"*Con mucho gusto*" (with much pleasure), replied Sandoval after steadily surveying me for a long moment.

"But he needs a third person," continued Feret.

"I know," answered Sandoval. "If the Señor Inglés will

come around to the committee room tonight at eight o'clock I will present him to the Jefe General of the Group – Señor Parra – and he will fix up something."

On leaving the draper's shop I learnt from Paul Feret that Pépé Sandoval was a prominent member of a mountaineering association known as *Neuvos Horizontes*, founded in 1944, and considered one of the foremost climbers in Ecuador.

That afternoon I kept my appointment and I not only found the ex-President's sister "in" but also kind and helpful; I no longer felt the necessity of throwing myself at her feet and begging for assistance because I was far too elated to do any such thing after the successful meeting with Sandoval earlier on.

That night – Friday – I went to the committee room of the mountaineering association. I felt frightened for I thought my great lack of experience would run against me, but no! I was taken for what I was, rather than for what I had not done. I was immeasurably grateful when it was agreed that Pépé Sandoval and his friend, Edmundo Pazmino, would climb Cotopaxi with me in about a week's time. My plan of sleeping on the crater was also accepted. I went back to my hotel that night a very contented man. Meanwhile it was decided that I should go for a practice climb on Pichincha, the extinct volcano that rises 6,000 ft above Quito to the westward. I was to set out early on Sunday morning. Pichincha, by any comparative standard, is not a difficult climb, indeed a party of strong-legged picnickers could scramble to its highest summit (there are two) without extraordinary fatigue.

Therefore I did not dare hope, or expect, to gain much mountain technique upon its gentle, grassy slopes; indeed, it is possible to ride a sure-footed mule to within a thousand feet of the top. This last lap sometimes produces momentary hesitation of balance and dizziness upon the ultimate rock face that is undeniably precipitous, and doubtless if it were covered with snow and ice, as it occasionally is, the best of climbers would have to step warily. At 5.30 a.m. on the morning of Sunday I met two members of the *Neuvos Horizontes* (not Sandoval or Pazmino) in the cold and totally deserted Central Plaza that is so busy in the daytime. With hardly a word exchanged between us we walked out of the suburbs of the capital and on to the undulating and cultivated slopes of Pichincha before daylight came. I led to begin with until we reached a height of about 12,000 ft at which point I was unaccountably smitten with a nasty attack of diarrhoea and a splitting headache. I was absolutely determined to shake off this nausea that swept over me – I had never been similarly affected at 12,000 ft. I knew that the *Neuvos Horizontes* had put me on trial; all depended on how I "made out" on Pichincha.

A hundred times as we scrambled ever higher I felt I had taken my last step and a hundred times I persuaded myself to carry on, until we arrived at a point some 6,000 ft directly above Quito which lay like a little toy town far below us. At this point we were about 900 ft under the highest of Pichincha's twin summits. From here on it looked as if we would be scrambling on all fours as the hitherto gentle, grassy slopes had given place to sheet rock-faces of loose, dry granite around which the prevailing wind lashed with a ferocity that stung the face. My companions decided it wasn't worth employing a rope, although I am sure none of us would have had opportunity for a second slip had we slipped once, which fortunately we did not, and we reached the highest point, 15,918 ft, safely, at 10.45 a.m.

We seated ourselves in some rocky outcrops and one of the Ecuadorians extracted a tin brief-case from a convenient crevice in between two rocks where a little snow had drifted and collected. Taking a "log" from this metal document case he proceeded to note down the following items about the ascent, in triplicate: The names of the successful climbers, their respective addresses, their nationalities, the time of arrival, the route they followed, the current atmospheric conditions, finishing with a brief matter-of-fact *résumé* of the hazards encountered and overcome during the ascent. We each kept a copy, bearing three signatures, and I noted that the number of mine was 000198. Therefore even if I was not the very first to reach the top, I was certainly not going to be the last!

Afterwards, when the tin case was safely back in its

corner, we cheered lustily three times to the memory of Edward Whymper, followed by three "hurrahs" for the memory of a famous Ecuadorian mountaineer, Nicolas Martínez. This is an established custom among the members of the *Neuvos Horizontes* and whenever a peak in "the waistline of the world" is successfully scaled the sound of three cheers rings from the mountain tops. From the summit of Pichincha we had a good view of a snow-capped cone, slewed off at the top some forty miles to the southeast. This was my very first sight of the volcano Cotopaxi. It looked beautifully symmetrical from where we stood, and I found it hard to make myself believe I would be climbing upon it in eight days' time; the future filled me with awe. After viewing three other peaks, those of Antisana, Corazon and the twin pinnacles of Illiniza, we left the summit of Pichincha and made our way down to Quito where we finally arrived at about 4.30 p.m. after relating the circumstances of our ascent to little parties of Quito residents, who had climbed up to the lower slopes to pass the lazy afternoon, picnicking. They all seemed very friendly, and regarded our small achievement with an admiration it did not deserve; cheerfully disregarding the fact that their unhurried after-luncheon Sunday stroll had led them to an eminence at least 3,000 ft above the capital. That evening, having changed, I went to a Sunday movie, at the Ciné Bolivar, with one of my companions, to see *Call Me Madam*.

Before this story goes farther, I must give an account of former explorations upon Chimborazo and Cotopaxi.

In 1802, after three years of travelling in South America, Alexander von Humboldt came to Ecuador and together with two friends, Aimié Boupland and Carolos Montufar, attempted an ascent of Chimborazo. They reached an alleged height of 19,286 ft before they were halted by an impassable ravine – some 400 ft deep (or high!) and 60 ft wide, which presented an insurmountable barrier. "We could see clearly that the ridge on which we stood continued in the same direction on the other side of the ravine . . . There was no means of getting round the cleft . . . The softness of the snowy mass prohibited such an attempt." It was apparent that they had a bad time for they continue to speak of being indisposed, experiencing nausea and giddiness . . . "Blood exuded from their lips and gums."

At this time Chimborazo was thought to be the highest mountain on earth; the Himalayas had not been surveyed nor the heights of the mighty mountains in Southern Chile – Aconcagua, Tupungato Mercedario – evaluated. In fact to the end of his long life Humboldt held Chimborazo to be "the grandest mountain in the world".

The next attempt was made in 1831 by Joseph Dieudonné Boussingault in company with an American, Colonel Hall, and a Negro. They were equally unsuccessful, suffering similar torments as Humboldt's party. "As we went on, we felt extreme fatigue from the want of consistency in the snowy soil, which gave way continually under our feet, and in which we sank sometimes up to our waists. We were convinced of the impossibility of proceeding." Nevertheless on their second attempt they reached a height a few hundred feet above that of Humboldt.

It was not until 1880 that Edward Whymper and his two Swiss guides, Jean Antoine and Louis Carrel, conquered the fabulous Chimborazo for the first time. Since that day it has been climbed, perhaps, eight times.

In 1872 a German named Reiss ascended to the crater of Cotopaxi and in 1877 it erupted – to such an extent that in Quito (only forty miles distant) it became dusk at eight o'clock in the morning, remaining so until midday, at which time it was pitch dark. A man returning home could not find his own door although standing immediately opposite it; another couldn't see his hand when he held it close to his face. The volcano – which can be seen from Quito – was completely invisible, and to quote Whymper, "in a few minutes the whole of it was enveloped in smoke and steam – but out of the darkness a moaning noise arose, which grew into a roar, and a deluge of water, blocks of ice, mud and rock rushed down, sweeping away everything that lay in its course. It was estimated to have travelled as far as Latacunga (about sixty miles) at the rate of fifty miles an hour."

The first news that Europe received of the eruption was from the volcanic dust that settled upon the decks of steamers which plied southwards up the coast, at least 200 miles from the volcano.

At the base camp – about 15,800 ft – we met four other Ecuadorians – all very youthful, and associates of the *Neuvos Horizontes* organization, who on hearing of our plan to spend the night on the crater-lip of the volcano decided that opportunity was too good to be missed. This decision was frightening; we tried hard to dissuade them for there was a good chance of them freezing solid before morning could come again. They had only one tent – too awkward to carry up to the summit, and there were then – that auspicious evening – still four of them.

"What will you do then – when you get up there?" we asked.

"We will dig ourselves foxholes and curl up in our sleeping-bags."

"You won't last the night, you won't wake in the morning. It's your responsibility; we'll have nothing to do with it."

Next morning at eight o'clock we set out in two parties, on two separate ropes. My own party carried only emergency equipment – a little two-man tent, which one enters on all four through a hole in the side; some preserved fruit, a thermos of coffee, chocolate biscuits and barley sugar. The other four had thin sleeping-bags and iron rations.

For the first half-hour after leaving camp climbing was of the scrambling nature, amounting to no more than a breathless trudge over loose, volcanic shale. The first moment came when we arrived at the snow-line – here both parties solemnly sat on an outcrop of rock and started getting out crampons – ice-spikes – and ropes. This was frightening, for neither of these articles had to my conscious knowledge graced either my feet or waist.

Edmundo led, with myself in the centre and Pépé in the rear. We climbed cautiously along a traverse in steady relays, Edmundo employing his ice-axe with dexterous precision to cut steps for those behind by which we made the slow ascent.

With infinite care he would cut steps ahead of him, climbing sometimes thirty feet at a time while Pépé and

I would pay out the rope – I was not good at this and would frequently hold up progress by getting it entangled around the spikes in my crampons. When this happened I perspired with frantic embarrassment and that in its turn meant that moisture obscured my spectacles and goggles – and before we continued I had to take them off and wipe them both. This happened many times.

When Edmundo had proceeded about ten yards he would drive his ice-axe into the snow, belay the rope around it and again around his body for double security and then take the strain while I climbed up the steps towards him. Reaching him I would belay and he (Edmundo) would proceed upwards for another thirty feet hacking out further ice-steps until he would belay once more to allow Pépé to join me. Then the manoeuvre would be repeated all over again and in this way we painstakingly ascended the dome of the world's highest volcano. It was very tiring for Edmundo.

Although it was toilsome work, it was also dangerous, for we all knew that one moment's relaxation or carelessness might plunge all three of us a thousand feet headlong below. I was just beginning to properly understand what mountaineering meant.

We had been climbing in this manner for perhaps half an hour when suddenly there was a cry from the party behind. Turning, I expected to witness someone falling. But no! – they were all on their feet. Pépé shouted a question across the intervening furrow between the two parties – his voice sounded strangely sinister in the silence of the Andean mountain air. A very few seconds later a voice replied, "Snow blindness," and the next moment two of them – one leading the other – were taking the first steps down towards the base camp. Now there were two. The hand of Providence must have been upon us, for if this incident had not occurred when and where it did – this account would not have been written. But we did not then know what the future held.

We watched the two going slowly down for a few minutes then we turned and faced what would lie ahead. Now, as we started again, my leg muscles began to ache intolerably and I thought I could never go on. But I did, I did . . .

At about 18,000 ft we came upon the first of the two crevassed areas – most dangerous part of the climb.

The first crevasse loomed up ahead – a six-foot fissure which doubtless went down into unimaginable depths.

We halted. Pépé drove his ice-axe hard into the frozen snow, tested it, hitched the rope around it, and took the strain. A second later Edmundo had leapt across the gap – the soft vibration of his landing on the far side caused the snow overhangs at the treacherous and uneven edge to crumble and fall in little sparkling lumps into the crevasse. It was fascinating. Then came my turn. I waited while Edmundo had me belayed on his side. I was trembling – as he looked up from his work and nodded. I jumped. A leap of six feet is nothing at sea-level, it's an exertion at 18,000 ft with crampons encrusted with frozen snow to weight one's feet. I had never jumped a crevasse before. All across, we struggled on again, placing our feet carefully in the steps Edmundo cut, with such toil, ahead; the temperature was below zero, the wind was rising, the weather worsening. Where the slightest slip meant the loss of life, we crawled warily.

At this stage I called for very frequent rests for my lungs heaved like the bellows of the hearth, and my heart, wholly unaccustomed to extreme elevation, thundered, like an express train entering a long tunnel, my legs ached intolerably, as if I had a chronic fever. Edmundo and Pépé were very patient – but I sensed, rather than saw, through their dark goggles that they were worried – for time was running out, and it was absolutely essential we gain the crater before darkness came. I wondered if I would stick it out, but I had to – these men were risking their lives at my invitation, I could not let them down now.

Then suddenly, as so often happens when one is at the end of one's tether, something happened. Edmundo had come to a halt – frozen in his steps like a pointer in the snow. His experienced eyes had detected an unusual darker patch in the snow ahead which showed where frozen snow had formed a flimsy treacherous snow-bridge across the depths of a crevasse. To put foot on that bridge would have invited disaster. Again we jumped.

Now the snow was getting deeper, often above our thighs. The wind was still mounting; it moaned now. I wondered what it would be like on the crater, for down here it was almost the force of a gale as it drove frozen particles of snow into the uncovered parts of our faces like the points of a thousand pine-needles. The protective cream with which I had smothered every unprotected part did nothing to alleviate the pain. I had some more in my rucksack, but couldn't make the effort to do anything that was not automatic. At this point I believe all three of us were feeling the strain, resting every few yards, climbing up and up in a series of traverses, like an ambitious cyclist up a very steep gradient, tacking three or four yards one way then three or four back the other. So sheer was the climb that it was impossible to take it in a straight line. Our rate of ascent must have been well under 500 ft an hour – slower than that when the snow deepened.

Later the all-encompassing darkness began to close down upon us. The gale, still rising, whipped up the snow from the face of the mountain in a fury blizzard, blotting out everything ahead.

Edmundo was himself now stopping frequently – lying like a waif in the snow smitten with the unpredictable *soroche* (mountain sickness) that made him vomit continuously. Bravely he insisted on retaining the first place on the rope. But it was a mistake for isolated in his world of sickness he went off the course and all sense of direction left us. This was really my fault, for it was I who had insisted on frequent stops which initially had wasted the precious hours of light – now we were paying for my mistake.

I staggered on blindly wherever Edmundo was leading – in a world of gloom, wind, and drifting snow that to me was very sinister. All my extremities were frozen numb, they somehow seemed to obey like robots. I thought my face was going to be marked, horribly, for life.

We were all near to exhaustion, struggling like automatons, our breath coming in short, deep gasps as the altitude increased. But we had to go forward. To stop and rest meant collapse, dying of exposure in the white graves our warm bodies would imprint for themselves too easily in the ever-deepening snow. I did not know how the others felt but I was now desperately alarmed – grateful for the darkness as it withheld the sight of my tears from the eyes of Pépé – Edmundo would not have noticed, he was too ill. My one desire was to sit and never to rise; I wanted to leave my bones where we were, but I lacked the courage. Fear, coupled with the encouragements of Pépé, kept me going. Pépé was wonderful.

Suddenly there was a shout of triumph from Edmundo. Through a gap in the curtain of the blizzard he caught sight, momentarily, of the craggy outlines of the crater-lip itself. A wave of extreme jubilation swept through the party. Cold, fatigue, irritation were temporarily forgotten. We almost ran those last few yards . . . or what seemed at first to be the last few yards.

But our run quickly became a walk again, the walk a drunken stagger. Another five . . . ten . . . fifteen minutes passed, and still the elusive silhouette of what we so longingly sought eluded us – or was it that our eyes could not properly focus?

Again I fell over the frozen lengths of rope to lie spread-eagled, hopelessly, in the deep snow. I knew I had to make the effort to get up . . . to get up and go on . . . to get up and go on. I repeated the simple phrase over and over again for my brain had become irrevocably fixed in one groove and the gramophone kept playing . . . "Get up and go on," with unbearable monotony. I got to my feet and was just starting again when through the howling gale another shout came from Edmundo. He had reached the crater of Cotopaxi.

We struggled to join him on the marginal strip of loose, black lava, some thirty feet wide, where there was no snow.

Now, with the external side of the volcano no longer providing shelter, we caught the full force of the gale that came from the east.

Pépé and I struggled to pitch the two-man tent among the boulders and stones on the black patch of lava which separated the unpredictable depths of the volcano from the icy, snow-covered slope we had so painfully ascended.

The only way we could erect the tent was by Pépé

crawling in through the hole – like a participant in an obstacle race – and pushing up the hollow aluminium tent-pole from within. While outside, I, at the same moment, pulled out the base flaps to their full extent and hammered in the skewer-like stays. Poor Edmundo, too ill to take any active part, watched fascinated as though in the throes of a nightmare.

Somehow we got the fragile-looking shelter up at a ridiculously uneven angle, about five feet below the edge of the volcano, just sufficient to allow the worst of the raging wind to pass over the conical top of the canvas. Even so the pressure on the ground pegs was exacting, and before entering I dragged some heavy boulders into position to weight down the edges of the tent as I considered it probable we might find ourselves half-way down the way we had come before dawn. This was a great work at 19,650 ft, and once the boulders were in place, the hitherto two-man tent was reduced internally to a one-man dimension. Nevertheless we all three managed to ease ourselves inside together with our rucksacks, rope, crampons, etc. We scarcely expected sleep. Edmundo, ill with mountain sickness, lay in an inert heap. Pépé and I huddled close together, cramped, cold, and exhausted. The only food we had was a small carton of dried prunes – the ascent had taken much longer than anticipated and we had eaten everything else. We had no stove to "fabricate water".

Meanwhile the remaining two of the other party had also reached the crater, and even now we could hear sounds like a blacksmith's forge some ten yards away. They were digging their graves with vigour, their ice-axes crunching into the frozen, stony lava. Would they be able to dig deep enough holes? I wondered.

Some ten minutes after the noises of human endeavour had altogether ceased – there was a cry – almost theatrical in its tragic intensity, brought to us as it was through the moaning gale. I nudged Pépé.

"They'll freeze to death out there," I said. Whereupon I untied the flap by which we entered our tent and shouted. A minute or so passed before a wretched apparition dragging a sleeping bag after him appeared in the doorway. Unceremoniously Pépé and I helped him in; he was almost on the verge of collapse. He was only eighteen and, I noticed, had no gloves. Why did he come? A few minutes later there was a further cry, and a little later another figure appeared at the entrance – we got him in as well. How we did so I don't know.

It was then about seven o'clock in the evening and for the next sixteen hours the two-man tent (reduced to one-man in capacity) bulged with five frozen human beings. It was suffocating, yet freezing, and I kept making involuntary little lunges at the roof in quest of oxygen. If I'd had a knife I would have cut a hole and stuck out my nose. Instead I ran my fingers over the cold, moist canvas and applied them to my forehead. It helped for a few short seconds – it was like a self-baptism. But a little later I stood it no longer and dived bodily for the entrance flap, untied it, and ejected my head dartingly like a cobra in the act of striking, but brought it back into the tent as suddenly for outside the cold was equally insupportable. When circulation died in our feet we rubbed each other feverishly; two of us were too ill to bother. Perhaps they were fortunate – rubbing is very painful. We attempted two songs – they died as soon as they came to our lips. Two of us devoured the prunes, one did not want them and the other two did not know, I suppose, we even had them. Oh, the lassitude!

Even when dawn came again and the wind had dropped we could not get out for a blanket of mist enveloped the entire mountain. We had to wait until nearly eleven o'clock before the sun broke through.

By this time Edmundo had slightly recovered. It was decided now that we were on the crater we must try to scale a dangerous ice and snow pinnacle that rose some 150 ft above the lip. It has never been climbed. Accordingly, after an intense struggle to separate and find our various "dismembered" limbs, we crawled out and put on our boots and crampons. How hateful they were! Fearful objects that no longer seemed part of us.

Leaving the tent and the other two within it, we climbed the few feet to the crater, in enforced slow motion, and then walked carefully along the lip. The wind was unbelievably painful on our right cheeks. There was nothing to see within the "chimney" – nothing but scurrying mist and general murkiness. We moved for perhaps a hundred yards before the eminence that was our immediate goal came into view. It looked horribly sheer and full of predatory cornices. Soon we reached its base, but the mist, suddenly, totally obscured it. We couldn't remain where we were – the wind cut through as if we had no bone structure. We took cover behind a low line of frozen *séracs* – as though we were in a slit trench preparatory to a final assault. We remained crouched in this manner for twenty minutes without moving – the mist did not lift for more than a few seconds at a time. At last we could stand it no longer and we made our way back to the tent and hustled the others.

With the visibility again getting worse, we struck camp and started off down the mountain in two parties as before. We came upon the crevassed areas again; more dangerous this time for there had been a fresh fall of snow in the night and consequently many new "bridges" had been created.

Suddenly I felt the snow move underfoot, shuddering and sliding away. Stupidly I had ventured on to one of the "new bridges" although Edmundo ahead had missed it. I tried to throw myself forward to safety. Too late. I felt myself dropping, then happily came an agonizing jerk around the ribs, and the rope held.

It was Pépé who had saved me. Even as the snow gave way, expectant as ever, he had stopped dead in his tracks, driving his ice-axe hard into the ground, twisting the rope like lightning around and at the same time leaning back on his heels to take the strain.

But all I knew then as I hung suspended was an urgent shout from Pépé. I didn't understand all the words but knew well enough what they meant.

"Don't move! Whatever you do – don't move!"

I felt rather like a marionette on a string until I at last managed to get a firm grip on the marginal snow.

We reached the base camp – at 15,800 ft – at about three o'clock on the same afternoon, spent the night, went down to Hacienda Ilitio next day, and from thence we walked on to the main trunk road at Lasso and there picked up a long-distance bus for Quito where we arrived at about ten o'clock the same evening. It had been a hectic thirty-six hours. I nearly broke down in the street outside the bus-terminus while I awaited the arrival of a taxi. It was a very, very short wait perhaps of only fifteen minutes – but something within me broke and I lost the faculties of direction, decision, and initiative. I swayed towards the ground, but just as I was about to drop a cab appeared and I fell within into the back seat.

The residents of the *Residencia Lutetia* were not all in bed as I groped my way through the hall. Paul Feret extricated himself from a group of people collected around the warmth of the fire.

"Did you do it, Sebastian?"

"Yes."

"The bit of the top?"

"No."

Then Paul gave me an arm and I went to my room and fell into bed with all the clothes that had been around me on the crater. When I awoke to strong sunlight, I found someone had taken off my boots.

Ten days later – Friday the 4th of September – at nine o'clock on a brilliant sunny morning a gleaming blue-cream Chevrolet could have been seen speeding swiftly south through the last straggling suburbs of Quito, on its way to Chimborazo. Inside there were four people of three different nationalities; their mutual *lingua franca* was Spanish, but at nine o'clock in the morning they were not speaking, they were gazing out of the windows, idly aware of the thunderous, yet even, roar of the new tyres burning up the cobbled highway.

Let me introduce them. The driver and owner of the motor, with his dark hair cut *en brosse*, big black business-like spectacles, check shirt, fawn trousers and sandals, was a Frenchman, a technician attached to the United Nations Delegation to Ecuador, his name, Roger Ouvrard.

Next to him was a neat man – with neat dark hair, neat dark glasses, and neat dark moustache; his name was Cesár Morejon, an Ecuadorian photographer who had a studio a floor above the Committee Room of the *Neuvos Horizontes*. In the back seat was a man who spoke idiomatic American and colloquial French; his name Juan Elizade, an architect, and scion of one of Ecuador's most influential families, and the only one of the party who understood what all the others were trying not to say. Ouvrard spoke no English, Morejon no English or French, and I found ringing the changes in French and Spanish beyond my ability. Nevertheless we all had one word in common – Chimborazo.

After about two hours of fast, uneventful driving, we reached the small town of Latacunga where, after a quick snack of cheese and pig purchased hurriedly from a vagrant vendor, we arrived at the provincial capital of Ambato (population 34,000), a little after midday. Here, in a busy, narrow street, the Frenchman pulled up the big car and we lunched – thank God – at an unpretentious little restaurant inappropriately named *El Trocadero*. Although the advertisements adorning the four walls strongly advised us to take a couple of familiar purgatives and a glass of coca-cola, Ouvrard and I ordered steak and chips while Elizade and Morejon plumped for chicken soup, salad mess, and beer.

Chimborazo has been attempted many times; conquered comparatively few. It is a mountain that tests the physical stamina rather than the technical skill of the mountaineer. It has three principal difficulties that have overcome the assaults of past expeditions led by travellers of world renown.

The first difficulty is to locate a "breach" within the vast, sheer cliffs that practically encircle all approach to deep, snowy slopes that lie beyond and lead towards the two main summits – the "Western" and Southern or "Whymper" summit. This great natural rampart of rock – known as the Red Walls – rises vertically with startling grandeur four to five hundred feet (perhaps more) clear out of the less oblique slopes below; situated at 18,700 ft, they are capped overall by a 300 ft layer of ice and snow conglomeration, seemingly cut flush with the angle of rocks from whence giant icicles hang for a hundred feet. Very impressive. The great nineteenth-century explorers,

Alexander von Humboldt and Joseph Dieudonné Boussingault, were both beaten at this point.

The second difficulty is the uncertainty of whether or not the huge crevasse, found at 20,000 ft, and extending for hundreds of yards in either direction, is possible to jump. The German scientist Hans Meyer turned back here.

The third difficulty is the appalling strain of having to flounder through soft snow – sometimes neck-deep – at over 20,500 ft without oxygen.

All previous expeditions – I believe without exception – seemed to have pitched their highest camps at or around the 17,000 ft mark preparatory to the following day's assault. We thought this too low, being largely influenced by the lurid accounts of the horrifying rigours which overtook other parties that had tried to gain both summits within the short space of a single day. This involved them in at least 7,000 ft of climbing (ascent and descent) with the most arduous part above 20,000 ft; up to that point they had probably been making good progress – well up to schedule, but then they got trapped in the deep, soft snow through which they sank as if in quick-sands, sometimes having to continue on all fours. It is then that the race for survival starts; for each member of each expedition knows full well that he has to be below the Red Walls – 18,700 ft – before darkness comes, otherwise he will not survive the night, out on these pitiless, windswept slopes that lead to the summits of one of South America's greatest mountains.

We decided to camp, therefore, higher up, at 18,700 ft, directly beneath the Red Walls which meant only 4,000 ft of climbing; which we thought would be quite enough, especially for novices like myself. However, we did not know if it was possible to find a suitable site where the tents could be erected at that elevation. Morejon thought it possible. He had been previously on two expeditions that had climbed Chimborazo: he was the only man living who had conquered it twice – and now he was determined upon the hat-trick. Elizade and Ouvrard, like myself, had never set foot upon it. It was fortunate that such a man as Morejon was with us.

Next day, not very early, we left Pogyos mounted upon mules with full packs upon our shoulders. We were accom-

panied by the telegraphist and two *arrieros* (mule-drivers).
We closed with Chimborazo by riding across country –
known as the Arenal – of sandy soil and stunted vegetation
until we arrived at the bottom of a moraine full of boulders
where further progress on four-legged beasts was out of the
question. The height here was approximately 15,600 ft – the
most inhospitable spot imaginable – the wind cut through
us like well-aimed stilettoes. All around amongst the in-
animate, grey-black rocks there was an air of unspeakable
desolation. It seemed from the outset to rob one of all
courage to fight against this mighty mountain. The quiet-
ness was sinister.

We of the expedition gathered under the lee of a large
rock while the mule-drivers off-loaded our stores and
equipment from the beasts. Their hands must have been
frozen as they worked for they wore no gloves. Their only
protection against the icy blast that enfiladed them from the
slopes above were the pelts of deer (like cricket pads) that
covered their legs from ankle to loin; only the telegraphist
had a scarf and that was an inadequate one.

It was therefore no surprise when on finding we had not
sufficient backs to carry our baggage up to the High Camp
(18,700 ft) that they did not volunteer and would not be
bribed with tempting offers of inconceivable unheard-of
wealth. They left us with the airy promise that they would
be with us, at that very spot, at 8 a.m. on Monday, 7
September; by that time we would have put in our attack
and be starting down from High Camp. We hoped. Then
we began to sort out and readjust ourselves; each one of us
would be compelled to carry 40 lb of weight across his
shoulders as far as the Red Walls where we hoped to find
shelter for the night; next day, all being well, we could leave
all sleeping and cooking equipment within the camp and set
out for the summit with emergency rations only.

We still looked upon the establishment of a higher camp
as a possible idea, but it did have the disadvantage of a
greatly exhausting, preliminary day. I hoped we would not
be too spent on the morrow, the day that counted. As we
organized ourselves at this depressing place, here are some
extracts from my journal that I wrote up at the time.

It is about 11.15 a.m. I am leaning up against a huge grey-black boulder smothering my face with lashings of protective cream with one hand and writing this with the other. Ouvrard, a few paces to my right, attired in light brown anorak, fawn trousers (he doesn't appear to have any climbing breeches, they are absolutely unattainable in Ecuador, as is most equipment necessary for mountaineering) and kid gloves, is painstakingly folding up his eight blankets (he doesn't possess a sleeping bag either!). On my left Elizade is sorting out the food methodically. We have an incredible amount of noodle soup. "How many packets should we take?" he asks – no-one answers him, his guess is as good as ours; he takes the lot. A little farther over, near the edge of the great boulder, Morejon is, of all things, doing a strip-tease act, putting on extra underwear.

At last we are all ready and assembled. Morejon and Elizade carry the food; Ouvrard, his awkward-looking blankets; I, the two tents. We are leaving a crate of oranges and tangerines under a rock against our return on Monday – if we return!

Then we set off for the High Camp. I went into the lead with Morejon at my heels; Elizade and Ouvrard a little behind; they moved more slowly. We were not roped.

The moraine got steeper, and soon our cramponed feet crunched and imprinted themselves, a satisfying sound, against the first of the snow; our breathing became more and more difficult. Then a blanket mist swept down upon us from the direction of the Red Walls and enveloped us. I couldn't pick out Morejon only thirty yards behind; I heard the regular crunch, crunch, of his feet on the snow and his heavy breathing. I leant on my ice-axe, resting upon it, and watched him slowly emerge into my vision through the fog. When he caught up, he said:

"Where is Juan and Ouvrard?"

"Behind you?"

"No."

We shouted, "Juan! Juan!"

There was no reply – no sound but that of our lungs heaving after the exertion of yelling. We called again, louder this time. An answering cry came from far below – it was not one of distress; so we continued slowly on upwards.

"They will be all right now we are on the ridge (south-west ridge), they can follow our tracks, the snow will soon be getting deeper. We must go on if we are to reach the *Murallas Rojas* before night. If we don't it may be impossible to find a place to sleep," said Morejon.

After climbing for another few hundred feet we rested and shouted down again to our two companions. This time there was no acknowledgment.

"What's happened, no trouble, I hope?" I asked.

"No, I expect they have gone too far to the right – probably missed our tracks in the mist. They'll be all right; Elizade has done quite a bit of climbing on other mountains."

We then turned inwards to the slope, which was becoming increasingly steep, and climbed again. We were feeling the altitude and we started to zig-zag, tacking a little this way, a little that. Later we shouted again through the mist, but still no sound came from below.

Late in the afternoon the sun broke through and the mist cleared and we got our first good view of the *Murallas Rojas* which by now appeared quite close at hand. Deceptively close. At about this time I became absolutely exhausted. I had been going strongly, and had been feeling proud of the deliberate rhythmical tread I had maintained. Cotopaxi had done that for me. But suddenly, as the Great Ramparts loomed up above, I lost all power of controlled movement and I started to stagger as if I was drunk. Do what I would I could not master my legs, all the sinews and muscles seemed to have flopped. It was as if I were climbing on stilts, pushing one leg before the other, instead of using the muscles of the thighs. Morejon overtook and passed me; his pace did not slacken; his body and legs working automatically. He was determined to find a site for the erection of our tents before night. It was imperative that he did. There was still some way to go although the immense walls, with their thick layer of solid ice and snow conglomeration above, appeared almost within touch. This will give some idea of their magnitude.

Around five-thirty that evening we came to the head of the ridge we had been climbing all day. At this point we were faced with making a "traverse" across to the lower end of the walls, where the only possible sites for camp could be found. We should have roped up – but time, oh, so precious time! – was running out, and Morejon without hesitating went straight across; he had got within ten yards of the far side and was almost under the Red Walls when I, following uncertainly some twenty yards behind, along the traverse, fell. As my legs slipped from under me down the slope, I somehow, at the same moment, contrived to keep a grip on my ice-axe with my left arm and clutch a friable piece of rocky sandstone outcrop with my right. There I hung suspended; poised above a slope that would at any moment send me rolling over and over thousands of feet below towards the telegraphist post of Pogyos. I did not scream immediately; I didn't dare to breath for the slightest heave of my lungs would sever my two remaining contacts with this world; the ice-axe and the friable piece of sandstone. Instead, I cautiously peered upwards and saw, what I knew I would see, the point of my ice-axe burrowing its way, slowly but relentlessly, like a mole, upwards and along the little fissure of frozen snow where I had casually placed it before the accident occurred. Any moment the narrow point of steel would break surface; it was already at an incline of forty-five degrees with the slope and was proceeding with perceptible, if sadistic, certainty towards the horizontal. A fascinating little ring of widening redness of rust formed in the virgin whiteness, resembling the gore of a mortal wound . . . At the same time, all in a flash, I became aware, rather than actually felt, the friable rock supporting my right hand move a little every few seconds. Immediately I glanced at my boots and wondered (confused as I was) if I could kick a foothold, but decided such indulgence would be too risky.

It was then that I yelled to Morejon. Out of the tail of my

eye I saw him relieving himself of his rucksack and lodging it with much deliberation against a "safe" boulder. Then he started back across the twenty-five yards of life-line that separated us; edging himself along carefully; every few steps he called across to me in a calm voice, *Un momento, Un momento*. As the gap narrowed between us I found I could no longer look at him the suspense was too great. I wanted to scream: "For God's sake hurry up! Can't you see I'm lost if you don't hurry!" But I did not shout because I knew the ice-axe would break surface from its little frozen cavity and the piece of friable rock come away in my hand.

Nothing broke, however, and within about a minute or so Morejon had climbed down and placed his right foot under mine and given me support whereby I could regain control of my ice-axe and my right hand. It had been a close call.

A little after this incident Elizade came into sight, the first time for hours, perfectly silhouetted against the evening sky, staggering robot-like up the last fifty feet that led to the traverse. Ouvrard was not with him; we assumed he was following out of sight a little below the crest; we were wrong.

While I awaited Elizade, on the far side of the traverse, for news of Ouvrard, Morejon set off on an expedition of reconnaissance around the extreme right of the walls towards the breach that led to the upper slopes. A few minutes later Elizade joined me with no news of Ouvrard; he thought he was just behind. Morejon then reappeared at a corner of the walls and said he had found a ledge where he considered it possible to erect the big tent.

We had immense difficulty in pulling out the flaps and making fast the "stays". The ledge was too narrow; the final erection looked like an umbrella at half-mast. As Morejon and Elizade were completing the finishing touches I explored farther and located another "platform" a little above, much smaller, coated with sheet-ice and separated by three dangerous steps across frozen snow at the head of a gulley. I shouted to Morejon to pass around the smaller tent; the circular two-man tent that had saved lives upon Cotopaxi thirteen days before.

I began to sort it out. I had just slotted the last

extension into place when I knocked the upper part
against the over-hanging walls – an immediate gush of
dry soil crumbled down like an unexpected storm of hail
on the canvas, then stopped as quickly as it had begun. I
cursed silently, and bent down to shake it off, but was
interrupted by a low, subdued whistle followed by a loud,
dull thud. I looked up and was astonished to see a foot-
long boulder, one jagged end of which had fallen within
six inches of my head. I felt giddy, everything went
around in circles, but I recovered and heaved the rock,
with effort, over the edge down the bleak slopes, beneath.
I stood and watched it gathering speed; faster and faster it
rolled, and soon it was leaping high and far into the air,
like a medieval projectile . . . in a matter of five seconds it
had disappeared from sight. I still gazed, fixedly, at the
spot where it had pierced the encircling darkness that was
rapidly creeping over the mountain. I was wondering if a
human form would career and jump in the air with the
momentum of that boulder . . . This thought, as I stood
rooted to the lip of the narrow platform of sheet-ice,
fascinated me; in that moment of time I was not afraid to
die, I would almost have welcomed the experience of
doing so; almost a temptation.

I suddenly decided not to tell my companions of this
episode: they would not benefit by the knowledge that a
further avalanche was a possibility – for two of them were
utterly defenceless, tied in their sleeping bags on the very
spot where the stone had dropped. I was not going to sleep
there; why should I? I felt very frightened indeed. No
qualms of conscience affected my fear. I thought only of
my self-preservation.

Having fixed the two-man tent as best I could I carefully
eased myself across to the other ledge and rejoined the
others; Ouvrard was still missing! It was now completely
dark; no-one went out in search of him; we had been
anticipating his arrival at every moment for the past hour.
Elizade should not have left him. We shouted spasmodically, but receiving no reply, we gave up. "He'll come," we
said; we did not appreciate his danger.

At half-past seven out of the ghostly eeriness of the

mountain night, suspended as we were, almost literally, between heaven and earth, we heard a distant wail – yes, a wail – of chronic distress. When it occurred we three were forgathered at the entrance of the big tent, squatting cross-legged around the primus stove; glaring distractedly at the inert wad of frozen snow that refused to melt. Our eyes were casting a spell upon it, hypnotizing it; willing it to thaw, as we passed tongues across lips as dry as parchment.

While we waited another cry came across to us; we knew Roger Ouvrard had at last arrived at the far end of the "traverse". Elizade burrowed into his rucksack, pulled out a flashlight, and went off to guide him in . . .

Dealing with water is always a tedious process at great altitudes; the boiling point being so low, it often takes as much as an hour to melt the equivalent of half a cupful with the stove roaring at full blast. I can recall nothing more sadistic – on a mountain – than the inevitable interim period between the lighting of the stove and the final production of the liquid. Even although one knows it will take at least an hour, it is difficult to accept the fact after a gruelling day's climb during which time any form of beverage has been denied one; it is then, over the evening brew, that the basic animal lights up – perhaps only for an instant – in men's faces.

It was not until we had cooked some noodle soup, at about eight o'clock, that Roger Ouvrard appeared at the door of the tent – swaying. As we helped him into the big tent he continued to sway. He refused all nourishment, and we had the greatest difficulty passing a little medicinal whisky through his cracked lips into his mouth. Later he regained a little colour, but it was evident that he had been smitten by the dreaded *soroche* (mountain sickness). He was through – until he got to lower levels.

Then came the great question – which two of us were going to spend the night on the other platform? It had to be decided and it was now a matter for my conscience. As I looked at the tragic face of Ouvrard I knew I was on the fence and ready to take the cowardly way out. "Someone must look after him," I argued to myself, – and why shouldn't it be me – I invited him on the expedition, it is up to me to see him through, no doubt about it." Then suddenly the "balloon" popped as Elizade quietly said, "I'll look after him." I looked at Morejon and we filed off to the other ledge.

The warm presence of another human being was comforting and I began to realize I had done the right thing – come what might.

When we awoke the sky was overclouded and leaden, it was a grey, depressing day and chillingly cold around our "crow's nest"; but later, after we had spent too long boiling water for tea, the sun broke through and cast a different complexion upon everything.

Neither of us was feeling well – the extreme altitude had sown the seed of lassitude among us. Ouvrard had only slightly recovered, but he was still spent and the gruelling climb of the day before had left him without interest in the final assault upon the summit. All this made the disadvantages of establishing a high camp only too obvious.

After a huddled conversation with Ouvrard, it was decided that Morejon, Elizade and I would make an attempt. Ouvrard, as long as he did not move out of the tent, was safe and he had plenty of food. We would join him before nightfall; we had to. It would have been far too dangerous to have taken him with us. Nevertheless it was brave of him to let us all go; if we did not come back I do not believe he could have crossed the traverse and descended the south-west ridge alone.

The three of us roped up, descended from the ledge, and made a brief "traverse" across the head of the Stubel Glacier, and started upward. It was already nine o'clock; we had taken too long getting ready; it was going to be a race against the clock, the sun was mounting in the blue sky. We soon found and penetrated the famous "breach" within the "Red Walls" . . . "thus far and no farther a man may go who is not a mountaineer," wrote Edward Whymper. I recalled these words and speculated on what lay ahead . . . We climbed very slowly – Morejon in the lead, Elizade in the middle, myself in the rear. The incline was steep, its course intersected with slippery, ice-coated rock protuberances. Extreme caution was needed.

Then suddenly no more than 300 ft above the camp site, on the ledge, I was smitten and could go no farther. My dragging steps got slower and slower until I could scarcely force one toe in front of the other; my breathing came out in desperate gasps; a dreadful form of nausea swept over me in hot waves. *Soroche*. This is IT, I said to myself. You have had it. I was just about to shout to the others to tell them that it was all over with me – they must go on and I would go back, when suddenly, before I could make the effort to speak, I saw Elizade unrope himself, make a quiet gesture of capitulation, and start down the slopes to Ouvrard. Morejon and I remained – rooted in our tracks. "I have got to rest, I have just got to rest," I told Morejon.

At first, after Elizade had disappeared back to the High Camp, I couldn't register that he had been feeling as ill as I was. Strangely enough it gave me new hope, new zest to climb the fabulous Monarch. I suddenly felt I had passed the test, weathered the attack of nausea. I had passed through it without giving up – I would have given up if Elizade had not done so first – but now all my instincts told me to hold on, stick it out and go on – go on upward; I could not let Morejon down. In a way I was glad there were only two of us against Chimborazo – I felt I could give of my best with this number, but I am not sure why.

Starting again on a greatly shortened rope I managed for a short time to keep pace with the even, uniform steps of my companion. We went through an area of broken *séracs* and afterwards we ascended on to a glistening white slope that seemed to lead straight to heaven; it appeared endless but it was undoubtedly a false crest; the summit was far above this celestial ladder. The gradient got steeper. I began to tire again and my stride became uncontrolled, shuffling. Morejon was still climbing strongly, now at least thirty feet above.

"I don't think I can go on," I bleated.

"No! Come on, climb slowly to me . . . take your time . . . now climb to me. I'll wait . . . don't hurry."

Then I noticed that Morejon kept shaking his head – backwards and forwards. A terrible thought assailed me, "God, snow-blindness – now we are really through." My brain began to race in alarm. How can I get him down to safety, food, and warmth? But when I reached him, he said:

"I keep going to sleep; can't keep my eyes open."

"What's wrong?" I asked.

"I had a headache this morning when we started. Elizade gave me a pill – it was nice of him, but it was a pill for sleep, now I sleep."

However, after resting we drank tea from the thermos, and swallowed a Benzedrine tablet apiece and set off again. We were then above 19,600 ft up; I tried to make out the Pacific – one is supposed to be able to see it from Chimborazo – but I did not.

Now we closed with the great crevasse – one of the main obstacles on the mountain that has successfully defeated some previous expeditions. If we could find a place to jump, the key to the conquest was ours. However, when we finally arrived at this crucial point things did not look auspicious. We staggered wearily up the last slope and gazed into a huge ravine of ice and snow, certainly fifty feet wide. We were careful to keep away from the edge, undoubtedly undermined from the brim.

We then beat to the right, keeping parallel with the fissure; gradually as we made the traverse it narrowed and narrowed until it appeared no more than a crack a few feet wide, but of unimaginable depth. Morejon decided "it would go" and crept close to select a point for the jump. White I thrust my ice-axe into the soft snow up to the hilt, belaying the rope securely around it, Morejon made doubly sure of the knot at his waist. Then he nodded. I paid him out carefully, not too much, for fear he might get entangled in his crampons while in mid-air and consequently fall into the predatory jaws of the crevasse. He crept gingerly down to the edge, feeling his way like a man with a mine-detector, for he knew that he was almost certainly treading on an overhang that might crumble at any moment and send him into the unknown. Next moment he shouted, whereupon I threw out a long length of rope, and he leapt and landed noiselessly and safely on the far side, but he did not linger. A few seconds later he was three or four yards farther up the slope. He then belayed, pulled the rope taut, and I jumped . . . and rejoined him.

We then rested a little; jumping crevasses at 20,000 ft is a great exertion. While we waited there in the snow, alone, amid a wilderness of nothingness, my mental approach changed – perhaps it was the effect of the Benzedrine tablet – but now I was imbued with one purpose. Nothing in this world seemed to matter any more but the conquest of this mountain. Hitherto, up as far as the crevasse, my role had been that of a tourist being towed up by an experienced guide . . . The time factor had nagged me at every step. "Could we do it and get back to camp before night – surely it's not worth the risk – a great risk; after all it is only a sport, it's not war, not life and death. It doesn't matter." But now it did matter; it was total war. Having thus committed myself I felt much better – at peace and un-fettered. I expect Morejon was thinking on the same lines for already he was the only man living who had climbed Chimborazo twice; now there seemed a real chance that he would complete the hat-trick and thereby make himself one of the greatest climbers Ecuador has ever known.

The southern summit was now, numerically, so to speak, within our grasp – perhaps only a scant 500 ft above. But of a sudden the elements changed with vio-lence. Hell was unleashed, lashing us with its fury; it seemed staging a special performance for us. Cold mists floated and scurried around us, terrible, biting winds seared and ripped into our bodies through our clothing, and all the time the snow got softer and deeper; it was going to be a devil of a fight. On we went, slowly and inexorably flogging our way through the sea of virgin snow, like robots . . . ice-axe, right foot, left foot, and once again the same automatic motions.

We gained the southern summit before three o'clock; half a mile of hollow plateau, and 130 ft separated us from our goal. We were leaving it late.

As we started for it, everything hit us – never have I endured such utter torment. The wind rose now to a crescendo about us, biting into the skin of our exposed parts, knifing into the very marrow of our bones, until I fully expected the most hideous "third degree" burns. All our senses were numbed; it seemed to dispossess our souls, but like automatons we trudged on. Then there was the snow; it got deeper and deeper. When we left the southern summit it was only up to our thighs – now it was above our waists, and every so often I lost sight of Morejon altogether – perhaps it was bottomless!

Progress was almost at a standstill, and we both knew that if the depth of snow continued all the way to the top we stood very little chance of getting up and back before night. But nothing in this world was going to prevent us from conquest now. We had to zig-zag up the last hundred feet. I took the lead for the first time and pushed on with all the fervour of one obsessed; reaching far out with my ice-axe, sinking it into the snow up to my forearm, then I floundered two feet or so forward with one leg, then I would bring up the other and repeat the process all over again. It was desperate. Once I let myself be persuaded of the uselessness of this self-inspired suffering I believed I would be lost. I would have dropped where I was standing in the snow; physically I was at breaking point, mentally on the crown of Chimborazo. If I had hesitated and contemplated whether "To go back" or "Go forward", counted the cost and thought of the clock and all that it meant, I would have laid down and died. No man can live through such torment unless he has vision of success clear and strong within him and *before* him all the time. As we floundered and beat up the last few feet I was thinking of nothing but, "Go on! Go on, you're nearly there now. Go on. Go on."

At four-fifty-five exactly we reached the highest point on the dome; we could go no higher; Chimborazo was ours. Oh, joy of joys! I had fulfilled my hope; Morejon his ambition. We hugged each other rapturously; it was a wonderful moment. There was, alas! nothing to see but mist, nevertheless Morejon took out his camera and took a photograph of me with the ice-axes raised above my head in token of victory. It never came out!

We spent only five minutes on the summit before we started to descend, almost running for our lives. There was only an hour and a half before nightfall; it was 2,000 ft to the High Camp; the ascent had taken eight hours.

We fled down the dome of the Whymper summit, across the plateau in the grove of our ascent – over the crevasse and down to about the point where Elizade left us. When darkness fell we shouted to Elizade and soon his torch gave us our directions. We finally got into camp at about seven o'clock. We found Ouvrard better.

Next day we descended the south-west ridge to the waiting mules and the crate of oranges. At Pogyos I found I had frostbite; Elizade rubbed feverishly for a long time, then wrapped me in blankets and put me in the back of the car and we drove back to Quito. We arrived there at about midnight.

I was carried to my hotel room and once again only my boots were removed. Next day Paul Feret lent me a warm fur slipper.

The following week I was limping around New York in it on my way to London. I must send that slipper back to Paul – some day.

Thin Air

Greg Child

An Australian mountaineer, in 1986 he made, along with T. Macartney-Snape and T. Margis, the first ascent of Gasherbrum IV, 7,925 – (26,000 ft) in Trans-Himalaya via the North-West Ridge.

We continue up the ridge, Tim now in the lead. With every foot gained, the tempo of the wind increases. The slope steepens to 65 degrees. We follow Tim's footsteps, kicked into a frozen surface of perfect consistency. I marvel at the parking-lot size imprints his size 12 feet leave behind, but, as I stretch my shorter legs to match his lanky stride, I begin to hyperventilate from the effort.

The slope crests out on a narrow horizontal ridge at 24,500 ft. We catch the full force of the wind here, and crampon for 100 ft to shelter in a rocky outcrop at the ridge's end. We pause to examine the options. The continuation of the ridge above is steep, rocky, difficult. But to the left a band of ice curls toward another icefield. That is the way.

"Rope up?" I ask.

"No. Too slow. We can handle this," says Tim after a moment of consideration.

One by one we front-point across the traverse. Nothing holds us to the face but the inch-long steel fangs of our crampons and the tips of our ice tools. A slip and we'd be sliding down the Northwest Face, toward the glacier 5,000 ft below. Exposure and exertion create a tingling feeling that runs up the back of my neck. I try to relax. A nervous, thumping heart is an inefficient mechanism up here. Around the corner of the rocks Tim begins to climb up a 300 ft prow of 65 degree ice. Tom and I linger behind. The unroped climbing is increasingly unnerving. Our calves ache from front-pointing. I see Geoff and Andy 100 ft below. Their faces read a mixture of unease and intense concentration. Geoff, front-pointing on a broken crampon, looks particularly concerned.

"I don't like the looks of where Tim is going," I say to Tom.

"Me neither. I'll try out left."

He traverses 80 ft to a more gentle slope but ends up in waist-deep snow. He shakes his head. The wind-polished ridge crest is the only safe path. We return to Tim's prow. At 10.00 a.m. we exit the ice field and huddle into a wind-carved niche bounded by a ridge wall of sun-warmed orange-brown marble. The altitude is 25,000 ft. In front of us, the final 40 degree ice slope to the headwall glints in the sun. But for the snow ramps I'd seen from Broad Peak, switchbacking up the wall, interspersed by vertical cliffs, few weaknesses break the smooth headwall. Somewhere left of our line is Voytek's line of descent. One look at the wall tells us that we won't be back at the tents tonight. In the niche we brew up and talk turns to tactics.

"It looks like hard going above," says Tim. "I reckon we dump everything here and go light. We should be able to make it to the summit and back to here by nightfall."

Geoff, fiddling with his broken crampon, listens on with reservations. If Tim reasoned by leaps of optimism, Geoff reasoned by clear-headed pessimism. We had ten hours to climb 1,000 vertical feet to the North Summit and traverse 1,500 ft horizontally to the true summit. Just by looking at the headwall it was obvious that there'd be climbing as hard as grade 5.9. We'd be pushing to do all that, and abseil down, in ten hours. Even with our light packs, we'd move slowly, yet without bivouac gear up there, we'd be committed to bivouac in the niche. If we were caught out on the headwall, it wouldn't be pretty.

The water in the pot heats up and we share a drink of hot chocolate.

"Well?" Tim asks.

"Okay, we go light," I say.

We stash the stove and bivouac gear in the niche and head to the base of the headwall with only climbing gear and headlamps. We each carry a partially full water bottle stuffed inside our down suits. Tim carries the cine camera, shooting film as he goes.

The icefield butts against the headwall. We arrive at a steep crack in a fifty foot cliff. Above this, the snowramps begin. It seems like the best place to start. Tom hammers in a belay piton and I tie in to lead. After a few easy feet I stand beneath a bulge. I hammer in a piton, strip my mittens down to my liner gloves, and begin jamming my fists and feet into the crack, hauling myself around an overhang. The marble is glass smooth. Crampons scrattle and slip as I inch up, gloves become sodden, hands cold and wooden. The amount of oxygen I need is more than I can suck out of the air. A heady lightness, like a glimpse of unconsciousness, washes over me in waves. Gasping desperately, I pause above the bulge, with one foot wedged into the crack, the other stemmed out onto a flake. It's a rest, of sorts. I will myself to breathe more slowly, and suck on my fingers to warm them. I find myself thinking of Voytek's letter. "Do not fear the headwall, it is nice surprise," he'd written. Some surprise.

As I creep up I hear a shout from Geoff: "I'm going down."

I know what he's thinking. That we're too slow and we'll never make it before dark, that the weather has been good for five days and can't last much longer, that to be caught in a storm without bivvy gear on this wall will be the end of us, that with his snapped crampon it's too risky. I try to shout to him that I'm nearly on the snow ramp, that it looks easier for a long way above, but only a croak exits my dry throat. I see him zigzagging down the slope, toward the niche, where he will bivouac and await us. Watching him descend is like losing a piece of my own body. He'd given his all to get us here but he knew where to draw the line. I hoped we'd be as clear-headed as the day wore on.

I continue up the crack for twenty feet, to a point where

ice fills the cracks and the footing again becomes insubstantial. I try for ten minutes to rig protection but nothing works. Finally I take my ice hammer and swing it into the frozen crack. Half of the pick bites. I clip the hammer's wrist-loop to the rope and gasp and grasp onto a patch of snow ten feet above.

"I'm okay now," I shout, turning to crampon up the ramp.

"Well done. It looked hard," calls a voice over my shoulder."

I turn to see Andy, just a few feet away, wobbling onto the snow ramp after soloing up another crack.

"Jesus, Tuthill. Why didn't you tell me it was easier over there? I thought I was gonna die on this crack!"

"I thought I was gonna die on *this*."

I inspect the verglassed wall he'd just climbed. If anything, it looked more difficult than my crack. He just felt like moving, that's all. 150 ft later I reach a large block and secure the rope around it. Andy, followed by the others, jumars up. Tom is coughing wildly again, his lung infection back in full force.

Andy leads a second long pitch, then Tim takes over for two leads. The route alternates between steep ramps covered in snow and short vertical rock steps. Marble, limestone, and occasional lenses of diorite collide. Protection is minimal, the climbing tricky. We grow more and more tired, move slowly and slower. At 3.00 p.m. I join Tim on a ledge: 100 ft above us the headwall ends and the ridge to the smaller North Summit begins. I tie in to the lead end of the rope and begin to pull up over some blocks. After a few feet I return to the ledge and, gasping and weak, hand the task to Tim.

"You lead it. I'm exhausted. I need time to rest."

Tim disappears into a chimney. Thirty minutes later he reaches the ridge.

As the four of us jumar up and gather on the narrow crest at 25,850 ft, we consider our position. About 150 easy feet higher and some 700 horizontal feet east is the North Summit. From there, due south by 1,500 horizontal feet, we see the true summit, 40 ft higher than the North

Summit. The time is 4.00 p.m., the skies are still clear but on the ridgecrest we are exposed to a wind that makes conversation almost impossible. No one needs to be told that we will not make the summit and get back to the foot of the headwall before dark.

Our bodies burn with fatigue. We stand there, watching dusk gather over the Karakoram. The realization that we've blown it begins to sink in. If we descend, we'll never climb Gasherbrum IV, yet to press on seems like insanity. Everything seems about to turn to shit. Then the worm of unfinished ideas begins to twist in our heads. The crazy talk begins.

"I'm certain I can make it through the night without frostbite," says Tim, the words ripped out of his mouth by wind.

"Bivvy out?" I ask.

"Either that or go down."

We have nothing but the clothes on our backs. No water, food, or stove. I'd read long ago about Hermann Buhl sitting out a night just below the summit of Nanga Parbat. It seemed to me then something only a superman could endure or a madman conceive. I'd also heard the separate tales of Nazir Sabir and Jim Wickwire, both of whom had sat out nights near the summit of K2. Nazir had suffered memory loss for months. Jim's bivouac had cost him a piece of lung when fluid had frozen in his chest. And there was Bonatti and Mahdi on K2. Even with an oxygen cylinder, Mahdi had lost his feet. A bivouac here would be harsh, but at the same time I felt that our chances were good; the weather was clear, and we still had some strength left. Instinct condoned the idea, the ambition put words in my mouth.

"I'll risk it," I hear myself say.

Our own private epic begins to take shape.

Tom and Andy look with uncertainty about the clear horizon. That hacking cough is hammering Tom's ribs again. He's running on sheer determination. Andy, who'd frozen toes in years past, looks about the icescape, justly concerned.

"Don't be talked into this by us. It could be a bad night. Maybe frostbite. Think hard," I say.

They bat it about for a few moments, torn between the rationality of descent and the irrationality of success.

"I'm staying," says Tom.

"No, it's not worth it to me. I'm going down," says Andy, seeing the enormity of the gamble.

"Alone?" Descending the rock band unaccompanied seemed dangerous.

"You're worried about me? I'm more worried about you! Anyway, tonight is the summer solstice, the shortest night of the year."

"Yeah? At least we've got that going for us."

Andy rips a 12 in by 24 in foam pad out of the back of his rucksack and hands it to us. We divide the hardware: he takes three slings, five pitons, a wired chock, and a rope. We give him the larger share of the gear in order that he should have enough to make five or six abseils. We hope that the next day we'll find his anchors, maybe Voytek's as well . . .

"Good luck." He turns and leaves to descend to Geoff at the niche.

Now we are three.

"Well, this is a grand idea but what do we do now?" I ask, as if reproaching myself.

"Gotta dig a hole. That's the only way to make it through the night," Tim replies.

We continue along the narrow ridge for another hour, looking for a suitable site to claw out a snowcave. Just below the North Summit, we find a cluster of snow drifts and cornices. We poke our axes about, to see if the drifts allow a snowcave to be dug into them. All are solid ice. Time creeps by. Despite our leg-heaviness our search for a place to endure the night becomes laced with a certain desperation. To sit out the night on the bare ice and rocks could be fatal if the wind didn't drop. I begin to chop into the ice at my feet. Even crouching in a pit would be better than nothing.

Tim crampons down the side of the ridge to a point where a steep spur joins the Northwest Ridge. It's the ridge the Italians had climbed. Somewhere on that ridge, at the site of the Italian Camp VI, at 24,770 ft, the climber Giuseppe de Francesch had left a statue of the Madonna of Lourdes, given him by his wife, to invoke a blessing for the mountain. Perhaps even after all these years, the Madonna was still there, propped against the rock. It occurs to me that we could use a little divine intervention right now. Then Tim shoves his ice axe into a triangular mound of snow perched on the narrow crest of the Italian Ridge and the shaft sinks deeply.

"Hey, we can get a cave down here."

Tom and I descend. Digging begins.

We scratch out little handfuls of snow with the adzes of our ice axes, digging for five minutes each, then kicking and clawing the snowy payload toward the entrance for the others to remove. The effort is almost more than we are capable of. As I take my turn at digging I think of the bridge we have burned, of what might happen, and what might not. Framed in the entrance to the cave is Broad Peak, where Pete had died and where he still lay. It is almost three years to the day since our struggle to get down the mountain. As oxygen starved as my thoughts are, the essence of my reason for returning to the Karakoram falls clearly into place, as never before. It seemed that finishing that idea I had shared with Pete, to climb G4, would close a circle, would somehow set a cruel score a little more even. Why had I taken so long to understand that this was the fundamental reason I'd come here? And what of my two companions? What drew them here? The beauty? To be able to say they had done it? Did they too have hidden compartments inside them full of thoughts pounding for resolve? Or was adventure enough reason? No time for thoughts. I return to digging.

"Greg, come out here. Look at the sky," Tim calls.

Sky? How can he stand there looking at the sky when night will be on us in a matter of minutes and the snowcave is only half dug?

I back out of the cave. The wind has dropped. Gasherbrums I, II, and III poke up like huge tusks, their snows pearly white, their rocks shining amber. The shadow of Gasherbrum IV is cast across them and the sky is indigo blue, fading into a deeply pink upper atmosphere. Stars penetrate the fading daylight, led by Venus, glinting in the north. Low on the horizon the rising full moon blasts a surreal glow across the Karakoram, from the monsoon thunderheads over Indian Kashmir, to Nanga Parbat in the west.

We stand looking, breathing. For a moment all our doubts vanish. We are quite certain we have chosen the right place to be. As we settle into the cave I feel like a stranded astronaut bedding down for the night on a hostile planet. But no, it's our own wild and beautiful earth.

Cold is the immediate sensation that overcomes us as we seal the entrance to the snowcave with Tim's pack. Height, length, and width, the cave measures four feet in each direction. As the day's last light filters through the thin walls we remove our crampons, then take stock of the few possessions we have. The foam pad from Andy's pack goes beneath us. Whoever is in the middle gets a full seat, while those on either end get one buttock on the pad, the other on snow. We decide to rotate positions during the night.

A mouthful of water remains in each of our bottles. We mix the water with snow to stretch it further and sip it down. The water soaks into our tongues, then is gone. We search the pack and the pockets of our down suits for scraps of food. A mangled energy bar comes up from the bottom of the pack, and from Tim's pocket a stale, crumbling lump of fruitcake. He breaks the cake into three portions. Tom and I sample it and gag: it has the consistency of sawdust.

"Can't eat this shit up here," I grumble.

"That's my mother's fruitcake you're talking about," counters Tim.

"I'm sure it's very nice at Base Camp, but up here it's shit."

Nothing is palatable at altitude. We have no appetites, only a great thirst. Tom and I store the cake in our pockets till we can find a use for it. We contemplate the energy bar.

"Save it for 'ron," I mutter.

"Who?" Tom asks.

Tim chuckles at a familiar Australian wordplay.

"Later-ron," I explain.

We continue the search for anything useful. Tim checks

his cine camera. I notice the sheepskin insulation jacket surrounding the camera and suggest someone could sit on it, or we might take turns wearing it as a hat. Tim rejects the proposition, concerned that the motor in the camera might freeze. He is determined to film us on the summit, but if the temperature keeps dropping as fast as it was, we wouldn't see any summit. Teeth were already chattering. Tom was coughing at full force.

"What about the rope?" asks Tom. "We could sit on that."

"I anchored it in the rocks above us. I thought we'd want to be tied in," I reply, grabbing the strand that runs through the door. The snowcave was burrowed into a precarious mound of snow. Its walls were thin enough to knock down with a misplaced elbow. It didn't seem too remote a possibility that the entire cave might fall to bits during the night, emptying us out of it. With that thought, we keep our headlamps ready. We pull what slack is left in the rope into the cave, clip our harnesses into it, and put the rest behind our backs. Then, zipping our suits up and drawing our hoods and balaclavas tightly around our faces, we sit tight.

"What's the time?" Tom asks. His voice wakes me from a snatch of sleep. I notice that Tim is singing.

"Don't ask that, Tom," Tim begs.

I check my watch. Little more than an hour has passed since we entered the cave. I announce the discouraging fact. It seems as though we'd been there longer. Tim resumes his singing, louder, some school song by the sound of it. We begin to shiver violently. I rock my body back and forth, slapping my thighs to the beat of Tim's song, wriggling my toes at the same time. The movement produces a trancelike effect, takes the focus off the cold. I notice Tom moving to the same beat, see him rubbing his hands and banging his feet together, mumbling as he counts sets of a hundred wriggles, loses count, and starts over. My shivering gradually becomes a low wail that sounds very much like someone in constant pain. I begin to think about this pain, the pain we are feeling now, the pain of cold. What is it like, how to quantify it? Like having a tooth pulled without anaesthetic, all day.

"What's the worst bivvy you've ever had?" Tim asks, prompting me to think back on years of cold, wet bivouacs.

"This is," I reply without reservation.

Tom coughs again. Something like a pale green, blood-spattered tadpole flies out of his gullet, hits the wall, and freezes solid. He retreats into himself and takes on the countenance of a zombie. The luxury of conversation, even of the occasional caring "How are you feeling?" drops away. Suddenly I cannot feel my toes.

"My feet – they're going!"

I kick off my boots. Tim unzips his down suit. I put my socked and lifeless feet against his chest. We squirm and shift positions in the tiny hole, like a *ménage à trois* in deep freeze. All we need is a few more hours of windlessness to survive. As we sit shivering, a state, neither sleep nor wake but more like a sedative overdose, full of strange, restless dreams, carries us into our own worlds. All grasp of the flow of time falls away. The night fills with strange mumblings.

As 22 June dawns, sunlight creeps into the snowcave and onto our stiff, hurting bodies. A minuscule veil of frozen moisture momentarily clasps my eyelids together, then releases. We look at each other. Faces are puffed and bloated with mild edema. Capillaries bulge red and angry on our brows. Lips and noses look like peeling sausages. Icicles hang from beards and noses. I recognize none of this ugly crew. Still, the mountain has been kind to us. No one is frostbitten, our lungs breathe free, our heads are un-troubled by pain. Outside, the daily wind is building, but the skies remain clear. We enter the daylight, clip crampons to boots, and plod like machines to the nearby North Summit.

Between the North Summit and the summit proper is a long ridge of wind-polished ice that on our right drops over the two mile high West Face, and on our left plunges to a snow plateau 4,000 ft below. The wind from China slams into the East Face and tumbles over the ridge like surf pounding a seawall. At the end of the ridge, somewhere amongst a series of steep-faced limestone towers, is the summit.

We traverse the ice ridge unroped, reaching the cluster of towers in an hour, sheltering from the wind beside the first rocks, where we break out the rope. I tie in and lead off, traversing a snowfield beneath the 80 ft towers, peering through my iced-over goggles, looking for the highest tower. But any one of five separate points above me could be the one. It's a puzzle my altitude-addled brain can barely cope with. I decide we have two choices to the summit: either climb a crack directly in front of me and straddle the jagged summit crest until we reach the highest point, or traverse across the foot of the towers, over verglassed slabs, until we see the summit, and then climb directly up to it.

For some reason I choose the crack. The limestone is solid, 80 degrees steep, the wall sheltered from the brunt of the wind. In the half-hour the tower takes to climb I become so completely involved with the task of pulling up on handjams and flakes that I ignore the bigger picture I'm painting until I reach the summit crest and see a long double-corniced knife-edge ahead of me. I've climbed into a dead end.

"This is the wrong way!" I shout down to Tim and Tom. Spindrift blowing over the ridge sprays them. Watching through openings in their tightly drawn stormhoods, they've been aware I was heading into a dead end for several minutes, but, like me, have been too lost in their windy oxygen-starved dream-world to be overly concerned.

Cursing my mistake I drape one of our precious slings around a rock spike and abseil down. Tim takes over, heads toward the low traverse, balances unroped across the 50 ft wide verglassed slab beside us, toward a snowfield. His crampons creak shrilly against the rock. One mittened hand pads over the holdless wall, the other holds his ice axe, which he hooks into smears of ice. Neither Tom nor I like the look of the traverse. We rope up. Tom leads across, placing a piton for protection two-thirds of the way across.

On the other side of the traverse, the wind is moderate.

There, we stand in a small snowy bowl, directly beneath the true summit. Tim, ahead of us, is already at the end of the snow slope, clambering up the summit rocks. Tom and I follow, towing the rope behind us. Deep pockets in the rock form sure holds for the final steep moves. Meanwhile Tim sits sheltered from the wind by a boulder, the cine camera fast against his face, filming our every move. He holds his breath, shoots a sequence, then gasps wildly. A few steps to his right is a pointed crest of snow encrusted onto the summit rocks. I look around, expecting some final obstacle to surmount, but no, we are on the summit. It is 10.00 a.m.

Tom, coughing at every step, moves a few steps behind.

"He's a determined bastard," Tim says in admiration.

Seeing the end of the climb, Tom's ashen face breaks into a smile. The obscure object of desire is reached, the worm within us is satisfied. Too exhausted for clever words we simply clasp one mittened hand in another, shake, gaze about us, and turn to our own thoughts. We'd gone beyond words two days ago, forced by necessity into a state in which we functioned as a single being. Now on the summit, that being, drunk with euphoria, felt suddenly as if it had merged with sky and mountain as well to become a single, elemental entity, like some rare particle, formed in an atom smasher, existent for a millisecond in time.

The catenulate shapes of Broad Peak, K2, the Gasher-brums, and Chogolisa loom around us. The Trango Towers stand like distant castles at the head of the Baltoro. The sky is cloudless right up to Nanga Parbat. A few photographs later, we jam a stone in a crack on the summit rock-fin, sling it, loop the rope through this, and abseil off the summit. As I back down the rope I feel a moment of regret for not having left something up there in memory of Pete, for the summit we never reached. Instead, I leave a fond thought. It's the best thing I had to give.

It's still there.

The Devil's Thumb

Jon Krakauer

Born in 1954, Krakauer is an American climber and journalist famous for his account of the 1996 Everest disaster, Into Thin Air. *Here he recalls a 1977 solo ascent of The Devil's Thumb, a peak on the Stikine Icecap in Alaska.*

I awoke early on May 11 to clear skies and the relatively warm temperature of twenty degrees Fahrenheit. Startled by the good weather, mentally unprepared to commence the actual climb, I hurriedly packed up a rucksack nonetheless, and began skiing toward the base of the Thumb. Two previous Alaskan expeditions had taught me that, ready or not, you simply can't afford to waste a day of perfect weather if you expect to get up anything.

A small hanging glacier extends out from the lip of the icecap, leading up and across the north face of the Thumb like a catwalk. My plan was to follow this catwalk to a prominent rock prow in the centre of the wall, and thereby execute an end run around the ugly, avalanche-swept lower half of the face.

The catwalk turned out to be a series of fifty-degree ice fields blanketed with knee-deep powder snow and riddled with crevasses. The depth of the snow made the going slow and exhausting; by the time I front-pointed up the overhanging wall of the uppermost *bergschrund*, some three or four hours after leaving camp, I was whipped. And I hadn't even gotten to the "real" climbing yet. That would begin immediately above, where the hanging glacier gave way to vertical rock.

The rock, exhibiting a dearth of holds and coated with six inches of crumbly rime, did not look promising, but just left of the main prow was an inside corner – what climbers call an open book – glazed with frozen melt water. This ribbon of ice led straight up for two or three hundred feet, and if the ice proved substantial enough to support the picks of my ice axes, the line might go. I hacked out a small platform in the snow slope, the last flat ground I expected to feel underfoot for some time, and stopped to eat a candy bar and collect my thoughts. Fifteen minutes later I shouldered my pack and inched over to the bottom of the corner. Gingerly, I swung my right axe into the two-inch-thick ice. It was solid, plastic – a little thinner than I would have liked but otherwise perfect. I was on my way.

The climbing was steep and spectacular, so exposed it made my head spin. Beneath my boot soles, the wall fell away for 3,000 ft to the dirty, avalanche-scarred cirque of the Witches Cauldron Glacier. Above, the prow soared with authority toward the summit ridge, a vertical half-mile above. Each time I planted one of my ice-axes, that distance shrank by another twenty inches.

The higher I climbed, the more comfortable I became. All that held me to the mountainside, all that held me to the world, were six thin spikes of chrome-molybdenum stuck half an inch into a smear of frozen water, yet I began to feel invincible, weightless, like those lizards that live on the ceilings of cheap Mexican hotels. Early on a difficult climb, especially a difficult solo climb, you're hyperaware of the abyss pulling at your back. You constantly feel its call, its immense hunger. To resist takes a tremendous conscious effort; you don't dare let your guard down for an instant. The siren song of the void puts you on edge, it makes your movements tentative, clumsy, herky-jerky. But as the climb goes on, you grow accustomed to the exposure, you get used to rubbing shoulders with doom, you come to believe in the reliability of your hands and feet and head. You learn to trust your self-control.

By and by, your attention becomes so intensely focused

that you no longer notice the raw knuckles, the cramping thighs, the strain of maintaining nonstop concentration. A trance-like state settles over your efforts, the climb becomes a clear-eyed dream. Hours slide by like minutes. The accrued guilt and clutter of day-to-day existence – the lapses of conscience, the unpaid bills, the bungled opportunities, the dust under the couch, the festering familial sores, the inescapable prison of your genes – all of it is temporarily forgotten, crowded from your thoughts by an overpowering clarity of purpose, and by the seriousness of the task at hand.

At such moments, something like happiness actually stirs in your chest, but it isn't the sort of emotion you want to lean on very hard. In solo climbing, the whole enterprise is held together with little more than *chutzpa*, not the most reliable adhesive. Late in the day on the north face of the Thumb, I felt the glue disintegrate with a single swing of an ice-axe.

I'd gained nearly 700 ft of altitude since stepping off the hanging glacier, all of it on crampon front-points and the picks of my axes. The ribbon of frozen melt water had ended 300 ft up, and was followed by a crumbly armour of frost feathers. Though just barely substantial enough to support body weight, the rime was plastered over the rock to a thickness of two or three feet, so I kept plugging upward. The wall, however, had been growing imperceptibly steeper, and as it did so the frost feathers became thinner. I'd fallen into a slow, hypnotic rhythm – swing, swing; kick, kick; swing, swing; kick, kick – when my left ice-axe slammed into a slab of diorite a few inches beneath the rime.

I tried left, then right, but kept striking rock. The frost feathers holding me up, it became apparent, were maybe five inches thick and had the structural integrity of stale cornbread. Below was 3,700 ft of air, and I was balanced atop a house of cards. Waves of panic rose in my throat. My eyesight blurred, I began to hyperventilate, my calves started to vibrate. I shuffled a few feet farther to the right, hoping to find thicker ice, but managed only to bend an ice axe on the rock.

Awkwardly, stiff with fear, I started working my way back down. The rime gradually thickened, and after descending about eighty feet I got back on reasonably solid ground. I stopped for a long time to let my nerves settle, then leaned back from my tools and stared up at the face above, searching for a hint of solid ice, for some variation in the underlying rock strata, for anything that would allow passage over the frosted slabs. I looked until my neck ached, but nothing appeared. The climb was over. The only place to go was down.

Heavy snow and incessant winds kept me inside the tent for most of the next three days. The hours passed slowly. In the attempt to hurry them along I chain-smoked for as long as my supply of cigarettes held out, and read. I'd made a number of bad decisions on the trip, there was no getting around it, and one of them concerned the reading matter I'd chosen to pack along: three back issues of *The Village Voice*, and Joan Didion's latest novel, *A Book of Common Prayer*. The *Voice* was amusing enough – there on the icecap, the subject matter took on an edge, a certain sense of the absurd, from which the paper (through no fault of its own) benefited greatly – but in that tent, under those circumstances, Didion's necrotic take on the world hit a little too close to home.

Near the end of *Common Prayer*, one of Didion's characters says to another, "You don't get any real points for staying here, Charlotte." Charlotte replies, "I can't seem to tell what you do get real points for, so I guess I'll stick around here for awhile."

When I ran out of things to read, I was reduced to studying the ripstop pattern woven into the tent ceiling. This I did for hours on end, flat on my back, while engaging in an extended and very heated self-debate: Should I leave for the coast as soon as the weather broke, or stay put long enough to make another attempt on the mountain? In truth, my little escapade on the north face had left me badly shaken, and I didn't want to go up on the Thumb again at all. On the other hand, the thought of returning to Boulder in defeat – of parking the Pontiac behind the trailer, buckling on my tool belt, and going back to the same brain-dead drill I'd so triumphantly walked away from just a month before – that wasn't very appealing, either. Most of all, I couldn't stomach the thought of having to endure the smug expressions of condolence from all the chumps and nimrods who were certain I'd fail right from the get-go.

By the third afternoon of the storm I couldn't stand it any longer: the lumps of frozen snow poking me in the back, the clammy nylon walls brushing against my face, the incredible smell drifting up from the depths of my sleeping bag. I pawed through the mess at my feet until I located a small green stuff sack, in which there was a metal film can containing the makings of what I'd hoped would be a sort of victory cigar. I'd intended to save it for my return from the summit, but what the hey, it wasn't looking like I'd be visiting the top any time soon. I poured most of the can's contents onto a leaf of cigarette paper, rolled it into a crooked, sorry looking joint, and promptly smoked it down to the roach.

The reefer, of course, only made the tent seem even more cramped, more suffocating, more impossible to bear. It also made me terribly hungry. I decided a little oatmeal would put things right. Making it, however, was a long, ridiculously involved process: a potful of snow had to be gathered outside in the tempest, the stove assembled and lit, the oatmeal and sugar located, the remnants of yesterday's dinner scraped from my bowl. I'd gotten the stove going and was melting the snow when I smelled something burning. A thorough check of the stove and its environs revealed nothing. Mystified, I was ready to chalk it up to my chemically enhanced imagination when I heard something crackle directly behind me.

I whirled around in time to see a bag of garbage, into which I'd tossed the match I'd used to light the stove, flare up into a conflagration. Beating on the fire with my hands, I had it out in a few seconds, but not before a large section of the tent's inner wall vaporized before my eyes. The tent's built-in rainfly escaped the flames, so the shelter was still more or less weatherproof; now, however, it was approximately thirty degrees cooler inside. My left palm began to sting. Examining it, I noticed the pink welt of a burn. What troubled me most, though, was that the tent wasn't even mine – I'd borrowed the shelter from my father. An expensive Early Winters Omnipo Tent, it had been brand new before my trip – the hang-tags were still attached – and had been loaned reluctantly. For several minutes I sat dumbstruck, staring at the wreckage of the shelter's once-graceful form amid the acrid scent of singed hair and melted nylon. You had to hand it to me, I thought: I had a real knack for living up to the old man's worst expectations.

The fire sent me into a funk that no drug known to man could have alleviated. By the time I'd finished cooking the oatmeal my mind was made up: the moment the storm was over, I was breaking camp and booking for Thomas Bay.

Twenty-four hours later, I was huddled inside a bivouac sack under the lip of the *bergschrund* on the Thumb's north face. The weather was as bad as I'd seen it. It was snowing hard, probably an inch every hour. Spindrift avalanches hissed down from the wall above and washed over me like surf, completely burying the sack every twenty minutes.

The day had begun well enough. When I emerged from the tent, clouds still clung to the ridge tops but the wind was down and the icecap was speckled with sunbreaks. A patch of sunlight, almost blinding in its brilliance, slid lazily over the camp. I put down a foam sleeping mat and sprawled on the glacier in my long johns. Wallowing in the radiant heat, I felt the gratitude of a prisoner whose sentence has just been commuted.

As I lay there, a narrow chimney that curved up the east half of the Thumb's north face, well to the left of the route I'd tried before the storm, caught my eye. I twisted a telephoto lens onto my camera. Through it I could make out a smear of shiny grey ice – solid, trustworthy, hard-frozen ice – plastered to the back of the cleft. The alignment of the chimney made it impossible to discern if the ice continued in an unbroken line from top to bottom. If it did, the chimney might well provide passage over the rime-covered slabs that had foiled my first attempt. Lying there in the sun, I began to think about how much I'd hate myself a month hence if I threw in the towel after a single try, if I scrapped the whole expedition on account of a little bad weather. Within the hour I had assembled my gear and was skiing toward the base of the wall.

The ice in the chimney did in fact prove to be continuous, but it was very, very thin – just a gossamer film of verglas. Additionally, the cleft was a natural funnel for any debris that happened to slough off the wall; as I scratched my way up the chimney I was hosed by a continuous stream of powder snow, ice chips, and small stones. One hundred twenty feet up the groove the last remnants of my composure flaked away like old plaster, and I turned around.

Instead of descending all the way to Base Camp, I decided to spend the night in the 'schrund beneath the chimney, on the off chance that my head would be more together the next morning. The fair skies that had ushered in the day, however, turned out to be but a momentary lull in a five-day gale. By mid-afternoon the storm was back in all its glory, and my bivouac site became a less than pleasant place to hang around. The ledge on which I crouched was continually swept by small spindrift avalanches. Five times my bivvy sack – a thin nylon envelope, shaped exactly like a Baggies brand sandwich bag, only bigger – was buried up to the level of the breathing slit. After digging myself out the fifth time, I decided I'd had enough. I threw all my gear in my pack and made a break for base camp.

The descent was terrifying. Between the clouds, the ground blizzard, and the flat, fading light, I couldn't tell snow from sky, nor whether a slope went up or down. I worried, with ample reason, that I might step blindly off the top of a serac and end up at the bottom of the Witches Cauldron, a half-mile below. When I finally arrived on the frozen plain of the icecap, I found that my tracks had long since drifted over. I didn't have a clue how to locate the tent on the featureless glacial plateau. I skied in circles for an hour or so, hoping I'd get lucky and stumble across camp, until I put a foot into a small crevasse and realized I was acting like an idiot – that I should hunker down right where I was and wait out the storm.

I dug a shallow hole, wrapped myself in the bivvy bag, and sat on my pack in the swirling snow. Drifts piled up around me. My feet became numb. A damp chill crept down my chest from the base of my neck, where spindrift had gotten inside my parka and soaked my shirt. If only I had a cigarette, I thought, a single cigarette, I could summon the strength of character to put a good face on this fucked-up situation, on the whole fucked-up trip. "If we had some ham, we could have ham and eggs, if we had some eggs." I remembered my friend Nate uttering that line in a similar storm, two years before, high on another Alaskan peak, the Mooses Tooth. It had struck me as hilarious at the time; I'd actually laughed out loud. Recalling the line now, it no longer seemed funny. I pulled the bivvy sack tighter around my shoulders. The wind ripped at my back. Beyond shame, I cradled my head in my arms and embarked on an orgy of self-pity.

I knew that people sometimes died climbing mountains. But at the age of 23 personal mortality – the idea of my own death – was still largely outside my conceptual grasp; it was as abstract a notion as non-Euclidian geometry or marriage. When I decamped from Boulder in April, 1977, my head swimming with visions of glory and redemption on the Devil's Thumb, it didn't occur to me that I might be bound by the same cause-effect relationships that governed the actions of others. I'd never heard of hubris. Because I wanted to climb the mountain so badly, because I had thought about the Thumb so intensely for so long, it seemed beyond the realm of possibility that some minor obstacle like the weather or crevasses or rime-covered rock might ultimately thwart my will.

At sunset the wind died and the ceiling lifted 150 ft off the glacier, enabling me to locate Base Camp. I made it back to the tent intact, but it was no longer possible to ignore the fact that the Thumb had made hash of my plans. I was forced to acknowledge that volition alone, however powerful, was not going to get me up the north wall. I saw, finally, that nothing was.

There still existed an opportunity for salvaging the expedition, however. A week earlier I'd skied over to the south-east side of the mountain to take a look at the route Fred Beckey had pioneered in 1946 – the route by which I'd intended to descend the peak after climbing the north wall. During that reconnaissance I'd noticed an obvious unclimbed line to the left of the Beckey route – a patchy network of ice angling across the south-east face – that struck me as a relatively easy way to achieve the summit. At the time, I'd considered this route unworthy of my attentions. Now, on the rebound from my calamitous entanglement with the nordwand, I was prepared to lower my sights.

On the afternoon of 15 May, when the blizzard finally petered out, I returned to the south-east face and climbed to the top of a slender ridge that abutted the upper peak like a flying buttress on a gothic cathedral. I decided to spend the night there, on the airy, knife-edged ridge crest, 1,600 ft below the summit. The evening sky was cold and cloudless. I could see all the way to tidewater and beyond. At dusk I watched, transfixed, as the house lights of Petersburg blinked on in the west. The closest thing I'd had to human contact since the airdrop, the distant lights set off a flood of emotion that caught me completely off guard. I imagined people watching the Red Sox on the tube, eating fried chicken in brightly lit kitchens, drinking beer, making love. When I lay down to sleep I was overcome by a soul-wrenching loneliness. I'd never felt so alone, ever.

That night I had troubled dreams, of cops and vampires and a gangland-style execution. I heard someone whisper, "He's in there. As soon as he comes out, waste him." I sat bolt upright and opened my eyes. The sun was about to rise. The entire sky was scarlet. It was still clear, but wisps of high cirrus were streaming in from the southwest, and a dark line was visible just above the horizon. I pulled on my boots and hurriedly strapped on my crampons. Five minutes after waking up, I was front-pointing away from the bivouac.

I carried no rope, no tent or bivouac gear, no hardware save my ice-axes. My plan was to go ultralight and ultrafast, to hit the summit and make it back down before the weather turned. Pushing myself, continually out of breath, I scurried up and to the left across small snowfields linked by narrow runnels of verglas and short rock bands. The climbing was almost fun – the rock was covered with large, in-cut holds, and the ice, though thin, never got steep enough to feel extreme – but I was anxious about the bands of clouds racing in from the Pacific, covering the sky.

In what seemed like no time (I didn't have a watch on the trip) I was on the distinctive final ice field. By now the sky was completely overcast. It looked easier to keep angling to the left, but quicker to go straight for the top. Paranoid about being caught by a storm high on the peak without any kind of shelter, I opted for the direct route. The ice steepened, then steepened some more, and as it did so it grew thin. I swung my left ice-axe and struck rock. I aimed for another spot, and once again it glanced off un-yielding diorite with a dull, sickening clank. And again, and again. It was a reprise of my first attempt on the north face. Looking between my legs, I stole a glance at the glacier, more than 2,000 ft below. My stomach churned. I felt my poise slipping away like smoke in the wind.

Forty-five feet above the wall eased back onto the sloping summit shoulder. Forty-five more feet, half the distance between third base and home plate, and the mountain would be mine. I clung stiffly to my axes, unmoving, paralyzed with fear and indecision. I looked down at the dizzying drop to the glacier again, then up, then scraped away the film of ice above my head. I hooked the pick of my left axe on a nickel-thin lip of rock, and weighted it. It held. I pulled my right axe from the ice, reached up, and twisted the pick into a crooked half-inch crack until it jammed. Barely breathing now, I moved my feet up, scrabbling my crampon points across the verglas. Reaching as high as I could with my left arm, I swung the axe gently at the shiny, opaque surface, not knowing what I'd hit beneath it. The pick went in with a heartening *THUNK*! A few minutes later I was standing on a broad, rounded ledge. The summit proper, a series of slender fins sprouting a grotesque meringue of atmospheric ice, stood twenty feet directly above.

The insubstantial frost feathers ensured that those last

twenty feet remained hard, scary, onerous. But then, suddenly, there was no place higher to go. It wasn't possible, I couldn't believe it. I felt my cracked lips stretch into a huge, painful grin. I was on top of the Devil's Thumb.

Fittingly, the summit was a surreal, malevolent place, an improbably slender fan of rock and rime no wider than a filing cabinet. It did not encourage loitering. As I straddled the highest point, the north face fell away beneath my left boot for 6,000 ft beneath my right boot; the south face dropped off for twenty-five hundred. I took some pictures to prove I'd been there, and spent a few minutes trying to straighten a bent pick. Then I stood up, carefully turned around, and headed for home.

The Ascent of Nanda Devi

H.W. Tilman

Bill Tilman made the first ascent of India's Nanda Devi – 7,817 m (25,655 ft) – in 1936, aged 38. After a lifetime of mountaineering and adventuring, he disappeared in 1977 sailing a cutter from Rio de Janeiro to the Falkland Islands.

Our plan now was for two of us to occupy Camp II or the Gîte, as it was appropriately called, and on the following day, while those two went up higher to look for a Camp III, two Sherpas would join them at the Gîte. We assumed that a site for Camp III would be found on the snow saddle, and on the third day the Sherpas would assist in establishing the two Sahibs there while two more of us in turn occupied the Gîte.

It was a fine morning on the 14th, but we did not get away until 10 a.m. Graham Brown and Houston, who were going to sleep at Camp II, had to pack up the bivouac tent and their own gear and then someone dropped a mug down the *khud* and Houston very sportingly went down after it. The task looked hopeless in all the new snow, but he got it. Odell stayed in camp to catch up with his geological notes, but six of us started with Pasang and Nima.

At the roping-up place Carter went back as he had not yet acclimatised, and from there we climbed on three ropes, Lloyd and Nima, Pasang and myself, and Graham Brown, Houston, and Loomis. As usual the steps had to be cleared of snow and in places they were now not very reliable, but by cutting deep in they held sufficiently well. The passage round and up the projecting nose below the Gîte roused so much misgiving that we talked of putting a fixed rope there. But it was an awkward place to fix anything and in the end familiarity bred sufficient contempt for us to do without. A rope of two can move quicker than one of three, so Lloyd and I got there well ahead of the others and Pasang and Nima began making a platform; it now looked as though there would just be room for the bivouac tent and a big one. When they had finished I took them down on my rope, Lloyd waiting for the others, who had not yet arrived. By six o'clock it was snowing again.

The journey to Camp II, though now a daily routine, was never boring however unpleasant it might be in other ways. The unstable rocks of the lower half still lay in wait to punish any carelessness, and on the upper section the daily snow-fall made it at least look like a new ascent.

The next day all started except Phuta and, when we reached the roping-up place, we descried what looked like two flies crawling up the steep snow arête above the Gîte. These of course were Graham Brown and Houston, and we watched them anxiously, making ribald remarks about their rate of progress and their frequent halts. The fact that we were ourselves sitting down eating chocolate by no means lessened our enjoyment of this spectacle and certainly increased the flow of wit. We felt like dramatic critics eating their chocolates in the stalls, and sharpened the pencils of our wit accordingly.

It was a fine day for a change and the bright sun on the snow sapped our energy. We were up by 2 p.m. and having seen the tent pitched, for which there was just room enough, and Pasang and Nima safely established there, Lloyd and I went down, while Odell and Loomis waited to hear the news from above. An hour later Graham Brown and Houston got back to Camp II, and reported that there were a couple of hundred feet of difficult climbing before the snow arête was reached, that this was steep and long, but that a good site for a camp had been found where the arête merged into the broad saddle. They had felt the sun even more severely than we had.

We got down to Camp I at four o'clock and Phuta requested that he might go to the Base Camp that evening. It was no use keeping him, so I gave him a chit to Emmons and sent him down. There were now five of us at Camp I, two Sahibs and two Sherpas at Camp II, and Emmons, Kalu, and three Sherpas at the Base Camp.

Next day, the 16th, two more Sahibs had to occupy Camp II, and at half-past nine we all started, Odell and I carrying our personal kit and some odds and ends. Some student of human nature has remarked that "no one can do an act that is not morally wrong for the last time without feelings of regret", but now I was doing the climb from Camp I to Camp II for the fifth and last time and can very positively refute that statement. Of course devout Hindus might say that in climbing Nanda Devi we *were* committing an immoral act and that would account satisfactorily for my absence of regret.

Before reaching the roping-up place, we were bothered by seeing two tents still standing at the Gîte and it looked as though no move was in progress. Later we made out somebody on the arête but could see only two instead of the four we expected. We puzzled our heads over this and made many wild conjectures. If Graham Brown and Houston were not moving up to Camp III there would be some congestion at the Gîte, but Odell and I were determined to sleep there, even if it meant four in a tent. We could not face yet another ascent from Camp I.

It was no use speculating, and as Odell was going slowly, and I was not unwilling to do the same, he and I went along together while the other three pushed on as fast as they could to find out what the matter was. We two continued in leisurely fashion, not arriving until three o'clock. Perhaps we were carrying heavier loads; Odell certainly was, for he was cluttered up with hypsometers, clinometers, and thermometers, and was so attached to certain favourite but unnecessary articles of clothing that his personal kit was a portentous affair – nor was Da Namgyal there to carry it as he should have been. I remember particularly a hideous yellow sweater, a relic of the War, which weighed more than the five Shetland woollies carried by us all; and at the highest camp he produced a hat which none of us had ever seen before and which, I suppose, had some attributes peculiarly fitting it for wear at 24,000 ft.

The mystery of the two tents was solved by a note and the presence of both Sherpas. Nima was sick and Pasang was completely snow-blind. The note told us that they had gone up with food and kit and asked us to bring on the tent and their sleeping bags. Loomis and Lloyd had already left with these when we arrived and halfway up the snow arête they were met by Houston and Graham Brown. For these four it was a hard day.

Houston's note went on to say that the necessary dope for alleviating snow-blindness had been unaccountably left at Camp I, and suggested that strong tea should be tried in the interim. Tea was at a premium, for we were carefully conserving our solitary ounce for higher up, but we brewed some and did what we could for Pasang, who was in considerable pain. He was lying on his face in the tent and quite unable to open his eyes, but by forcing the lids apart we managed to get some tea in. This treatment was continued until the medicine arrived two days later, but had little effect; nor had the medicine either for that matter, and, though we did not then suspect it, Pasang was now out of the hunt.

It was not easily understood how he had managed to get such a severe attack. Yesterday had been very bright and sunny but no one noticed him with his glasses off, nor were these any different from Nima's which were perfectly efficient. While he was preparing the platform here, I noticed he was working without glasses and it must have been then that his eyes were affected, although the platform was in shadow and there was more rock than snow. But a rarefied atmosphere makes the light more dangerous in this respect and we read that on Everest in 1924 Norton was snow-blind merely from the glare off rocks. In 1930 Shipton and I climbed Kilimanjaro (19,700 ft), and on snow near the summit we both took off our glasses to see where we were, for there was a thick mist and not a sign of the sun. Nevertheless that same night we both went snow-blind and suffered great pain, but in twenty-four hours it passed off without any treatment and this led me to think that Pasang's would do the same.

When Lloyd and Loomis returned, we agreed that they should please themselves whether they came up tomorrow with the little that was left at Camp I to bring. They would not be able to sleep here because Odell and I would still be in residence. Another tent, more food, and our own kits had to be carried to Camp III before we could move up, and for reasons of acclimatisation it was a sound plan to sleep two nights at a camp before going on to the next.

When they had gone, we took stock of our surroundings. These consisted of blank rock wall and thin air in equal proportions; there were about four feet of terra firma between the two tents and one could walk, without a rope, for about ten paces round the corner where the exit lay. All view of the ridge was cut off and only a little of it immediately below the Gîte was visible, but to the east a wide field of vision included East Nanda Devi, "Longstaff's Col" now well below us, a great crescent of fluted ice wall on the rim to the south of it, and, beyond, the beautifully proportioned Nanda Kot. The height was about 20,400 ft.

Having brewed the tea for Pasang's eyes and drunk some ourselves, we tried to instil some life into Nima, who seemed very lugubrious and lethargic – in much the same frame of mind as a passenger in the last stages of seasickness, who having prayed long and earnestly for the ship to sink has almost abandoned hope that it will. I think they had not eaten since they got there, so we made him light his stove and cook some pemmican, which the Sherpas relish far more than we do. They were in the roomy 6 ft × 7 ft tent while we occupied the small bivouac tent vacated by Graham Brown and Houston, who had taken up one of the larger ones. We graciously allowed the Sherpas to remain in the enjoyment of their luxurious quarters, but this generosity will not be counted unto us for righteousness because the atmosphere in their tent was such that no tent at all would have been preferable.

I forget the exact dimensions of our tent, but it was very long and narrow and the two occupants lay, literally, cheek by jowl – that is if the human face has a jowl; or is it confined to pigs? It was admirably suited to Odell, who is also long and a bit narrow, and I think this was the first night that he was able to lie at full length since he had left Ranikhet. On this expedition we were experimenting with air beds as insulation when lying on snow, instead of the usual rubber mats, half an inch thick and 3 ft × 4 ft. The extra room they took up was very noticeable in a small tent and apart from that they were not altogether successful. Punctures were numerous and unless they amounted to bursts, as they sometimes did, they were not easy to locate; situated as we were, the method of plunging them into a bath and watching for bubbles was seldom practicable. If your bed did go flat, it was a serious matter because no protection at all was afforded, and the result was a cold and sleepless night. Again, if you blew them up too hard you rolled off, and if they were too soft you were in contact with the ground and therefore cold. The Sherpas used to blow them up as if they were blowing up a dying fire, with the result that one bounded about like a pea on a drum, and if two people sat on it when in that state the whole thing exploded. Pasang got a lot of amusement out of the operation of blowing up and deflating beds by making them produce discordant noises like ill-played bagpipes. Now that only two of the Sherpas were left, and those two incapable of raising even a zephyr, we had to blow our own up, and this process provided yet another example of the perfection of natural laws which can even legislate for the remote association of a mountaineer and an air bed; as we gained in altitude and lost breath, the beds required less air to fill them owing of course to the diminution of pressure.

There was a storm in the night but, packed as we were, it was easy to keep warm and difficult to keep cool. Pasang was still blind and very sorry for himself, but Nima was brighter and offered to come with us to Camp III. Odell and I took a tent and paraffin, and Nima 40 lb of sugar. Care was required on a short stretch above the camp and an upward traverse on rather shaky snow took us on to the ridge. We left it again where it suddenly stood on end and got into trouble on the rocks which would, when climbed, bring us out above this steep bit which had so frightened us.

Odell led over a steep ice-glazed traverse which Nima and I resolved mentally to have nothing to do with, and when he was securely placed we had ourselves more or less pulled up in a direct line.

We were now at the foot of the steep snow arête which was such a prominent feature from below, and we settled down to kicking steps up it very slowly and methodically, the steps made by our forerunners having vanished. It was a narrow ridge, but we were able to stick to the crest, or slightly on the Rishi side, which was now less steep than the east side, though both fell away sharply, and the upward angle was 40 or 45 degrees; it will be remembered that from Camp I to Camp II the route lay always on the east flank and that the Rishi side was a precipice. As might be expected after the persistent falls of the last week, there was a lot of fresh snow to kick through before solid footing was obtained, and when we reached the tent at Camp III Graham Brown told us exactly how many of these steps we had kicked out, he having counted them. As far as I remember, the figure was disappointingly small for we felt that it must be something astronomical, but in sober fact there were only about 700 ft of snow ridge. Approaching the tent, the angle eased off and we found it pitched snugly under the shelter of a steep snow bank.

It was after midday, but Graham Brown and Houston were still in bed and evidently intended "lying at earth" after their efforts of yesterday. Going back we rattled down in an hour, and this time reversed our upwards procedure by descending the very steep snow patch in order to avoid the rocks. Nobody had come up from below, Pasang was still blind, we both had slight headaches, it was snowing again, and there was a big sun halo; but all this was forgotten in the warm glow of self-righteousness induced by our virtuous activity.

Having thus acquired enough merit for the time being by working while others slept, we sat about next morning until Graham Brown and Houston came down from Camp III for more loads. We found it such a pleasant occupation that we sat about some more until the other three came up from Camp I. As soon as the first man's head appeared round the corner of the bulge below us, a shout went up to know if they had found the tea. They had no tea, but they brought the zinc-sulphate medicine and we now hoped that Pasang's recovery would be speedy; at present his eyes were as firmly closed as ever. Nima too had relapsed into his former state of misery, but even yet we did not despair of getting some useful work out of these two. There was still a load to come up from Camp I, so it was arranged that Carter and Nima should go down tomorrow for this and as much more food as they could carry.

At three o'clock four of us started back for Camp III, Odell and Houston on one rope, Graham Brown and myself on the other. We had the advantage of the steps made by them on the way down and, in spite of heavy loads, were up in two hours. Our tent platform was ready for us, so the others had not been so idle yesterday as we thought, and it was pleasant to have some room again, room outside as well as in. I was sorry we had not got a cat to swing.

As Odell and I lay that night with our cheeks and our jowls at a reasonable distance apart, we wondered happily whether the three below were suffocating in the bivouac tent or succumbing to asphyxiation in the overripe atmosphere of the Sherpas.

We flattered ourselves that the height of this camp was about 21,500 ft but, if it was, it seemed highly improbable that from here we could put a bivouac within striking distance of the summit. It postulated a carry of 2,000 ft, at the very least, 2,500 would be better, and on the difficult going below we had not done a carry of more than 1,500. The climbing was likely to get harder rather than easier and, of course, the increasing altitude would slow us up progressively. Repeated trials with the hypsometer made things appear even more discouraging by giving Camp III a height of only 21,200 ft, and though we knew by now that this instrument was, to put it mildly, subject to error, we had perforce to accept the lower figure in making future plans.

The question of the height of our camps bothered us a lot and, quite early on, the hypsometer had earned for itself an opprobrious name of a like sound which may not be printed. For some reason or other we omitted to bring an aneroid barometer graduated for reading height; possibly our numerous scientists scorned an instrument which even the half-wits of the party could read. I remember in 1934 Shipton and I, having no scientific training, took with us an aneroid barometer out of an aeroplane. I think it cost ten shillings at one of those miscellaneous junk shops in Holborn. Our Sherpas conceived a great affection for it and called it "Shaitan", probably because we consulted it so frequently. It worked very well until we dropped it. But this hypsometer, or boiling-point thermometer, while not giving us any very precise information, afforded everyone a lot of fun and the scientists food for thought. The results it gave were always interesting, sometimes amusing, and seldom accurate. For example, after several hours of exhausting climbing in what we foolishly thought was an upward direction, it was startling to learn that we had in reality descended a hundred feet from where we started. The learned scientists explained with bland assurance that such vagaries were to be expected, and were accounted for quite simply by the presence of a "column of cold air"; the unlearned oafs on the contrary thought that it must be something to do with "hot air", and plenty of it.

But there is generally some use to be found for the most unlikely things, and so it was with the hypsometer. It had as part of its equipment a small bottle of methylated spirits, and when we ran out of solid methylated for priming the stoves, this came in very handy. Priming a stove with paraffin is both noisome and inefficient.

On the 19th Graham Brown and Houston went down again to Camp II for loads while Odell and I went to spy out the land higher up. At the point we had reached, our ridge had widened out into a great hog's-back, so wide that it was in reality the south face, though up the middle of this face a ridge was still discernible, and 1,000 ft higher up it again stood out prominently. We struck straight up the middle of the face over what we called the "snow saddle", avoiding the steep bank above the camp by a short traverse to the left. The snow was in good condition and the angle of slope about thirty degrees for the first 700 ft, after which it began to steepen. Above this was a sort of glacis of snow-covered rock lying at an angle of forty-five to fifty degrees. In the steep places outcrops of rock appeared through the snow. This broad glacis appeared to stretch upward for 1,000 ft until it narrowed again to a sharp ridge. On our immediate right was a forbidding gully, a trap for falling stones and ice, and beyond that the tremendous cirque which forms the connecting ridge between East Nanda Devi and Nanda Devi itself. Some two or three hundred yards to the left was a wide shallow depression, scarcely a gully, and on the far side of it the horizon was bounded by a very bold and steep ridge, probably the same which we had looked at from Pisgah.

We attacked the glacis in the centre and worked upwards and to the left, making for what looked like a slight ridge overlooking the shallow gully. As we mounted, the angle grew steeper and the climbing more difficult. At first a good covering of snow overlay the rocks, but presently this became thinner and the outcrops of rocks more numerous. For mountaineering as well as geological reasons we were keenly interested to reach the first of these outcrops, for the line we should take, and our progress, depended greatly upon its quality. We hoped that at this height it might have changed to something more honest than the treacherous rock of the lower ridge, and that the strata might lie in a more favourable direction. Technically it may have differed, but for a climber it was substantially the same crumbling yellow stuff upon which no reliance could be placed, and, though the dip of the strata was now more in our favour, little comfort was to be derived from that on rock of such rottenness.

When we had climbed about 500 ft from the foot of the glacis, it became apparent that the supposed ridge we were making for was no ridge at all. To go straight up was still possible, but with loads on it would be both difficult and dangerous, for nowhere was there enough snow for an anchorage with an axe, or any rock round which a rope could be belayed. We decided to traverse to the left and go for the shallow gully which appeared to offer a safe route on snow for at least 1,000 ft. But shortly after putting this resolve into practice, we contrived to get ourselves into such a mess on the ice-glazed face of a rock outcrop that all our attention was concentrated on getting out of it, and instead of continuing the traverse to the left we were compelled to embark upon a long and tricky traverse in the opposite direction. By sticking wherever possible to snow, and avoiding any rock like the plague, we worried a way back down the glacis until we rejoined our earlier track.

A lower route was obviously the best line for the gully, but it was now too late for any more and we hurried back to camp, where we arrived in time to avoid the start of a blizzard. Two days had elapsed since the warning of the sun halo.

Lloyd and Loomis had come up here to sleep after only one night at Camp II in defiance of our self-imposed rule of two at each camp. No one, however, with experience of the Gîte would doubt their wisdom in making that camp an exception to the rule.

The results of our reconnaissance were mainly negative but not without value. It was clear that a route directly up the glacis should only be tried as a last desperate resource, and also that whichever way we went it was going to be a painfully long carry before a place where a tent could be pitched would be found. The conclusions were that further reconnaissance was needed, that the most promising line was the broad gully, and that in any case it would be advantageous to move the present camp to a new site at the foot of the glacis.

The night was cold and windy and no one turned out until nine o'clock. Lloyd and Loomis started out to have a look at the way to the gully, and the rest of us went down to Camp II for loads. All the tracks down had to be remade after the blizzard and we had long ceased to expect any tracks to last for twenty-four hours. To anticipate, they did not last so long to-day, and when we returned in the afternoon all were once more obliterated.

We found Pasang still blind and Nima not well, and it was pretty clear that neither would be any use. Nima's single journey to Camp III, the highest reached by any of the porters, was but a dying kick. The almost total failure of the Sherpas is easily explained, for, as I have pointed out, we had to take the leavings of several other expeditions. The only two I expected to go high were Pasang and Kitar. Of the others three were past their best and one was too young and inexperienced. Pasang of course was unlucky to be struck down with snow-blindness, but it cannot be said that it was not his own fault. Kitar was a victim to disease.

The medicine seemed to be having little effect on Pasang's eyes, and Nima's cheery grin was a thing of the past. That they should both go down was now the best course, but this was not possible until Pasang could see something. Apart from their rather miserable mode of existence at the Gîte, I was anxious to have them safely down at the Base Camp before we lost touch with them entirely by going higher up the mountain. We left them there, alone now, in the big tent, having told them that two of us would come down again tomorrow, and we started back, Carter with us, taking the small bivouac tent. Carter had a note which he had found at Camp I telling us that Emmons had moved the Base Camp down to the foot of the scree slope and that he was busy with the plane table, but only Kalu was able to help him by carrying loads.

It was cold and windy when we reached Camp III in a flurry of snow. There was a halo round the sun and two mock[1] suns, and I have seldom seen a more ominous-looking sky. The report of the reconnoitring party was more cheering than the weather. Taking a line below and to the left of ours, they had reached a point from where they could see into and up the gully. They had not got into it, but they reported that it could be reached by a route which lay almost entirely on snow, and that the going up the near side of it looked straightforward enough. Like us, they had seen no promise of a camp site higher up, and it was agreed to move this camp to the top of the snow saddle and to press the attack by the gully.

It was a quiet night in spite of all the signs of approaching

1 Mock suns are coloured images of the sun which appear on either side of the sun and at the same altitude. They probably result from the intersection of two halos and are fairly common in high latitudes.

storm, but the morning of the 21st dawned dull, misty, and snowy. We had a late breakfast and spent the morning in one tent discussing ways and means. Now that the thing was to be put to the test, it was clear that some difficult decisions would have to be made, and the upshot of our talk was that the responsibility for these decisions was put upon the writer. The too frequent use of the word "I" in this narrative will not have escaped the notice of the reader. The reason for this is that up to now I may have had most to say in our affairs; but that was merely through the accident of my being the only one who knew the country or the porters. We had no official leader, and managed very well without, until at this crisis the need was felt for some kind of figure-head.

After a cup of cocoa additional to our lunch which, by the way, was usually a slab of chocolate and nothing else, Lloyd, Carter, and I went down again to Camp II for more loads, and the others took a first instalment of loads up to what would presently be Camp IV.

Pasang and Nima still appeared to be immovable, but I told them that two of us would come down again tomorrow and see them safely over the worst of the route to Camp I. Until they were down they were merely a source of anxiety, and, after tomorrow, we expected to be out of reach. We climbed up again in one and a quarter hours and it was satisfactory to see that our time on the snow arête became faster, indicating that we were still acclimatising and not deteriorating. The other party had found a good camp site on the snow saddle near the foot of the glacis, and had dug out one tent platform.

The sunset was again threatening, with greasy-looking cigar-shaped clouds hanging low over East Nanda Devi, a greenish watery haze to the west, and, to the south, black banks of cumulus tinged with copper.

We woke to find the tent shaking and banging to the blasts of a fierce blizzard. The wind was coming out of the south-east, some snow was falling, but it was impossible to tell what was new snow and what was drift, for outside was nothing but a whirling cloud of driving snow. The three tents were close together and guyed to each other for mutual support. Six of us occupied the two big ones and

Carter was by himself (a doubtful privilege under these conditions) in the small bivouac tent, pitched on the weather side. Odell, Lloyd, and I held the baby in the shape of the Primus stove, but it was conceivable that the inconvenience of fetching ice and breathing paraffin fumes was outweighed by the advantage of getting the food hot without having to fetch it. Going from the comparative warmth of the sleeping bag and the tent out into the blizzard was a breath-taking experience. Breathing was almost impossible facing the wind and nothing could be handled without mittens, while the act of leaving or entering the tent by the small sleeve entrance required the quick co-operation of all, unless the inside was to be covered with a layer of snow.

There was nothing to be done but lie in our bags, with one eye on a book and the other on the furiously flapping fabric and the quivering tent pole. The pole was of very light aluminium and we were rather nervous about it, but it stood the strain well, as did the tents, for which we forgave them all our past discomforts. At five o'clock, when we cooked our evening pemmican, conditions were unchanged. The wind still maintained a steady roar with occasional gusts of gale force, and we discussed the advisability of sleeping with windproofs on in case the tent went in the night. However, we pinned our faith to the fabric and did not resort to these extreme measures.

Morning brought no change in these unpleasant conditions; and we wondered whether it was blowing as hard at the Gîte and how the Sherpas were faring. Anyhow, with the direction of the wind as it was, the rock wall would stop them being blown off their ledge.

The snow was being blown away as soon as it fell, and round our tent it had not accumulated to any great depth. The other big tent had not fared so well and there was a high bank of snow around it by morning. The pressure of this snow had reduced the space inside by half, so that the unfortunate residents were sleeping almost on top of each other. They had the consolation of knowing that their tent was now securely anchored. Carter too, in the bivouac, was experiencing trouble in keeping the snow-laden walls off his face.

Another weary day of inactivity and torpor passed, but towards evening the wind began to moderate and we were able to get outside, clear the accumulated snow away from the doors, and attend to the guys. Snow was still falling lightly and a leaden pall hid everything but the snow at our feet and three forlorn-looking tents.

Followed another cold and stormy night, but the morning of Monday the 24th dawned fine, calm and sunny. Had it been black as night, we would not have complained, for stillness was all we asked for after the battering of the last two days. The loss of this valuable time was disturbing, and though it may seem strange that two days in bed could be anything but beneficial, there was no doubt that the strain and the inaction had done us harm physically. Nor could we tell what effect the blizzard might have had on the snow of the upper slopes. It was imperative now to push on with all speed, and surely after such a snorter we might expect several days of fine weather.

These blizzards which we experienced, three of them lasting for thirty-six, twelve, and forty-eight hours respectively, all came from between east and south-east. Monsoon weather in the hills generally comes from between south and west, but these storms may have been deflected by the mountain. Such blizzards are more to be expected prior to the break of the monsoon, and during two previous monsoon periods in the Himalaya, one in Garhwal and one in the Everest region, I do not recollect one of any severity. This year the monsoon broke early and ended late, and was exceptionally severe in the United Provinces and Garhwal.

At nine o'clock Lloyd and I started out for Camp II in accordance with our promise to the Sherpas, the fulfilment of which the blizzard had compelled us to postpone. We left to the others the cold work of breaking out the tents from their frozen covering and digging out the buried stores, preparatory to carrying one big tent and the bivouac to the new Camp IV site. Five of us were to sleep up there tonight in readiness for carrying up a bivouac for the first summit party next day.

The presence of a lot of powder snow made conditions on the arête bad, and we both felt weak and got progressively

weaker as we descended. Arrived at the Gîte, we were
surprised to find it empty; evidently the Sherpas had tired
of waiting for us and left early. It was comforting to know
that the tent had weathered the storm, that Pasang's eyes
must be better, and that we ourselves had not to descend
any farther. Indeed, we were now in such a state of languor
that our chief concern was how on earth we were going to
get up again. We lolled about on the ledge, assailed by a
violent thirst, feeling complete moral and physical wrecks;
and it was evident that two days and nights in our sleeping
bags had taken more out of us than a really hard day's work.

The Sherpas had taken the stove and cooking pot with
them, but there was some food here and we opened a tin
with an ice-axe – not for the sake of the food but for the tin,
in which to catch the elusive drips from the rock wall. We
had to sleep at the higher camp that night, so at midday we
summoned up all our resolution and, taking with us all the
food that was left here, we crawled weakly away from the
Gîte.

I should be ashamed to say how long it took us to get back
to Camp III, but by the time we arrived we were feeling
better and our strength was beginning to return. Graham
Brown and Carter, who were spending the night here, came
down from Camp IV just as we arrived and informed us
that up there it was perishing cold. Carter thought his toes
were slightly touched with frost-bite.

Adding some more food to our loads, Lloyd and I went
off once more and an hour of steady plodding brought us to
the new camp. They had evidently started late that morning
owing to the frozen tents, and, when we got up, the second
tent was just being pitched. There was a bitter wind
blowing and Loomis was inside attending to his feet, which
also had been slightly affected by cold.

In spite of the cold, it was difficult to turn away from the
astonishing picture painted by the fast-sinking sun. Nanda
Kot still shone with dazzling purity like an opal, and
beyond to the east was range upon range of the snow peaks
of Nepal, looking like rollers breaking in white foam on a
sunny sea. From the snow slope falling away out of sight at
our feet, the eye swept across a great void till arrested by the

castellated ivory wall of the Sanctuary, dominated by Tri-sul, up which the shadows were already stealing. And to the west was the dark chasm of the Rishi gorge, the clear-cut outline of the "Curtain", and the blue-green swell of the foothills.

The height of Camp IV we estimated to be 21,800 ft, and with five of us here and food for nearly a fortnight we were in a strong position. If we could push a bivouac up another 2,000 ft, the summit would be within reach, and, big "if" though this was, the time had come to make the attempt. Of the five now at this camp, it was not difficult to decide which two should have the privilege of first shot. Odell was going very well and his experience, combined with Hous-ton's energy, would make a strong pair. Assuming that we could place the bivouac high enough tomorrow, they were to have two days in which to make their attempt, and on the third day a second pair would take their place, whether they had been successful or not. The form shown tomorrow would indicate which two would have the second chance, and, provided the weather held, it might be possible to send up a third pair.

The 25th broke fine, but it was ten o'clock before we had made up our loads of 15 lb each, which included food for two men for six days. During the blizzard, not very much snow had actually settled, and since then sufficient time had elapsed for this new snow to consolidate. We found it in good condition. After gaining some height by kicking steps, we approached the gully by a long traverse where steps had to be cut and great care exercised. The snow covering grew thinner and we came to an uncomfortable halt on the steep lip of a minor hollow, cutting us off from the main gully. This was the farthest point reached by Lloyd and Loomis, and they had seen that this difficult little gully could be avoided by working round the head of it, 200 ft higher.

We sat here for a little, but it was no place for a long sojourn without prehensile trousers. There was not enough snow to afford a step, much less a seat, and the angle of the rock was such that mere friction was of no avail – boots, hands, and ice-axe were all needed to prevent the beginning of a long slither which would only end on the glacier 6,000 ft below. Turning up the slope, the next few feet were of the same precarious nature that Odell and I had experienced on the glacis, but this was as yet the only part of the route where we had to forsake the security of the snow for the uncertainty of the rock. Once over this, we settled down to a long steady grind, kicking and cutting our way up very steep snow, and having rounded the head of this minor hollow, we took a line up the true left bank of the broad gully.

We were climbing on two ropes, so by changing the leading rope and also the leading end of each rope, the work was divided among four. It was a beautiful day, but in our perverse way we were not content, and were captious enough to wish the sun obscured so that we could climb in more comfort. Nanda Kot, 22,500 ft, sank below us and we began to cast jealous eyes on Trisul, which still looked down upon us majestically from its height of 23,400 ft. Meantime we began to search the snow above us for the slightest break in the relentless angle of the slope which might afford a site for a tent. We were tempted momentarily by the broken outline of the skyline ridge away across the gully, but we decided it was too far off and the approach to it too steep.

As we gained height, the curve of the face to our right grew rounder and narrower and the central ridge was beginning to stand out again like the bridge of a Roman nose. We edged over towards it, thinking that the rocks might provide easier going than the snow, and aiming for the foot of a rock tower where there might be a platform. Knowing by now the sort of rock we might expect, it was curious that we should so think, but such was the distorting effect on our minds of five hours of laborious step-kicking. The change of course was for the worse and we had some awkward moments before we dragged ourselves to the foot of the tower, to find it sloping away as steeply as the rest of the mountain.

The time was now three o'clock and our height something over 23,000 ft, practically level with Trisul. Loomis had an attack of cramp, but when he had recovered we turned our attention to the rock tower at our backs, on top of which we hoped to find better things. Lloyd did a grand lead up a steep rock chimney with his load on and was able to give the rest of us some much needed moral and, in my case, physical encouragement with the rope. This took some time and it was four o'clock before we were all on top of the tower, where there was barely room for five of us to stand, much less pitch a tent. Looking up the ridge, it was impossible to say where such a place would be found, but it was sufficiently broken to offer considerable hope. Meantime three of us had to get back to Camp IV and at this time of the afternoon of a bright sunny day the snow would be at its worst. With the assent of all, it was decided to dump our loads here leaving Houston and Odell to shift for themselves. It seemed a selfish decision at the time and it seems so now; no doubt we could have cut it a bit finer and yet got down before dark, but it was likely that they would not have to go far before finding a bivouac, and, in any case, with sleeping bags and warm clothing they could not come to much harm.

We learnt afterwards that they had an uncommonly busy evening. They had to climb another 150 ft before even the most imaginative could discern the makings of a platform, and then they had to make two journeys up and down with the loads. It was dark before they were finally settled.

Oblivious of this activity and the curses which were being bestowed, rather unjustly, on us for our premature desertion, we climbed hastily but cautiously down, reaching the camp at sundown. There was no sign of Graham Brown and Carter, so we assumed they were having a day off at Camp III.

Discussing the results of this day's work, we decided the bivouac was about 23,500 ft, probably too low for an attempt on the summit, but as high as we could push it in the day. We thought they would probably move it higher tomorrow and make their bid on the following day. The closer view of the upper part of the mountain which we had obtained had not made it look any easier, and it was a puzzle to make out where exactly the peak lay. I began to fear we had not allowed them enough time, but now it was too late to alter plans.

Next day was fine, but mist shrouded the upper moun-

tain from our anxious gaze. We felt slack, and took the
morning off before going down to Camp III to give Graham Brown and Carter a hand with their loads. As their tent
was the one which had been half-buried by the blizzard, it
took them a long time to dig it out, so we returned before
them and prepared a platform.

The 27th was to be for us at Camp IV another day of
idleness. That at least was the plan, but the event was
different, and for some of us it was a day of the greatest
mental and physical stress that we had yet encountered.

I had been worrying all night over the waste of this day,
trying to devise some scheme whereby the second pair
could go up at once to the bivouac. The trouble was that
a second tent was essential, and having seen something of
the extraordinary difficulty of finding a site even for the
small tent, to go up there on the slim chance of finding a site
for the big one as well was incurring the risk of exhausting
the party to no purpose. While we were having breakfast,
debating this knotty point and wondering how far the
summit party had got, Loomis disclosed the fact that all
was not well with his feet, the toes being slightly frost-
bitten, and that henceforward we should have to count him
out. This loss of carrying power knocked the scheme for a
second tent on the head and a few moments later we had
something else to think about.

We had just decided they must be well on the way to the
top when we were startled to hear Odell's familiar yodel,
rather like the braying of an ass. It sounded so close that I
thought they must be on the way down, having got the peak
the previous day, but it suddenly dawned on us that he was
trying to send an S.O.S. Carter, who had the loudest voice,
went outside to try and open communication, and a few
minutes later came back to the tent to announce that
"Charlie is killed" – Charlie being Houston. It was impossible to see anyone on the mountain, but he was certain
he had heard correctly. As soon as we had pulled ourselves
together, I stuffed some clothes and a bandage into a
rucksack and Lloyd and I started off as fast as we could
manage, to be followed later by Graham Brown and Carter
with a hypodermic syringe.

It was a climb not easily forgotten – trying to go fast and realizing that at this height it was impossible to hurry, wondering what we should find, and above all what we could do. The natural assumption was that there had been a fall, and that since they were sure to be roped, Odell was also hurt, and the chance of getting a helpless man down the mountain was too remote to bear thinking about. As if to confirm this assumption, we could get no answer to repeated calls on the way up.

Remembering our struggles yesterday on the ridge and in the chimney, we took a different line and tackled a band of steep rock directly above us, in between the gully and the ridge. It proved to be much worse than it looked and, when we had hauled ourselves panting on to the snow above, we vowed that the next time we would stick to the gully, which here narrowed and passed through a sort of cleft in the rock band.

The time was now about two o'clock, and traversing up and to the right over snow in the direction of the ridge, the little tent came in sight not thirty yards away. Instinctively we tried almost to break into a run, but it was no use, and we advanced step by step, at a maddening pace, not knowing what we should find in the tent, if indeed anything at all. The sight of an ice-axe was a tremendous relief; evidently Odell had managed to crawl back. But when another was seen, conjecture was at a loss. Then voices were heard talking quietly and next moment we were greeted with, "Hullo, you blokes, have some tea." "Charlie is ill" was the message Odell had tried to convey!

Lloyd and I experienced a curious gamut of emotions; firstly and naturally, of profound relief, then, and I think not unnaturally, disgust at having suffered such unnecessary mental torture, and, of course, deep concern for Houston. While we swallowed tea, tea that reeked of pemmican but which I still remember with thankfulness, we heard what they had done and discussed what we were to do.

They had devoted yesterday to a reconnaissance. Following the ridge up they found, at a height of about 500 ft above the bivouac, a flat snow platform capable of holding two tents comfortably. Beyond that the climbing became interesting and difficult, but they had reached the foot of a long and easy snow slope leading up to the final rock wall. Here they turned back, having decided to move the bivouac next day to the higher site. Both were going strongly, but early that night Houston became violently ill, and in the cramped quarters of the tent, perched insecurely on an inadequate platform above a steep slope, both had spent a sleepless and miserable night. Houston attributed his trouble to the bully beef which both had eaten; Odell was unaffected, but it is possible that a small portion was tainted and certainly the symptoms pointed to poisoning of some kind.

Houston was still very ill and very weak, but it was he who suggested what should be done, and showed us how evil might be turned to good. It was only possible for two people to stay up here, and his plan was that he should go down that afternoon and that I should stay up with Odell, and thus no time would have been lost. We demurred to this on the ground that he was not fit to move, but he was so insistent on the importance of not losing a day and so confident of being able to get down that we at last consented.

We all four roped up, with Houston in the middle, and started slowly down, taking frequent rests. We struck half-right across the snow and joined the gully above the rock band according to our earlier resolution, and there the two rear men anchored the party while Lloyd cut steps down the narrow cleft, which was very icy. Houston was steady enough in spite of his helpless state of weakness, and having safely negotiated this awkward bit, we kicked slowly down to the left and found our up-going tracks. Presently Graham Brown and Carter hove in sight, and I imagine their amazement at seeing four people coming down was as great as ours had been at the sight of the two ice-axes. When we met, Lloyd and Houston tied on to their rope and continued the descent, while Odell and I climbed slowly back to the bivouac.

This illness of Houston's was a miserable turn of fortune for him, robbing him as it did of the summit. Bad as he was, his generous determination to go down was of a piece with the rest of his actions.

Scenically the position of the bivouac was very fine but residentially it was damnable. It was backed on two sides by rock, but on the others the snow slope fell away steeply, and the platform which had been scraped out in the snow was so narrow that the outer edge of the tent overhung for almost a foot, thus reducing considerably both the living space and any feeling one yet had of security. Necessity makes a man bold, and I concluded that necessity had pressed very hard that night when they lit on this spot for their bivouac. Odell, who had had no sleep the previous night, could have slept on a church spire, and, as I had Houston's sleeping bag and the extra clothing I had fortunately brought up, we both had a fair night. Odell, who was the oldest inhabitant and in the position of host, generously conceded to me the outer berth, overhanging space.

The weather on the 28th still held and without regret we packed up our belongings and made the first trip to the upper bivouac. The snow slope was steeper than any we had yet met but, at the early hour we started, the snow was good and in an hour we reached the spacious snow shelf which they had marked down. It was about 20 ft × 20 ft, so that there was room to move about, but on either side of the ridge on which it stood the slope was precipitous. After a brief rest the increasing heat of the sun warned us to be on the move again and we hurried down for the remaining loads. The snow was softening rapidly under a hot sun nor was this deterioration confined only to the snow. We already knew, and it was to be impressed on us again, that at these altitudes a hot sun is a handicap not to be lightly assessed.

Guessing the height of this camp, aided by the absence of the hypsometer, we put it at about 24,000 ft. Trisul was well below us and even the top of East Nanda Devi (24,379 ft) began to look less remote. The condition of the wide belt of snow which had to be crossed, the difficulties of the final wall, and the weather were so many large question marks, but we turned in that night full of hope, and determined to give ourselves every chance by an early start.

We were up at five o'clock to begin the grim business of cooking and the more revolting tasks of eating breakfast and getting dressed. That we were up is an exaggeration, we were merely awake, for all these fatigues are carried out

from inside one's sleeping bag until it is no longer possible
to defer the putting on of boots. One advantage a narrow
tent has, that at lower altitudes is overlooked, is that the two
sleeping bags are in such close proximity that boots which
are rammed into the non-existent space between them
generally survive the night without being frozen stiff. It
worked admirably on this occasion so that we were spared
the pangs of wrestling with frozen boots with cold fingers.
Frozen boots are a serious matter and may cause much
delay, and in order to mitigate this trouble we had, since the
start, carefully refrained from oiling our boots. This notion
might work well enough on Everest in pre-monsoon conditions where the snow is dry, but we fell between two
stools, rejoicing in wet feet down below and frozen boots
higher up.

By six o'clock we were ready, and shortly after we
crawled outside, roped up, and started. It was bitterly
cold, for the sun had not yet risen over the shoulder of
East Nanda Devi and there was a thin wind from the west.
What mugs we were to be fooling about on this infernal
ridge at that hour of the morning! And what was the use of
this ridiculous coil of rope, as stiff as a wire hawser, tying
me for better or for worse to that dirty-looking ruffian in
front! Such, in truth, were the reflections of at least one of
us as we topped a snow boss behind the tent, and the
tenuous nature of the ridge in front became glaringly
obvious in the chill light of dawn. It was comforting to
reflect that my companion in misery had already passed
this way, and presently as the demands of the climbing
became more insistent, grievances seemed less real, and
that life was still worth living was a proposition that might
conceivably be entertained.

This difficult ridge was about 300 yards long, and though
the general angle appeared slight it rose in a series of abrupt
rock and snow steps. On the left was an almost vertical
descent to a big ravine, bounded on the far side by terrific
grey cliffs that supported the broad snow shelf for which we
were making. The right side also fell away steeply, being
part of the great rock cirque running round to East Nanda
Devi. The narrow ridge we were on formed a sort of

causeway between the lower south face and the upper snow shelf.

One very important factor which, more than anything, tended to promote a happier frame of mind was that the soft crumbly rock had at last yielded to a hard rough schistose-quartzite which was a joy to handle; a change which could not fail to please us as mountaineers and, no doubt, to interest my companion as a geologist. That vile rock, schist is, I believe, the technical term, had endangered our heads and failed to support our feet from the foot of the scree to the last bivouac. It was a wonder our burning anathemas had not caused it to undergo a geological change under our very eyes – metamorphosed it, say, into plutonic rocks. But, as has been said – by others, there is good in everything, and, on reflection, this very sameness was not without some saving grace because it meant that we were spared an accumulation of rock samples at every camp. A bag of assorted stones had already been left at the Glacier Camp, and I tremble to think what burdens we might have had to carry down the mountain had the rock been as variegated as our geologist, and indeed any right-minded geologist, would naturally desire.

Thanks to the earlier reconnaissance by him and Houston, Odell led over this ridge at a good pace and in an hour and a half we had reached the snow mound which marked the farthest point they had reached. It was a ridge on which we moved one at a time.

In front was a snow slope set at an angle of about 30 degrees and running right up to the foot of the rock wall, perhaps 600 or 700 ft above us. To the west this wide snow terrace extended for nearly a quarter of a mile until it ended beneath that same skyline ridge, which below had formed the western boundary of the broad gully. On our right the shelf quickly steepened and merged into the steep rock face of the ridge between East Nanda Devi and our mountain. We were too close under the summit to see where it lay, but there was little doubt about the line we should take, because from a rapid survey there seemed to be only one place where a lodgement could be effected on the final wall. This was well to the west of our present position, where a snow rib crossed the terrace at right angles and, abutting against the wall, formed as it were a ramp.

We began the long snow trudge at eight o'clock and even at that early hour and after a cold night the snow was not good and soon became execrable. The sun was now well up. After it had been at work for a bit we were going in over our knees at every step, and in places where the slope was steeper it was not easy to make any upward progress at all. One foot would be lifted and driven hard into the snow and then, on attempting to rise on it, one simply sank down through the snow to the previous level. It was like trying to climb up cotton wool, and a good deal more exhausting, I imagine, than the treadmill. But, like the man on a walking tour in Ireland, who throughout a long day received the same reply of "20 miles" to his repeated inquiries as to the distance he was from his destination, we could at any rate say, "Thank God, we were holding our own."

The exertion was great and every step made good cost six to eight deep breaths. Our hopes of the summit grew faint, but there was no way but to plug on and see how far we could get. This we did, thinking only of the next step, taking our time, and resting frequently. It was at least some comfort that the track we were ploughing might assist a second party. On top of the hard work and the effect of altitude was the languor induced by a sun which beat down relentlessly on the dazzling snow, searing our lips and sapping the energy of mind and body. As an example of how far this mind-sapping process had gone, I need only mention that it was seriously suggested that we should seek the shade of a convenient rock which we were then near, lie up there until evening, and finish the climb in the dark!

It is noteworthy that whilst we were enjoying, or more correctly enduring, this remarkable spell of sunshine, the foothills south and west of the Basin experienced disastrous floods. As related in the first chapter, it was on this day that the Pindar river overflowed sweeping away some houses in the village of Tharali, while on the same day nineteen inches of rain fell at the hill station of Mussoorie west of Ranikhet.

We derived some encouragement from seeing East Nanda Devi sink below us and at one o'clock, rather to our surprise, we found ourselves on top of the snow rib moving at a snail's pace towards the foot of the rocks. There we had a long rest and tried to force some chocolate down our parched throats by eating snow at the same time. Though neither of us said so, I think both felt that now it would take a lot to stop us. There was a difficult piece of rock to climb; Odell led this and appeared to find it stimulating, but it provoked me to exclaim loudly upon its "thinness". Once over that, we were landed fairly on the final slope with the summit ridge a bare 300 ft above us.

Presently we were confronted with the choice of a short but very steep snow gully and a longer but less drastic route to the left. We took the first and found the snow reasonably hard owing to the very steep angle at which it lay. After a severe struggle I drew myself out of it on to a long and gently sloping corridor, just below and parallel to the summit ridge. I sat down and drove the axe in deep to hold Odell as he finished the gully. He moved up to join me and I had just suggested the corridor as a promising line to take when there was a sudden hiss and, quicker than thought, a slab of snow, about forty yards long, slid off the corridor and disappeared down the gully, peeling off a foot of snow as it went. At the lower limit of the avalanche, which was where we were sitting, it actually broke away for a depth of a foot all round my axe to which I was holding. At its upper limit, forty yards up the corridor, it broke away to a depth of three or four feet.

The corridor route had somehow lost its attractiveness, so we finished the climb by the ridge without further adventure, reaching the top at three o'clock.

The summit is not the exiguous and precarious spot that usually graces the top of so many Himalayan peaks, but a solid snow ridge nearly 200 yards long and 20 yards broad. It is seldom that conditions on top of a high peak allow the climber the time or the opportunity to savour the immediate fruits of victory. Too often, when having first carefully probed the snow to make sure he is not standing on a cornice, the climber straightens up preparatory to savouring the situation to the full, he is met by a perishing wind and the interesting view of a cloud at close quarters, and with a muttered imprecation turns in his tracks and begins the descent. Far otherwise was it now. There were no cornices to worry about and room to unrope and walk about. The air was still, the sun shone, and the view was good if not so extensive as we had hoped.

Odell had brought a thermometer, and no doubt sighed for the hypsometer. From it we found that the air temperature was 20 degrees F, but in the absence of wind we could bask gratefully in the friendly rays of our late enemy the sun. It was difficult to realize that we were actually standing on top of the same peak which we had viewed two months ago from Ranikhet, and which had then appeared incredibly remote and inaccessible, and it gave us a curious feeling of exaltation to know that we were above every peak within hundreds of miles on either hand. Dhaulagiri, 1,000 ft higher, and 200 miles away in Nepal, was our nearest rival. I believe we so far forgot ourselves as to shake hands on it.

After the first joy in victory came a feeling of sadness that the mountain had succumbed, that the proud head of the goddess was bowed.

At this late hour of the day there was too much cloud about for any distant views. The Nepal peaks were hidden and all the peaks on the rim, excepting only Trisul, whose majesty even our loftier view-point could not diminish. Far to the north through a vista of white cloud the sun was colouring to a warm brown the bare and bleak Tibetan plateau.

After three-quarters of an hour on that superb summit, a brief forty-five minutes into which was crowded the worth of many hours of glorious life, we dragged ourselves reluctantly away, taking with us a memory that can never fade and leaving behind "thoughts beyond the reaches of our souls".

If our thoughts were still treading on air, the short steep gully, swept by the avalanche bare of steps, soon brought us to earth. We kicked slowly down it, facing inwards and plunging an arm deep into the snow for support. Followed another exhausting drag across the snow, hindered rather than helped by the deep holes we had made coming up, and then a cold hour was spent moving cautiously, one at a time, down the ice and the benumbing rocks of the long ridge above the bivouac. We paused to watch a bird, a snow pigeon, cross our ridge and fly swiftly across the grey cliffs of the ravine beneath the snow terrace, like the spirit of Nanda Devi herself, forsaking the fastness which was no longer her own.

At six o'clock we reached the tent and brewed the first of many jorums of tea. After such a day nothing could have tasted better and our appreciation was enhanced by our long enforced abstinence. There was but a pinch left and we squandered it all recklessly, saving the leaves for the morning. Food was not even mentioned.

We paid for this debauch with a sleepless night to which no doubt exhaustion and a still-excited imagination contributed. Each little incident of the climb was gone over again and again, and I remember, in the small hours when the spark of life burns lowest, the feeling which predominated over all was one of remorse at the fall of a giant. It is the same sort of contrition that one feels at the shooting of an elephant, for however thrilling and arduous the chase, however great has been the call upon skill, perseverance, and endurance, and however gratifying the weight of the ivory, when the great bulk crashes to the ground achievement seems to have been bought at the too high cost of sacrilege.

It was very cold next morning when we packed up and started down. Near the bottom of the gully we were met by Lloyd and Loomis, who were coming up to help us down and who were overjoyed when they heard that success had crowned the efforts of the whole party. Houston and Graham Brown had already gone down and we decided to stop the night at Camp IV. There were still three or four days' food left in hand but Loomis and Carter were both troubled with their feet, which must have been touched with frost the day Camp IV was occupied. Lloyd was going stronger than ever and it was much to be regretted that we could not make up a second party.

The weather, which during this crucial period had been

so kind, now broke up and on the morning of the 31st it was blowing half a gale out of a clear sky. Lloyd, Loomis, and I started some time before the other two, all carrying heavy loads because we left nothing but the two big tents, some snow-shoes, and two pairs of crampons or ice-claws. The snow-shoes had been lugged up to assist us on soft snow and the crampons for use on hard snow, but the slopes were, of course, all too steep for snow-shoes, and the only time we might have used the crampons was now when they had been abandoned.

It was bitterly cold, and the snow on the arête was hard and dangerous – the mountain had not finished with us yet. We started to descend in the usual way, plunging the heel in at each step with a stiff leg. When one or two "voluntaries" had been cut, we should have taken warning that the snow was not right for such tactics, but we were all pretty tired and in a hurry to get down, and it is in such circumstances that care is relaxed and the party comes to grief. Fortunately before this happened we had another warning which could not well be ignored. The leader's heels went from under him and he slid down the slope pulling the second man after him until checked by the rope belayed round the end man's axe, which fortunately held firm. We all felt rather ashamed of ourselves after this exhibition and abandoned that method in favour of the slower but safer one of cutting steps and moving one at a time, which should have been adopted at the start.

There was another slip, quickly checked, when one of the snow steps above the Gîte gave way, and we reached this camp in a chastened frame of mind and hoping that the mountain had now exhausted its spite. After a brief rest we pushed on, unroped gladly when we were off the snow, and picked our way with great caution down the unstable rocks to Camp I. On the way we noticed with concern that Odell and Carter were still high up on the arête and moving very slowly.

We found here Graham Brown and Pasang. The former's leg was troubling him, so he had spent the night here where there were still two tents, and Pasang had come up from below to take his load. We heard that Graham Brown and

Houston too had narrowly escaped disaster on the previous day by the breaking of a step above the Gîte. Pasang had completely recovered his sight, but he was not yet his former bright self, for I think he felt keenly the disability which prevented him from helping his Sahibs at grips with the mountain.

It was now midday and after a drink of cocoa, which served only to bring home to us the loss we had suffered, we continued the descent. The cocoa so wrought upon Lloyd that, with a desperation born of thirst, he turned aside to prosecute a last and unsuccessful search for the tea. On the Coxcomb ridge I met Phuta going up to help Pasang and was shocked to hear that Kitar had died in the night. We got down to the new Base Camp at the foot of the scree at two o'clock and but for the melancholy news of Kitar's death there was nothing to mar our contentment. Twenty-one days had elapsed since we left.

The Long Grind

Sir Edmund Hillary

*New Zealand mountaineer and explorer, born in 1919. A
member of Sir John Hunt's 1953 Himalayan expedition,
Hillary, together with Sherpa Tenzing, made the first
ascent of Everest on 29 May of that year.*

I looked at the way ahead. From our tent very steep
slopes covered with deep powder snow led up to a
prominent snow shoulder on the South-East ridge about
a hundred feet above our heads. The slopes were in the
shade and breaking trail was going to be cold work. Still a
little worried about my boots, I asked Tenzing to lead off.
Always willing to do his share, and more than his share if
necessary, Tenzing scrambled past me and tackled the
slope. With powerful thrusts of his legs he forced his
way up in knee-deep snow. I gathered in the rope and
followed along behind him.

We were climbing out over the tremendous South face of
the mountain, and below us snow chutes and rock ribs
plummeted thousands of feet down to the Western Cwm.
Starting in the morning straight on to exposed climbing is
always trying for the nerves, and this was no exception. In
imagination I could feel my heavy load dragging me backwards down the great slopes below; I seemed clumsy and
unstable and my breath was hurried and uneven. But
Tenzing was pursuing an irresistible course up the slope,
and I didn't have time to think too much. My muscles soon
warmed up to their work, my nerves relaxed and I dropped

into the old climbing rhythm and followed steadily up his tracks. As we gained a little height we moved into the rays of the sun, and although we could feel no appreciable warmth, we were greatly encouraged by its presence. Taking no rests, Tenzing ploughed his way up through the deep snow and led out on to the snow shoulder. We were now at a height of 28,000 ft. Towering directly above our heads was the South Summit – steep and formidable. And to the right were the enormous cornices of the summit ridge. We still had a long way to go.

Ahead of us the ridge was sharp and narrow, but rose at an easy angle. I felt warm and strong now, so took over the lead. First I investigated the ridge with my ice-axe. On the sharp crest of the ridge and on the right-hand side loose powder snow was lying dangerously over hard ice. Any attempt to climb on this would only produce an unpleasant slide down towards the Kangshung glacier. But the left-hand slope was better – it was still rather steep, but it had a firm surface of wind-blown powder snow into which our crampons would bite readily.

Taking every care, I moved along on to the left-hand side on the ridge. Everything seemed perfectly safe. With increased confidence, I took another step. Next moment I was almost thrown off balance as the wind-crust suddenly gave way and I sank through it up to my knee. It took me a little while to regain my breath. Then I gradually pulled my leg out of the hole. I was almost upright again when the wind-crust under the other foot gave way and I sank back with both legs enveloped in soft, loose snow to the knees. It was the mountaineer's curse – breakable crust. I forced my way along. Sometimes for a few careful steps I was on the surface, but usually the crust would break at the critical moment and I'd be up to my knees again. Though it was tiring and exasperating work, I felt I had plenty of strength in reserve. For half an hour I continued on in this uncomfortable fashion, with the violent balancing movements I was having to make completely destroying rhythm and breath. It was a great relief when the snow conditions improved and I was able to stay on the surface. I still kept down on the steep slopes on the left of the ridge, but plunged ahead and climbed steadily upwards. I came over a small crest and saw in front of me a tiny hollow in the ridge. And in this hollow lay two oxygen bottles almost completely covered with snow. It was Evans' and Bourdillon's dump.

I rushed forward into the hollow and knelt beside them. Wrenching one of the bottles out of its frozen bed I wiped the snow off its dial – it showed a thousand-pounds pressure – it was nearly a third full of oxygen. I checked the other – it was the same. This was great news. It meant that the oxygen we were carrying on our backs only had to get us back to these bottles instead of right down to the South Col. It gave us more than another hour of endurance. I explained this to Tenzing through my oxygen mask. I don't think he understood but he realized I was pleased about something and nodded enthusiastically.

I led off again. I knew there was plenty of hard work ahead and Tenzing could save his energies for that. The ridge climbed on upwards rather more steeply now, and then broadened out and shot up at a sharp angle to the foot of the enormous slope running up to the South Summit. I crossed over on to the right-hand side of the ridge and found the snow was firm there. I started chipping a long line of steps up to the foot of the great slope. Here we stamped out a platform for ourselves and I checked our oxygen. Everything seemed to be going well. I had a little more oxygen left than Tenzing, which meant I was obtaining a slightly lower flow rate from my set, but it wasn't enough to matter and there was nothing I could do about it anyway.

Ahead of us was a really formidable problem, and I stood in my steps and looked at it. Rising from our feet was an enormous slope slanting steeply down on the precipitous East face of Everest and climbing up with appalling steepness to the South Summit of the mountain 400 ft above us. The left-hand side of the slope was a most unsavoury mixture of steep loose rock and snow, which my New Zealand training immediately regarded with grave suspicion, but which in actual fact the rock-climbing Britons, Evans and Bourdillon had ascended in much trepidation when on the first assault. The only other route was up the snow itself and still faintly discernible here and there were traces of the track made by the first assault party, who had come down it in preference to their line of ascent up the rocks. The snow route it was for us! There looked to be some tough work ahead, and as Tenzing had been taking it easy for a while I hard-heartedly waved him through. With his first six steps I realized that the work was going to be much harder than I had thought. His first two steps were on top of the snow, the third was up to his ankles and by the sixth he was up to his hips. But almost lying against the steep slope, he drove himself onwards, ploughing a track directly upwards. Even following in his steps was hard work, for the loose snow refused to pack into safe steps. After a long and valiant spell he was plainly in need of a rest, so I took over.

Immediately I realized that we were on dangerous ground. On this very steep slope the snow was soft and deep with little coherence. My ice-axe shaft sank into it without any support and we had no sort of a belay. The only factor that made it at all possible to progress was a thin crust of frozen snow which tied the whole slope together. But this crust was a poor support. I was forcing my way upwards, plunging deep steps through it, when suddenly with a dull breaking noise an area of crust all around me about six feet in diameter broke off into large sections and slid with me back through three or four steps. And then I stopped; but the crust gathering speed, slithered on out of sight. It was a nasty shock. My whole training told me that the slope was exceedingly dangerous, but at the same time I was saying to myself: "Ed my boy, this is Everest – you've got to push it a bit harder!" My solar plexus was tight with fear as I ploughed on. Half-way up I stopped, exhausted. I could look down 10,000 ft between my legs, and I have never felt more insecure. Anxiously I waved Tenzing up to me.

"What do you think of it, Tenzing?" And the immediate response, "Very bad, very dangerous!" "Do you think we should go on?" and there came the familiar reply that never helped you much but never let you down: "Just as you

wish!" I waved him on to take a turn at leading. Changing
the lead much more frequently now, we made our unhappy
way upwards, sometimes sliding back and wiping out half a
dozen steps, and never feeling confident that at any moment
the whole slope might not avalanche. In the hope of some
sort of a belay we traversed a little towards the rocks, but
found no help in their smooth, holdless surfaces. We
plunged on upwards. And then I noticed that a little above
us, the left-hand rock ridge turned into snow and the snow
looked firm and safe. Laboriously and carefully we climbed
across some steep rock, and I sank my ice-axe shaft into the
snow of the ridge. It went in firm and hard. The pleasure of
this safe belay after all the uncertainty below was like a
reprieve to a condemned man. Strength flowed into my
limbs, and I could feel my tense nerves and muscles
relaxing. I swung my ice-axe at the slope and started
chipping a line of steps upwards – it was very steep, but
seemed so gloriously safe. Tenzing, an inexpert but en-
thusiastic step cutter, took a turn and chopped a haphazard
line of steps up another pitch. We were making fast time
now and the slope was starting to ease off. Tenzing gallantly
waved me through, and with a growing feeling of excitement I cramponed up some firm slopes to the rounded top
of the South Summit. It was only 9 a.m.

With intense interest I looked at the vital ridge leading to
the summit – the ridge about which Evans and Bourdillon
had made such gloomy forecasts. At first glance it was an
exceedingly impressive and indeed a frightening sight. In
the narrow crest of this ridge, the basic rock of the mountain had a thin capping of snow and ice – ice that reached
out over the East face in enormous cornices, overhanging
and treacherous, and only waiting for the careless foot of the
mountaineer to break off and crash 10,000 ft to the Kangshung glacier. And from the cornices the snow dropped
steeply to the left to merge with the enormous rock bluffs
which towered 8,000 ft above the Western Cwm. It was
impressive all right! But as I looked my fears started to lift a
little. Surely I could see a route there? For this snow slope
on the left, although very steep and exposed, was practically
continuous for the first half of the ridge, although in places

the great cornices reached hungrily across. If we could make a route along that snow slope, we could go quite a distance at least.

With a feeling almost of relief, I set to work with my ice-axe and cut a platform for myself just down off the top of the South Summit. Tenzing did the same, and then we removed our oxygen sets and sat down. The day was still remarkably fine, and we felt no discomfort through our thick layers of clothing from either wind or cold. We had a drink out of Tenzing's water-bottle and then I checked our oxygen supplies. Tenzing's bottle was practically exhausted, but mine still had a little in it. As well as this, we each had a full bottle. I decided that the difficulties ahead would demand as light a weight on our backs as possible so determined to use only the full bottles. I removed Tenzing's empty bottle and my nearly empty one and laid them in the snow. With particular care I connected up our last bottles and tested to see that they were working efficiently. The needles on the dials were steady on 3,3000 lb per square inch pressure – they were very full bottles holding just over 800 litres of oxygen each. At three litres a minute we consumed 180 litres an hour, and this meant a total endurance of nearly four and a half hours. This didn't seem much for the problems ahead, but I was determined if necessary to cut down to two litres a minute for the homeward trip.

I was greatly encouraged to find how, even at 28,700 ft and with no oxygen, I could work out slowly but clearly the problems of mental arithmetic that the oxygen supply demanded. A correct answer was imperative – any mistake could well mean a trip with no return. But we had no time to waste. I stood up and took a series of photographs in every direction, then thrust my camera back to its warm home inside my clothing. I heaved my now pleasantly light oxygen load on to my back and connected up my tubes. I did the same for Tenzing, and we were ready to go. I asked Tenzing to belay me and then, with a growing air of excitement, I cut a broad and safe line of steps down to the snow saddle below the South Summit. I wanted an easy route when we came back up here weak and tired. Tenzing came down the steps and joined me, and then belayed once again.

I moved along on to the steep snow slope on the left side of the ridge. With the first blow of my ice-axe my excitement increased. The snow to my astonishment – was crystalline and hard. A couple of rhythmical blows of the ice-axe produced a step that was big enough for our oversize high-altitude boots. But the best of all the steps were strong and safe. A little conscious of the great drops beneath me, I chipped a line of steps for the full length of the rope – forty feet – and then forced the shaft of my axe firmly into the snow. It made a fine belay and I looped the rope around it. I waved to Tenzing to join me, and as he moved slowly and carefully along the steps I took in the rope as I went on cutting steps. It was exhilarating work – the summit ridge of Everest, the crisp snow and the smooth easy blows of the ice-axe all combined to make me feel a greater sense of power than I had ever felt at great altitudes before. I went on cutting for rope length after rope length.

We were now approaching a point where one of the great cornices was encroaching on to our slope. We'd have to go down to the rocks to avoid it. I cut a line of steps steeply down the slope to a small ledge on top of the rocks. There wasn't much room, but it made a reasonably safe stance. I waved to Tenzing to join me. As he came down to me I realized there was something wrong with him. I had been so absorbed in the technical problems of the ridge that I hadn't thought much about Tenzing, except for a vague feeling that he seemed to move along the steps with unnecessary slowness. But now it was quite obvious that he was not only moving extremely slowly, but he was breathing quickly and with difficulty and was in considerable distress. I immediately suspected his oxygen set and helped him down on to the ledge so that I could examine it. The first thing I noticed was that from the outlet of his face-mask there were hanging some long icicles. I looked at it more closely and found that the outlet tube – about two inches in diameter – was almost completely blocked up with ice. This was preventing Tenzing from exhaling freely and must have made it extremely unpleasant for him. Fortu-

nately the outlet tube was made of rubber and by manip-
ulating this with my hand I was able to release all the ice and
let it fall out. The valves started operating and Tenzing was
given immediate relief. Just as a check I examined my own
set and found that it too, had partly frozen up in the outlet
tube, but not sufficiently to have affected me a great deal. I
removed the ice out of it without a great deal of trouble.
Automatically I looked at our pressure gauges – just over
2,900 lb (2,900 lb was just over 700 litres; 180 into 700 was
about 4) – we had nearly four hours' endurance left. That
meant we weren't going badly.

I looked at the route ahead. This next piece wasn't going
to be easy. Our rock ledge was perched right on top of the
enormous bluff running down into the Western Cwm. In
fact, almost under my feet, I could see the dirty patch on the
floor of the Cwm which I knew was Camp IV. In a sudden
urge to escape our isolation I waved and shouted and then
as suddenly stopped as I realized my foolishness. Against
the vast expanse of Everest, 8,000 ft above them we'd be
quite invisible to the best binoculars. I turned back to the
problem ahead. The rock was far too steep to attempt to
drop down and go around this pitch. The only thing to do
was to try to shuffle along the ledge and cut handholds in
the bulging ice that was trying to push me off it. Held on a
tight rope by Tenzing, I cut a few handholds and then
thrust my ice-axe as hard as I could into the solid snow and
ice. Using this to take my weight I moved quickly along the
ledge. It proved easier than I had anticipated. A few more
handholds, another quick swing across them, and I was able
to cut a line of steps up on to a safe slope and chop out a
roomy terrace from which to belay Tenzing as he climbed
up to me.

We were now fast approaching the most formidable
obstacle on the ridge – a great rock step. This step had
always been visible in aerial photographs, and in 1951 on
the Everest Reconnaissance we had seen it quite clearly
with glasses from Thyangboche. We had always thought of
it as the obstacle on the ridge which could well spell defeat.
I cut a line of steps across the last snow slope, and then
commenced traversing over a steep rock slab that led to the

foot of the great step. The holds were small and hard to see, and I brushed my snow-glasses away from my eyes. Immediately I was blinded by a bitter wind sweeping across the ridge and laden with particles of ice. I hastily replaced my glasses and blinked away the ice and tears until I could see again. But it made me realize how efficient was our clothing in protecting us from the rigours of even a fine day at 29,000 ft. Still half blinded, I climbed across the slab, and then dropped down into a tiny snow hollow at the foot of the step. And here Tenzing joined me.

I looked anxiously up at the rocks. Planted squarely across the ridge in a vertical bluff, they looked extremely difficult, and I knew that our strength and ability to climb steep rock at this altitude would be severely limited. I examined the route out to the left. By dropping fifty or a hundred feet over steep slabs, we might be able to get around the bottom of the bluff, but there was no indication that we'd be able to climb back on to the ridge again. And to lose any height now might be fatal. Search as I could, I was unable to see an easy route up to the step or, in fact, any route at all. Finally, in desperation I examined the right-hand end of the bluff. Attached to this and overhanging the precipitous East face was a large cornice. This cornice, in preparation for its inevitable crash down the mountainside, had started to lose its grip on the rock, and a long narrow vertical crack had been formed between the rock and the ice. The crack was large enough to take the human frame, and though it offered little security, it was at least a route. I quickly made up my mind – Tenzing had an excellent belay and we must be near the top – it was worth a try.

Before attempting the pitch, I produced my camera once again. I had no confidence that I would be able to climb this crack, and with a surge of competitive pride which unfortunately afflicts even mountaineers, I determined to have proof that at least we had reached a good deal higher than the South Summit. I took a few photographs and then made another rapid check of the oxygen – 2,550 lb pressure. (2,550 from 3,300 leaves 750. 750 over 3,300 is about two-ninths. Two ninths off 800 litres leaves about 600 litres. 600 divided by 180 is nearly 3½.) Three and a half hours to go.

I examined Tenzing's belay to make sure it was a good one and then slowly crawled inside the crack.

In front of me was the rock wall, vertical but with a few promising holds. Behind me was the ice-wall of the cornice, glittering and hard but cracked here and there. I took a hold on the rock in front and then jammed one of my crampons hard into the ice behind. Leaning back with my oxygen set on the ice, I slowly levered myself upwards. Searching feverishly with my spare boot, I found a tiny ledge on the rock and took some of the weight off my other leg. Leaning back on the cornice, I fought to regain my breath. Constantly at the back of my mind was the fear that the cornice might break off, and my nerves were taut with suspense. But slowly I forced my way up – wriggling and jambing and using every little hold. In one place I managed to force my ice-axe into a crack in the ice, and this gave me the necessary purchase to get over a holdless stretch. And then I found a solid foothold in a hollow in the ice, and next moment I was reaching over the top of the rock and pulling myself to safety. The rope came tight – its forty feet had been barely enough.

I lay on the little rock ledge panting furiously. Gradually it dawned on me that I was up the step, and I felt a glow of pride and determination that completely subdued my temporary feelings of weakness. For the first time on the whole expedition I really knew I was going to get to the top. "It will have to be pretty tough to stop us now" was my thought. But I couldn't entirely ignore the feeling of astonishment and wonder that I'd been able to get up such a difficulty at 29,000 ft even with oxygen.

When I was breathing more evenly I stood up and leaning over the edge, waved to Tenzing to come up. He moved into the crack and I gathered in the rope and took some of his weight. Then he, in turn, commenced to struggle and jam and force his way up until I was able to pull him to safety – gasping for breath. We rested for a moment. Above us the ridge continued on as before – enormous overhanging cornices on the right and steep snow slopes on the left running down to the rock bluffs. But the angle of the snow slopes was easing off. I went on chipping a line of steps, but thought it safe enough for us to move together in order to save time. The ridge rose up in a great series of snakelike undulations which bore away to the right, each one concealing the next. I had no idea where the top was. I'd cut a line of steps around the side of one undulation and another would come into view. We were getting desperately tired now and Tenzing was going very slowly. I'd been cutting steps for almost two hours, and my back and arms were starting to tire. I tried cramponing along the slope without cutting steps, but my feet slipped uncomfortably down the slope. I went on cutting. We seemed to have been going for a very long time and my confidence was fast evaporating. Bump followed bump with maddening regularity. A patch of shingle barred our way, and I climbed dully up it and started cutting steps around another bump. And then I realized that this was the last bump, for ahead of me the ridge dropped steeply away in a great corniced curve, and out in the distance I could see the pastel shades and fleecy clouds of the highlands of Tibet.

To my right a slender snow ridge climbed up to a snowy dome about forty feet above our heads. But all the way along the ridge the thought had haunted me that the summit might be the crest of a cornice. It was too late to take risks now. I asked Tenzing to belay me strongly, and I started cutting a cautious line of steps up the ridge. Peering from side to side and thrusting with my ice-axe, I tried to discover a possible cornice, but everything seemed solid and firm. I waved Tenzing up to me. A few more whacks of the ice-axe, a few very weary steps, and we were on the summit of Everest.

It was 11.30 a.m. My first sensation was one of relief – relief that the long grind was over; that the summit had been reached before our oxygen supplies had dropped to a critical level; and relief that in the end the mountain had been kind to us in having a pleasantly rounded cone for its summit instead of a fearsome and unapproachable cornice. But mixed with the relief was a vague sense of astonishment that I should have been the lucky one to attain the ambition of so many brave and determined climbers. It seemed

difficult at first to grasp that we'd got there. I was too tired
and too conscious of the long way down to safety really to
feel any great elation. But as the fact of our success thrust
itself more clearly into my mind, I felt a quiet glow of
satisfaction spread through my body – a satisfaction less
vociferous but more powerful than I had ever felt on a
mountain top before. I turned and looked at Tenzing. Even
beneath his oxygen mask and the icicles hanging from his
hair, I could see his infectious grin of sheer delight.

Annapurna, Mon Amour

Maurice Herzog

Born in France in 1919, Herzog led the 1950 conquest of Annapurna, 8,075 m (26,493 ft) in Nepal, the first 8,000-metre peak to be scaled. Unfortunately for the French team, the descent turned into a disaster when the monsoon broke around them.

A fierce and savage wind tore at us.

We were on top of Annapurna! 8,075 metres, 26,493 feet.

Our hearts overflowed with an unspeakable happiness.

"If only the others could know . . ."

If only everyone could know!

The summit was a corniced crest of ice, and the precipices on the far side, which plunged vertically down beneath us, were terrifying, unfathomable. There could be few other mountains in the world like this. Clouds floated half way down, concealing the gentle, fertile valley of Pokhara, 23,000 ft below. Above us there was nothing!

Our mission was accomplished. But at the same time we had accomplished something infinitely greater. How wonderful life would now become! What an inconceivable experience it is to attain one's ideal and, at the very same moment, to fulfil oneself. I was stirred to the depths of my being. Never had I felt happiness like this – so intense and yet so pure. That brown rock, the highest of them all, that ridge of ice – were these the goals of a lifetime? Or were they, rather, the limits of man's pride?

"Well, what about going down?"

Lachenal shook me. What were his own feelings? Did he simply think he had finished another climb, as in the Alps? Did he think one could just go down again like that, with nothing more to it?

"One minute, I must take some photographs."

"Hurry up!"

I fumbled feverishly in my sack, pulled out the camera, took out the little French flag which was right at the bottom, and the pennants. Useless gestures, no doubt, but something more than symbols – eloquent tokens of affection and goodwill. I tied the strips of material – stained by sweat and by the food in the sacks – to the shaft of my ice-axe, the only flag-staff at hand. Then I focused my camera on Lachenal.

"Now, will you take me?"

"Hand it over – hurry up!" said Lachenal.

He took several pictures and then handed me back the camera. I loaded a colour-film and we repeated the process to be certain of bringing back records to be cherished in the future.

"Are you mad?" asked Lachenal. "We haven't a minute to lose: we must go down at once."

And in fact a glance round showed me that the weather was no longer gloriously fine as it had been in the morning. Lachenal was becoming impatient.

"We must go down!"

He was right. His was the reaction of the mountaineer who knows his own domain. But I just could not accustom myself to the idea that we had won our victory. It seemed inconceivable that we should have trodden those summit snows.

It was impossible to build a cairn; there were no stones, and everything was frozen. Lachenal stamped his feet; he felt them freezing. I felt mine freezing too, but paid little attention. The highest mountain to be climbed by man lay under our feet! The names of our predecessors on these heights chased each other through my mind: Mummery, Mallory and Irvine, Bauer, Welzenbach, Tilman, Shipton. How many of them were dead – how many had found on these mountains what, to them, was the finest end of all.

My joy was touched with humility. It was not just one party that had climbed Annapurna today, but a whole expedition. I thought of all the others in the camps perched on the slopes at our feet, and I knew it was because of their efforts and their sacrifices that we had succeeded today. There are times when the most complex actions are suddenly summed up, distilled, and strike you with illuminating clarity: so it was with this irresistible upward surge which had landed us two here.

Pictures passed through my mind – the Chamonix valley, where I had spent the most marvellous moments of my childhood. Mont Blanc, which so tremendously impressed me! I was a child when I first saw "the Mont Blanc people" coming home, and to me there was a queer look about them; a strange light shone in their eyes.

"Come on, straight down," called Lachenal.

He had already done up his sack and started going down. I took out my pocket aneroid: 8,500 metres. I smiled. I swallowed a little condensed milk and left the tube behind – the only trace of our passage. I did up my sack, put on my gloves and my glasses, seized my ice-axe; one look round and I, too, hurried down the slope. Before disappearing into the couloir I gave one last look at the summit which would henceforth be all our joy and all our consolation.

Lachenal was already far below; he had reached the foot of the couloir. I hurried down in his tracks. I went as fast as I could, but it was dangerous going. At every step one had to take care that the snow did not break away beneath one's weight. Lachenal, going faster than I thought he was capable of, was now on the long traverse. It was my turn to cross the area of mixed rock and snow. At last I reached the foot of the rock-band. I had hurried and I was out of breath. I undid my sack. What had I been going to do? I could not say.

"My gloves!"

Before I had time to bend over, I saw them slide and roll. They went further and further straight down the slope. I remained where I was, quite stunned. I watched them rolling down slowly, with no appearance of stopping.

The movement of those gloves was engraved in my sight as something ineluctable, irremediable, against which I was powerless. The consequences might be most serious. What was I to do?

"Quickly, down to Camp V."

Rébuffat and Terray should be there. My concern dissolved like magic. I now had a fixed objective again: to reach the camp. Never for a minute did it occur to me to use as gloves the socks which I always carry in reserve for just such a mishap as this.

On I went, trying to catch up with Lachenal. It had been two o'clock when we reached the summit; we had started out at six in the morning; but I had to admit that I had lost all sense of time. I felt as if I were running, whereas in actual fact I was walking normally, perhaps rather slowly, and I had to keep stopping to get my breath. The sky was now covered with clouds, everything had become grey and dirty-looking. An icy wind sprang up, boding no good. We must push on! But where was Lachenal? I spotted him a couple of hundred yards away, looking as if he was never going to stop. And I had thought he was in indifferent form!

The clouds grew thicker and came right down over us; the wind blew stronger, but I did not suffer from the cold. Perhaps the descent had restored my circulation. Should I be able to find the tents in the mist? I watched the rib ending in the beak-like point which overlooked the camp. It was gradually swallowed up by the clouds, but I was able to make out the spearhead rib lower down. If the mist should thicken I would make straight for that rib and follow it down, and in this way I should be bound to come upon the tent.

Lachenal disappeared from time to time, and then the mist was so thick that I lost sight of him altogether. I kept going at the same speed, as fast as my breathing would allow.

The slope was now steeper; a few patches of bare ice followed the smooth stretches of snow. A good sign – I was nearing the camp. How difficult to find one's way in thick mist! I kept the course which I had set by the steepest angle of the slope. The ground was broken; with my crampons I went straight down walls of bare ice. There were some patches ahead – a few more steps. It was the camp all right, but there were *two* tents.

So Rébuffat and Terray had come up. What a mercy! I should be able to tell them that we had been successful, that we were returning from the top. How thrilled they would be!

I got there, dropping down from above. The platform had been extended, and the two tents were facing each other. I tripped over one of the guy-ropes of the first tent; there was movement inside – they had heard me. Rébuffat and Terray put their heads out.

"We've made it. We're back from Annapurna!"

Rébuffat and Terray received the great news with excitement and delight.

"But what about Biscante?" asked Terray anxiously.

"He won't be long. He was just in front of me! What a day – started out at six this morning – didn't stop . . . got up at last."

Words failed me. I had so much to say. The sight of familiar – faces dispelled the strange feeling that I had experienced since morning, and I became, once more, just a mountaineer.

Terray, who was speechless with delight, wrung my hands. Then the smile vanished from his face: "Maurice – your hands!" There was an uneasy silence. I had forgotten that I had lost my gloves: my fingers were violet and white, and hard as wood. The other two stared at them in dismay – they realized the full seriousness of the injury. But, still blissfully floating on a sea of joy remote from reality, I leant over towards Terray and said confidentially, "You're in such splendid form, and you've done so marvellously, it's absolutely tragic you didn't come up there with us!"

"What I did was for the Expedition, my dear Maurice, and anyway you've got up, and that's a victory for the whole lot of us."

I nearly burst with happiness. How could I tell him all that his answer meant to me? The rapture I had felt on the summit, which might have seemed a purely personal, egotistical emotion, had been transformed by his words into a complete and perfect joy with no shadow upon it. His answer proved that this victory was not just one man's achievement, a matter for personal pride; no – and Terray was the first to understand this – it was a victory for us all, a victory for mankind itself.

"Hi! Help! Help!"

"Biscante!" exclaimed the others.

Still half intoxicated and remote from reality, I had heard nothing. Terray felt a chill at his heart, and his thoughts flew to his partner on so many unforgettable climbs; together they had so often skirted death, and won so many splendid victories. Putting his head out, and seeing Lachenal clinging to the slope a hundred yards lower down, he dressed in frantic haste.

Out he went. But the slope was bare now; Lachenal had disappeared. Terray was horribly startled, and could only utter unintelligible cries. It was a ghastly moment for him. A violent wind sent the mist tearing by. Under the stress of emotion Terray had not realized how it falsified distances.

"Biscante! Biscante!"

He had spotted him, through a rift in the mist, lying on the slope much lower down than he had thought. Terray set his teeth, and glissaded down like a madman. How would he stop? How would he be able to brake, without crampons, on the wind-hardened snow? But Terray was a first-class skier, and with a jump turn he stopped beside Lachenal, who was concussed after his tremendous fall. In a state of collapse, with no ice-axe, balaclava, or gloves, and only one crampon, he gazed vacantly round him.

"My feet are frost-bitten. Take me down . . . take me down, so that Oudot can see to me."

"It can't be done," explained Terray regretfully. "Can't you see we're in the middle of a storm . . . It'll be dark soon."

But Lachenal was obsessed by the fear of amputation. With a gesture of despair he tore the axe out of Terray's hands and tried to force his way down, but soon saw the futility of his action, and resolved to climb up to the camp. While Terray cut steps without stopping, Lachenal, ravaged and exhausted as he was, dragged himself along on all fours.

Meanwhile I had gone into Rébuffat's tent. He was appalled at the sight of my hands and, as rather incoherently I told him what we had done, he took a piece of rope and began flicking my fingers. Then he took off my boots, with great difficulty, for my feet were swollen, and beat my feet and rubbed me. We soon heard Terray giving Lachenal the same treatment in the other tent.

For our comrades it was a tragic moment: Annapurna was conquered, and the first "eight-thousander" had been climbed. Every one of us had been ready to sacrifice everything for this. Yet, as they looked at our feet and hands, what can Terray and Rébuffat have felt?

Outside the storm howled and the snow was still falling. The mist grew thicker and darkness came. As on the previous night we had to cling to the poles to prevent the tents being carried away by the wind. The only two air-mattresses were given to Lachenal and myself while Terray and Rébuffat both sat on ropes, rucksacks and provisions to keep themselves well off the snow. They rubbed, slapped and beat us with a rope; sometimes the blows fell on the living flesh, and howls arose from both tents. Rébuffat persevered; it was essential to continue, painful as it was. Gradually life returned to my feet as well as to my hands, and circulation started again. It was the same with Lachenal.

Now Terray summoned up the energy to prepare some hot drinks. He called to Rébuffat that he would pass him a mug, so two hands stretched out towards each other between the two tents and were instantly covered with snow. The liquid was boiling though at scarcely more than 60° Centigrade (140° Fahrenheit). I swallowed it greedily and felt infinitely better.

The night was absolute hell. Frightful onslaughts of wind battered us incessantly, while the never-ceasing snow piled up on the tents.

Now and again I heard voices from next door – it was Terray massaging Lachenal with admirable perseverance, only stopping to ply him with hot drinks. In our tent

Rébuffat was quite worn out, but satisfied that warmth was returning to my limbs.

Lying half-unconscious I was scarcely aware of the passage of time. There were moments when I was able to see our situation in its true dramatic light, but the rest of the time I was plunged in an inexplicable stupor with no thought for the consequences of our victory.

As the night wore on the snow lay heavier on the tent, and once again I had the frightful feeling of being slowly and silently asphyxiated. Occasionally in an access of revolt I tried, with all the strength of which I was capable, to push off with both forearms the mass that was crushing me. These fearful exertions left me gasping for breath and I fell back into the same state as before. It was much worse than the previous night.

"Hi! Gaston! Gaston!"

I recognized Terray's voice.

"Time to be off!"

I heard the sounds without grasping their meaning. Was it light already? I was not in the least surprised that the other two had given up all thought of going to the top, and I did not at all grasp the measure of their sacrifice.

Outside the storm redoubled in violence. The tent shook and the fabric flapped alarmingly. It had usually been fine in the mornings: did this mean the monsoon was upon us? We knew it was not far off – could this be its first onslaught?

"Gaston! Are you ready?" Terray asked again.

"One minute," answered Rébuffat. He did not have an easy job: he had to put my boots on and do everything to get me ready: I let myself be handled like a baby. In the other tent Terray finished dressing Lachenal, whose feet were still swollen and would not fit into his boots. So Terray gave him his own, which were bigger. To get Lachenal's on to his own feet he had to make some slits in them. As a precaution he put a sleeping bag and some food into his sack and shouted to us to do the same. Were his words lost in the storm? Or were we too intent on leaving this hellish place to listen to his instructions?

Lachenal and Terray were already outside.

"We're going down!" they shouted.

Then Rébuffat tied me on to the rope, and we went out.
There were only two ice-axes for the four of us, so Rébuffat
and Terray took them as a matter of course. For a moment,
as we left the two tents of Camp V, I felt childishly ashamed
at abandoning all our good equipment.

Already the first rope seemed a long way down below us.
We were blinded by the squalls of snow and we could not
hear each other a yard away. We had both put on our
cagoules, for it was very cold. The snow was apt to slide and
the rope often came in useful.

Ahead of us the other two were losing no time. Lachenal
went first and, safeguarded by Terray, he forced the pace
in his anxiety to get down. There were no tracks to show
us the way, but it was engraved on all our minds – straight
down the slope for 400 yards then traverse to the left for
150 to 200 yards to get to Camp IV. The snow was
thinning and the wind less violent. Was it going to clear?
We hardly dared to hope so. A wall of seracs brought us up
short.

"It's to the left," I said, "I remember perfectly."

Somebody else thought it was to the right. We started
going down again. The wind had dropped completely, but
the snow fell in big flakes. The mist was thick, and, not to
lose each other, we walked in line: I was third and I could
barely see Lachenal, who was first. It was impossible to
recognize any of the pitches. We were all experienced
enough mountaineers to know that even on familiar ground
it is easy to make mistakes in such weather – distances are
deceptive, one cannot tell whether one is going up or down.
We kept colliding with hummocks which we had taken for
hollows. The mist, the falling snowflakes, the carpet of
snow, all merged into the same whitish tone and confused
our vision. The towering outlines of the seracs took on
fantastic shapes and seemed to move slowly round us.

Our situation was not desperate, we were certainly not
lost. We would have to go lower down: the traverse must
begin further on – I remembered the serac which served as a
milestone. The snow stuck to our cagoules, and turned us
into white phantoms noiselessly flitting against a background equally white. We began to sink in dreadfully,

and there is nothing worse for bodies already on the verge of exhaustion.

Were we too high or too low? No one could tell. Perhaps we had better try slanting over to the left! The snow was in a bad state, but we did not seem to realize the danger. We were forced to admit that we were not on the right route, so we retraced our steps and climbed up above the serac which overhung us – no doubt, we reflected, we should be on the right level now. With Rébuffat leading, we went back over the way which had cost us such an effort. I followed him jerkily, saying nothing, and determined to go on to the end. If Rébuffat had fallen I could never have held him.

We went doggedly on from one serac to another. Each time we thought we had recognized the right route, and each time there was a fresh disappointment. If only the mist would lift, if only the snow would stop for a second! On the slope it seemed to be growing deeper every minute. Only Terray and Rébuffat were capable of breaking the trail and they relieved each other at regular intervals, without a word and without a second's hesitation.

I admired this determination of Rébuffat's for which he is so justly famed. He did not intend to die! With the strength of desperation and at the price of superhuman effort he forged ahead. The slowness of his progress would have dismayed even the most obstinate climber, but he would not give up, and in the end the mountain yielded in face of his perseverence.

Terray, when his turn came, charged madly ahead. He was like a force of nature: at all costs he would break down these prison walls that penned us in. His physical strength was exceptional, his will-power no less remarkable. Lachenal gave him considerable trouble. Perhaps he was not quite in his right mind. He said it was no use going on; we must dig a hole in the snow and wait for fine weather. He swore at Terray and called him a madman. Nobody but Terray would have been capable of dealing with him – he just tugged sharply on the rope and Lachenal was forced to follow.

We were well and truly lost.

The weather did not seem likely to improve. A minute ago we had still had ideas about which way to go – now we had none. This way or that . . . We went on at random to allow for the chance of a miracle which appeared increasingly unlikely. The instinct of self-preservation in the two fit members of the party alternated with a hopelessness which made them completely irresponsible. Each in turn did the silliest things: Terray traversed the steep and avalanchy slopes with one crampon badly adjusted. He and Rébuffat performed incredible feats of balance without the least slip.

Camp IV was certainly on the left, on the edge of the Sickle. On that point we were all agreed. But it was very hard to find. The wall of ice that gave it such magnificent protection was now our enemy, for it hid the tents from us. In mist like this we should have to be right on top of them before we spotted them.

Perhaps if we called, someone would hear us? Lachenal gave the signal, but snow absorbs sound, and his shout seemed to carry only a few yards. All four of us called out together: "One . . . two . . . three . . . Help!"

We got the impression that our united shout carried a long way, so we began again: "One . . . two . . . three . . . Help!" Not a sound in reply!

Now and again Terray took off his boots and rubbed his feet; the sight of our frost-bitten limbs had made him aware of the danger and he had the strength of mind to do something about it. Like Lachenal, he was haunted by the idea of amputation. For me, it was too late: my feet and hands, already affected from yesterday, were beginning to freeze up again.

We had eaten nothing since the day before, and we had been on the go the whole time, but man's resources of energy in face of death are inexhaustible. When the end seems imminent, there still remain reserves, though it needs tremendous will-power to call them up.

Time passed, but we had no idea of it. Night was approaching, and we were terrified, though none of us uttered a complaint. Rébuffat and I found a way we thought we remembered, but were brought to a halt by the extreme steepness of the slope – the mist turned it into a vertical wall. We were to find, next day, that at that moment we had been almost on top of the camp, and that the wall was the very one that sheltered the tents which would have been our salvation.

"We must find a crevasse."

"We can't stay here all night!"

"A hole – it's the only thing."

"We'll all die in it."

Night had suddenly fallen and it was essential to come to a decision without wasting another minute; if we remained on the slope, we should be dead before morning. We should have to bivouac. What the conditions would be like, we could guess, for we all knew what it meant to bivouac above 23,000 ft.

With his axe Terray began to dig a hole. Lachenal went over to a snow-filled crevasse a few yards further on, then suddenly let out a yell and disappeared before our eyes. We stood helpless: would we, or rather would Terray and Rébuffat, have enough strength for all the manoeuvres with the rope that would be needed to get him out? The crevasse was completely blocked up save for the one little hole where Lachenal had fallen through.

"Hi! Lachenal!" called Terray.

A voice, muffled by many thicknesses of ice and snow, came up to us. It was impossible to make out what it was saying.

"Hi! Lachenal!"

Terray jerked the rope violently; this time we could hear.

"I'm here!"

"Anything broken?"

"No! It'll do for the night! Come along."

This shelter was heaven-sent. None of us would have had the strength to dig a hole big enough to protect the lot of us from the wind. Without hesitation Terray let himself drop into the crevasse, and a loud "Come on!" told us he had arrived safely. In my turn I let myself go: it was a proper toboggan-slide. I shot down a sort of twisting tunnel, very steep, and about thirty feet long. I came out at great speed into the opening beyond and was literally hurled to the bottom of the crevasse. We let Rébuffat know he could come by giving a tug on the rope.

The intense cold of this minute grotto shrivelled us up, the enclosing walls of ice were damp and the floor a carpet of fresh snow; by huddling together there was just room for the four of us. Icicles hung from the ceiling and we broke some of them off to make more head room and kept little bits to suck – it was a long time since we had had anything to drink.

That was our shelter for the night. At least we should be protected from the wind, and the temperature would remain fairly even, though the damp was extremely unpleasant. We settled ourselves in the dark as best we could. As always in a bivouac, we took off our boots; without this precaution the constriction would cause immediate frostbite. Terray unrolled the sleeping-bag which he had had the foresight to bring, and settled himself in relative comfort. We put on everything warm that we had, and to avoid contact with the snow I sat on the cine-camera. We huddled close up to each other, in our search for a hypothetical position in which the warmth of all bodies could be combined without loss, but we could not keep still for a second.

We did not open our mouths – signs were less of an effort than words. Every man withdrew into himself and took refuge in his own inner world. Terray massaged Lachenal's feet; Rébuffat felt his feet freezing, too, but he had sufficient strength to rub them himself. I remained motionless, unseeing. My feet and hands went on freezing, but what could be done? I attempted to forget suffering, to forget the passing of time, trying not to feel the devouring and numbing cold which insidiously gained upon us.

Terray shared his sleeping-bag with Lachenal, putting his feet and hands inside the precious eiderdown. At the same time he went on rubbing.

"Anyhow the frost-bite won't spread further," he was thinking.

None of us could make a movement without upsetting the others, and the positions we had taken up with such care were continually being altered so that we had to start all over again. This kept us busy. Rébuffat persevered with his rubbing and complained of his feet; like Terray he was thinking: "We mustn't look beyond tomorrow – afterwards we'll see." But he was not blind to the fact that "afterwards" was one big question mark.

Terray generously tried to give me part of his sleeping-bag. He had understood the seriousness of my condition, and knew why it was that I said nothing and remained quite passive; he realized that I had abandoned all hope for myself. He massaged me for nearly two hours: his feet, too, might have frozen, but he did not appear to give the matter a thought. I found new courage simply in contemplating his unselfishness; he was doing so much to help me that it would have been ungrateful of me not to go on struggling to live. Though my heart was like a lump of ice itself, I was astonished to feel no pain. Everything material about me seemed to have dropped away. I seemed to be quite clear in my thoughts and yet I floated in a kind of peaceful happiness. There was still a breath of life in me, but it dwindled steadily as the hours went by. Terray's massage no longer had any effect upon me. All was over, I thought. Was not this cavern the most beautiful grave I could hope for? Death caused me no grief, no regret – I smiled at the thought.

After hours of torpor, a voice mumbled, "Daylight!" This made some impression on the others. I only felt surprised – I had not thought that daylight would penetrate so far down.

"Too early to start," said Rébuffat.

A ghastly light spread through our grotto and we could just vaguely make out the shapes of each other's heads. A queer noise from a long way off came down to us – a sort of prolonged hiss. The noise increased. Suddenly I was buried, blinded, smothered beneath an avalanche of new snow. The icy snow spread over the cavern, finding its way through every gap in our clothing. I ducked my head between my knees and covered myself with both arms. The snow flowed on and on. There was a silence. We were not completely buried, but there was snow everywhere. We got up, taking care not to bang our heads against the ceiling of ice, and tried to shake ourselves. We were all in our stockinged feet in the snow. The first thing to do was to find our boots.

Rébuffat and Terray began to search, and realized at once that they were blind. Yesterday they had taken off their glasses to lead us down, and now they were paying for it. Lachenal was the first to lay hands upon a pair of boots. He tried to put them on, but they were Rébuffat's. Rébuffat attempted to climb up the shoot down which we had come yesterday, and which the avalanche had followed in its turn.

"Hi, Gaston! What's the weather like?" called up Terray.

"Can't see a thing. It's blowing hard."

We were still groping for our things. Terray found his boots and put them on awkwardly, unable to see what he was doing. Lachenal helped him, but he was all on edge and fearfully impatient, in striking contrast to my immobility. Terray then went up the icy channel, puffing and blowing, and at last reached the outer world. He was met by terrible gusts of wind that cut right through him and lashed his face.

"Bad weather," he said to himself, "this time it's the end. We're lost . . . we'll never come through."

At the bottom of the crevasse there were still two of us looking for our boots. Lachenal poked fiercely with an ice-axe. I was calmer and tried to proceed more rationally. We extracted crampons and an axe in turn from the snow, but still no boots.

Well – so this cavern was to be our last resting-place! There was very little room – we were bent double and got in each other's way. Lachenal decided to go out without his boots. He called out frantically, hauled himself up on the rope, trying to get a hold or to wriggle his way up, digging his toes into the snow walls. Terray from outside pulled as hard as he could: I watched him go; he gathered speed and disappeared.

When he emerged from the opening he saw the sky was clear and blue, and he began to run like a madman, shrieking, "It's fine, it's fine!"

I set to work again to search the cave. The boots *had* to be found, or Lachenal and I were done for. On all fours, with nothing on my hands or feet, I raked the snow, stirring it round this way and that, hoping every second to come upon something hard. I was no longer capable of thinking – I reacted like an animal fighting for its life.

I found one boot! The other was tied to it – a pair! Having ransacked the whole cave I at last found the other pair. But in spite of all my efforts I could not find the camera, and gave up in despair. There was no question of putting my boots on – my hands were like lumps of wood and I could hold nothing in my fingers; my feet were very swollen – I should never be able to get boots on them. I twisted the rope round the boots as well as I could and called up the shoot:

"Lionel . . . boots!"

There was no answer, but he must have heard, for with a jerk the precious boots shot up. Soon after the rope came down again. My turn. I wound the rope round me; I could not pull it tight so I made a whole series of little knots. Their combined strength, I hoped, would be enough to hold me. I had no strength to shout again; I gave a great tug on the rope, and Terray understood.

At the first step I had to kick a niche in the hard snow for my toes. Further on I expected to be able to get up more easily by wedging myself across the runnel. I wriggled up a few yards like this and then I tried to dig my hands and my feet into the wall. My hands were stiff and hard right up to the wrists and my feet had no feeling up to the ankles; the joints were inflexible and this hampered me greatly.

Somehow or other I succeeded in working my way up, while Terray pulled so hard he nearly choked me. I began to see more distinctly and so knew that I must be nearing the opening. Often I fell back, but I clung on and wedged myself in again as best I could. My heart was bursting, and I was forced to rest. A fresh wave of energy enabled me to crawl to the top. I pulled myself out by clutching Terray's legs; *he* was just about all in and I was in the last stages of exhaustion. Terray was close to me and I whispered:

"Lionel . . . I'm dying!"

He supported me and helped me away from the crevasse. Lachenal and Rébuffat were sitting in the snow a few yards away. The instant Lionel let go of me I sank down and dragged myself along on all fours.

The weather was perfect. Quantities of snow had fallen the day before and the mountains were resplendent. Never had I seen them look so beautiful – our last day would be magnificent.

Rébuffat and Terray were completely blind; as he came along with me Terray knocked into things and I had to direct him. Rébuffat, too, could not move a step without guidance. It was terrifying to be blind when there was danger all round. Lachenal's frozen feet affected his nervous system. His behaviour was disquieting – he was possessed by the most fantastic ideas:

"I tell you we must go down . . . down there . . ."

"You've nothing on your feet!"

"Don't worry about that."

"You're off your head. The way is not there . . . it's to the left!"

He was already standing up; he wanted to go straight down to the bottom of the glacier. Terray held him back, made him sit down, and though he couldn't see, helped put his boots on.

Behind them I was living in my own private dream. I knew the end was near, but it was the end that all mountaineers wish for – an end in keeping with their ruling passion. I was consciously grateful to the mountains for being so beautiful for me that day, and as awed by their silence as if I had been in church. I was in no pain, and had no worry. My utter calmness was alarming. Terray came staggering towards me, and I told him: "It's all over for me. Go on . . . you have a chance . . . you must take it . . . over to the left . . . that's the way."

I felt better after telling him that. But Terray would have none of it: "We'll help you. If we get away, so will you."

At this moment Lachenal shouted: "Help! Help!"

Obviously he didn't know what he was doing . . . Or did he? He was the only one of the four of us who could see Camp II down below. Perhaps his calls would be heard. They were shouts of despair, reminding me tragically of some climbers lost in the Mont Blanc massif whom I had endeavoured to save. Now it was our turn. The impression was vivid: we were lost.

I joined in with the others: "One . . . two . . . three . . . *Help*! One . . . two . . . three . . . *Help*!" We tried to shout all together, but without much success; our voices could not have carried more than ten feet. The noise I made was more of a whisper than a shout. Terray insisted that I should put my boots on, but my hands were dead. Neither Rébuffat nor Terray, who were unable to see, could help much, so I said to Lachenal: "Come and help me put my boots on."

"Don't be silly, we must go down!"

And off he went once again in the wrong direction, straight down. I was not in the least angry with him: he had been sorely tried by the altitude and by everything he had gone through.

Terray resolutely got out his knife, and with fumbling hands slit the uppers of my boots back and front. Split in two like this I could get them on, but it was not easy and I had to make several attempts. I lost heart – what was the use of it all anyway since I was going to stay where I was? But Terray pulled violently and finally he succeeded. He laced up my now gigantic boots, missing out half the hooks. I was ready now. But how was I going to walk with my stiff joints?

"To the left, Lionel!"

"You're crazy, Maurice," said Lachenal, "it's to the right, straight down."

Terray did not know what to think of these conflicting views. He had not given up, like me: he was going to fight; but what, at the moment, could he do? The three of them discussed which way to go.

I remained sitting in the snow. Gradually my mind lost grip – why should I struggle? I would just let myself drift. I saw pictures of shady slopes, peaceful paths, there was a scent of resin. It was pleasant – I was going to die in my own mountains. My body had no feeling – everything was frozen.

"Aah . . . aah!"

Was it a groan or a call? I gathered my strength for one cry: "They're coming!" The others heard me and shouted for joy. What a miraculous apparition! "Schatz . . . It's Schatz!"

Barely 200 yards away Marcel Schatz, waist-deep in snow, was coming slowly towards us like a boat over the surface of the slope. I found this vision of a strong and invincible deliverer inexpressibly moving. I expected everything of him. The shock was violent, and quite shattered me. Death clutched at me and I gave myself up.

When I came to again the wish to live returned and I experienced a violent revulsion of feeling. All was not lost! As Schatz came nearer my eyes never left him for a second – twenty yards – ten yards – he came straight towards me. Why? Without a word he leant over me, held me close, hugged me, and his warm breath revived me.

I could not make the slightest movement – I was like marble. My heart was overwhelmed by such tremendous feelings and yet my eyes remained dry.

"Well done, Maurice. It's marvellous!"

I was clear-headed and delirious by turns, and had the queer feeling that my eyes were glazed. Schatz looked after me like a mother, and while the others were shouting with joy, he put his rope round me. The sky was blue – the deep blue of extreme altitude, so dark that one can almost see the stars – and we were bathed in the warm rays of the sun. Schatz spoke gently:

"We'll be moving now, Maurice, old man."

I could not help obeying him with a good grace, and with his assistance I succeeded in getting up and standing in balance. He moved on gradually, pulling me after him. I seemed to make contact with the snow by means of two strange stilt-like objects – my legs. I could no longer see the others; I did not dare to turn round for fear of losing my balance, and I was dazzled by the reflection of the sun's rays.

Having walked about a couple of hundred yards, and skirted round an ice wall, without any sort of warning, we came upon a tent. We had bivouacked 200 yards from the camp. Couzy got up as I appeared, and without speaking held me close and embraced me. Terray threw himself down in the tent and took off his boots. His feet, too, were frost-bitten; he massaged them and beat them unmercifully.

The will to live stirred again in me. I tried to take in the situation: there was not much that we could do – but we should have to do whatever was possible. Our only hope lay in Oudot; only he could save our feet and hands by the proper treatment. I heartily agreed to Schatz's suggestion that we should go down immediately to the lower Camp IV which the Sherpas had re-established. Terray wanted to remain in the tent, and as he flailed his feet with the energy of despair he cried out:

"Come and fetch me tomorrow if necessary. I want to be whole, or dead!"

Rébuffat's feet were affected, too, but he preferred to go down to Oudot immediately. He started the descent with Lachenal and Couzy, while Schatz continued to look after me, for which I was deeply grateful. He took the rope and propelled me gently along the track. The slope suddenly became very steep, and the thin layer of snow adhering to the surface of the ice gave no foothold; I slipped several times, but Schatz, holding me on a tight rope, was able to check me.

Below there was a broad track: no doubt the others had let themselves slide straight down towards the lower Camp IV, but they had started an avalanche which had swept the slope clear of snow, and this hardly made things easier for me. As soon as we drew in sight of the camp the Sherpas came up to meet us. In their eyes I read such kindliness and such pity that I began to realize my dreadful plight. They were busy clearing the tents which the avalanche had covered with snow. Lachenal was in a corner massaging his feet; from time to time Pansy comforted him, saying that the Doctor Sahib would cure him.

I hurried everyone up; we must get down – that was our first objective. As for the equipment, well it could not be helped; we simply must be off the mountain before the next onslaught of the monsoon. For those of us with frost-bitten limbs it was a matter of hours. I chose Aila and Sarki to escort Rébuffat, Lachenal and myself. I tried to make the two Sherpas understand that they must watch me very closely and hold me on a short rope. For some unknown reason, neither Lachenal nor Rébuffat wished to rope.

While we started down, Schatz, with Angtharkay and Pansy, went up to fetch Terray who had remained on the glacier above. Schatz was master of the situation – none of the others were capable of taking the slightest initiative. After a hard struggle, he found Terray:

"You can get ready in a minute," he said.

"I'm beginning to feel my feet again" replied Terray, now more amenable to reason.

"I'm going to have a look in the crevasse. Maurice couldn't find the camera and it's got all the shots he took high up."

Terray made no reply; he had not really understood, and it was only several days later that we fully realized Schatz's heroism. He spent a long time searching the snow at the bottom of the cavern, while Terray began to get anxious; at last he returned triumphantly carrying the camera which contained the views taken from the summit. He also found my ice-axe and various other things, but no cine-camera, so our last film shots would stop at 23,000 feet.

Then the descent began. Angtharkay was magnificent, going first and cutting comfortable steps for Terray. Schatz, coming down last, carefully safeguarded the whole party.

Our first group was advancing slowly. The snow was soft and we sank in up to our knees. Lachenal grew worse: he frequently stopped and moaned about his feet. Rébuffat was a few yards behind me.

I was concerned at the abnormal heat, and feared that bad weather would put an end here and now to the epic of Annapurna. It is said that mountaineers have a sixth sense that warns them of danger – suddenly I became aware of danger through every pore of my body. There was a feeling in the atmosphere that could not be ignored. Yesterday it had snowed heavily, and the heat was now working on these great masses of snow which were on the point of sliding off. Nothing in Europe can give any idea of the force of these avalanches. They roll down over a distance of miles and are preceded by a blast that destroys everything in its path.

The glare was so terrific that without glasses it would have been impossible to keep one's eyes open. By good luck we were fairly well spaced out, so that the risk was diminished. The Sherpas no longer remembered the different pitches, and often with great difficulty, I had to take the lead and be let down on the end of the rope to find the right way. I had no crampons and I could not grasp an axe. We lost height far too slowly for my liking, and it worried me to see my Sherpas going so slowly and carefully and at the same time so insecurely. In actual fact they went very well, but I was so impatient I could no longer judge their performance fairly.

Lachenal was a long way behind us and every time I turned round he was sitting down in the track. He, too, was affected by snow-blindness, though not as badly as Terray and Rébuffat, and found difficulty in seeing his way. Rébuffat went ahead by guess-work, with agony in his face, but he kept on. We crossed the couloir without incident, and I congratulated myself that we had passed the danger zone.

The sun was at its height, the weather brilliant and the colours magnificent. Never had the mountains appeared to me so majestic as in this moment of extreme danger.

All at once a crack appeared in the snow under the feet of the Sherpas, and grew longer and wider. A mad notion flashed into my head – to climb up the slope at speed and reach solid ground. Then I was lifted up by a superhuman force, and as the Sherpas disappeared before my eyes, I went head over heels. I could not see what was happening. My head hit the ice. In spite of my efforts I could no longer breathe, and a violent blow on my left thigh caused me acute pain. I turned round and round like a puppet. In a flash I saw the blinding light of the sun through the snow which was pouring past my eyes. The rope joining me to Sarki and Aila curled round my neck – the Sherpas shooting down the slope beneath would shortly strangle me, and the pain was unbearable. Again and again I crashed into solid ice as I went hurtling from one serac to another, and the snow crushed me down. The rope tightened round my neck and brought me to a stop. Before I had recovered my wits I began to pass water, violently and uncontrollably.

I opened my eyes, to find myself hanging head downwards, with the rope round my neck and my left leg, in a sort of hatchway of blue ice. I put out my elbows towards the walls in an attempt to stop the unbearable pendulum motion which sent me from one side to the other, and caught a glimpse of the final slopes of the couloir beneath me. My breathing steadied, and I blessed the rope which had stood the strain of the shock.

I simply *had* to try to get myself out. My feet and hands were numb, but I was able to make use of some little nicks in the wall. There was room for at least the edges of my boots. By frenzied, jerky movements I succeeded in freeing my left leg from the rope, and then managed to right myself and to climb up a yard or two. After every move I stopped, convinced that I had come to the end of my physical strength, and that in a second I should have to let go.

One more desperate effort, and I gained a few inches – I pulled on the rope and felt something give at the other end – no doubt the bodies of the Sherpas. I called, but hardly a whisper issued from my lips. There was a death-like silence. Where was Gaston?

Conscious of a shadow, as from a passing cloud, I looked up instinctively; and lo and behold! two scared black faces were framed against the circle of blue sky. Aila and Sarki! They were safe and sound, and at once set to work to rescue me. I was incapable of giving them the slightest advice. Aila disappeared, leaving Sarki alone at the edge of the hole; they began to pull on the rope, slowly, so as not to hurt me, and I was hauled up with a power and steadiness that gave me fresh courage. At last I was out. I collapsed on the snow.

The rope had caught over a ridge of ice and we had been suspended on either side; by good luck the weight of the two Sherpas and my own had balanced. If we had not been checked like this we should have hurtled down another 1,500 ft. There was chaos all around us. Where was Ré-buffat? I was mortally anxious, for he was unroped. Looking up I caught sight of him less than a hundred yards away:

"Anything broken?" he called out to me.

I was greatly relieved, but I had no strength to reply. Lying flat, and semi-conscious, I gazed at the wreckage about me with unseeing eyes. We had been carried down for about 500 ft. It was not a healthy place to linger in – suppose another avalanche should fall! I instructed the Sherpas:

"Now – Doctor Sahib. Quick, very quick!"

By gestures I tried to make them understand that they must hold me very firmly. In doing this I found that my left arm was practically useless. I could not move it at all; the elbow had seized up – was it broken? We should see later. Now, we must push on to Oudot.

Rébuffat started down to join us, moving slowly; he had to place his feet by feel alone, and seeing him walk like this made my heart ache; he, too, had fallen, and he must have struck something with his jaw, for blood was oozing from the corners of his mouth. Like me, he had lost his glasses and we were forced to shut our eyes. Aila had an old spare pair which did very well for me, and without a second's hesitation Sarki gave his own to Rébuffat.

We had to get down at once. The Sherpas helped me up, and I advanced as best I could, reeling about in the most alarming fashion, but they realized now that they must hold me from behind. I skirted round the avalanche to our old track which started again a little further on.

We now came to the first wall. How on earth should we get down? Again, I asked the Sherpas to hold me firmly:

"*Hold me well because . . .*"

And I showed them my hands.

"Yes, sir," they replied together like good pupils. I came to the piton; the fixed rope attached to it hung down the wall and I had to hold on to it – there was no other way. It was terrible; my wooden feet kept slipping on the ice wall, and I could not grasp the thin line in my hands. Without letting go I endeavoured to wind it round them, but they were swollen and the skin broke in several places. Great strips of it came away and stuck to the rope and the flesh was laid bare. Yet I had to go on down; I could not give up half way.

"Aila! *Pay attention*! . . . *Pay attention*!"

To save my hands I now let the rope slide over my good forearm and lowered myself like this in jerks. On reaching the bottom I fell about three feet, and the rope wrenched my forearm and wrists. The jolt was severe and affected my feet. I heard a queer crack and supposed I must have broken something – no doubt it was the frost-bite that prevented me from feeling any pain.

Rébuffat and the Sherpas came down and we went on, but it all seemed to take an unconscionably long time, and the plateau of Camp II seemed a long way off. I was just about at the limit of my strength. Every minute I felt like giving up; and why, anyway, should I go on when for me everything was over? My conscience was quite easy: everyone was safe, and the others would all get down. Far away below I could see the tents. Just one more hour – I gave myself one more hour and then, wherever I was, I would lie down in the snow. I would let myself go, peacefully. I would be through with it all, and could sleep content.

Setting this limit somehow cheered me on. I kept slipping, and on the steep slope the Sherpas could hardly hold me – it was miraculous that they did. The track stopped above a drop – the second and bigger of the walls we had equipped with a fixed rope. I tried to make up my mind, but I could not begin to see how I was going to get down. I pulled off the glove I had on one hand, and the red silk scarf that hid the other, which was covered in blood. This time everything was at stake – and my fingers could just look after themselves. I placed Sarki and Aila on the stance from which I had been accustomed to belay them, and where the two of them would be able to take the strain of my rope by standing firmly braced against each other. I tried to take hold of the fixed rope; both my hands were bleeding, but I had no pity to spare for myself and I took the rope between my thumb and forefinger, and started off. At the first move I was faced at once with a painful decision: if I let go, we should all fall to the bottom: if I held on, what would remain of my hands? I decided to hold on.

Every inch was a torture I was resolved to ignore. The sight of my hands made me feel sick; the flesh was laid bare and red, and the rope was covered with blood. I tried not to tear the strips right off: other accidents had taught me that one must preserve these bits to hasten the healing process later on. I tried to save my hands by braking with my stomach, my shoulders, and every other possible point of contact. When would this agony come to an end?

I came down to the nose of ice which I myself had cut away with my axe on the ascent. I felt about with my legs – it was all hard. There was no snow beneath. I was not yet down. In panic I called up to the Sherpas:

"Quick . . . Aila . . . Sarki . . .!"

They let my rope out more quickly and the friction on the fixed rope increased.

My hands were in a ghastly state. It felt as though all the flesh was being torn off. At last I was aware of something beneath my feet – the ledge. I had made it! I had to go along it now, always held by the rope; only three yards, but they were the trickiest of all. It was over. I collapsed, up to the waist in snow, and no longer conscious of time.

When I half-opened my eyes Rébuffat and the Sherpas were beside me, and I could distinctly see black dots moving about near the tents of Camp II. Sarki spoke to me, and pointed out two Sherpas coming up to meet us. They were still a long way off, but all the same it cheered me up.

I had to rouse myself; things were getting worse and worse. The frost-bite seemed to be gaining ground – up to my calves and my elbows. Sarki put my glasses on for me again, although the weather had turned grey. He put one glove on as best he could; but my left hand was in such a frightful state that it made him sick to look at it, and he tried to hide it in my red scarf.

The fantastic descent continued and I was sure that every step would be my last. Through the swirling mist I sometimes caught glimpses of the two Sherpas coming up. They had already reached the base of the avalanche cone, and when, from the little platform I had just reached, I saw them stop there, it sapped all my courage.

Snow began to fall, and we now had to make a long traverse over very unsafe ground where it was difficult to safeguard anyone: then, fifty yards further, we came to the avalanche cone. I recognized Phutharkay and Angdawa mounting rapidly towards us. Evidently they expected bad news, and Angdawa must have been thinking of his two brothers, Aila and Pansy. The former was with us all right – he could see him in the flesh – but what about Pansy? Even at this distance they started up a conversation, and by the time we reached them they knew everything. I heaved a deep sigh of relief. I felt now as if I had laid down a burden so heavy that I had nearly given way beneath it. Phutharkay was beside me, smiling affectionately. How can anyone call such people "primitive", or say that the rigours of their existence take away all sense of pity? The Sherpas rushed towards me, put down their sacks, uncorked their flasks. Ah, just to drink a few mouthfuls! Nothing more. It had all been such a long time . . .

Phutharkay lowered his eyes to my hands and lifted them again, almost with embarrassment. With infinite sorrow, he whispered: "Poor Bara Sahib – Ah . . ."

These reinforcements gave me a fresh access of courage, and Camp II was near. Phutharkay supported me, and Angdawa safeguarded us both. Phutharkay was smaller than I, and I hung on round his neck and leant on his shoulders, gripping him close. This contact comforted me and his warmth gave me strength. I staggered down with little jerky steps, leaning more and more on Phutharkay. Would I ever have the strength to make it even with his help? Summoning what seemed my very last ounce of energy, I begged Phutharkay to give me yet more help. He took my glasses off and I could see better then. Just a few more steps – the very last . . .

At Camp II Marcel Ichac had been following our movements for the past two days, noting down the sequence of events, minute by minute. Here are some extracts from his log:

Saturday June 3rd[1] (I) – Camp II:
Oudot and Noyelle left at 9 o'clock;[2] at 10.30 Noyelle arrived back.

1 The day Lachenal and I left Camp V and were going up towards the summit.
2 Oudot and Noyelle were intending to go up to Camp III to pitch tents to replace those taken on by Gaston and Lionel to Camp IV. For Oudot this ascent was to be a vitally important experiment in the use of oxygen.

Something to do with the oxygen? Possibly the mask didn't allow a sufficient flow? Oudot and the three Sherpas are going very slowly up the funnel.

Meanwhile I am playing hide and seek with the clouds looking through the telescope of the theodolite, and also watching the parties above the seracs of the Sickle through field-glasses. There are four of them; Lionel and Rébuffat, and behind them Couzy and Schatz. No sign of Maurice. He must be on the final slopes which are less steep, and so invisible from here. The wind is blowing the powder snow violently. But he can't be far from the summit now, perhaps even . . .

Sunday, June 4th

A dull day. Snow fell during the night – sleet, then fine snow with a strong north wind. Annapurna is hidden in the mist. Tired and anxious. What's happening to the others? By midday eight inches of powder snow. Continual avalanches, visibility nil.

Heard voices about 4 o'clock and in the mist, which continues for about a hundred yards below the camp, four forms appeared – Oudot and his three Sherpas. Obviously sinking in up to their waists. Nothing to do but to get boiling water ready for them.

They arrived at 7 o'clock: that morning Oudot had remained in his tent. Towards 1 o'clock the bad weather got worse and Ajeeba had come to him and said: "It's the monsoon! If we stay here we're done for."

Monday, June 5th

Will today end better than it has begun? What alarms there have been – for us, anyway! At one time I thought Oudot and myself were the sole survivors of the party of eight who left Le Bourget on March 30th!

At 6 o'clock thought I heard someone calling and went outside: the sun was rising through threatening clouds. Nothing to be seen. Got back into my sleeping-bag; immediately heard two distinct shouts and through the field-glasses saw two men on a patch of ice at the height of Camp IV, but well over to the left. They kept on shouting and signalling with their arms. Who could they be – Oudot thought Schatz and Couzy. Their immobility – particularly one of them – was most alarming. Frost-bitten feet no doubt. What did they want? Normally it takes six hours to get up so far in fine weather. But in powder snow and with the monsoon striking repeatedly . . . They're still shouting . . . things are getting urgent. Where are the other eight? Higher up near the summit? Their position must be pretty precarious at Camp IV, but what can they be waiting for to descend to Camp III?

8 o'clock: Oudot is preparing a rescue party. He has no ice-pitons, etc. Noyelle is going down to Camp I with Ajeeba to bring up reinforcements (equipment and Dawathondup). Up here the Sherpas are uneasy. Three of them belong to the same family: Pansy, Aila and Angdawa.

8.30: Shouting continues. On the off-chance I'm tracing out the letters "VU" in the snow. A few minutes later a man moves quickly towards the seracs which must shelter Camp IV. He's stopped 300 yards away from it – on the same level – is making signs and has now gone back again. The others are getting up, apparently without difficulty, and are tra-versing across to Camp IV. Not two of them but four.
So there are four, plus the one who went to meet them, plus his companion or companions. The position of Camp IV near the funnel of the Sickle is more sheltered, and from there one can get down quickly to Camp III or Camp II. The avalanches have now stopped.

9.30: Saw Noyelle arrive at Camp I.

10 o'clock: At last – three men have appeared in the funnel of the Sickle coming down towards Camp III (one Sahib, two Sherpas?) Miraculously the weather is holding, with a west wind. Annapurna is completely clear – if only it lasts! *11 o'clock*: Two men, unroped and therefore Sahibs, appear and come quickly down the former party's track. At the pace they're going, they should be here by evening. At last we'll know everything!

11.15: A man has appeared exactly at the spot where we saw one this morning, going *towards* Camp V. He has stopped and is evidently looking up. His appearance is comforting in one way, for he is certainly not alone at Camp IV. So that he and his probable companion make two, plus those coming down – three and two – seven in all. Seven out of ten. It looks, then, as if one party must still be somewhere higher up.

12.20: I'm watching the group of four crossing a very steep slope above Camp III. Behind them is one man alone, lagging a bit. Now, very high up, another man has just left Camp IV and is quickly descending: perhaps one of those I saw a short time ago? Suddenly a cloud of snow – like a volcano – appears to spurt out beneath the feet of the four near Camp III. They are knocked down and go rolling over and over. Then the avalanche passes on, leaving three figures stretched out on the snow; the lowest, who has been swept down 150 ft[3] is now climbing up the slope again; now two more – ah, thank God! – they have separated and revealed a fourth. So they are all safe.
Our Sherpas have realized what's happened. Angdawa and Phutharkay have gone off to meet them with ice-axes and glasses which they have lost. The others are continuing to descend. At 3 o'clock they meet the two Sherpas at the top of the avalanche cone. At last we shall know everything . . .

We were now quite near the tents of Camp II and Ichac, Noyelle and Oudot rushed up to meet us. I was in a fever to tell them the good news.

"We're back from Annapurna," I shouted. "We got to the top yesterday, Lachenal and I." Then, after a pause: "My feet and hands are frost-bitten."

They all helped me; Ichac held something out to me, and Noyelle supported me, while Oudot was examining my injuries.

My responsibility was now at an end. We had succeeded, and I knew that the others would all be with us in a few minutes.

3 In fact it was 500 ft.

We were saved! We had conquered Annapurna, and we had retreated in order. It was now for the others to take the initiative, above all Oudot, in whom lay our only hope. I would put myself entirely in their hands; I would trust myself to their devotion. Henceforth only one thing would count – the victory that we had brought back, that would remain for ever with us as an ecstatic happiness and a miraculous consolation. The others must organize our retreat and bring us back as best they could to the soil of France.

My friends all rallied round – they took off my gloves and my cagoule and settled me into a tent already prepared to receive us. I found this simplification intensely comforting: I appreciated my new existence which, though it would be short-lived, was for the moment so easy and pleasant. In spite of the threatening weather the others were not long in arriving: Rébuffat was the first – his toes were frost-bitten, which made it difficult for him to walk and he looked ghastly, with a trickle of blood from his lips, and signs of suffering writ large on his face. They undressed him, and put him in a tent to await treatment.

Lachenal was still a long way off. Blind, exhausted, with his frost-bitten feet, how could he manage to follow such a rough and dangerous track? In fact, he got over the little crevasse by letting himself slide down on his bottom. Couzy caught up with him on his way down and, although desperately weary himself, gave him invaluable assistance.

Lionel Terray followed closely behind them, held on a rope by Schatz, who was still in fine fettle. The little group drew nearer to the camp. The first man to arrive was Terray, and Marcel Ichac went up towards the great cone to meet him. Terray's appearance was pitiful. He was blind, and clung to Angtharkay as he walked. He had a huge beard and his face was distorted by pain into a dreadful grin. This "strong man", this elemental force of nature who could barely drag himself along, cried out:

"But I'm still all right. If I could see properly, I'd come down by myself."

When he reached camp Oudot and Noyelle were aghast.

Once so strong, he was now helpless and exhausted. His appearance moved them almost to tears.

Immediately after, Schatz and Couzy arrived, and then Lachenal, practically carried by two Sherpas. From a distance it looked as though he was pedalling along in the air, for he threw his legs out in front in a most disordered way. His head lolled backwards and was covered with a bandage. His features were lined with fatigue and spoke of suffering and sacrifice. He could not have gone on for another hour. Like myself, he had set a limit which had helped him to hold on until now. And yet Biscante, at such a moment, still had the spirit to say to Ichac:

"Want to see how a Chamonix guide comes down from the Himalaya?"

Ichac's only reply was to hold out to him a piece of sugar soaked in adrenalin.

It was painful to watch Terray groping for the tent six inches from his nose: he held both hands out in front of him feeling for obstacles. He was helped in, and he lay down; then Lachenal, too, was laid on an air mattress.

Everyone was now off the mountain and assembled at Camp II. But in what a state! It was Oudot's turn to take the initiative, and he made a rapid tour of inspection. Faced with the appalling sight that we presented, his countenance reflected, now the consternation of the friend, now the surgeon's impersonal severity.

He examined me first. My limbs were numb up to well beyond the ankles and wrists. My hands were in a frightful condition; there was practically no skin left, the little that remained was black, and long strips dangled down. My fingers were both swollen and distorted. My feet were scarcely any better: the entire soles were brown and violet, and completely without feeling. The arm which was hurting me, and which I was afraid might be broken, did not appear to be seriously injured, and my neck was all right.

I was anxious to have Oudot's first impression.

"What do you think of it all?" I asked him, ready to hear the worst.

"It's pretty serious. You'll probably lose part of your feet and hands. At present I can't say more than that."

"Do you think you'll be able to save something?"

"Yes, I'm sure of it. I'll do all I can."

This was not encouraging, and I was convinced that my feet and hands would have to be amputated.

Oudot took my blood pressure and seemed rather concerned. There was no pressure in the right arm, and the needle did not respond at all on my left arm. On my legs the needle oscillated slightly, indicating a restricted flow of blood. After putting a dressing over my eyes to prevent the onset of ophthalmia, he said:

"I'm going to see Lachenal. I'll come back in a moment and give you some injections. I used them during the war and it's the only treatment that's any use with frost-bite. See you presently."

Lachenal's condition was slightly less serious. His hands were not affected, and the black discoloration of his feet did not extend beyond the toes, but the sinister colour reappeared on his heels. He would very likely lose his toes, but that would probably not prevent him from climbing, and from continuing to practise his profession as a guide.

Rébuffat's condition was much less serious. His feet were pink except for two small grey patches on his toes. Ichac massaged him with Dolpyc for two hours and this appeared to relieve him; his eyes were still painful, but that was only a matter of two or three days. Terray was unscathed: like Rébuffat he was suffering from ophthalmia – most painful, but only a temporary affliction. Couzy was very weak, and would have to be considered out of action. That was the balance sheet.

Night fell gradually. Oudot made his preparations, requisitioned Ichac and Schatz as nurses, and Camp II was turned into a hospital. In cold and discomfort, and to the accompaniment of continual avalanches, these men fought, late into the night, to save their friends. Armed with torches, they passed from tent to tent, bending over the wounded and giving them emergency treatment, at this minute camp, perched 20,000 ft up on the flanks of one of the highest mountains in the world.

Oudot made ready to give me arterial injections. The lamp shone feebly and in the semi-darkness Ichac sterilized the syringes as best he could with ether. Before starting operations, Oudot explained:

"I am going to inject novocaine into your femoral and brachial arteries."

As I could not see a thing with the bandage over my eyes, he touched with his finger the places where he would insert the needle: both groins and in the bends of my elbows.

"It's going to hurt. Perhaps I shan't get the right place first shot. But in any case you mustn't move, particularly when I have got into the artery."

I was not at all reassured by these preparations; I had always had a horror of injections. But it would have to be done, it was the only thing possible.

"Go ahead," I said to Oudot, "but warn me when you are going to stab."

Anyhow, perhaps it would not hurt all that much in my present condition. I heard the murmur of voices – Oudot asking if something was ready, and Ichac answering: "Here you are. Got it?"

Oudot ran his fingers over my skin. I felt an acute pain in the groin and my legs began to tremble; I tried to control myself. He had to try again, for the artery rolled away from the needle. Another stab, and my whole body was seized with convulsions, I stiffened when I should have relaxed, and felt all my nerves in revolt.

"Gently!" I could not help myself.

Oudot began again: my blood was extremely thick and clotted in the needle.

"Your blood is black – it's like black pudding," he said in amazement.

"That's got it!" This time he had succeeded in spite of my howls which, I knew very well, made the operation all the more difficult to perform. The needle was now in position:

"Don't move!" Oudot shouted at me. Then to Ichac: "Hand it over!"

Ichac passed him the syringe; I felt the needle moving in my flesh and the liquid began to flow into the artery. I should never, until then, have believed so much pain to be possible. I tried to brace myself to the utmost to keep myself from trembling: it simply had to be successful! The liquid went on flowing in.

"Can you feel any warmth?" asked Oudot, brusquely, while he was changing the syringe. Again the liquid went in; I gritted my teeth.

"Does it feel warm?"

Oudot was insistent – the point was evidently crucial; yet still I felt nothing. Several times the syringe was emptied, filled up, and emptied again:

"Now, do you feel anything?"

"I seem to feel a little warmth, but it's not very definite."

Was it auto-suggestion? The needle was withdrawn abruptly, and while Ichac sterilized the instruments, I had a few moments' respite.

"It's excruciating, the way it hurts," I said, just as if Oudot needed telling!

"Yes, I know, but we must go on."

The performance was repeated on the other leg. My nerves were all to pieces, and to brace myself like this took all my strength. In went the needle and I howled and sobbed miserably, but tried in vain to keep still. I could see nothing because of the bandage. If only I could have seen the faces of my friends it might perhaps have helped me. But I was in the dark – a terrible darkness – with nowhere to look for consolation but within myself. It was late and we had all had more than enough. Then for that day it was over and the first-aid party moved on to Lachenal's tent. Perhaps he would have more courage in face of physical pain.

It seemed to me, when I vaguely became aware of the end of the session, that things had gone more quickly for him. Terray slept in Lachenal's tent and Couzy and Ichac slept beside Rébuffat, who was delirious and moaned about his feet all night. Oudot came and lay down next to me. If anything were to happen, he would be there.

Next day plans were completed for the evacuation of the entire camp: the three injured men would be taken down on sledges, two would be able to walk, with assistance, and four were all right. There were miles of glacier to cover, rock barriers to get down, interminable moraines and screen slopes to skirt round or to traverse, a river to cross, and a pass of over 13,000 ft to negotiate – and all this in the monsoon!

It was now June 6th, and Ichac was worried; he remembered the Tilman expedition to Nanda Devi, which was held up for three weeks by rivers swollen by the torrential monsoon rains. Should we have time to reach the Gandaki Valley where the easier gradient would put fewer obstacles in our way? In a week's time we must be clear of the mountains. Soon Couzy would be fit again, Terray cured of his ophthalmia and Rébuffat able to walk. But there were two serious casualties who would have to be carried on the porters' backs under the most appalling conditions, as far as the main valley.

"I can't believe it," remarked Ichac, "it's actually fine today."

The medical supplies urgently demanded by Oudot had arrived from Camp I. He began his rounds with me, and was pleased because the injections had been effective and warmth had returned as far as my insteps. He put fresh dressings on my hands, and though I felt no real pain, there was, nevertheless, some sort of feeling in my fingers. Again I put my question:

"What shall I have left?"

"I can't exactly say. Things have not completely settled down yet and I hope to be able to gain an inch or so. I think you'll be able to use your hands. Of course," and he hesitated for a moment, "you'll lose one or two joints of each finger, but if there's enough of the thumbs left, you'll have a pinch hold, and that's of prime importance."

It was grim news, but still, only yesterday I had feared that the consequences would be far worse. For me this meant goodbye to a great many plans, and it also implied a new kind of life, perhaps even a new conception of existence. But I had neither the strength nor the wish to look into the future.

I appreciated Oudot's courage and was grateful to him for not being afraid to tell me the extent of the amputations which he foresaw would be necessary. He treated me as a man and as a friend, with courage and frankness which I shall never forget.

The injections, which had already done so much good, had to be repeated. This time the session would be even worse and I was terrified at the prospect. I am ashamed to say that the thought of this treatment daunted me – and yet so many people have had to endure it. This time it was to be an injection not of novocaine but acetyl-choline, of which a few ampoules had been brought up from Camp I. Terray joined me in the tent and stood close beside me. He, too, could see nothing under his bandage, and he had to be guided if he wanted to move about at all. I pictured his face, and touched his features with my forearms while Ichac and Oudot prepared the needles, ether and ampoules. I whispered to Lionel what a fearful ordeal I found it all, and begged him to stay close.

"Oudot will warn me before inserting the needle; I mustn't budge then, and you must hold me as tight as you can in your arms."

I hoped that Terray's presence would help me bear the agony. Oudot began with my legs; as on the day before, it was too awful for words. I howled and cried and sobbed in Terray's arms while he held me tight with all his strength. I felt as if my foot was burning – as if it had been suddenly plunged into boiling oil. Professionally, Oudot was in the seventh heaven and everybody shared his delight in my suffering, which was proof of the success of the treatment. This gave me courage and at last, after the fourth syringeful, the necessary 100 cc had been injected.

"Now for the arms," announced Oudot.

This session seemed to go on for ever and I was utterly worn out, but there was distinctly more feeling in my right arm. Oudot stormed away – the needles were either too thick or too small, too thin or too long: never just right, and each time it meant a fresh stab. I began to howl like a dog again.

"Hold me tighter," I gasped between sobs to Terray, who was already holding me as tightly as he could. I tried hard not to tremble, but Oudot was still not satisfied:

"Don't move, *nom d'une pipe*! We'll go on as long as we must. It's *got* to succeed."

"Sorry, I'm doing all I can; I'll bear it, never fear."

I held out my arm for a fresh attempt. When Oudot did find the artery, then it was the needle that got blocked – the too-thick blood clotted inside. From the bend of the elbow Oudot gradually tried higher and higher up towards the shoulder so as not always to stab in the same place. Twice he touched a nerve: I did not cry but sobbed spasmodically. What an eternity of suffering! I could do nothing. Oudot stopped for a moment. "We'll manage all right," Ichac assured me.

"Stick it, Maurice!" Terray whispered. "It'll soon be over; it's dreadful, I know, but I'm here beside you."

Yes, he was there. Without him I could never have borne it all. This man whom we thought hard because he was strong, who made himself out to be a tough peasant, showed a tenderness and affection towards me that I have never seen equalled. I hid my face against him and he put his arms round my neck.

"Come on! Get on with it!"

"Too small and too fine," shouted Oudot.

He began to lose patience. All this fuss with the instruments exasperated me, and I wondered if they would have succeeded "first go" in a nursing home.

After several hours, and goodness knows how many attempts, the injection was successfully made. In spite of frightful pain I remained still as the syringe was emptied. Deftly Oudot replaced it with another without removing the needle from the artery. With the second syringeful, I felt the warmth spreading, and Oudot was exultant. But this warmth became unbearable. I howled and clung to Terray in desperation, holding my arm out stiff, without, so I hoped, moving it a fraction of an inch. Then I felt the needle being withdrawn and cotton wool applied.

"Right arm finished! Now for the left!"

Oudot could not find the artery, and this puzzled him. I told him that when I was young I had seriously damaged this arm, and that explained everything: that was why there had been no blood pressure, and why he could feel no pulse.

The position of the artery was not normal, and it was not possible to make an injection in the bend of the elbow; it would have to be done at the shoulder – much more difficult. I thought of what it had been like for the right arm! Suddenly, at the fifth or sixth attempt, Oudot shouted:

"I've got it!"

I kept absolutely still: syringeful after syringeful went in.

"I'll have to do a *stellaire*."

I had no idea what this was. Oudot explained that it meant injecting novocaine into the nerve ganglion to dilate the arteries and make them easier to find, and improve the blood supply. A long needle was necessary, to stick into the neck in the region of the pleura. I was in despair. It was just too much. For hours and hours I had endured this agony – I should never have the strength for more. But Oudot lost no time, the needle was ready, and he began to explore my neck:

"This is a tricky bit of work. You have to insert the needle in a certain direction, then, when you come up against an obstacle you have to push to the left, and you're bound to be in the right spot."

"Warn me before you stick it in."

In the silence that followed I heard things being moved around.

"I'm going to insert the needle," Oudot announced.

I braced myself immediately, and resolved to keep perfectly still. The needle went in – it must have been a tremendous length; it touched a very sensitive part and the pain made me cry out in Terray's arms. Oudot was now manoeuvring to get the needle into the ganglion, and I could feel it moving deep down. It was in! First shot! The liquid must have started flowing in, but I could not feel it.

"Will it take long?" I asked faintly.

"It's almost finished," he replied holding his breath. "Only another 20 cc to go in."

I felt the awful needle being pulled out: it was over, and now I could relax. Oudot was very pleased: it had been almost a whole day's work, but he had managed to do everything he wanted. Never had I suffered so much in my life; but if my feet and hands were saved it was thanks to

Oudot and his perseverance. Ichac helped him collect the instruments to take along to Lachenal's tent. For the time being he was satisfied with my general condition, but what effect this generalized frost-bite would have on my body in the next few days remained to be seen. The camp was becoming more and more like a hospital: everybody's thoughts and actions were dictated by the condition of the casualties, and everybody hung on the surgeon's lips. From now on his word was law.

That same day began the incredible work of transporting the injured, which ended only after a long and painful retreat, lasting five weeks, beneath torrential rain and over dangerously steep ground. This retreat, during which all the injured slowly recovered, will for ever remain an achievement of the highest order, and it reflects great honour upon all the members of the Expedition.

The sledge we had at our disposal was an extra-light-weight Dufour *luge* mounted on two skis for runners. Naturally, the Sherpas were not familiar with this contraption, so Oudot and Ichac decided to make the least injured of us, Rébuffat, the victim of the first try-out. Schatz took charge of operations, with four Sherpas whom he placed in V formation round the sledge, and the procession started off about 2.30. Rébuffat was well wrapped up and firmly tied to the sledge in case it should tip over. As night fell the four Sherpas arrived back in camp, bringing a note from Schatz advising the use of six men for subsequent descents.

Meanwhile Oudot had given all his patients injections and the evening was spent in changing the dressings. Soon after nightfall the weather worsened, and again it snowed heavily. The others were alarmed and decided to get the rest of the casualties down before it became too late. As luck would have it next morning, when we woke up, it was fine. I was to be taken down first, and before I left Oudot inspected my feet and hands and changed the dressings. He was very satisfied and described my progress as "spectacular"! I was dressed, put in a sleeping-bag and laid on the Dufour sledge, and Angtharkay directed the team of Sherpas. I could see nothing under my bandage, but I felt the air was warm and so knew it must be fine; I hated the thought of being transported without being able to see what was going on. I was very glad to hear that Ichac would accompany me down so that I should not be alone if I needed anything. In my heart I dreaded this descent, particularly the passage over the rock barriers. How would they manage? But the Sherpas were intelligent chaps and never had to be shown anything twice. Afterwards, when we were in camp, Ichac told me how much he had admired them: "It would have been difficult to find a team like this in France," he said; "every one of them did his utmost and every move was perfectly coordinated."

With a few jerks the sledge started off. I was weak and slightly deaf, but I recognized Oudot's voice in the climber's familiar *Bonne descente*! No doubt he was there behind us, waving a hand. Swaddled in all my clothes, I began to sweat; the sun must have been beating down. Sometimes my back skimmed the surface of the snow; now and again Ichac came close and said something, and it did me good to hear him and know he was there. Suddenly the slope steepened, and in spite of the straps holding me in position, I slipped forward. The Sherpas took up their positions in an inverted V in order to brake the sledge. We had reached the big rock band, and as far as I could remember the angle here was steep. I guessed that Ichac had driven his axe in to keep me in balance.

I heard a hollow echo – seracs – and the pace had to be forced now for there was danger of their collapsing. We came to the rocks – and how these Sherpas managed, I shall never know. The wall was very steep yet I was carried on the sledge itself; Ichac told me later that if my eyes had not been blindfolded I should never have been able to stand the sight of such acrobatics and of such impossible positions. I heard sighs of relief – we must have reached the glacier at last. The sledge reverted to a horizontal position, and I was on the snow. A few minutes rest, and on we went at what seemed to me a breakneck pace; I pictured the Sherpas pulling on the ropes all round me and running in the snow, though no doubt this was only imagination. Then we slowed up – we had reached the moraine of Camp I.

I was left alone for a moment while the Sherpas put up a big valley tent into which they carried me a few minutes later. Ichac settled himself beside me – from now on we always shared the same tent and he watched over me, day and night, like a brother. The descent had taken two hours and twenty minutes, and the Sherpas had been marvellous. What should we have done without them?

Ichac briefly explained what was going on. Being blind was most demoralizing; I felt I was nothing but a chattel to be carted about. I knew my ophthalmia was less serious than that of the others and I kept asking for the bandage to be taken off. But since I was nothing but a chattel I had no right to speak.

Although it had clouded over and had begun to sleet, the Sherpas went up again to Camp II with Schatz and Noyelle to fetch Lachenal. About 3 o'clock snow started to fall. Time dragged as I lay in my tent alone with my thoughts. The silence was broken only by the persistent sound of cracking ice, which rather alarmed me: where had they placed the tent? Suppose a crevasse suddenly opened? I was ashamed of these childish fears – surely a mountaineer of many years' experience should know very well that a crevasse does not yawn open like that in a second!

Ichac, the only fit Sahib, supervised the organization of Camp I. Towards the end of the afternoon, at about 5 o'clock, he saw, to his great surprise, Noyelle and Lachenal's convoy emerge through the mist, covered in snow. This time the Sherpas had taken only an hour-and-three-quarters to come down – they had had a terrific day and were worn out. This resulted in some complaints: there was not enough food, and part of their equipment had remained up at Camp III and Camp IV! This last point especially bothered them, for on Himalayan expeditions the normal practice is for the Sherpas to keep their personal equipment as a perquisite. They bitterly regretted these clothes, which had to be considered as lost, and Angtharkay even declared his intention of going up to Camp III again.

I summoned Angtharkay and warned him that I expressly forbade anyone to return higher than Camp II to fetch anything whatsoever. But at the same time I told him of my very great satisfaction at the magnificent behaviour of the Sherpas under his orders, and assured him that they were not to worry about the clothes, for they would all receive generous compensation. Angtharkay went off to give the others the good news.

There was tremendous activity all over the camp, where Lachenal was being made as comfortable as possible. Tents seemed to have sprung up as if by magic, and what looked like a little village was formed at the foot of the great wall of ice.

The next day, after a fine start, the clouds collected again towards 11 o'clock, and it was not long before snow began to fall. Oudot had not yet come down from Camp II. I could hear the avalanches rumbling down in ever closer succession, making an appalling row which wore my nerves thin. Ichac tried to make a joke of it.

"Here we are – that's the 3.37 goods! Now for the 4 o'clock express!" He succeeded in making me smile.

Through the telescope he saw, towards the end of the morning, the last tents of Camp II being taken down, and in the afternoon our MO arrived with his Sherpas, laden like donkeys. Before even putting down his sack he asked about the condition of his patients: any developments since yesterday?

There was marked improvement: Rébuffat could now walk and his ophthalmia was nearly cured. As for Lachenal, circulation had been restored to his feet, and warmth had returned, except to his toes, though the black patches on his heels would probably leave scars. Improvement was visible on my limbs, too, and Oudot was well pleased. He spoke with a frankness that touched me far more than he will ever know:

"I think that the fingers of your left hand will have to be amputated, but I hope to be able to save the end joints of your right hand fingers. If all goes well, you'll have passable hands. As for your feet, I'm afraid that all your toes will have to go, but that won't prevent you from walking. Of course to begin with it'll be difficult, but you'll adapt yourself all right, you'll see."

I was aghast at the thought of what would have happened

if Oudot had not given me the injections so promptly and efficiently. Perhaps they had not yet produced all their effect. More sessions would be necessary and I wondered whether I should be able to overcome the immense lassitude that came over me after all these painful ordeals. In any case I wanted to take every advantage of the respite, and celebrate our success with due ceremony. For the first time since our victory the whole Expedition was assembled together and the condition of the casualties was now such as to warrant a little festivity. We gathered round the one and only tin of chicken in aspic and we uncorked the one bottle of champagne. There were already a lot of us who wanted a drink of it but I was determined that the Sherpas should, somehow or other, join in the general rejoicing. I invited Angtharkay and we drank with him to our victory. Ichac put our thoughts into words:

"You've taken a lot of punishment, but our victory will remain."

Aurora

Jonathan Waterman

An American climber and writer. In 1982 Waterman made a winter assault on Alaska's Mount McKinley, at 6,194 m (20,320 ft) the highest peak in North America. (The mountain is also well-known by its Indian name of Denali). A previous winter bid, in 1967, had left one team member dead and three frost-bitten.

On February 17, 1982, we flew onto the Kahiltna Glacier as Mike muttered about white beaches in the Caribbean. As we vaulted out of our ski-plane another team barrelled into a second plane, so grim-faced after their failed winter ascent that they stared straight ahead, refusing to acknowledge our ebullient waves.

The wind blew a thirty-below-zero chill through my zippers and into my crotch like liquid ice. Since Mike and Roger pretended not to notice my coughing, I pretended that the spasms were mere sneezes. True to form, Mike strutted around without a hat, remarking on how warm it was. And Roger discovered a *Penthouse* stashed in his haulbag by some joking torturer.

We set up a tent and promptly snapped a pole. The cold would continue to break stoves and lanterns and zippers and boots and cameras. Even removing a mitten to tie a knot could cost you your fingers. Because our cockiness was the only way to disguise the layers of terror in our hearts, we never openly discussed the cold, which shadowed us like an omniscient being.

Denali's winter mood was completely unlike the more benign and sun-kissed summer pastels. Even the sunset was violent: the orange light was plucked right off the mountain as it pulsed into abrupt nightfall. Unlike the perpetually lit summer climbing season, the sixteen-hour winter nights meant that camp chores began and ended in the dark. That night the Cassin Ridge stretched taut and arrow-straight beneath the rounded summit bow, tinted violet by stars.

In the morning we put our heads down and trudged into the relentless north wind, pulling loaded sleds ten miles toward the Cassin. We made pitiful progress. I coughed and limped behind Mike and Roger on the end of the rope, tilting back a bottle of cough syrup and chewing its frozen shards. Images of hot showers, warm beaches, and an ex-girlfriend plagued me like a toothache, while my ankle rode fat and unforgettable in its double-boot cast.

On the third morning our ten-foot-long snowcave tunnel filled in with wind-blown snow. Feeling a burgeoning morning urgency, I slipped out of my warm sleeping bag and struggled into my climbing suit, bracing myself for the inevitable hell outside. I wormed my way into the tunnel, shoveling and kicking back chunks of snow into our living quarters.

After twenty minutes of burrowing I poked my head up into a ground blizzard. When I stood up the wind blew me to my knees. Leaning into the gale, I staggered away from the cave and futilely searched for a windbreak. In this nether winter world where fantasy merges with reality. I imagined a toilet flushing; so I yanked off my mittens, unzipped my suit, and squatted until that loathsome wind blew me over and I was back in kindergarten, shame-faced, helpless, reduced to whimpering as I crawled back stinking into the cave. Unwilling to bear witness, Mike and Roger promptly exited and performed jumping jacks in the wind while I boiled my clothing.

Eventually, Mike tried to define the wind. As it whipped and whistled out in the tunnel, he waxed Shakespearean. With a sweeping gesture of his arms he announced that the wind was the breath of God. I never heard anything so untrue in my life.

On our fifth night we dug a palatial snowcave, with a customised "Quick Jonnie" chamber carved into the tunnel. Inside, Mike disgustedly swatted at Roger's clouds of burning dope – Roger assured us he would stop once we began climbing.

My bronchitis dried up and optimism warmed us as we approached the Cassin. Ten thousand feet above, the wind was like storm-driven surf. Its waves crashed and broke over the summit, swirling giant banners of foaming snow over the southwestern face. Our route, however, laid still and taunting.

Early on February 27 we emerged from a snowhole beneath the Japanese Couloir. Roger couldn't get over the bergschrund, so he stood on his pack, reached over the gap, and mantled up. We hoisted the packs up, chinned ourselves over, and pumped our legs, calf muscles screaming under huge packs, spurred on by the fear of changing weather.

It was impossible to avoid knocking plates of ice onto each other. When someone in the lead screamed "Ice!" the unhelmeted followers tried to duck beneath their packs. Four hundred feet up, Roger took a hit in the face and swore violently; his dark blood speckled the opaque ice like graffiti.

We swung our axes and kicked our feet repeatedly into the cold belly of the mountain. We were jumpy, nervous, yelling at each another to hurry. My left ankle felt good while frontpointing, but at each flatfooted twist electrical jolts shot up my leg.

We finished the 1,200-ft gully fumbling with our headlamps. The night hung above as if it were the mid-Atlantic becalmed: vast and black and mirror-still. We tied ourselves into pitons and made our beds on a narrow rock shelf, swinging and clomping our feet over the void with great delight. Getting off the avalanche-fired glacier and coming to grips with the climbing felt so nice that we temporarily forgot the business above.

The stove's flames licked at a pot full of ice. Two hours later we slurped down freeze-dried swill, and when Mike and Roger hurled my home-baked fruitcake into the void,

I feigned indifference. We slept fitfully, wiggling toes and adjusting hoods, ogling the full moon as if it could offer the warmth of a lover.

Several hours before dawn we started melting ice for tea. Getting out of warm sleeping bags and pulling on frozen boots made us shut our eyes, clench our stomachs, and flutter our breath. Packing up was awkward with mittens, so we would take them off, make an adjustment, then rewarm our fingers in our armpits; our feet felt blocky and sore and distant.

Mike and Roger raced to the east, axes squeaking in the Styrofoam snow. As Roger led a hundred-foot cliffband with down-sloping 5.8, Mike and I looked away, cringing as we thought of Roger's 70 lb pack. His crampons raked the rock like fingernails screeching on a blackboard. Then, after a dutiful curse, he was up.

We followed him onto a long ridge that sliced the sky and, to my delight, made the wind hum in subjugation. *Au cheval* along this corniced arête, we kicked steps into the snow and ice for hours, weaving around cornices, oblivious to the space beneath. We laughed and taunted one another; I sang at belays. The mountain gave us what we had come for, and as we straddled it and held it and gently kicked it, I loved it more than I have ever loved a mountain before or since.

On such days you can see every snow crystal sparkle. You can even hear music, although the most elegant orchestra could play here and be horribly underdressed. Some might say that we had too many endorphins rushing around in our heads or that we were surfing a tsunami and staring down at our own reef of mortality, but those people will never hug sun-warmed granite in sub-zero cold, gnaw icicles from their moustaches, or hazard that a mountain and its wind have become a living, breathing entity.

We knew that we would suffer soon enough, but we did not know that the winter climb would prove to be a link to our later lives. Climbing the Cassin in winter put Mike's medical schooling in perspective, developed the pacing for Roger's march to the South Pole, and inspired my writing career. Even a decade later, I am still a captive of this climb.

Our competitiveness was one unfortunate by-product of both the climb and our personalities. The tension surged like a hot current along our climbing rope. If we didn't flash the Cassin, we would have to answer to weather conditions beyond any of our experiences. So, fervently kicking around a cornice, then running across a knife-edge, I pulled Roger off his feet behind me; snatches of blasphemy attached to my name blew past me in a fiery breeze.

That night's campsite was the only flatness of the route. Instead of pitching our tiny tent we jumped into a crevasse and chopped out a snowcave. Later, bathed in eerie ultraviolet glow, Mike and Roger gagged on freeze-dried chili and dumped it into the crevasse's bowels. I forced mine down, hoarding every calorie.

As we slept the wind gusted and swirled and shook at the cave entrance like a wolf worrying a caribou's flank. By morning our sleeping bags were frosted with snow.

There, at 13,500 ft, the climb became our only focus. We were married, chained, and bonded to Denali because a lesser dedication would have been dangerous luxury. Once we climbed higher, retreating during a winter storm, or even surviving a storm, seemed unthinkable. We had to get up.

That day the climbing was superb, albeit strenuous. After fun moves I'd shout, "Boy, that'd be great with light packs!" Roger and Mike replied with glowering anxiety on their faces. We clambered over tawny granite and gray ice, pinching rock with one hand, swinging an axe with the other. We rested on ledges, calves burning, chests heaving.

Because we couldn't afford to rest and acclimatise properly, we all had minor altitude illness. It was a question of getting pummelled by a storm, weakening to the cold, and being kited off by the wind versus dealing with headaches, weakness, and loss of appetite. We took the latter course, and if the cold had only tickled before, now we could feel its talons prickling our skin. Fear actually constipated me.

At the end of our third day of climbing we chopped a tent ledge into steep ice. Since it was too crowded for three, I built a separate platform with snow blocks and clipped into an ice screw. Then I lit the stove, put on a pot of ice, and hid inside my bag. Either gusts of wind blew out the stove, or the pot needed more ice, so I would emerge from my embryonic cocoon, shivering and hating the cold. My fingers turned wooden and the blood crept back all too slowly as I winced and thrust icy digits into my crotch.

When the northern lights first appeared, I dropped the lighter in astonishment. A single ghostly strobe swept the horizon. Then the entire sky filled with tracers. I yelled, nearly knocking off the stove, while Roger opened the tent. Outer space was raining translucent bands of jade and saffron, stealing time and the cold away from us, reeling us beyond the bounds of our banal earthbound existence. Dinner somehow got cooked but had no taste; I no longer felt the cold.

Sleep was an elusive pursuit, so I gave a running commentary of the colors to Mike and Roger, burrowed inside their sleeping-bag wombs. I studied the heavens, raving like a lunatic.

I refuted Mike by saying that the wind is not God's breath, but Lucifer's; the northern lights are the aura of God. Every manmade monument – from Buddhist temples to cathedral frescoes to Louvre paintings – will remain forever artifices, forever cast into the shadow of this night and its aurora.

Although Roger and Mike kept rolling onto one another inside the tilted tent, their grumbling – like the neon glow of Anchorage – was eclipsed by the sublime spectre that blazed above and around us. I felt lifted and freed from earthly cares, while my anxiety about the next day was replaced by exhilaration and spiritual awe. Finally, the world was born anew as the northern lights dimmed into dawn.

The days blurred into one another. We grunted up rock pitches, leaning heads and knees wearily on the ice, always guessing how much further. I kept looking over my shoulder, wondering when the Great Fly Swatter in the sky would squash us like the insignificant insects that we were.

When Roger dislodged a boulder from a long chimney, he screamed "Rock!" and I shrunk under my pack. The 40-lb missile crashed a foot away and bounced fifty feet down, then crashed and gathered more rocks, pounding down until I could no longer see them. Ozone filled my nostrils. I imagined falling with the rocks as if I had become the clipped bird of my nightmares, down past the blinking blue eyes of tottering seracs, feeling the air burst from my lungs as I cartwheeled through wreaths of cloud and bounced off slabs of pebbled granite and slammed into the maws of the crevassed glacier below, finally free.

The falling rock had come and gone in a flash, but when fear is constantly thrown in your face and adrenalin surges through your vessels all day, you no longer recognize when you are supposed to be afraid. Roger shouted "Sorry!" and we blithely continued up the chimney together.

As the climbing became less difficult we grew weaker from the altitude. The thermometer read forty below at 16,500 ft, so Roger hid our "negativity indicator" in the bottom of his pack. Though we wore every piece of clothing we had, the wind came right through our customized suits. I didn't envy Roger, who was harassed by a headache and nausea that evening, taking his turn outside the tent like a Third World cur.

Morning fell loud and clear. We packed the rope away and I began stepkicking up a long couloir. Mike and Roger followed on my heels, grousing about the distance between my hard-won steps. So I cursed back at them – our tacit mode of climbing communication. Near the couloir's top, I felt dizzy and let them pass.

Stomach acid clung to the back of my throat. After a brief rest, panting over my ice-axe, I raced upward with a pulse drumming in my head. Lost in an other-worldly spell, I stepped on a patch of windslab snow, which broke away beneath my sore ankle and started me sliding. The world flashed around me: distant icefalls and endless peaks and cobalt sky whirled with flying saucer clouds. I jammed in my axe pick and clawed to a stop. Through the fog of my pom-pom head and my now-throbbing ankle, I forced myself to concentrate, then climb.

I caught up to them at 18,000 ft only because they had stopped. We chopped out a platform, then set up the tent, continually looking over our shoulders at the sky.

Inside my sleeping bag I assumed a praying position and whispered, "Please, please, please give us one more good day." In the grip of forces beyond your control, righteousness and prayer come to agnostic lips as if you had been born thumping the Bible. Such alchemy is frequently denied afterward, but during the heat of action it shrinks your skin with all the swiftness of a frigid baptism. No one could deny that Denali rose higher and whiter than any church on Earth.

We slept deeply and it dawned miraculously clear.

Up, up we went. The tempo of the drumbeat increased in my head. My feet turned leaden. I could not find a rhythm, let alone go more than one step at a time. Mike and Roger yelled for me to hurry up but I could barely move, so after cursing like brigands they pulled gear out of my pack to lighten my load. Still, I stumbled back and forth, woozy with Denali's thin air, a derelict destined for the gutter.

Finally, after a paltry thousand feet, they stopped and chopped a platform. When I arrived, their anger hung indelibly, like the calm before a great storm. They could have gone on to the top. Bivouacs this high on the mountain were foolhardy, maybe even deadly. But short of being dragged I could not go on.

We piled into the tent. I was too weak to talk. My world spun and dipped and hovered as I held my head and tried to find my breath. Mike plied me with tea while Roger looked out the door and analyzed the sky; they took turns looking out the tent as if something were coming to get us. I'll never forget their wide eyes, the creases on their foreheads, the tension that shook the tent like the wind. Even sick, I knew how worried and scared and tiny we were.

I had destroyed our speedy climbing formula, so I closed my eyes and let sickness spin me away from the bitter realities into unconsciousness. That night the tent became a frozen coffin. We tossed and turned and rolled onto each other throughout the long, long night.

Just before the dawn I dreamed of drowning. I came alive thrashing and lunging for my sleeping-bag zipper, desperate for air. I sat up and realized that fluid had infiltrated my lungs; I could only steal panting breaths.

While the stove roared, Mike changed socks. His two big toes were black with frostbite, but when Roger peered closer, Mike yanked the socks back on. "Oh," he said, "it's nothing."

Stuffing my sleeping bag seemed to take hours. After breakfast, they left the tent, so I zipped the door shut, steepled my hands together, and begged for good weather and the strength to survive the coming ordeal.

Mike overheard me. He knew. "You say something, Jon?"

"No," I said, my breath bubbling. "Nothing."

I followed their steps, oblivious to the sea of clouds that had arrived, oblivious to the passage of time, and acutely aware of the terrible heaviness of the gravity that repeatedly sent me sprawling to the snow.

After several hours Mike and Roger topped out, dropped their packs, and walked the anticlimactic fifty yards to the summit. When they returned, they were not amused to see me crawling down below.

Mike jogged down and relieved me of my pack. Twenty minutes later, I finished my crawl to the summit ridge. I looked briefly upward, but on this day my success would be measured in survival, not a summit. I could manage only two steps before collapsing over my axe and fighting for the privilege of breathing. The wind was mild but the cold was vivid, and despite wearing three sets of layered mittens we couldn't touch our metal-topped axes. Somehow it registered that my toes had frozen.

We plungestepped down and after a dozen strides I was completely winded. Even the descent of Denali's standard route was going to be a battle. Roger and Mike were too cold to wait, so I urged them onward. After several minutes I caught my breath, although sitting down in the hundred-below temperature didn't seem to improve my mood. I shivered violently.

I had to pace myself. Breathe twice for each step, then rest for ten breaths. Again, again, and again. I forced myself into the rhythm, eyes locked on my feet. It became a game: how do you move forward when you can barely breathe?

Mike and Roger watched and waited as long as they could

in the cold. They shouted at me in shrill voices, alternately mad and caring, then left me behind to keep me walking and ward off their own chill.

At Denali Pass I rested a long time, terrified I would fall asleep and never wake up. Just before dark, I caught up to them at 17,000 ft. Roger was curled outside the tent, so I crawled in with Mike. The tent shuddered with the cold, so I didn't bare my skin for more than a few seconds. Even while exhausted I could still enact my preprogrammed warming functions: brush off snow; remove Gore-Tex suit, mittens, boots; get in bag; dry feet; warm toes with hands. I turned on my headlamp. "Wait a minute," I thought. "White toes! Frostbite?" I massaged my swollen bluish ankle and toes until I fell into a sleep racked by coughing.

Strong winds blew in daylight and clouds as we fixed cocoa in the tent. Mike looked me in the eyes and told me I would die if I didn't get down. Then he dressed me like a child. I stumbled off into the wind as they pulled down the tent.

The sky darkened. Taking only three or four steps at a time was disheartening, but I thought I might get down. Mike caught up, then passed me, while Roger stayed with me, cajoling and coaxing me downward. At 16,200 ft I batmanned madly down the fixed ropes, stopping constantly to catch my breath, not sure how much longer I could continue. I tried to downclimb the bergschrund neatly, but in my sickened torpor I fell and landed next to Mike. He laughed – I'll never forget his laughter and the emptiness of our fallen friendship.

In the past, our partnership had rarely suffered because we had always been strong together. For seven years I had envisioned us laughing and hurting and starving and lusting after ice-blasted mountains that no one else gave a rat's ass for. Although we would later be hounded by the media and receive letters and phonecalls of congratulations, as I recoiled below the bergschrund I thought our expedition was a rout.

I lay gasping on my pack. In my delirium I suggested calling for a helicopter; Mike suggested leaving me. No sooner than the words left our mouths, the swirling clouds parted and we saw climbers below. The seriousness, the commitment, and the isolation all disappeared. We smiled for the first time in a week.

As we stumbled down, some Brits walked uphill with congratulations and hot tea. I stared at them, speechless, exhausted, elated. They pumped our hands. We looked up at the mountain wondering if we were dreaming. Someone helped me untie from the rope. "We're alive," I said to no one in particular. Later, in a snowcave, we warmed up and the mountain disappeared. While their nurse massaged my toes, the Brits confessed that when they had first seen us they thought we were crazed because our expressions had been those of asylum escapees.

In the morning Mike was angry, no longer willing to wait for me. His blackened toes mandated immediate descent. Fortunately, I had recovered in the thicker air, so we roped up and raced one another down the low-angled slopes.

We reached our 7,800-ft cache that afternoon and dug out some food. Mike apologized and said the frostbite was his own fault. But I wondered how we could ever set things straight. The words froze in my mouth and we both acknowledged without speaking that this climb had wrecked our friendship. Concealing our disappointment, we glutted ourselves with canned ham and pineapples. Then Mike reminded us of his toes, so with distended stomachs we packed up and trudged toward Base Camp in the gathering dusk.

Darkness hit quickly, and we became puppets jerking along to the pull of the rope. Unlike Mike, Roger and I had no snow-shoes and often broke through the crust, floundering in deep snow. Mincing strides seemed to give us a few more yards without smashing through the crust. Sometimes we crawled, which was slow, but this prevented us from wallowing. On the final Heartbreak Hill Mike snowshoed ahead to dig out our landing-strip snowcave and fix hot drinks. Roger collapsed several times, and I went back to cajole and coax him onward. He murmured the name of Sir Robert Scott, who had died crawling back from the South Pole in 1912.

Recovering in the snowcave, I couldn't believe we had

climbed the Cassin in winter. Roger came alive too, so we dug out a Walkman and listened to Judy Collins while sipping steaming cocoa. The music stirred me deeply. When I realized the extent of our sensory deprivation, how much we had suffered, how far the cold and the dark and the altitude had twisted us, I ducked into my sleeping bag and let the briny tears wash my face.

When I came out, Roger was grinning contagiously, holding his breath. Smoke filled the cave and Mike was coughing, trying to wave the cloud away. Mike said the climb hadn't really been difficult and he had never felt extended; I half-believed him. Roger's lungs were close to bursting and his eyes were narrow slits. He offered me the joint, but I waved it off, because I could scarcely control my emotions.

By our second day of waiting, our various irritations with one another and our tardy bush pilot would no longer permit normal conversation. The cave turned into a soot-blackened repository for all of our frostbitten misery. We ached to leave this frozen hell and endlessly fantasized of the pleasures we would own once we escaped.

Unbeknownst to us, our pilot flew in three Spanish climbers on our third afternoon of waiting. Although he saw our ice-axes and crampons lining the cave entrance, we could not hear his shouts, so he flew back out.

At dawn I hobbled out into the arctic gloom and discovered the Spanish tent. At this point I no longer knew what was real, so I shuffled over, yanked off my mittens, then rubbed the tent fabric between my fingers. The Spaniards woke up, unzipped their door, and jumped back when they saw my terrified face.

From then on the only subject Mike and Roger and I talked about with any mutual accord was our pilot's rationale in leaving us stranded in sub-zero anguish. Although Roger had been the only uninjured one among us, on the fifth day of waiting he fell into a crevasse and destroyed his knee cartilage so badly he could not stand. Thereafter, three derelicts grunted monosyllabically at one another, limping out of the cave only for matters of the toilet. Food rationing began.

Fortunately, the Spaniards swore they would not begin climbing Mount Hunter until we were successfully evacuated. On the eighth day, after our *compadres* dug the word *HELP* in forty-foot-high letters, a passing bush pilot came to our rescue.

The depressive ennui that followed our unsuccessful high adventure totalled me. Next to climbing Denali in winter, everything – relationships, work, exercise – seemed worthless. It took me months to readapt to normal living. While I recovered from my frost-bite (and inertia) in Colorado, a friend loaned me a room and a car, which I promptly crashed into the garage. Because I had squandered all on Denali, I had neither a cent nor a job.

Other climbers heard of our "success" and invited me on the big Himalayan trips I had always dreamed of. I told them that Denali had defeated me; I told them that I had quit climbing and I told them that summits had lost all meaning.

My inability to quit the climb, even with the red flags of injury and sickness waving in my face, can be written off as the shining brashness of youth. But I am still haunted by a partnership that never happened, by a cold with claws, and by a wind so corrupt I could smell its breath as it knocked me onto the glacier, my pants fouled with shit. I did not lose my innocence in 1964 when I saw my grandfather's corpse, nor with my first lover in 1973. I lost my innocence on the Cassin Ridge in the winter of 1982.

In the ensuing years my back stiffened as I heard about other winter climbers on Denali. In February 1983, Charlie Sassara was knocked off by his partner, Robert Frank. Sassara self-arrested on the fifty-degree ice, then watched Frank plummet thousands of feet, spraying flecks of bone and skin and blood on the way down the west rib.

In January 1984, the Japanese soloist Naomi Uemura disappeared after trudging down alone from the storm-washed summit on his birthday. That April I helped twenty Japanese search for his body, but we never found it.

And in the winter of 1986, Vern Tejas soloed the west buttress. Tejas, who had been inspired by Uemura, not only showed the world that the mountain could be soloed in winter, but he climbed it during a stormy February, sans frost-bite or epics.

The following winter, Dave Staeli walked in to solo the Cassin. He took one look and wisely proceeded up the west rib.

Meanwhile, three Japanese alpinists, who had climbed several 8,000-metre peaks, were blown off the west buttress and killed. Staeli abjectly snuck up to the summit a day later. Although the Japanese autopsies read "hypothermia," anyone who has withstood the breath of Denali in winter knows that the wind murdered them.

During these climbs, I envied the climbers not a whit; I worried about them a lot. Now I see Art and Dave and Charlie and Vern and Dave infrequently. But when we greet one another in Anchorage, we stop and look into each other's eyes and beam at one another with little talk. We know full well what we got away with.

Climbing changed for me because of the Cassin. Now I like to revel in the mountain's virility rather than my own. I like to say that in ten trips, I have gone to the summit only once, via the west rib in 1981 – which is true and feels quite fair.

I like to say that we climb because mountains are sacred places and climbing is a form of worship. We climb because the mountains are our church. Indeed, *It* – the Creator, Allah, God, the Great Fly Swatter, or Buddha – can't be any greater than the sight of the aurora borealis at fifty below, where the wind hums over a fin of ice and the light cuts right through to your soul.

Roger wrote and expressed the "hollow feelings" the Cassin had left him with. After surgeons overhauled his knee, he returned to Alaska and limped up an unclimbed, sabre-edged ridge on coveted Mount Deborah. Afterward, he was nearly arrested in Cantwell for counting his own change out of the cash register, and when he got to Talkeetna his smile lit my afternoon.

Several years later, still gimpy, Roger pulled a sled to the South Pole, retracing the footsteps of Scott. He refused to carry a radio, his support ship sank with their plane, and he went into six-figure debt.

Meanwhile, Mike bagged a new route on Annapurna IV, got married, splintered his leg as a result of a long fall in the Alps, and fathered a daughter. In 1989, just before the sap ran in northern Vermont, we met again. He was 36, I was 32. Encountering Mike that day was extraordinary and unplanned. He lived in California and I lived in Colorado. Our spontaneous rendezvous at the house of some mutual friends could only be explained as one of the inescapable circles that connect climbers' lives. His arrival at the remote place I was staying was announced by four whitetail deer charging out of the clearing and into the forest. When he came through the doorway, surprise painted our faces because it had been a long time.

My skin prickled with terrible and textured remembrances: the acrid smell of falling rocks, Mike's anger when I dropped his water bottle into a crevasse, and the mountain trembling as an avalanche crashed down beside us.

The timbre of Mike's voice was as familiar as an old rock-and-roll tune from high school, and he telegraphed his thoughts before he spoke. Undoubtedly I did the same for him. I could scarcely imagine him playing the respectable faculty member at a Palo Alto hospital. His stately eyebrows jitterbugged above an unlined face, and he had the same untended chocolate mop of curls. I said that he looked no different than before.

"What did you expect," he asked, "an old man?"

Still, the climb would not go away, and we were held apart as if Denali sat between us on the table. We exchanged stilted formalities for a long hour. Finally I asked him if he wanted to go for a walk. He pulled on his boots.

We strolled side by side up the trail and sank into the snow rather than walk behind one another. Neither one of us knew exactly how or where to begin, although our intended destination was clear.

As a preamble, I called it providential that we had met again. Without knowing what my next words would bring, I told him I had been trying to forget what happened to us on Denali. I told him that nothing would make me happier than to go climbing or skiing together. In turn, Mike told me that he had recently climbed an ice gully on Mount

Washington, our old stomping grounds. He had stopped midway and remembered our having climbed all of the gullies twice in five hours. Mike said that he treasured these memories, and I instantly recognized the kinder and higher-pitched burr to his voice. We both laughed. Too soon we were standing at the trailhead exchanging addresses.

A year and a half later, at the American Alpine Club meeting in San Diego, we met again. I was surprised to see him because he used to declare that formal climber gatherings – with all their attendant glad-handing and self-congratulation – were a waste of time. But he let it slip that he had come to be with friends. I knew that family dilemmas and city life offered him much more difficult mountains to climb, yet he never breathed a complaint.

Through all of the lectures about other climbers and different mountains, we hung close to one another and endured the weekend. It felt as if we were still relying upon one another, but uncomfortably so, as if still jailed in that putrid, soot-smeared cave during the winter of our discontent. Because of our competitiveness and our numbed toes and our mutual betrayals, we know one another better than I know any other climber, or any climber knows me. As those around us basked in their own deeds on warmer and higher peaks, Denali preyed on both of us. Finally, when no one could overhear, he said it: "You know, we really pulled off a coup up there, didn't we?"

The Climb

René Desmaison

Born in 1930, Desmaison was a French Alpinist and guide. He became a figure of controversy in 1966 when, aided by Mick Burke and Gary Hemming, he made an "unofficial" rescue of two German climbers from the West Face of the Dru – an "insuburdination" for which he was dismissed from the Guides Bureau. There was more controversy five years later when, accompanied by Serges Gousseault, he sought a new winter route on the left side of the Walker Spur of Grande Jorasses.

When daylight finally came, it was dull, sullen, overcast. A wan light filtered through the snow and the mist. When the clouds cleared momentarily, we could catch a glimpse of long trails of fresh snow across the face. And when the cloud closed in, all sound was muffled and deadened, and the snow fell softly, soundlessly, ominously. There would be a few moments' grace, then the wind would get up again and howl round the face, whirling, swirling, the snowflakes dancing round us in a mad dervish-dance. Then there would be another short lull, during which we could sense the storm gathering itself together, to hurl itself with demoniac energy against the immovable granite of the mountains, which had resisted storm and wind for aeon upon aeon of time.

Huddled in our sleeping bags, we watched the spindrift swirling round and over us, at the whim of the winds. For a long moment we lay there silent, appalled, unable to bring ourselves to move.

Today, we must get off. At all costs, WE MUST GET OFF THE FACE. I could feel the phrase echoing round and round in my brain like a rat in a trap. But one step at a time – first, I had to get out of my sleeping bag.

"Serge, how do you feel? Did you get some sleep?"

"Yes, I slept for a bit. I'm not feeling too bad. How far do you think we are from the top?"

"No distance at all, really."

I struggled out of my sleeping bag and into the howl of the wind, then pushed what little gear we had left into my own rucksack. There was not very much: the stove, now on its last gas cylinder, three big channels, the sack-hauling rope, my crampons. All we had left to eat were four sachets of honey and six pieces of nougat. I divided them meticulously in half, gave half of them to Serge and thrust the other half into my anorak pocket. Then I threw the extra rucksack out into space – it was no longer serving any useful purpose. It whirled away into the air, swept along horizontally by the force of the wind.

Serge, too, was getting ready. I helped him to roll up his gear and pack it away, then to buckle his rucksack. I checked on our belay pegs and ropes.

"What did you do with the pegs from yesterday?"

"They're over there on that sling, clipped to the belay peg."

"What do you mean? Are you sure? There's only two of them!"

"That was all I managed to get out."

"How many have we got left, then?"

I did a very rapid count: there were the two we had used to belay for the night, then the two Serge had managed to bring up with him and five more clipped to my harness. That meant that we had just nine blade pitons and six big channels, counting the one I had left at the top of the flake before coming back down again the previous evening. But there were very few cracks on this face large enough to take a big channel. That meant that the channels were virtually useless, and what I needed, principally, were blades. What sort of problems was I likely to meet on the rest of the climb? How many pegs would I need to get up them?

"Serge, I know your hands are very painful, and believe me I do understand, but you must get the pitons out, you *must*, do you understand? All of them, every single one. I'll manage with as few as I possibly can, I'll hammer them in no farther than is absolutely necessary, but you must get them out, however much your hands hurt. If you don't, we've had it. Have you got that? – we've had it, we'll freeze to death on the face or else we'll fall. I know your hands are in a bad way, but how do you feel in yourself? Not too bad?"

"Apart from my hands, I'm feeling all right. Do you think it's still far to the top?"

"No, we should make it by this evening. All right, belay me now. We'd better get started."

Snow was still driving out of the cloud, sweeping over the pall of ice on the dièdre; when it met the overhanging wall it swirled upwards, caught in a violent updraught.

I used the yellow rope as a fixed rope, grasped the edge of the flake with both hands, set both feet on the rock, swung out and waybacked up the flake. I jammed my leg behind the flake, clipped into the peg and rubbed my hands together. They were already numb. The wind was whipping snow into my face, and I could feel my eyes watering and aching. I buried my face in my hands and rested for a moment, waiting for the burning sensation to go away. Would this wind never stop? I would have to get out my goggles.

Ten or twelve feet higher up was a little ledge. It looked as though it would make a good stance; if I could get a decent belay, I would be able to give Serge a tight rope. But there was one problem; how in heaven's name was I to stand up on the top of the flake?

The wind died away for a moment. It was now or never . . .

I grabbed the karabiner with my right hand, unjammed my left leg, twisted it out of the crack and got a foot up on top of the flake. My left hand groped frantically upwards and found a hold on a block a bit further up. I stood up . . .

"Watch out, Serge!! Below!!"

The block had come out. It shot over my shoulder, rebounded once or twice from the slabs and flew out into the storm. I was hanging from my right hand only, my fingers hooked through the karabiner, both my feet dangling and scrabbling at the face. With no time to spare, I clawed my left hand over the top on the flake, pulled up with the strength of desperation and jammed my leg back in the crack.

"Are you okay, René?"

"Yes thanks. Wait a minute, I need time to recover. What about you, are you okay? The block didn't get you?"

"No, but I'm afraid it's cut right through the yellow rope. You can see the cut end dangling behind you if you look down. Watch it, you're not belayed any longer."

"Right, hang on a minute . . . All right, take in on red, I'm coming down."

Once again I used the rope for an impromptu rappel and went down to Serge's stance. The yellow rope was in an even worse state than the red one had been: it was cut right through at about one-third its length. We had just seventy-five feet of sound climbing rope.

We untied from the shorter of the pieces of rope, coiled it and put it away in my rucksack. I tied Serge by his harness to the very end of the yellow rope.

"All right, Serge, I'll make a start. This time it should go. After all, I've got rid of that loose block, so at least it shouldn't happen again!"

Where the block had been was a little flat hold already beginning to fill up with snow. I scrabbled under the snow, found a little finger-hold, hooked my fingers round it. I pulled up, mantelshelfed on to the little flat area on top of the flake and stood up gingerly, with just enough space for the tips of my boots.

I was now standing at the foot of a dièdre, rigorously vertical for the first few feet and sheathed with ice. There were a few thin holds, the odd flake or spike sticking out of the ice. But there was not a single peggable crack. It looked as if it might be possible to get a peg into the back of the dièdre fifteen or twenty feet higher up, but first I would have to get that far. The dièdre, visibly, could not be taken direct. A little to the right was the little ledge where I had intended to belay. And just above that there was another little dièdre, rather smaller than the first, separated from it by a rock corner and more or less parallel to it. Might that be the solution? Or could I start up the second dièdre, and then traverse back left into the first a few feet higher up? I could only try . . .

"Serge, give me a bit of slack, I'm going to try moving up a bit right."

"All right, René, carry on."

Ten feet or so of relatively easy climbing, and I was on the ledge. I hammered in a piton and clipped in. I rubbed my hands together, slapped them against my body and put on my gloves. The movement brought some feeling back to my hands and took the stiffness out of the joints, so that I could use my hands. That was better: I could last out a bit longer yet. Provided that Serge remembered to get all the pitons out, we might yet make it. It was still snowing, true, but the wind was strong enough to blow the spindrift off the face and there was no drifting. On my right, a nose of rock prevented my seeing the rest of the face. I took off my belay, edged my way round the nose on small holds, leant out and peered round it. A violent gust of wind blew snow into my face and blinded me. No, it was a pointless exercise: what with the wind, the blizzard and the buffeting of the storm, it was impossible to make a leisurely study of the face. I retreated back to the peg.

And yet, back there, I thought I had glimpsed a giant groove slashing down the face, quite different from anything on our own route. If only I had been able to see more clearly! I was sure that the groove could only be part of the Cassin route on the Walker Spur. I tried to conjure up a mental re-run of the guidebook: the couloirs, the chimneys, the corners and dièdres. Yes, surely the groove I had glimpsed must be the big gully between us and the summit ridge on the Cassin. It might well make a safer, easier route to the top. So why not traverse over to it? Perhaps I ought to try and abseil down and across into the groove? But suppose I was wrong? And besides it was all very well to talk of abseiling, but what were we to abseil on? A couple of ropes cut through and knotted halfway along? No, thank you very much. There was only one way out: up.

In the very back of the dièdre was a thin, shallow crack, with a few little chockstones. We would have to use aid to climb it, but how much aid? How soon before a stance? Through the whirling snowflakes, the shreds and tatters of cloud, I could not even make a guess. It might be a very long pitch, and if so, Serge with his damaged, swollen hands would never be able to get the pegs out. We had so few, so desperately few of them left. I made the only possible decision: I would have to go back to the first of the dièdres. And somehow or other claw my way up that. Surely there must be something, some little hairline crack for a peg or two?

To get back to the first dièdre, I would have to go down a few feet. I took out the peg to which I had been belayed and yelled down to Serge to take in, very gently, very carefully, so as not to drag on me and pull me off.

Had he heard? More to the point; had he understood? Yes, I could feel very slight movements in the rope as he took in and it tightened a little.

My hopes were dashed: the first dièdre would not go either. If I did try to fight my way up it, I would only, inevitably, come off, and Serge was no longer strong enough to arrest a fall. There was nothing for it: I would have to go back up right again. I was annoyed with myself for dithering and wasting so much time. You're losing your touch, I told myself, you're going bananas, and you couldn't have chosen a worse time.

There was only one thing for it: we would have to go up the second dièdre so far, then traverse across back left to the first one. So be it: there was no point in hanging about any longer.

A gust of wind brought a gush of fresh snow down on my face, filling the dièdre. I felt myself suffocating.

I went back to the foot of the second dièdre and put the peg in again. "You can come up now, Serge!"

The wind carried my voice away; Serge had not heard.

"Serge, come on! Climb now! Can you hear me? Climb! Climb now!"

"Yes . . . coming . . ."

Thank God for that.

I clipped a jumar to the peg and put Serge's rope through it.

In lulls in the storm, I could hear occasional sounds of hammering. It sounded as though it was taking Serge a long time to get the belay piton out. I could tell that he was not managing very efficiently: the blows sounded feeble and inaccurate. Nevertheless, the pitons were indispensable.

Long minutes passed. The storm howled on.

Serge reached me. He was exhausted by the pull up over the overhang, although I had been able to hold him on a tight rope, had even pulled him up, inch by inch, hold by hold.

But at least there was now some legitimate grounds for a very faint hope. The overhang we had just surmounted was part of a rock band which marked the transition between two slab systems on the face, each more or less identical as to angle and seriousness. What was left should be no more difficult than the ramp we had earlier climbed. I turned to Serge and said: "Serge, I don't think there should be another overhang now. Once we're up this dièdre, there'll just be the summit cornice. You've got to hold out, do you hear, got to!"

"Not to worry, René. I'll do it. I'll hold out."

That morning, Simone[1] had not gone up to La Flégère. She had supposed, reasonably enough, that our radio set was broken, or even that we had dropped it.

Leo Filippo, a friend of ours who has a charming small hotel in Entrèves just over the Italian border, had telephoned. "Serge and René should be down very soon. I should think they'll be there by tomorrow evening at the latest. Why don't you come and wait for them here?"

Simone, on whom by now the strain was beginning to tell, was only too ready to take his advice. All of a sudden, she was able to feel almost optimistic. Yes, of course, that

1 Desmaison's wife. She manned a "walkie-talkie" in Chamonix during the ascent.

was it, they would soon be back. In fact, they might be already on their way down.

She glanced at herself in the mirror. She looked like death warmed up. The result of so many sleepless nights, so many hours of worry. René certainly musn't see her like that! At three o'clock, she went to the hairdresser's. At five, along with Pierre and Marie-Claude, she took the Mont Blanc tunnel through to Entrèves.

At Leo's, there was quite a crowd; journalists, television crews, a real circus. The hotel buzzed with an atmosphere of almost feverish impatience. God, what awful weather conditions up on the face! They must be having one hell of a struggle! By the following evening, they would be down.

"Where are your goggles, Serge?"

"In the front pocket of my rucksack."

I got out the goggles, brushed caked snow and ice off his eyebrows and eyelashes, and put them on for him. Then I found my own and put them on.

"Did you manage to get all the pegs out of the stance?"

"Yes, here they are, I even managed to get the big channel."

"Well done, that's great! How about your hands? All right?"

"Not so bad. But don't hammer the pegs in too hard, will you?"

"I'll do my best, but there's not much point if they pop out as soon as I put my weight on them!"

I untied Serge from the red rope and tied it firmly to the belay piton.

"When I get up to a belay, I'll call you. Then I'll hold you on the yellow rope, and you can jumar up the red one. But until then, you can belay me on both."

I traversed diagonally upwards for about thirty feet, taking out most of my own pegs as I went. But some I had to leave for Serge, about four of them, so that as he prussicked, or if he came off, he would not pendulum across left out of control. And now there was a new problem: I had to make a tension traverse into the first of the dièdres, fifteen or twenty feet below me.

I explained to Serge what I intended to do. In short lulls in the blizzard, through blinding swirls of snow, I cold see his face, intent, looking up at me. Had he understood?

"When you get up to where I am now, you can let yourself slide down the rope from the karabiner I'll leave in the peg here. We'll have to leave the peg and the krab in place, but don't bother about them. I'll hold you from below. Give me some slack on yellow."

I gripped the red rope with both hands and let myself slide slowly down into the back of the dièdre. I felt both feet land on a patch of sheer ice where they could get no purchase at all. For several heart-stopping moments, my feet scrabbled and slid, trying to find some pebble sticking out of the ice, some little rugosity in the ice, so that my feet would grip. Finally I managed it. There was a crack just to my right. I hammered in a piton and belayed myself securely.

"Taking in on yellow . . . I'm on belay."

The rope came inching in. I pulled it determinedly until it came taut. Now for my crampons; at all costs I must not drop them down the mountain. I entrusted all my weight to the peg and hung my rucksack on it while I got out my crampons. What a position to try to fasten crampons on to your boots! Finally I managed it, taking infinite precautions to avoid dropping them.

"Okay, Serge! Climb when you're ready."

"Yes."

"The pitons – for God's sake don't forget the pitons!"

Whatever time could it be now? Serge seemed to be crawling up the face like a snail on a leaf. We were in an insane world, a world in which every minute seemed an hour, but where the hours were hurrying past at terrifying speed. Suddenly I heard a shout:

"I can't get the pegs out. I can't . . ."

Just those few terrible words, floating up out of nothingness, blown by the wind.

"Serge, you *must* get the pegs out! Do you hear me? You *must!*"

Finally he reached the last peg.

"Just let yourself go. I'll lower you on the rope."

Serge let himself hang on the rope. Very slowly, using the

friction of the rope over my shoulder to provide a brake, I let him down to the stance beside me. I tied his ropes to the peg and took in both ropes.

"I've left two of the pegs behind. I just couldn't get them out."

Serge was exhausted, at the end of his tether. There was no point in blaming him. And anyway, it was probably quite true – his hands must have been virtually useless.

"Look, Serge, if you look up it seems a bit less steep. It'll be easier from now on, you'll see. I'll help you get your crampons on."

I got his crampons out of his rucksack and strapped them securely to his boots. Out of my anorak pocket I took three pieces of nougat and unwrapped them.

"Here, open your mouth. And here's another one. And here's a sachet of honey."

I took one piece of nougat and one sachet of honey myself. We would have to conserve the rest; they would be needed that night and the next day.

"Right, I'm carrying on."

I passed the rope round Serge's shoulder and under one arm, then turned to continue my struggle upwards, in quest of the summit which seemed to be becoming more elusive, less attainable with every foot we climbed.

The storm had eased momentarily, but now it came on again worse than ever. Would this face ever have an end? Were we condemned to a hell in which we would go on climbing endlessly, laboriously, upward?

The worn front points of my crampons bit less and less into the ice. To my right was rock; I had hoped to find it climbable, but it was disappointingly compact and smooth. No escape that way. I could only kick my front points into the ice as securely as possible, and use each piton as I placed it as a foot-hold on which I could stand to place the next.

By the time I had done forty feet or so, I had just one peg left, one blade: the channels were useless here in any case. There was a crack just in front of me. I hammered the blade in securely. A crack like that was a real piece of good luck. Real good luck – for once fate was on our side.

A decent crack! Suddenly I saw the irony of what I was thinking. Luck, indeed! If we had had any luck, we would have been off the face and down in the valley hours ago. Hours ago . . .

I cut a step in the ice to use as a stance.

"Come on, Serge! And don't forget the pegs! Hey, Serge, Can you hear me? Serge! Come on! Come on, come up now!"

No reply from Serge. Perhaps he had not heard me.

"Hey, Serge! Serge, you can climb! Come on!"

What in God's name was he up to? Why wasn't he replying?

"Can . . . you . . . hear . . . me? Come on!!"

Serge did not seem to be moving; he was standing there motionless, his arms by his sides, staring into the void. Through the howling of the wind I could not hear him.

"What's going on, Serge? What's the matter?"

And then, finally, I caught a few words as his voice floated up to me.

"Not coming . . . can't make it . . . hands . . . completely dead."

An icy hand clutched my heart; my blood drummed in my ears. A feeling of intense grief, nameless horror swept over me, and left me momentarily helpless. Serge had given up. I could see him not far away below me, a remote and motionless figure silhouetted against the whirling snow, resigned and apathetic before the assaults of the storm. I found it difficult to believe that this was really happening. It must be a nightmare! And yet could any nightmare be as detailed, as complete, as this? Never, never as long as I live will I forget that second, that instant of searing, appalling realization.

Serge had given up. He had no more fight left in him, and he could no longer climb.

Despair and fear swept over me. I felt helpless, broken. It was too much. I stood there motionless too, as if turned to stone, my forehead pressed to the ice. We were finished. The ship was foundering in the still, dark, sinister waters of death. For the first time I felt truly afraid.

But no! I had to go on. I had to. I could not give in, not

when I at least still had some fight left in me. My hands after all were undamaged. If necessary, I could let myself down on the rope as far as the stance where Serge was standing, climb up again de-pegging as I went, and then haul Serge up bodily foot by foot, inch by inch, to the stance. Every little inch we made would be one inch nearer to the cornice, which so short a time before – could it really be only twenty-four hours? – we had seen shining like a friendly beacon in the sun.

We had to get off. Somehow or other, by hook or by crook, we had to get off.

I untied both ropes from my harness, threaded them through the belay peg and abseiled down to Serge.

"Come on, mate, this is no time to be giving up. We're very nearly at the top."

"I can't go on. My hands are finished. If you want to go on, you'll have to pull me up. Don't be angry. I've done my best."

"Don't worry, Serge, I'm not angry. I'll pull you up, and you'll see, it'll all be quite easy and comfortable. All you have to do is walk up the ice on your front points, and I'll do the rest. Come on, cheer up. We'll be out of here before very long."

My heart ached as I spoke. I could feel weak tears gathering in my eyes. But this of all times was no time to start weeping; now, if ever, was the time to be strong, stronger than ever before. Death in circumstances like these is merciless, pitiless. You must gird yourself up and fight back with everything you've got – fight it every inch of the way, until it draws back, defeated.

I unclipped Serge's rope from the peg. He was held firmly now on the yellow rope tied off to the peg at the stance fifty feet or so higher up. I tied on to the red rope, and started to prussick up it, step by step, de-pegging as I went.

"All right, Serge, come on, I'm taking in. I've got you, all you have to do is walk up on your front points."

I took in the rope, heaving on it with all my strength, in a back-breaking, muscle-tearing, last effort.

"Come on, Serge, just one more step . . . and another . . . and another."

All fear had left me. No longer was I mesmerized by the tragedy that menaced us, the probable uselessness of these last efforts. I was fighting back – no, *we* were fighting back. And if we were to succeed, I must generate hope. Nobody can fight properly on a diet of despair.

The following pitch was even more harrowing than the previous one, even more desperately dangerous. My second was no longer in any fit state to give me a belay. The ropes hung loose behind me. This time, I simply de-pegged as I went. I held on to the latest piton with one hand, leant out and down and removed the previous one. It only needed one peg to give way, just one, and that would be the end: a last, fearful fall into nothingness and oblivion.

The ice as it formed had glued my eyelashes and my eyelids to my goggles. I tore them off and threw them out into the void. Almost immediately I regretted my action and realized it had been one of those meaningless gestures of defiance in the face of fate.

And then another realization swept over me. Night would fall before too long, and I could see no sign of a ledge, no sign even of a marginally flatter spot.

Despairing of finding a ready-made bivouac, I set to and cut a little scoop where the ice was thickest, a small refuge where we could wait for the next day.

"Go on, sit down – there, in the little scoop. I'll tie you on. There, that's it, you can relax, you're belayed."

I organized the bivouac tent round us. Snow fell, softly, with deadly persistence. I took off Serge's crampons and fastened them to the belay peg, along with our rucksacks. We must not lose those, above all we could not afford to lose our crampons. I got out Serge's sleeping bag.

"Put your feet in the sleeping bag, I'm holding it. Sit up a bit so that I can get it under you. What? You can't quite manage it? All right then, put your arms round my neck . . . yes, that's right, now hold on tight and I'll raise you up a bit. There you are, the sleeping bag's on, you can sit down again now. Put your arms in the bag. All right? You're comfortable? Is the rope okay? Sure? All right, then, just hang on a minute while I get comfortable."

I wriggled into my sleeping bag and curled up on the

little scoop in the side. Then I jammed the stove between my knees and the ice and got it alight.

"I've got a few mints left in my anorak pocket," said Serge, "you could put them in the hot water, it would make it taste better . . ."

Only later, a long time later, was I to understand what was the matter. Months later, some friends of Serge told me: "But Serge wasn't at all well, you know. He'd been suffering all winter from a calcium deficiency, he'd been having medical treatment."

Everyone knew about it; everyone but me.

"But why on earth didn't he say anything?"

"Because you wouldn't have taken him with you, of course!"

Yes, it was only months later that they were to tell me the truth, the incredible, the unbelievable truth. Oh yes, yes indeed, certainly I would never have taken him with me.

"All right, Serge, you can have a drink now, here's the pan, I'm holding it. The water's really quite hot. That'll feel better. And with the mints in it, you're right, it does taste better. Wait a moment, here's a piece of nougat, and a sachet of honey. We'll have to keep a few for tomorrow. You're not feeling too cold? We'll be at the top tomorrow. If you're not too cold, you'd better try to get a bit of sleep. Don't worry, you'll feel much better tomorrow. We'll be all right. Yes, of course we'll get off the face. And then we'll be able to eat as much as we want. And we'll be able to sleep. You'll see – for days on end we'll just eat and sleep, eat and sleep."

They'll be up at the top by tomorrow night. Down in the valley, in the little hotel, there were comings and goings, cigarette smoke, reassuring words, the beginnings of a crowd. Yes, of course, no question, they'll be at the top. After all, yesterday, they were only 600 ft from the summit.

"Look, Simone," said Leo, "there's no point in worry-ing, they can't possibly come down this evening, it's too late and too dark. If they're somewhere on the way down, they'll be bivouacking. You might as well go and get some sleep, there's a bedroom ready."

But . . . the night was a succession of buts. But what
about the weather? Anything can happen, up there.

It was to be a long, a weary night.

Would daylight never come? My legs were cramped and
painful, curled up under me. I could no longer stand the
foetal position I had had to adopt. Only one thing would
bring some relief; I stood up, carefully, gingerly, hunching
over almost double to avoid dislodging the bivouac tent.
The scoop I had hollowed out in the ice was not big enough
for both of us to be able to sit down at once.

When, *when* would it be daylight? An act of faith told me
it would come – difficult, impossible to believe, but it would
come.

Friday, 19 February
Daylight came. Creeping, pale, and sullen, but it came,
through the driving snow, the mist and cloud. The wind
had dropped a little during the night, but now it rose again,
blinding, tearing, exhausting.

We shared about a pint of tepid water, no more. We had
very little fuel left, and that evening we would need enough
to heat a little more water.

Serge, superficially, seemed no worse. But I was aware,
terrifyingly aware, of how every hour, every minute that
passed must be sapping the little strength he had left,
wearing away his resistance, weakening his muscles.

Suddenly, my own courage drained away. I sat there,
motionless, beaten, defeated, overcome by a wave of panic
fear at the realization of all the difficulties that I would have
to overcome single-handed, with no physical or moral
support. I had no hope left; there could be no way out,
no ground for optimism. But even in that blackest of
moments I was conscious, deep inside me, of a will to live.
And if I wanted to live, I must climb on. I must not give in –
I must carry on the fight, even if it seemed hopeless, crazy. I
must carry on, over the ice and the rock, up to the summit
whose whereabouts above me was by now only an article of
faith. I could scarcely remember what we were doing here,
scarcely even remember the name of the face. Life was

reduced to the elemental, to the endless, hopeless battle for survival. How long had we been here? A week? A month? An eternity? How much longer would we have to spend in this hell?

And then, by a supreme effort, I turned my thoughts elsewhere. I looked back into my past and tried to remember other occasions. Just as hopeless, just as desperate, from which I had emerged alive and which might provide some ground for hope. If I had done it once, I could do it again . . . But there was nothing; never had I been in a situation so terrible, so desperate. In twenty years of climbing at the highest standard of difficulty, never had the prospect of survival seemed so black. Nothing; never; never, except yesterday. What I had done yesterday, I would have to do today. The waves of fear had to be overcome . . . I would have to get my head up, conquer gloom and despair. Bloody hell, René, you're not finished yet. If the only way out is to climb, climb! And the only way I could do that was to take it one step at a time, forget the future, forget the past, simply climb.

The face here was a jumble of boulders, rounded, ice-covered. You wondered why they didn't simply cataract down the mountain, away from this featureless, murderously steep face.

That was another three feet gained, anyway, and even three feet was something. But there were so many feet to the summit cornice high above us. And even if we got there, what would the summit mean for us? Life? Death? Or just nothingness?

"Simone Desmaison, how do you rate your husband's chances of survival now?"

"How long do you think they can last out without food or drink?"

"Are you worried?"

"They'll come back," said Simone, "of course they will, they'll come back."

It is hard to believe the sort of questions that get asked at times like these. But we musn't grumble: the journalists are only doing their job. Their role is to be there so that the overfed "general public", smugly asleep in its warm, cosy bed, does not miss out on anything: happiness and suffering, peace and war, poverty and riches, starvation and glut, the gallows and the firing squad, death and despair.

During the course of the morning, Nanouk, Serge's fiancée, came over to be with Simone. She was alarmed, of course, but still confident. Patiently, gently, Pierre with his instinctive kindness did his best to reassure.

"Look, Serge, there's the cornice, not so far above us. It's only about 300 feet away. All right, we won't make it this evening, but we'll be there by tomorrow. Just one more night, and that'll be it."

Serge looked up, but made no reply.

"Can you see it all right, the cornice?"

"Yes, I can see it. Do you really think we'll be there tomorrow?"

"Yes, of course we shall. Look, we're not going to spend the rest of the winter perched on this bloody face!"

Seventy feet above us I could see a bulge of granite, and a few feet further on there was a big block. At last we would be able to sit down, sheltered from the wind by the big block. There was an overhanging wall just above, and once we won over that, two pitches should take us to the top.

There was a very steep, difficult pitch between ourselves and the top of the bulge. I struggled up it. My arm was painful. There was a recurrent stabbing pain up my spine. And when I got there, there was no terrace; the top of the rock bulge was downward sloping. Not even a ledge big enough to sit down. Just as disappointing, the big block which had looked so promising from below was actually almost ridiculously small. Everything on this face was deceptive, nothing was what it seemed; no hope was ever fulfilled. And yet we had no choice: we had to bivouac as best we could, get through the night somehow. Life seemed to be turning into one long waiting game . . .

"Come on, Serge, you can take off your belay now."

Serge could no longer take his belay off; his fingers were not strong enough to open the gate of the karabiner. I had to go down, unclip him, then climb up again. That night I was exhausted but at least, thanks to that last effort, Serge was beside me.

Each of us hung from his separate piton, slung from a series of nylon webbing slings under his thighs and round his waist. Each of us had a precarious foot-hold on the edge of the rock bulge. So suspended, we embarked on the night, the night I could only pray would be our last on the face.

I had used my peg-hammer to break off some little slivers of ice from the rock around us. We would be able to melt them, and that night, at least, we would each have an inch or two of water to drink.

There was no point in even thinking of sleep. The webbing slings would eventually cut off the circulation and, where they went under our thighs, we would begin to feel first an uncomfortable throbbing, then real pain. We would have to keep moving, shifting the slings, relieving the aches in our muscles. It was agonizing, even more trying and more exhausting in fact than the febrile activity of the day.

Saturday, 20 February
A pale daylight filtered through the cloth of the bivouac tent. Pale, but clear and bright with no haze.

"Serge, it's a fine day. The good weather's back. We'll make it, do you hear? We're going to make it, we'll be at the top today."

Serge groaned, rolled his head from side to side, made no answer. I turned to him, took him by the shoulders, shook him slightly.

"Serge, wake up!"

"No, I don't want to. I've had enough, I can't go any further!" his voice finally came, slow, dragging.

"Oh, come on, Serge! It can't be more than a couple of pitches, it may even be less. We've got to get out of here!"

"No, I've had enough, I'm not moving."

"Don't worry, I'll pull you up as I did yesterday. You won't have to make the slightest effort, just hang on the rope and walk up on your crampons. Look, we're not just going to give up here, a couple of pitches from the top!"

"Had enough . . . Don't want to . . ."

That did it. "Serge, you chose to come here – I didn't make you. So you can damn well climb, you can put one bloody foot in front of another until we get off this mountain, do you hear? Once we're up, we're all right, friends will come and get us off, but until then, until we get to the top, you'll climb, and no bloody arguing!"

It was no use. Serge was no longer open to curses or pleas. He had sunk into a silent, deadly lethargy from which nothing could rouse him, and which simply became deeper and deeper. And so that was it. We could go no further. There was nothing more I could do. We had simply to give up and wait. Wait for the inevitable helicopter. Today was fine, clear, almost windless. Almost certainly a helicopter would come. They would see us and guess that we were stuck just below the summit. They would realize from our immobility that something was wrong; you don't sit around resting just a short distance from the top, not if the weather is good and after ten days on the climb. Never in my climbing career had I sat around, even in the worst conditions. That had always been my rule: never wait, go either up or down.

The sky was clear at last. At last, those in the valley could make out what was going on on the face. At Entrèves, everyone was up at dawn. Binoculars and telescopes were focused on the South Face of the Jorasses. Watchful, experienced eyes raked up and down the descent. Nothing. Not the slightest trace, no small black dots between the summit and the Boccalatte Hut 5,000 ft below. They must still be on the North Face.

At eleven o'clock, Simone telephoned the Chamonix police force in charge of mountain rescue and made a formal request for a helicopter reconnaissance flight. She was told: "We'll try to land somewhere near them and speak to them by loud-hailer."

"Serge, listen! Can you hear that? It's a helicopter and it's coming nearer."

Louder and louder came the characteristic noises of the helicopter: the turbo-prop engine, the clatter of the rotor, almost deafening after the long silence of the face. The machine came nearer, and hovered level with our belay, very close, certainly no more than 150 ft away and maybe even less. It hung there motionless for a few seconds. I could see the passengers looking at us. One of them waved an arm at us, first with his thumb up, then with it turned down.

I was more accustomed to the signals used in underwater diving than to those used by pilots. I took them to mean: up or down, or more precisely, are you going up or going down? I flapped my arms horizontally across my chest then outwards, in a wide extravagant gesture intended to convey that we were stuck, that in fact we could go neither up nor down. Then, again making an exaggerated gesture, I pointed several times to my companion, immobile, slumped beside me.

It seemed to me perfectly obvious, inevitable, that the passengers in the helicopter would see what was wrong. They were quite close enough to see that we were not comfortably and securely installed in our bivouac tent on a good ledge, but perched precariously on a spider's web of slings and pegs, and wrapped only approximately in the tent – so approximately that it could give us scarcely any protection from the wind and the cold. And surely they would be aware that after ten days on the face, two of them in the most appalling weather conditions, it would be absurd of us to sit around inactive only a short distance below the summit, on the very day when the weather had finally improved.

Later they were to claim that I had made a thumbs-up sign, which in the gesture language of aeroplane pilots would have implied that everything was all right. I don't remember having done so, but if I did, I certainly did not mean to imply that everything was all right, but rather that I thought our only hope of escape was upwards.

It is true enough that on that occasion I did not make the recognized mountain distress signal: moving my arm slowly and regularly up and down six times in a minute. As I have already said, the helicopter was so close that I was absolutely sure that the passengers would see for themselves what was the trouble.

Every year, dozens, hundreds maybe, of rescue operations in the Alps are performed by helicopter. I took part in a number myself when I was a guide-instructor at the Ecole Nationale in Chamonix, and I can state categorically that never, in all my experience, had it been necessary for climbers in difficulty to use the recognized distress signal. Anybody of any experience realizes very quickly and easily, from their position on the face and their lack of movement, that the climbers need help. And it is worth adding that up to that time the recognized distress signal had never been taught at the Ecole Nationale on the guides' course.

The helicopter veered away. Of course it would come back – we never doubted it for a second. The wind was not particularly strong, and any pilot used to flying in these mountains would be quite undeterred by it. It should be perfectly possible to land in the brèche between the Pointe Walker and the Pointe Whymper.

An hour later, the mountain-rescue service telephoned Simone at Filippo's hotel: "We weren't able to land, but we saw them all right. They're about 300 feet below the summit. We waved to them and then communicated with gestures. They waved back very enthusiastically. They looked quite well and happy. There's a fair amount of wind up there."

As a result, Simone and our friends could only suppose that we were waiting for the wind to drop before making a final push for the summit.

And yet, in spite of herself, Simone was not quite convinced. She was restless, uneasy, tense. She tried to hang on to one certainty: at least we were alive: alive, and the weather was good, and we were not far from the summit. We would make it, we would soon be off the face, it could only be a matter of a few hours.

She decided to go back to Chamonix. She would come back when Leo telephoned to say that she should.

Why, *why* had the helicopter not come back?

Vainly, hopelessly, I peered into the empty sky; vainly, I strained my ears for any murmur of sounds other than the usual ones of wind and flapping canvas.

Night fell. Nobody would come now. The helicopter would not return. I told myself that of course it takes time to get together a rescue team, get it equipped and organized, get it up to the top of the Jorasses: more time than I had allowed.

The next morning they would be there. For us it was a simple matter of surviving the night. We would make it. Serge would make it. We had no choice.

The slings and rope-loops in which we sat became more and more agonizing. All restraint lost, we moaned aloud, groaned, muttered. Every minute, every second, dragged past, and every hour seemed endless, an eternity. That night was the torture of the damned.

Sunday, 21 February

Cold, bleak, grey, daylight filtered back on our eleventh day on the face. Gusts of wind blew sudden flurries of snow from the ridge. It was over; the long night was over. Serge's condition was worsening. His lips and nose were swollen with the cold. He could no longer feel anything, and I could only be grateful that he could no longer suffer. He was hungry and thirsty. All our food had gone. We had nothing whatsoever left. There was just a little gas in the bottom of one cylinder. I managed to melt just one more cupful of water before the stove finally gave out. Very gently, I poured a little of the warm water between my companion's lips. I was no longer thirsty or hungry. My stomach felt knotted, hard, completely insensible. Physically, I could feel nothing but a dull, continuous ache. Much more insistent was my gnawing sense of urgency. If no one came today, Serge would be finished. I could not imagine he would survive another night.

What *could* they be doing down there in the valley? Yesterday the weather had been good. They must surely have guessed something was wrong, otherwise we would hardly be sitting motionless like that, cramped and contorted on our little cornice.

What time could it be? Was it morning, or was it already afternoon?

Serge could not survive long like this. I would have to go

and get help. Perhaps I could go and meet the mountain-rescue caravan which must already be winding up the South Face. Perhaps I could get down to the valley and get together a team of friends. Come and give me a hand – Serge is dying.

Even alone I could do something. I could take the last few pitons, five or six of them, scramble down to get the ones ten feet below, get up to the summit – I might even make it before nightfall – and then at least start down. By evening on the following day. I should be down in the valley. And then I could hurry up again with a rescue-team!

But they might already be on their way. And how long would it take me, all this? Serge would not last out. So what was I to do? Save my own skin, get out while there was still time? Get off the face, get down to the valley, and safety, and Simone? No; there is a law of the mountains, just as there is a law of the jungle: until death us do part. You don't leave your companion to die alone. And this was no longer some boy-scout code: it was a question of simple humanity. Serge needed me: he had no defence, now, against the cold and the wind. I had no choice: I must stay, look after him, protect him, help him to hold out. And yet – for how long *could* be hold out? How long could I survive myself?

That morning, at nine o'clock, Edouard arrived. Edouard Martin, a friend, a pillar of strength – a sort of elder brother whose sympathy and affection gave Simone a much-needed feeling of confidence. Together they went to see Charly Dessertenne. He runs a café in Chamonix which we usually use for telephone calls, and where messages are left for us. They decided that in the next clear spell they would ask for another helicopter reconnaissance flight. They were all quite clear in their minds: something was wrong, and our immobility just a few feet below the summit was alarming. At eleven o'clock, Simone rang the mountain-rescue service.

"They're coming back, Serge, I can hear them! Didn't I tell you? They're coming back!"

I pushed back the bivouac tent which I had pulled over

our heads. I could see the machine edging closer to the face, athough it could not come as close as yesterday's. There was more turbulence today, and I could see that the pilot was having trouble. I pulled a red anorak out of my rucksack and held it up at arm's length over my head. It flapped in the wind, then streamed out horizontally. Had they seen it? Had they been able to distinguish it from the red of the bivouac tent? The helicopter veered away, circled once and came back. I put my anorak back in the rucksack, waited until the machine came back close enough, then stuck out my arm and waved it slowly up and down six times. The helicopter seemed to come a little closer, then went away. Even now, Serge's voice comes back to me as he registered what was happening: clear, composed, calm: "René, the helicopter's gone away. It's gone again . . ."

"No, Serge, don't worry, it'll come back. I swear it'll come back."

Of course it would come back; I had no doubt of that. But if the weather got any worse, the helicopter would not be able to come back. That knowledge, that painful truth, I kept to myself.

At midday, Simone telephoned the police mountain-rescue service.

"They're still in the same place, but you can see that everything's fine. They were waving at us quite happily, and you could see they were quite all right. There's nothing wrong with René, don't you worry."

"But look here," replied Simone, "that can't be right, there *must* be something wrong. René isn't the sort of man to just sit there waiting a few feet below the summit. There *must* be something wrong."

And it was then that they asked the unbelievable, the unforgivable question: "Your husband couldn't just be putting it on, could he?"

Simone was so flabbergasted, so horrified, that she thought she must be hearing things.

"*What* did you say?"

"I said, your husband couldn't just be putting it on, could he?"

"What do you mean? You surely can't imagine that René is 'putting it on' after eleven days on that face, and when they can't have any food or water left?"

Shocked and shaken by such hostility, Simone hung up. She was distraught, unable to decide what was going on and what she ought to do. The day before they had told her that everything was fine. Today, apparently, everything was still all right. So what ought she to do? Should she call out the rescue service immediately? But nothing could be done that night: the weather was getting worse. She made up her mind: she would wait until the following morning, and then, come what might, she would call out a rescue team. If René was really refusing to be rescued, as the police rescue service seemed to be claiming, then he must have gone quite mad. It would not be the first time that a climber had gone mad in the mountains. The next morning, a rescue team would be sent up to get him off the face, to drag him off bodily, if necessary.

"Will it soon be dark, René?"

"Yes, quite soon, Serge."

"Why hasn't the helicopter come back?"

"The cloud is right down. But don't worry, there'll be a team coming up the South Face. They know we're stuck."

"Do you really think they'll be here tomorrow?"

"Oh, come on, Serge, of course they will! What would you do if you were in their place?"

"Yes, of course, you're right."

"The rope isn't hurting you too much?"

"Actually, it feels more comfortable than it did yesterday."

"Your sleeping bag is slipping off. Try to raise yourself a bit, I'll tuck it round you again."

I tucked the bivouac tent around us again like a sort of blanket, hoping that the wind would not tear it off us.

Yet another long night began, cramped and painful, during which I hovered in and out of nightmare. From time to time, Serge dozed off, then jerked awake again, moaning softly. I wriggled and shifted constantly, trying to find a less painful position, and every few minutes tucking in the bivouac tent that the wind threatened to tear away.

Monday, 22 February

My eyes strained towards the horizon where I knew that, eventually, day must come. And than at last, at long last, I could see, dimly, a line of contrast between earth and sky, then a faint, a very faint band of grey; finally, a pale blurred light spread from the east.

As we hung there suspended between earth and sky, my mind wandered off. Our planet was hurtling through space at some 1,250 mph. And life went on. Just as the earth would turn and turn eternally, so life would come and go, bringing deaths and endings, new beginnings and new life. At this very moment thousands of workers all over France would be setting off to earn their daily bread. They would be condemning themselves to a long eight hours shut up in gloomy workshops, deafened by noise, suffocated by fumes and dust. Did I, in the last analysis, envy them?

And nearer at hand, down in the valley, workmen would be setting cable-cars and ski-tows in motion; the sno-cats would be lurching out to prepare the pistes. Life would be going on, peacefully, heedlessly, to a prearranged and regular pattern.

But up there, on the Jorasses, time had come to a halt. There was no longer any such thing as time – only an eternity of waiting . . .

The faint, grey, diffused light turned to a golden, rosy glow. The sun, the life-giving sun was not yet in sight. We could only guess at its presence behind the Hirondelles Ridge, but we could see evidence of it on the gilded sky, the far bright peaks of the Matterhorn and Monte Rosa. On the South Face of the Jorasses, there must now be dazzling sunshine. But for us, on the North Face, there was no light, no warmth, only the harsh, freezing, deadly shadows. We could only wait, patiently, nursing the small remaining spark of life, putting our trust in the self-sacrifice and goodwill of our fellows.

We might be content to wait, but the time had come when Simone could no longer bear to do so. The reassuring words, the placating phrases were no longer enough. She had made up her mind. At eleven o'clock, she made an official request for a rescue.

Serge's parents had arrived the previous day. They were out of their element, uncomfortable in the mountains, in this bleak landscape and cruel climate which they could only admire without affection, and which they found profoundly disquieting. Gentle and a little lost, they felt isolated in the atmosphere of unease and alarm of which they soon became conscious.

How had it come about that Serge, a product of the quiet, tranquil countryside of the Touraine, with its sleepy rivers and lush orchards, had fallen in love with mountains?

Mme Gousseault talked freely about her son. That winter, she told Simone, Serge had not been well – had not been himself at all . . .

Once again a sound of turbo-prop engines, once again the clatter of the screws, echoed in the cold clear air of the face. I felt a surge of renewed hope. The helicopter soared up to us, disappeared, came in again. A gust of wind brought the smell of kerosene wafting over to our bivouac. The machine seemed so close I almost felt I could put out a hand and touch it. And with a sudden pang I realized that there, a few yards away, was life itself, sealed and apart in that bubble of perspex and metal.

Endlessly, unstoppably, the bivouac tent flapped noisily in the wind. It was the wind that was our enemy, sapping what little strength we had. We must not give in, we must hold out.

Serge was in a worse state than ever. He had sunk into a torpor, his head bent forward and resting on his folded arms which in turn rested on his bent knees. When I spoke to him, he no longer heard, no longer answered. All I could do for him now was to tuck the bivouac tent round him over and over again, and retrieve his sleeping-bag every time it threatened to slip off and disappear into space. He moaned gently, fell silent, moaned, fell silent, moaned . . .

We seemed to have travelled out of normality altogether, to be living in a timeless, featureless hell which could offer no hope to man. We had dared too much, gone too far, broken the barriers decreed by fate. And inexorably the barriers had closed behind us: we could not go back.

Serge suddenly raised his head and looked at me. I shall never forget his face as it looked at that moment; as long as I live, his expression will be engraved on my heart. "René, we'd better get on. If we don't get up to the meadows soon, we'll not have time to go to the café for lunch. We can always come back later."

My heart turned over. Serge had lost his reason. In spirit he was no longer with me, but somewhere off in the Calanques on the Mediterrean coast, in one of his favourite climbing grounds. Somewhere there, there must be a climb with meadows at the top and a café not too far away where after a climb in the blazing southern sun you could go and get a long cool drink.

"Yes, Serge, of course, we'll take the easy route up to the meadow, and then we'll come back later."

In 1961, on the Frêney Pillar, I had heard that Pierrot Kohlmann and Antoine Vieille, too, had lost their reason just before they died.

Serge had fallen silent again. He lowered his head back on to his folded arms.

I have never known how many more minutes or hours went past before Serge raised his head again. He looked up and gestured wildly. "My helicopter! Look, René, it's coming back for me, my helicopter is!"

This with a joy and enthusiasm that was even harder to take than his torpor of earlier on.

"Yes, Serge, of course it's coming. It's almost here! I can see it. It's here, waiting for you! It's like a great dome of glass, with golden blades!"

Serge straightened. His back arched, then he fell back, slowly, and sat unmoving, his eyes wide open, staring into space and into worlds beyond my seeing.

My heart ached. My head felt empty. I felt nothing. I sat there unmoving, unable to think, my head on my knees.

Serge had gone. Serge had gone. I was alone, quite alone. And all of a sudden a wave of despair and rage swept over me, and something like madness took me. I screamed into the wind, at the top of my lungs: "You bastard! You hear me? You bastard! I stayed with you, didn't I? I didn't leave you, and now you've left me. You bastard, you've left me all alone."

And then suddenly I came back to myself. I too was losing my reason. I chided myself: "Come on, René, pull yourself together. You'd better tuck in the bivouac tent, it's come untucked and the wind will blow it away." I pulled it down, tucked it round the pair of us and jammed it in behind my back. Now I could only wait for the night.

Serge is dead. Serge is dead. The words echoed and re-echoed round my head. Except for that one terrible thought, my head was an empty drum.

The wind had dropped. To the east, the darkness rose and spread. A great calm grew in me. I felt completely indifferent, unconcerned about myself. Yet every so often I would become aware again of the agony of the slings and the rope-loops round my thighs. Physical suffering was the only thing of which I was now conscious, the only thing that had any reality for me. Before you die, you must suffer. Such is the law of life . . .

Why, at that moment, did I not think of escaping from the face? Why, the next day, did I not make a last, hopeless, desperate dash for the summit? I had at least a little physical strength left – after all, I had enough strength to be aware of my suffering. So why?

It would be difficult to give any coherent answer.

It was not, as people might imagine, some sort of ex-piatory self-sacrifice, a penance paid to God or to man because I had been unable to save Serge. It was not some sort of death-wish, inspired by a tragic sense of personal failure. No, it was that some spring had broken in me.

By dying, Serge had given me back my freedom of action, and yet I could not leave him. Alive or dead, he was there, beside me. We were still, in some mysterious way, one flesh.

At six o'clock that evening, down in a little room in the Chamonix town hall, a meeting was held. At one end of the room was a platform, and there a few public figures from the valley, among them Gérard Devouassoux, held a press conference. They described the events of the day. A helicop-ter pilot called Nogues had tried to land on the summit of the

Grandes Jorasses, but there had been serious air-pockets and turbulence, and the helicopter had had considerable trouble. The pilot and his passengers had not surprisingly had a fright. There would be further attempts the following day.

Simone had been present at the conference, one of quite a crowd. That night she went back to our chalet and wrote me a letter begging me to accept any offers of rescue made; like everyone else she believed that I was refusing help. "Please come back, we need you." Simone was convinced of one thing at least: if either of us was still alive to make signals, it must be me. She handed the letter over, the next day, to the rescue-team on the helicopter which was to try to land on the Jorasses, but she made one mistake, as it later turned out: she sealed the letter. That she should not have done: she should have left it open so that it could be generally read. In any case, the letter was never given to me; it was never necessary. It was given back later to Simone, who threw it in the wastepaper basket. Later, during the police inquiry, they asked me what had been in the letter, and I repeated exactly what is written here.

"Well, of course, you would say that, but what guarantee have we that that is really what was in the letter?"

What else in Heaven's name would poor Simone have written? Did they imagine she'd written me a little note suggesting I make myself comfortable and stay up there a few days longer? Incredible as it seems, that may have been the thought in their minds: they were saying in the valley that every day I stayed up there on the face meant another thousand pounds or so in my pocket. And it was for that, apparently, they thought I had played fast and loose with Serge's life, and risked my own neck – a few miserable extra noughts on the francs in my bank balance.

Robert Flematti came to see Simone. Along with Lieutenant Marmier and Sergeant Georges Nominé, both of them from the crack Alpine troops of the Chasseurs Alpins, they wanted to go up the Italian side of the Jorasses, that is the *voie normale* on the South Face. All three were Alpine guides attached as instructors to the Ecole Militaire de Haute Montagne, the premier training school in France for Alpine troops. Nominé and Marmier, in fact, had just come off the

winter ascent of the North Face of the Grandes Jorasses by
the Croz Spur. Of all those at that time in the valley, they
were undoubtedly the most experienced, the best-qualified
and the fittest, as well as the most accustomed to winter
ascents. Moreover, because of their work at the Ecole Militaire, they were particularly well qualified in all the techniques of mountain rescue. But in order to absent themselves
from the Ecole Militaire and take part in a rescue, they
needed permission from their commanding officers.

It was night. The sky was a profound black pricked with
stars, like diamonds on a black velvet dress. High up, way
above the Jorasses and directly above the Hirondelles
Ridge, I watched an aeroplane wing across the sky from
south to north. I could just catch the sound of its engines – I
listened hungrily, avidly. It seemed in a hurry – to escape
from the dark, perhaps. I could visualize the warm, well-lit
cocoon of the cabin, the passengers leaning back at their
ease. In just a few minutes, the air-hostess would be saying:
"Fasten your seat-belts, please, we are beginning our
descent to Paris Orly." Unimaginable world. Could it be
real? For several evenings now I had heard the plane go
over, and I knew it would be the last before morning. The
morning plane usually went over at dawn. I could always
distinguish it from the night plane – its engines sounded
more muffled and its drone more leisurely. Maybe it was
simply at a higher altitude.

The friendly little winking light of the plane had gone,
disappearing at last into the far, far distance. Now there
would be only a long, dark tunnel until morning. A long
silent tunnel, its silence broken only by the whine of the
wind and the incessant, irritating flap of the bivouac tent.

I was neither hungry nor thirsty. Simply, I knew that my
throat was very sore. It felt as though it was being slowly
squeezed in a red-hot, relentless iron neck-ring.

I was not even conscious of the cold. It was just that my
body, every so often, was racked by fits of convulsive
shivering.

"Poor old lump of flesh! We've been through a lot
together, you and I. You've not done too badly – you

deserved better than this. Now look what I've got you into!"

I became aware that I was talking aloud. Now come on, mate, watch it; just pull up your sleeping-bag, otherwise the wind will have it off you. I realized dimly that I was now slipping from delirium to consciousness and back again almost without noticing the transition. I dragged up my sleeping bag and tried to relax on the rope loops, my head leaning on Serge's shoulder. Was it day? Or night? I could no longer be sure . . .

Ah, there it was, the dawn plane going over. I recognized the distinctive sound of the engines, but I could no longer tell if it was coming from the north or from the south.

Oh God, now I'd lost the bivouac tent! This time the wind must have got it. No, there it was, on the other side of Serge. Luckily it was securely guyed to Serge's belay peg. When it was light I'd bring it over and tuck it round me. It would be a good idea to tie it to my belay peg so that it wouldn't fly away again – but that would be no good; if I did that I wouldn't be able to shift around any more, and the slings were an agony. I must just sit there, staring into space, patiently waiting for the first sign of dawn: a faint ribbon of grey light over beyond the Matterhorn and Monte Rosa.

Patiently, vacantly I stared at the horizon, hoping for that first sign. The wind had dropped long before. There were tears trickling from my eyes. It must be the cold – after all, it must be very cold . . . Agonizing, endless wait for the dawn. And suppose dawn never came? No, that was impossible. In any imaginable world, dawn must come. Nothing, no human agency, no natural disaster, could prevent the dawn. The cosmic clock works perfectly, always. Man may come and man may go, but dawn goes on for ever . . .

At last! There it was. Suddenly the peaks in the distance looked blacker, silhouetted against the paler sky. I remembered a legend from my childhood – somewhere out there, over the great oceans, a little black boy was sitting on a hill playing a pipe, and as he played the sun rose, rose, rose . . .

Tuesday, 23 February
At 6.30 in the morning, Simone, clutching her letter, was waiting patiently in front of the police mountain-rescue

headquarters. Finally, at 7.30, a man appeared. He was to be one of the team in the helicopter on the first overflight on the Jorasses that morning. Simone gave him the letter and explained what it was for.

"Okay, then, we'll give it to him – if he's not already dead, that is."

Simone burst into tears. With Edouard Martin, who was looking after her, she went into the helicopter landing pad. They waited – there was nothing else to do . . .

Daylight. The mountains emerging from the blue haze. A magnificent sight, a fairyland. They are the mountains I have loved for years, my own playground: the Argentières, the Chardonnet, the Weisshorn, Monte Rosa. They look on impassive, stare uncaring at the last act of our tragedy. I look up – and there above me is the cornice, the promised land, dark still but soon to be touched by the golden fingers of the sun. To my left is Serge, stiff and still in his blue down jacket. He used to smile and call it his sunsuit. I'll wake up in a moment – in my own bed, in my own chalet, with my friends, with Simone. It's just a nightmare – if I rub my eyes, pinch myself, I'll wake up. But no. However hard I pinch, I'll never wake up. It's no nightmare – or rather it's a sort of living nightmare. Horror of horrors, life itself has become a living nightmare.

How long has it been daylight? Now the wind's getting up. Wait a minute – there's a noise. Yes, it's the helicopter all right – it's coming closer – it's only a few feet away. If I don't watch out they'll think I'm dead. I'd better get up, get on my feet – that'll show them!

Why haven't they come back? It's odd – after all, there wasn't that much wind. If only the helicopter had got here a bit earlier this morning!

But I expect they were just flying over to check up on the latest situation. Because of course, by this time, there must be rescue teams coming up the South Face.

Chamonix, nine o'clock
"There was too much wind, we couldn't land."

Simone realized that they should never have placed all

their reliance on the helicopters. They should have sent off a team on foot, as Robert Flematti had wanted. And now it was too late.

In the course of the morning, Simone telephoned the French War Office. Very soon afterwards Flematti, Nominé (who was to be killed soon afterwards on the Aiguille du Midi) and Lieutenant Marmier were given leave to take part in a rescue attempt. The three of them were among the best guides of their generation, trained to the highest standard and very experienced in mountain rescue. But there was a problem: they were soldiers, not Chamonix guides. Maurice Herzog, conqueror of Annapurna, president of the mountain-rescue services in the Chamonix valley and Mayor of Chamonix said: "We've already got a full team. And I know all about you, of course, but you must remember that a good climber doesn't necessarily make a good mountain-rescue man."

But when exceptional measures are called for, good climbers are precisely what are needed. Herzog should have remembered Annapurna, and recalled just what sort of men saved him then, rescuing him from certain death.[2]

It might have been possible, and it certainly would have been worth trying, to land three men not on the summit of the Jorasses where the wind made it impossible, but 600 ft lower down on the South Face on the glacier. The helicopter would surely have been able to hover for a few seconds above the snow, long enough for the men to jump out safely into the snow, and then once they were down they could have scrambled fairly easily up to the summit. That part of the South Face is nearly always sheltered, and in any case it's easier for the helicopters to land there than on the narrow summit.

In February 1963, when I had done the Walker Spur by the Cassin route with Jacques Batkin, we had gone down that way to the valley. On the summit there had

---

2 On the successful French Annapurna expedition of 1950, the summit party consisted of Louis Lachenal and Maurice Herzog. Both were seriously frostbitten and were brought to safety in terrible conditions by Lionel Terray and Gaston Rébuffat.
Editor's note: see pp. 170–213.

been a howling gale, but 600 ft further down it had been almost still.

In January 1973 Giorgio Bertone, Michel Claret and I were to be caught in bad weather and bivouac on the South Face of the Jorasses. As before, there was to be a hundred-mile-an-hour gale on the summit; and as before, 600 ft down, we were quite comfortable.

In my opinion they should have brought in the most experienced helicopter pilots. They had only to call on Jean-Louis Lumper, for instance, from the Protection Civile, who had spent the previous seven years piloting helicopters around the Mont Blanc range. Not only would he not have refused but I know for a fact that he volunteered. Or they could have tried Georges Rigaud, a pilot of quite exceptional skill who used a helicopter more powerful than those on normal service in Chamonix. In the event Rigaud was forbidden to try, on the pretext that he was under contract to the French television service and that meant he must take a photographer with him on any flight he might make. "No free publicity from mountain rescue", the authorities stated – this despite the fact that the television photographers swarmed quite unchecked around the Chamonix helicopter pad.

Towards the end of that morning, another machine arrived in Chamonix: the SA 330 known as the Puma. It was piloted by a remarkable man: Jean Boulet, chief engineer and chief pilot for Sud-Aviation who had for some years held the helicopter altitude record.

Simone dared to feel a little whisper of hope.

At the helicopter pad, they had set up barriers and brought in police to control the crowds. No one was allowed through – except of course the camera crews. Simone was kept outside, as if she had been one of the sensation seekers or souvenir hunters who surged round the barriers. For hour upon hour, she stood waiting in the cold, trying to find out what she could from gossip, rumour, second-hand sources . . .

I can't see it but this time I know it's not an Alouette III. The beat of the engine seems slower, more powerful. Ah, there it is! I can just see it, at the extreme range of my field of vision, just above the summit ridge of the Walker Spur. It's a fair size – much bigger than the Alouette III. It's camouflage-coloured – an army helicopter, perhaps? But that's odd – it's got wheels, not skis. You can't land a helicopter on a glacier on wheels! Through the cabin windows, I can see faces peering out at me. The machine hangs motionless for a moment or two, soars upwards again, then disappears. It must have come up to do an equipment drop for the rescue teams on the South Face.

Simone had been too long without any real news. She decided to go down to the police mountain-rescue head-quarters. Surely there they'd be able to give her some definite news. She hovered patiently for a while in a corridor. Nobody. She opened a door at random and peered in.

"Excuse me, do you think perhaps today . . .?"

No reaction. They simply shut the door in her face. There are some things it is very difficult to forgive.

Meanwhile, at last, something was being done. A team composed of French and Italian guides had been dropped by helicopter at the Boccalatte Hut, which is at about 9,000 ft on the South Face of the Jorasses; that meant about 5,000 ft of vertical height below the summit, but about two miles in distance to cover.

The Boccalatte Hut, after all that time! You'd have thought they could do better than that, better than wasting precious time trudging up a track, when the helicopter could have dropped them a good 4,000 ft higher up. Was it just a gesture? Did they want to give the impression that at least *something* was being done?

A pink glow steals over the mountains. A last golden ray of sunlight lingers on the snow-capped summit of Monte Rosa, then, abruptly, is gone. Day is coming to an end. Great violet shadows come creeping stealthily over the glaciers, crawling up the couloirs. Upwards and upwards, engulfing each summit in turn. Already the valleys are invisible, swamped in a tide of darkness. Like sandcastles that children build in the path of the incoming tide, one after another the mountain-tops sank into the ocean of the dark.

What am I doing, still up here on the face? I ought to have gone on this morning. Serge doesn't need me any longer. What has come over me? I can't understand why I'm feeling so lethargic, so unwilling to move . . . I should have gone on, should have put everything into a last dash for the summit. This is not how I want to die, sitting hunched up on a lump of rock. If I must die, I want to die on my feet, on the move – a fall perhaps, a last flashing fall, not a long, slow lingering death from cold and starvation. I ought to have tried to get out, so that I could explain what had gone wrong . . . And yet – it was not a question of failure. We had fought to the very end. To lose a fight is not dishonour. The mountain had won, that was all. And sometimes, after all, the mountain must win, or where's the point of it all?

Ah, there you are – there's the aeroplane back again with its little winking light. You might wait for me . . .

Let's have a look at my right hand – it's feeling worse. Yes, very swollen, and there's a sort of big spot just on top of the swelling. Must be an abscess. God – you wouldn't think you could get an abscess when it's as cold as this. Tomorrow, as soon as it's light, I'd better do something about it. And tomorrow I'd better get out of here. Oh, hell, the wind's got under the bivouac tent again – it's blown off me and over beyond Serge. Don't worry, Serge, I'll soon have us both comfortable and warm again, we can't sit here all night without the bivouac tent, can we? There we are, Serge, that's nice and comfy, isn't it? Yes, I know, I know, you can't hear me – but I've got to talk to someone, haven't I? Haven't I, Serge? Now let's both have a nice little sleep. Down there in the valley, they must all be fast asleep. Except Simone, of course – Simone won't be asleep – how could she be? But I don't feel she's real any more . . . So I'll just put my head on your shoulder, shall I? You don't mind do you? That's better!

A long column of men, like black ants, trudge on and on along a dusty road. A grey sky. Endless grey, endless despair. Hundreds of us – thousands of us. When did we start? Where are we going? Why are we here? I no longer know. All I know is that we must keep walking, walking. We can sleep sometimes, for a moment or two, only chained together, chained to stakes on the long road – to a piton on the vertical rock-face . . . Yes, you can see that's how it's done – you have to hang in a sort or rope hammock. If you let yourself hang flat, it's a lot more comfortable. The really important thing is to have a good long anorak, that'll keep your back warm . . .

I shiver uncontrollably and wake up. Out of the nightmare. I have fallen off the scoop in the ice and I'm hanging from the peg. My sleeping bag is round my knees. I come back to myself and realize where I am. The bivouac tent is still not tucked in – good job it's tied on. And now I've only the one sleeping-bag left – the other has disappeared, finally and completely, down the face. Whatever happens, I must not lose the other one. How can I prevent it from slipping off? Sitting in a spider's web of slings like this, I can't pull it up properly and zip it. I tug it back over my shoulders. I mustn't go to sleep again. I mustn't go to sleep, otherwise I'll probably never wake up.

Wednesday, 24 February
That's odd. It's daylight and I haven't heard the morning plane going over. Surely I can't have been asleep?

There's the big helicopter back again. What can have happened to the others? My hand is agonizing. Let's have a look at it. Yes, very swollen. I'd better do something about that big white spot. Fingers pretty sore too. Frostbite, perhaps? Silk gloves aren't really enough protection. So what's happened to my woollen mittens? They must have got lost. When? I don't know.

And what's that yellow slimy stuff running out of my nose? It's all clogged up round my mouth. I don't know. Well, I suppose it must mean it'll soon all be over. Can't be long, now . . . I'll have to remember to keep on wiping my mouth on my sleeve. I don't want them to find me up here dead with my face all covered with yellow slime. I must make sure I stay conscious as long as possible . . . What

shall I do about my hand? If I rub the big white spot on the
back of my hand on the rough granite – rub it hard – really
hard, just once, like that – God that hurt! – but that's done
it, it's broken. That's odd, nothing's coming out, no pus,
just a bit of blood. Strange, that, after all the hand's really
swollen. What's that helicopter up to? I can just see its tail
over the edge of the cornice. I suppose it's too much to hope
it's landed? No, there it goes, disappeared again over the
other side, can't see it any longer. Considering how long it's
been, there ought to be an army of them up there. Still,
mate, you're on your own now. Better make a little collection of bits of ice to suck, soon you won't be able to move.
Can't? Hands hurt? Too bad, mate: just get on with it,
break off bits of ice with your peg-hammer, and put them in
the rucksack ready. Too bad if they're cold, too bad if they
hurt your throat, you've got to suck them. Your body needs
moisture, and the wind and the cold are drying you up.

Back at our chalet it was bedlam. All our friends were
gathering to support Simone. My little sister Marie-Lou
had travelled up from Périgueux. She didn't understand the
mountains and had very little idea of what it was all about.
She was frightened by all the tension, all the comings and
goings. What could she do to help? Nothing. Why wasn't
anything being done? Nanouk, Serge's fiancée, was staying
at the chalet, too, but that night nobody slept much.
   Down in the village, the helicopter circus went on.
Behind the police barriers, our friends waited, in growing
anguish and despair. It was now our fourteenth day on the
face. Could we still, possibly, be alive?

My mouth is now so dehydrated that the bits of ice stick to
my lips, then to the roof of my mouth, and only then begin
to melt. The moisture trickles down into my burning
throat. I am no longer really conscious of the agony of
thirst; the larger agony, the agony of cold, is more immediate.
   Each little morsel of ice melting in my mouth will pro-
long my life at least for a minute or two and, God knows
why, I cling to those few minutes. Death's icy fingers are

crawling over my face, and death is too close now for me to have any real hope left. Just a few hours more, and it could all be over. If I just sat here quietly and shut my eyes, I could slip down into a long peaceful sleep, full of dreams, full of illusions, a long sleep which would lead unnoticed into the sleep of death, into the light or into the dark, whichever would be waiting for me. But it's not that simple; in my heart, death is now a fact, but my head is still clinging on to a spark of life, still refusing to give up and lie down and sleep. I must not give up, I must not go to sleep, I must meet death still awake and in my right mind.

And I am still conscious enough to be capable of self-analysis, to notice what is happening to me, to be aware when I have slipped over into delirium and hallucination. I'm too well-acquainted with the symptoms, too experienced not to realize what is going on: the toxins are gradually poisoning my body. The nightmare I have just had is, as I know only too well, a foretaste of the crisis which will finish me off.

As madness had threatened, as I had seemed to be slipping quietly over the edge of reason, I had felt a sudden overwhelming sense of serenity. Now that I am myself again, aware once again of the horrors of my situation, I am still calm, still oddly relaxed, in spite of the physical agonies. And my hallucinations are now more like mirages in the desert; in my mind's eye I can see that enormous Tokyo skyscraper, with its neon sign advertising beer: beer in gigantic glasses, capped with monstrous foaming heads.

As that hallucination fades, I can see another: a deep gorge and on its floor a crystal, cool mountain stream – the stream where we used to swim after a long hot day's climbing.

Way up above me, a jet leaves a white vapour-trail across the sky. I am back in a plane . . . flying and swooping far above the earth . . . I'm on my way to India . . . Nepal . . . I can smell the acrid, overpowering smell of the East. I can hear the mountain rivers soaring in my ears . . . I can see Jannu soaring, perfect and white, into the sky. "Whisky and soda, please . . ." I'd like to die up there, up in the sunshine. If only I could get away, cast off my body. Then

I'd go off down to Simone and tell her: "Here I am, don't worry, it's all over now. Up there it's all over, but here I am."

Watch it, mate, you're going mad. Look, you're standing up, leaning out. If you carry on like that, you'll have the peg out – you know the peg's none too sound. And your sleeping-bag's round your ankles. If you don't do something, you'll lose it.

In the valley nerves were beginning to crack under the strain. A friend took Simone back home: she had fainted and was in a state of collapse. At the end of the afternoon she insisted on going back to the helicopter launch pad. As often happens morning and evening, the wind had almost completely dropped. It was about 5.30. As Simone sat there in the car, Maurice Herzog passed by. Simone said: "But why have you stopped the helicopter flights? The wind's almost dropped and it's still light enough."

"I'm sorry, madame," he replied, "but those are my orders. No risks are to be taken."

I know, of course, that according to the rulebook helicopter take-offs and landings must take place at sun-up, not at first light. But in a place like Chamonix, in the bottom of a valley, the sun sinks below the horizon much earlier than it would on the plain. And so I have often seen the helicopters taking off at the first glimmer of light and coming in to land in the dark.

Simone was thinking: "René is going to die up there on a clear day, in bright sunlight, with no wind to speak of. An absurd, an unnecessary death."

The blue haze on the North Face darkens, the grey of the rock goes black. For a few hours there has been no wind. The bivouac tent dangles limply from its peg. There is a stony, terrible silence, a biting cold.

All of a sudden I am afraid. Afraid of the silence, of the cold. Afraid of the agony I have already undergone, the agony ahead. I can no longer face the nightmare night again, no longer risk slipping into hallucinations from which I may never awake. How long will I be able to resist

this intolerable urge to sleep? I must keep my brain working
. . . I must not stop thinking . . . And indeed perhaps I
should think – after all there may still be time, still time
before I cross over to the other side – think about God. And
why not? You were born a Christian, so why not . . .? Too
easy? Too obvious? Belief, faith, coming a bit too pat . . .?
And yet there have been times, out on the seared yellow
plains of India, in the lush and secret valleys of the Himalayas, when you thought you caught a glimpse of a sort of
truth, when you wondered if the peasants might not have
something you had not. They *could* just have been poor
fools, of course, convincing themselves of the existence of
unreal gods. And you're not really very convinced, are you?
But it's difficult to resign yourself to the thought of nothing, of a great non-being . . . It would be nice to *know*.
Perhaps it's all a great big cosmic joke – not with a bang but
with a whimper. But what's the point of the joke? It would
take a supernatural, a "divine" sense of humour to enjoy a
joke for aeons of time and not get bored with it.

Look up at the stars – their beauty, their everlasting
dance. Each could be a new, a fantastic world. And even the
mountains which will kill you are a part of a vast, an
awesome creation. Is that *it*? Is that what it all means?

Little light up there, aeroplane light twinkling up there
like one of the stars, don't go away! Please, please, wait for
me, come and get me. Don't leave me alone. I can't stand
any more.

Odd, I've forgotten what I'm doing here. Why am I
hanging here on the face with my arms jammed behind me
through the bars of the gate? The gate over the mouth of the
tunnel; if I could just get into the tunnel it would bring me
out on the South Face. My legs are dangling, my arms are
aching, my hand is agonizing. I don't think I'll be able to
hang on much longer, I'll have to leave go. That's what I'm
trying to tell all those people milling about in the tunnel-
mouth, behind the gate. But they won't even listen.

"Nothing we can do – you'll just have to stay there."

I can hear them muttering, whispering, behind their
hands, and I can't hear what they're saying, and I can't
even turn round to get a good look at them.

"Get me out of here – save me – I'm cold – oh God, I'm cold!"

I'm flailing around, struggling. I'm shivering with cold. The peg! If I don't keep still, the peg will come out of the crack. Too bad if the peg does come out, I don't want to stay here like a coat on a hook any longer. My God! The sleeping-bag! Where in God's name is it? Gone! The last disaster. And the bivouac tent? That at least is still there, on Serge's other side. I must wrap it round me, it's all I've got left.

Uneasily wandering between dream and reality, I search, despairingly, for the gate into the tunnel, unable to kill the faint hope that that at least is real, not part of the nightmare.

Thursday, 25 February
Through the bivouac tent tucked round me and over my face, I can see the first faint glimmers of daylight. I put my head on Serge's shoulder and feel almost comfortable. I am almost oblivious to the pain from the cat's cradle of slings and ropes. My flesh must have become hardened, and perhaps the cold has made me less sensitive. I am shivering, but I can no longer really feel the cold biting into my hands, my feet. The only thing that worries me is the horrible yellow slime oozing out of my nose so that I can't breathe properly. I wipe if off, slowly with my sleeve. My throat is dry, burning, painful. I put a hand in my rucksack to get a bit of ice. Nothing – empty. Sometime in the night, as I tossed and turned, I must have tipped the rucksack up. To get some more bits of ice would mean getting up and edging over several feet to my left. I don't feel strong enough – and anyway, what's the point? I know by now that no one is going to come up the South Face to get me down. Gary Hemming is dead, he won't come. It's a very long time since that rescue operation on the Drus, and perhaps, now, I'm having to pay the price for that long-past epic. It seems a bit hard to have a price to pay for rescuing two other men, two total strangers. But it had been worth it – yes, it had been worth it.

Over on the horizon, the outline of the mountains blurred and cleared, blurred and cleared. My eyesight was failing. I realized with perfect clarity, almost dispassionately, that it could not be very long now . . .

It was nothing short of a miracle that the weather was still good, thought Simone. She telephoned to the weather bureau. At 13,000 ft the wind speed was about 20 mph. At seven o'clock prompt she was at the helicopter landing pad.

"The wind has dropped a lot," she said to Gérard Devouassoux.

"You're quite right," he replied, "we ought to be able to land."

At 7.25, the SA 330 took off from Chamonix. Four guides were on board.

There they are – two of them. God, they're mad, if they fly that close together they'll collide. No, there's only one. No, there's the other one after all. No, I've lost him again where's he got to? Ah yes, I understand now, there *is* only one helicopter. It's me who's seeing double.

8.15
Total failure. The SA 330 arrived back at the landing pad. "Too much wind. We couldn't land."

The wind again – always the wind. And yet that morning it had felt as if there was scarcely a breath. Simone collapsed, exhausted and hopeless. They took her to a doctor, and then back home. They tried injections, sedatives, sleeping-tablets, but to no avail.

Back at our chalet, no one dared speak above a whisper. Simone was in a bad enough state already – how were they to give her the news that would so inevitably come, if not that day then the next, or the one after? How would they be able to tell her, when the two bodies were carried back to the valley: "Here they are." Of course they would make all the right comforting noises: "Would he have wanted to live, with no feet and no hands? Would life have meant anything to him?"

But for Simone, rather a René without hands and without feet than no René at all. Days ago in fact, she had faced up to that possibility. After fifteen days on the face, six of them totally immobile in sub-zero temperatures, she could not expect hands and feet to survive. But she would be able to help him adjust, she would make life happy and fulfilling even if he was crippled.

Poor Serge, now you've lost your sleeping-bag, too. Is it still morning? If I could be sure of the light over on the mountains, if I could see the sunlight, I'd be able to guess what sort of time it is. Everything is blurred. I can't remember Simone or the children. What do they look like? They seem to have receded into a dream. But I must try to remember . . . Their faces . . . No, it takes too much effort . . . No, it's coming back to me . . . I must hold on to the image, not let it slip away . . . I must work on it – what shape? what colour hair? I must remember – concentrate. There's nothing else to do now, anyway. I'll wrap the bivouac tent round me. I'll give up. I'll just think of Simone and the children – I'll never leave them again . . .

Grenoble, 9.10
On the helicopter pad at Versoud, an Alouette III is starting up. A long strident roar from its engine: 20,000 revs – 25,000 – 30,000. The automatic torque switches in, the long flexible blades turn, slowly at first and then quicker and quicker: 100,000–150,000. The machine vibrates and trembles on its skis. The rotor is now turning so fast it's invisible: 350,000 revs. The rev counters both reach maximum take-off revs. The helicopter, freed, soars up into the blue sky of the Isère. On board is the pilot Alain Frébault from the CRS and his technician Roland Pin, both of them accredited to the mountain-rescue service in Grenoble. Unlikely as it may seem, this was a miracle; there is no other word.

Alain Frébault had taken part in a number of rescues in the Dauphiné Alps as part of the CRS, sometimes in extreme conditions. He knew nothing whatsoever about the Grandes Jorasses. He had never even set eyes on them. At about 9.50 he flew directly over the summit of Mont Blanc, then over the Col du Géant where the CRS post gave him the wind speed (which incidentally had not changed since earlier that morning), and the bearings for the Grandes Jorasses. He could scarcely miss them. There in front of him was the great face. He saw the summit ridge and realized it was too narrow for him to land in those wind conditions. But just a little further on, between the two summits, was a brèche. He did not hesitate – calling on all his experience, all the skill of the great pilot which he was, he slipped quietly into the brèche and touched down lightly on the snow. It was exactly 10.15. At that precise second Alain Frébault saved my life. He stayed there for a few moments, then took off again and flew calmly down to Chamonix.

Alain Frébault landed, got out of his machine and announced calmly that he had just landed on the Grandes Jorasses. Consternation! Reactions varying from incredulous delight to sheer pique.

Alain Fréret, an old climbing partner of mine, exploded: "What the hell's going on around here? Wind conditions terrible, none of the helicopters can land, and this bloke comes straight up from Grenoble, doesn't even need to ask the way, just goes up there and lands."

At 10.45 Alain Frébault set off again with his technician and the guide Claude Ancey. A few minutes later he clattered composedly into the brèche, touched down, stayed down for about a minute, then took off again with his passenger still aboard to prove he could repeat the manoeuvre even if conditions became worse. Then he did it again. Another helicopter, this time piloted by a Chamonix pilot called Violeau, put down and left another guide on the brèche. Frébault circled, came in again touched down and dropped Claude Ancey.

By eleven o'clock there were five guides up at the brèche. At 11.30 they started up the Pointe Walker. It was only about 350 ft above the brèche. The ridge was windswept, bare ice. They had steps to cut, rescue gear to carry up to the summit. "Hello! Hello!"

From far away the call floated down to me. Dimly I thought I could hear it, but it didn't seem real.

"Hello! Hello!"

A call? Surely it couldn't be? No, just another hallucination. But what if it was real? And suddenly a feeling of wild hope swept over me. They were calling. They had come for me. Somewhere up there, someone was calling me. I got to my feet and looked up. There, above the overhang, was a man. A man, coming down on a cable.

"Hello! I'm here!"

He came down. He was beside me. I recognized him: Gérard Devouassoux.

"You're a hard man, René! God, but you're a hard man!"

"Yes, I'm still alive. Gérard, I'm glad it was you who got to me first."

I was remembering that epic rescue on the Drus, all those years ago, when Gérard and I had quarrelled after Gary Hemming and I insisted on bringing down the Germans from the West Face. Surely that old quarrel could be healed now? Nothing unforgivable, surely, had been said or done? Here I had been, lost and near death, and Gérard Devouassoux had come and got me; that made everything all right. In my naivety, in my state of physical weakness and heartfelt relief and gratitude, I was sure that it would all be as simple as that.

They clipped me on to the cable with Gérard Devouassoux. They pulled me up slowly, foot by foot; I had nothing to do but steady myself with my feet. The thin steel cable drew me up and up, out of the dark well into which I had fallen and back into the sunlight. I got my first proper look at those last 300 ft of face, and realized to my consternation that only the first 150 ft or so presented any difficulties at all. However had it happened that so small a distance had been fatal? It seemed a particular cruelty of fate; it made Serge's death seem more absurd than ever.

We stopped for a time while the guides made some adjustment to the steel cable. Then we went on. There were just a few more feet to the cornice, the almost transparent ice-barrier marking the frontier between light and shadow, life and death. I hungered for it, thirsted for it as if it had been a draught of pure, clear water from a crystal stream. Only six feet more – only three – and then suddenly I was over the edge, and a shaft of brilliant sunlight struck my face, and I fell to my knees on the ice, I was on my knees on the summit cornice. I wanted to look up, to raise my eyes to heaven, but I was twisted and wracked by emotion. Joseph Cornier put his strong arm round me and drew my head down to his shoulder. I felt sobs rising in my throat.

"Don't give way now, René, don't give way. You must hold out for a little longer. You remember me, don't you? We were in the same year on the guides' course."

"Yes, of course I remember. I'll hold out."

His mouth was working at the emotion of the moment. His eyes filled with tears. But don't worry, Joseph, I'll hold out, I'm not giving up now.

Olier and Zapelli from Courmayeur were there at the top, with Claude Ancey in charge of the stretcher.

Everything now took place in a dream. The brèche where I sat, the helicopter that lifted me off the mountain and took me down to the valley, the door opening, the friendly hands supporting me, helping me to walk across to the waiting ambulance. I could still stand, I wanted to walk under my own steam . . . friends supported me, Jean Franco gave me a shoulder to lean on. I looked everywhere for Simone, but she was not there. They had not yet dared to give her the news, because they did not yet know which of us it was who was still alive – were not yet sure, even, that one of us was still alive.

I lay down on a stretcher in the ambulance. The doors were slammed shut, the ambulance set off.

At the hospital they took me straight to intensive care. Seconds later, it seemed, I was undressed, laying down, with tubes up my nostrils and tubes into my bladder. They hung bottles of yellow and colourless liquids above me, pushed needles into my veins, stuck electrodes into my chest. Nothing had yet been said, no promises had been made. René Christen the surgeon was quite aware of the problems. Terminal renal failure could have been only an inch away; I ought to have been dead. The mere fact that I was still alive was miracle enough. I could only have lived for a few more hours, he told me later.

I could feel oxygen flooding into my lungs. My blood was

pumping itself back to normal. A delicious warmth stole over me. In the shaded room I felt good. I need no longer think of anything at all.

Simone came. René Christen had warned her.

"I'll do all I can, but I can't promise anything. The next forty-eight hours will be critical. He's in a state of extreme physical exhaustion."

I felt her presence before I actually saw her. She had not dared come too near. I turned my head slowly towards her and saw her drawn, weary face. How she too had suffered! And the fears were not over: I could read all her apprehension in her eyes.

"Don't worry, I'm back now, and I don't intend to die yet."

Through the window of my hospital room, warm and golden in the sunlight, I could see the Aiguilles dusted with frost and new snow. The temperature had fallen yet further.

Above and Beyond

Reinhold Messner

Messner was born in the Austrian Tyrol in 1944. One of the greatest mountaineers of all time, Messner first summitted Nanga Parbat 8, 125 m (26,666 ft) in the Punjab Himalaya in 1970 with his brother Gunther, who was killed by an avalanche on the descent. Eight years later, Messner returned to Nanga Parbat for a solo ascent.

I am sipping my soup from a pan hardly bigger than a cup. My throat feels as rough and sore as if someone had gone into it with a rasp. It is an effort to force down a piece of corned beef out of the tin.

That's a mistake. I must vomit, out of the tiny tent into the snow. In so doing I spew up half the liquid which cost me so much effort in the course of the morning. And without enough liquid in the body (six litres a day, to be exact) I would be finished right away. My altimeter points to just over 19,700 ft. I am on the West Face of Nanga Parbat in the Himalayas of Northern Pakistan.

I fetch in the socks and double boots which I had put outside the tent to dry in the sun. The fireball in the west dips amid a mass of clouds like atomic mushrooms, and sets.

It gets cold at once. As long as it was warm – even prickly hot in the sun – I melted snow in the bivvy tent. Before the meltwater can re-freeze in this sharp cold, I pour it carefully into a small pan and balance it over the gas flame. I must keep on drinking and replace the lost liquid so that my blood does not thicken. It's Monday, August 7, 1978 – the second day of my attempt to solo Nanga Parbat, 26,660 ft.

This morning I stepped on to the 13,000 ft West Face, without a rope, without protection; crampons on my feet, an ice-axe in my right hand and almost 40 lb on my back.

In six hours I have gained more than 3,000 ft. Hence I'm trembling with exhaustion; hence the cramp in my right forearm, which has been cutting steps continuously hacking out holes and pulling me over cravasse edges; hence the sickness. But I must go on drinking as darkness falls and the temperature drops to minus 15 degrees C; I have to go on drinking and must not be sick again. Vomit once more, and I'll have to turn back if I wish to survive.

Solo. The only man before me to attempt an 8,000 metre peak solo was Maurice Wilson. In 1934 he tried to climb Everest. Two years later his body was found at 21,000 ft.

Solo the nearest people are now already 8,000 ft beneath me in the tiny Base Camp. Waiting there are Ursula Grether, a 27-year-old medical student, and Major Mohammed Tahir – "Derry", my liaison officer.

Neither could help me in an accident. I have neither radio transmitter nor flares, nor any other emergency signal – there would be no point. The nearest place intermittently in touch with the outside world is Babusar, and is four days' walk away; they have a handcranked telephone which sometimes works.

To save weight, I have not even brought along a torch. The gas flame is my one source of light till I have drunk enough and prepare to sleep. And I sleep really well; at night nothing can happen to me. My mini-tent stands protected beneath an ice overhang and is tied to an ice screw. It ought even to resist being sucked away in the wake of any nearby avalanche. Ought to . . .

From Europe I had only brought 45 lb. Base Camp had been set up at about 13,000 ft, at the end of the valley where the meadow stops and the scree starts.

Three weeks passed in reconnaissance. Day after day, if the weather was fine, I scanned the Diamir Face of Nanga Pargat to discover a route where I could climb as quickly and as steeply as possible without committing suicide. On July 30–31 I climbed the neighbouring Ganalo Peak, more than 19,500 ft high – my final training.

On August 2 I climbed from Base to the foot of the West Face. I bivouacked, but had to return next morning as the weather had turned foul. Not till August 6 could I try again. I left Base alone and without any mountaineering support. Absolutely solo.

On Tuesday, August 8 I wake up at 5 a.m. My altimeter shows 150 ft more than the previous evening. I haven't been lifted up in my sleep – air pressure has fallen. Not a good sign. I breakfast on tea and soup.

In the icy stillness of dawn there is suddenly a noise as if from some huge distant waterfall.

I tear open the iced-up tent entrance and poke my head out. Beneath me half the ice-face must have broken off. Everything seems on the move. On my left ice avalanches roar to the valley. Beneath me a wide avalanche sweeps like a tidal wave to the foot of the mountain. It consists of the ice which I climbed yesterday, and it pours over the bivouac spot that I left 24 hours ago. Spellbound, I watch the end which would have overtaken me had I started today.

No panic, though the blood is throbbing in my temples. I say to myself: there goes your descent route. You won't get down that now. You'll have to think of something else for the way home.

In the chill blue shadow of the face I fold up my tent and pack everything into my sack: two finger-thick foam mats, a down sleeping bag, cooking things, seven beercan-sized gas canisters. I have food for eight to ten days. Then the ice-screw, camera, rock peg of lightest titanium (which I don't use), lip salve against cracked lips, sun cream, two pairs of strong glacier glasses. This time I really must avoid being snow-blinded, as on Everest.

In addition: toilet paper. But I only use it once – in fact this morning, after the avalanche. Plasters, too, for minor injuries – with serious ones it would be all over anyway. Lastly ten sleeping and pain-killing tablets, but no stimulants at all.

I already know that I shall get into such difficult situations that the temptation to take pills will be overwhelming. And if I take them at this height I'm finished.

Perhaps I would have swallowed them today. I have the feeling that no amount of movement will get me warm. The snow is uneven, at times pure ice, at times crusty or powdery, and my feet only feel secure when a firm base crunches under the crampons. In the western sky are cirrus clouds, and on Nanga Parbat summit a cloud is drooped in the colours of the rainbow. A cold wind blows across my face. I fear it's going to snow.

At about 9.30 the sun hits me for the first time shining down steeply from high up on the face. It turns warm, then hot. I feel the rays as through a burning glass, even though the air remains cool. I am now above 23,000 ft and reach gentler slopes surrounding the trapezoidal summit block of rock, a summit block which rears up in front of me, a whole separate peak by Alpine standards. This mountain begins at a height about 8,000 ft above the highest peaks in the Alps.

Gentler slopes – but as a result heavier, deeper snow where I sink in up to my thighs. Foot after foot I struggle on. Five steps. Pause. My breathing grates. Five steps. Pause. Pulse beats 130, 140.

In every cell of the body I now feel how alone I am. There's no one to take over making the steps. No one with whom I can exchange a few gasped curses and words of encouragement.

Finally I find a possible camp site on the rocks of the summit block. I am quite dehydrated, have no more strength, collapse in the snow. I am not going to manage putting up the tent.

What on earth brought me to this misery? As if the ascent of Mount Everest without oxygen equipment, which Peter Habeler and I had made only in May of this year, were not enough! But Pakistan sent me permission for Nanga Parbat this same year, and after staying only six weeks in Europe I was on my way again to the Himalayas.

I have dreamt for ages of conquering an 8,000 metre peak alone – considered by mountaineers to be "even more impossible" than the highest mountain on earth without breathing apparatus. My physical condition was in favour of making the attempt immediately, for after the many weeks on Everest my body was still acclimatised, and certainly more effective at altitude than it would be after a year's break.

Lying in the snow, I suck in the air and force it out in such a way that just before being exhaled it is briefly held again in the lungs. I must drink, melt more snow in the tent. With movements that seem very slow to me and must be even slower, I pitch my tent.

Beneath me is a sea of mist hiding all the valleys and mountains up to 21,000 ft. But on the western horizon a reddish-yellow bank of haze promises good weather. While cooking and drinking, and now and then storing the air in my lungs, I gradually regain confidence. Another night without sleeping tablets. Tomorrow is the crucial day; I must get up in time.

I sleep badly and do not leave the tent until 7 a.m. The sky is overcast but I can see the summit. If there were firm snow or ice in between I would be up in two hours, three at the most. But here I am ploughing through bottomless snow, which is treacherous as quicksand.

At 10 a.m., after three gruelling hours, I realize that I'll never reach the summit like this. I know too that I won't get down again if I wear myself out any more. I must either turn back at once, or risk the last remaining chance: climb the steep rock barrier towering up on my left in a direct line to the summit. Rock climbing has been my strength since childhood.

I climb carefully, but I give it everything, just as you must on a vertical Dolomite face. Dolomite faces, however, are unserious happy practice cliffs in comparison to this. Why I don't slip up here at 26,000 ft, with my unwieldy double boots and my poor vision through the goggles, is something I don't know.

I balance along ledges the width of a hand, and struggle up a snowy groove. All my instincts are alert; inner reserves are touched on that I no longer thought existed.

I am there. It's 4 p.m., August 9. Standing on the summit plateau of Nanga Parbat, I see the *Silbersattel* where Willo Welzenbach and Willy Merkl were killed, and which

Hermann Buhl crossed on the first ascent in 1953. On the right is the Rupal Valley, in between a vast precipice.

I, too, have stood here once before, eight years ago. My younger brother Günther was with me then and we embraced each other. It was our first 8,000 metre peak. On the descent my brother was killed by an avalanche.

I now feel surprisingly calm, not excited as I did then. I fix my camera on to the head of the ice-axe, which is fitted with a screw so that it can be used as a tripod.

I photograph myself in such a way that the background cannot fail to be recognized. Then with my unused peg I fasten a metal container to the summit rock. In it is a parchment reproduction of the first page of the Gutenberg Bible: "In the beginning God created . . ." It was given to me by a friend. I write the date and my name on the parchment and return it to the container.

I've often thought how it would be if I just remained sitting on an eight-thousander. Is it not a mountaineer's secret wish to stay up there? Not to return to the world which has only just been left behind with such an effort?

An hour later I descend, not down the rock barrier but round it – first along the South Ridge, then through the snow of the western slope. Descending the frosty quicksand is easier. Before dark I manage to reach the tent.

Next morning it's snowing, and thick mist. If I went on I would certainly lose my way like Franz Jäger and Andi Shlick, my two friends who disappeared when we descended Manaslu in a storm.

I wait. I have to ration fuel and food; the bad weather could last more than a week. I sit in the tent, dehydrated and very, very tired. Twice that day the full pan tips over. Part of my down sleeping bag is burned in the process. On the evening of August 10 the weather looks rotten. Three, four more days and I'll be too weak for the descent. I told Ursula Grether and Major Tahir: "If I am not back after ten days you can strike Base Camp and report me missing to the authorities in Islamabad. Nothing can be done. A search would be pointless."

Three-thirty next morning. The weather seems to be improving. I feel giddy, but it doesn't stop me. At five I'm out of the tent, determined to risk everything. I abandon the tent, sleeping bag and various pieces of equipment: soups, stove, everything. I must try to reach Base Camp today, in one single mammoth stage. 10,000 ft of height loss in the steepest direct line. If I don't make it, I won't survive the ensuing night.

Traversing diagonally, I suddenly slip and can only stop myself through sheer speed of reaction. A sprained ankle or broken tibia would have meant the end. The shock forces me to concentrate all my efforts.

On the left of a vertical rock spur exposed to stonefall – the Mummery Spur – I descend 6,500 ft in one section, facing inwards on bare ice at 50–60 degrees. No other incidents, no avalanches. In the late afternoon, in the lower, more level reaches of the face, I leap over a dozen crevasses. I feel both half-dead and reborn.

At Base Camp they have seen me sometime ago. Ursula comes towards me across the vast scree slopes carrying my training shoes. We meet. I take off my clubfoot-boots and throw them away, don't want to see them again. With the keen insight of a medic she states that I look "green" – like a mummy.

That's why there is not a photo of the return. Ursula thinks that a picture of me in this state would be "in bad taste".

The Loneliest Place on Earth

Hermann Buhl

Buhl was an Austrian mountaineer who, in 1953, made the first ascent of Nanga Parbat, 8,125 m (26,666 ft). This solo climb involved a tent-less, emergency bivouac at around 8,000 metres (26,000 ft), something previously considered impossible to survive.

"As I had been quite unable to sleep I was glad when it was 1 o'clock and time to get up. The storm had abated somewhat but it was still pitch-dark. Otto was well tucked into his sleeping bag and seemed oblivious to everything. He did not stir although I made a terrific clatter as I rooted around in the tent, brewed tea, dressed and packed my rucksack. Several times I urged him to get up, but he kept saying that it was too early and that yesterday I had said we would rise at 3 o'clock. I reminded him that we must make the fullest possible use of the day ahead of us and that we should be glad later on of every minute we gained now. I added that in any case I should be setting off at two and that if he were not ready I should have to go on alone. For the time being I packed everything necessary into my own rucksack, which made it quite a weight.

"Eventually Otto emerged from his chrysalis. I now thought that if I went on ahead and made the trail Otto would easily overtake me, and so that I should not have to carry everything myself I left some of the stuff behind for him, among other things Kuno's bacon, which was to be the summit ration. I was later to regret this bitterly. At 2.30 a.m. I crawled out of the tent and started on my way.

"The night was star-lit and the crescent moon threw her silvery light along the ridge which stretched away ahead of me. It was calm and cold. I put on everything I could. Across a hard, steep spur of compressed snow I regained the top of the ridge. Here on the spine the going was treacherous. I buckled on my crampons and felt able to move with greater freedom. In thrilling soaring leaps the ridge rose steeply before me. To the right giant snow slopes, broken by icy barriers, plunged to the plateau above Camp II; to the left my way was skirted by dark rock formations, while beyond the eye was lost in unimaginable depths. A biting wind came up from the south and forced me on to the Rakhiot side. At the start of the traverse to the Silver Saddle I paused for a rest. It was 5 a.m. and behind the Karakoram the sun was rising in golden splendour. Caught in the brilliance of the first rays an undulating sea of summits greeted me: beautiful Chogori, trapezoidal Masherbrum, the bishop's mitre of Rakaposhi, the black granite of the Mustag Tower. In the valleys a fine mist hovered, the best of weather portents. Blissfully I basked in the early sunshine as I took my morning refreshment. Otto was still a good way behind me – I estimated it at an hour's climb – but I never doubted for a moment that he would eventually catch up with me.

"The *Firn* was hard and in places patches of bare, bluish irridescent ice came to the surface. Distances were most deceptive. The rocks of Silver Crag stubbornly refused to come any nearer and another two hours had passed before I was standing on the Silver Saddle, at the edge of the great *Firn* plateau. How often had I dreamed of this moment!

"My altimeter registered 24,275 ft. So far I had made pretty good time. I was not terribly affected by the height. I was having to take two breaths for each step. After another short rest I continued on my way. The *Firn* plateau went on for about two miles, at first rising gently but later inclining steeply up to the Fore-Summit; the difference in height amounted to about 1,500 ft.

"The *Firn* had been ploughed by the high winds into

undulations three feet high. This meant a perpetual clambering up and down which greatly slowed down progress. At 25,000 ft I seemed to reach the limit of my capacity. Suddenly my body felt paralyzed, my lungs could not expand, and every step demanded tremendous effort. My pauses for rest became more and more frequent, and I was acutely conscious of the thinness of the air.

"Otto did not seem to be faring any better. It was quite some time before I caught sight of his figure on the Silver Saddle advancing slowly, silhouetted against the skyline. I saw him stop and then sink down. Otto had given up. This in itself was more or less immaterial to me but with my tongue parched and my stomach rumbling I could not but think of the bacon in Otto's rucksack which was now lost to me.

"On the Silver Plateau the sun was scorching, the air was terribly dry and not a breath of wind was stirring. After each rest I had to force myself to get up and carry on, so great was the temptation to go on lying where I was. The steep rise to the Fore-Summit seemed to get not one whit nearer although I had now been pegging away for hours. My idea that I should reach the summit by midday was completely set at naught. I now directed my steps over to the extreme edge of the plateau where it dropped away into the southern face. I hoped that a cool breeze might be coming up from the south. But here too the air was perfectly still.

"The weight of my rucksack became intolerable and when at length I reached the foot of the rise to the Fore-Summit I took it off and left it behind. I reckoned on being back there before nightfall. I tied my anorak round my waist by the sleeves, having first stuffed the summit flag, my camera, spare gloves and drinking flask in the pockets. I also stowed away some Pervitin, and also Padutin in case of frost-bite, picked up my ice-axe and continued on my way.

"The going was now decidedly easier; the pauses became less frequent and, summoning all my will-power, I tracked along below the Fore-Summit to the right in the direction of a declivity between the Fore-Summit and the Diamir depression. Once more the distance proved to be greater than it had appeared. I began to have doubts whether I should be able to keep going long enough, but in any case the Fore-Summit was within my grasp. It just missed being in the 26,000 ft class, but anyhow mine would be the first ascent. The Pervitin I was carrying gave me confidence; I felt I could rely on it in case of emergency. Just 300 ft below the Fore-Summit I set foot on the above-mentioned declivity."

Buhl had now reached the highest point hitherto attained. This was just about where Aschenbrenner and Schneider had stood when in 1934 they had climbed to within 150 ft of the Fore-Summit. It was also roughly the point where all possible ascent routes converged. Mummery in 1895 had aimed at the Bazhin Gap, and the route over the North Summit reconnoitered by Harrer, Aufschnaiter and Lobenhoffer in 1939 would also run into the Rakhiot route at approximately this point. From this juncture Schneider had conjectured that the route to the summit continued by a descent to the snowfield below the Bazhin Gap and then up the summit shoulder either by a central rib on its north-eastern flank or by a traverse of the main east ridge from the Bazhin Gap. Buhl decided to traverse direct from the declivity towards the Bazhin Gap and the main east ridge, without descending to the snowfield below. His narrative continues:

"My traverse across the rocks to the Bazhin Gap took me over snow and ice, deeply terraced and strewn with boulders. It was already 2 p.m. A steep rocky ridge crowded with snow towers, vertical pitches of sharp-edged granite, badly exposed cornices and steep flanks of compressed snow, now lay between me and the shoulder. Assessing all these difficulties I remembered the Pervitin and took two tablets. I should need every ounce of energy and will-power I could muster. I knew that the drug would remain effective for only six to seven hours and that I must reach some resting place by that time.

"A steep ridge of compressed snow led to the foot of the rocks. At this point the mountain-face plunged in a vertical drop of several miles direct from the ridge. Once or twice I looked through crevices which had formed between the rock and the ice into the gaping void below. Never had I seen such an abyss.

"I laboured doggedly on from one rise to the next, treating every single pitch as an objective in itself. When once more the summit revealed itself far above me I simply could not realize that that was my ultimate objective. Finally I had to scale a thirty-foot overhang which obstructed the access to a *couloir* which in turn led farther up. At the end of the ridge, which was in parts very severe, a massive and upright gendarme still barred the way. It was impossible to climb over it so I had somehow to circumvent it. The rock was very brittle and called for extreme care. The last rise before the shoulder consisted of a very steep and long slope of hard compressed snow. This presented no special problem but it demanded great exertion. With my last reserves of energy I managed to work myself up the few feet which still separated me from the ridge. At 6 p.m. I stood at last on the shoulder at an altitude of about 26,250 ft.

"I felt that I had reached the limit of my endurance.

"Naturally, as a climber, I realized that I was now on the last lap to the summit. But it might just as well have been any other summit in my native Tyrol. This may seem incredible but that was how I felt. I was simply not conscious of the fact that I was at that moment at grips with our own Nanga Parbat, an untrodden peak of over 26,000 feet, the summit to which no less than seven expeditions had gone forth, the mountain which had claimed so many lives . . .

"I took a last gulp of coca-tea, which offered some fleeting refreshment. Then I traversed into the northern face. Steep and rough, a tumbled mass of boulders now led up to the summit, still about 300 ft above me. I now left the ski-sticks behind and – I could do it in no other way – scrambled up on all fours.[1] Suddenly I realized that I could go no higher . . . I was on the summit.

1 Schneider had given warning that the climb to the shoulder, while quite within the bounds of possibility, might well prove to be technically the most difficult section of the whole ascent, but had declared that the stretch from the shoulder to the summit appeared to be a broad and easy rise negotiable by anything from "a handcart to a small motor-car". The experience of Hillary and Tenzing on Everest was the reverse of Buhl's. The summit was presumed to be rocky but they found it was a smooth, gentle snow-rise.

"I was not, I must confess, at the time fully conscious of the significance of that moment, nor did I have any feeling of elation at my victory. I simply felt relieved to be on top and to know that all the sweat and toil of the ascent were behind me.

"It was about 7 p.m. I at once took the small Tyrolese pennant from the pocket of my anorak, tied it to my ice-axe, took a photograph and tucked the pennant away again to take back to my club. Then I got out the flag of the country whose guests we were, Pakistan, fastened it to my ice-axe, changed films and took some more photographs – down towards Rakhiot Peak, towards the Fore-Summit, the Plateau and the Silver Saddle. My eye scanned the three mile drop into the Rupal valley where the setting sun was throwing the mighty shadow of the mountain on which I stood far out into the land. I looked all round me, eastward into the Himalaya, northward to the Karakoram with the Pamirs and the Hindukush adjoining farther west. To the south I could see over and beyond many 16,000 ft peaks.

"It was 7.10 p.m. when I left the summit pyramid. The sun was just disappearing on the horizon, and although the rocks still held some of the heat of the day, it immediately became very cold. The ridge seemed to me to be too difficult and dangerous for the purposes of descent, so I thought of trying to get down across the *Firn* flank facing the Diamir side. Unaccountably I had left my ice-axe on the summit so I had only the two ski-sticks with which to keep my balance. This carelessness might well have proved to be my undoing, for I was standing right in the middle of the traverse when suddenly my right crampon slipped off my boot. I just managed to grab it in time but the strap went overboard.

"I was left like a stork standing on the smooth, hard surface on one crampon, supporting myself on the two ski-sticks and without an idea as to how I should extricate myself. With extreme caution I finally succeeded in reaching some rocky ground.

"When I had dropped about 450 ft from the summit, night suddenly closed in on me. Some distance away I could just see the outline of a large rock and I now groped my way towards it. Supporting my body against the mountainside which inclined at an angle of about 50 degrees, I spent the night standing on this rock.

"I thought longingly of my bivouac equipment which was waiting for me in my rucksack at the foot of the Fore-Summit. I only had my thin pullover on; my heavy one, the tent-sack and my other spare clothing were all in the rucksack.

"Finally, as Karl had been at great pains to impress on me that I should do in case of an emergency bivouac, I took a few pills of Padutin.

"It was 9 p.m. when the darkness forced me to bivouac against the mountain, standing on that unsteady chunk of rock. To the west the last light of day was gradually being extinguished. My rest did me good, even if I was standing all the time. The hours passed surprisingly quickly. I dozed, nodding a little now and again, then jerking myself upright once more. Then a cold shiver would run through me. But it was all quite bearable. The only trouble was that my feet gradually lost all feeling, for I could not keep them moving sufficiently. It was not until nearly 2 a.m. that the moon appeared. Its silvery crescent hung just above the summit, lighting up miraculously the slopes of the North and Fore-Summits below me and casting its light right over to the Bazhin Gap. But I was not in its floodlit path; the flank remained in shadow. So I had to go on waiting until dawn should break.

"As the morning of 4th July approached it became increasingly cold. On the eastern horizon a pale streak showed in the sky. But it was still too dark for climbing and it was not until 4 a.m. that I was able to continue my descent. I had no feeling whatsoever in my feet, my boots were frozen stiff and the rubber soles were glazed with ice. All this called for extreme care. Every step had to be well considered even where the gradient was not particularly steep; the smallest error of judgment could have been fatal.

"If I did only one slight slip in the snow this took so much out of me that I needed minutes to collect myself again. After overcoming a difficult pitch which once again left me completely out of breath I stood at last on the steep iron-hard snowfield which led up to the Bazhin Gap. At around midday I eventually reached the rocks at the Diamir depression. As these offered but very slight hand-holds I took off both pairs of gloves and stuffed them in my pockets. When later I went to put them on again I found that one pair was missing. I have no idea what could have happened to them.

"Throughout this day I had the feeling that I was not alone, that someone was accompanying me. Many times I found myself in the act of turning round to address my companion, and when I was looking for my gloves he told me that I had lost them. It was only when I looked round that I realized that I was alone.

"The sun beat down without mercy. I took a rest and fell asleep for a short time. I awoke feeling ravenously hungry and with a raging thirst. I was so absolutely parched that I was obsessed with the thought of drinking. Now and again I heard voices above me and hoped it might be Hans or Walter coming to meet me with a flask of tea. But no one came. I continued to drag myself on with what help I could get from the ski-sticks, to the Diamir depression which lay about 100 ft up. It seemed quite incredible now, that only the day before I had been able to climb to the summit.

"At last I reached the Diamir depression. Before me lay once more the vast sweep of the Silver Plateau. I could no longer swallow nor speak. Bloodstained slaver oozed from my mouth. I longed to get at my rucksack, for hunger was torturing me no less than thirst. I stumbled about among the hard furrows. It was some time before I could locate the rucksack, then finally I fell down beside it. I could not swallow dry food, but I made myself a wonderfully refreshing concoction of Dextro-energen and snow and after a prolonged rest began to feel better again. Far away on the Silver Saddle I saw two specks. Oh, the joy of it! Someone was coming! I heard voices too, calling my name.

"But what was wrong? The two specks remained static. There was no movement in them. Then I realized that they were rocks. How bitter, how painful was this disillusion! My rests became more and more frequent, the pauses ever longer. I would struggle along for twenty or thirty yards then once more would I be fettered and held in total collapse. Two to three steps demanded ten rapid gasps for breath, then twenty, then still more, until eventually I could go on no longer. Then would follow another long rest, and then the agony would start all over again.

"In this fashion I reached the lowest point of the plateau. I was on the very brink of despair as I floundered among the petrified waves of this vast expanse of fluted *Firn*.

"The counter-gradient to the Silver Saddle seemed endless. I now resorted once more to Pervitin. Whatever reserves of energy were left must now be mobilized, otherwise I should be finished.

"At 5.30 p.m. I stood at last on the Silver Saddle and, looking down, saw two men standing near the Moor's Head. The sight of them gave me fresh impetus and as though buoyed up anew by some secret force I went ahead with greater ease."

The Gods Giveth, the Gods Taketh Away

Kurt Diemberger

*In 1957, Diemberger, an Austrian alpinist, accompanied
the legendary Hermann Buhl – the conqueror of Nanga
Parbat – on an expedition to the Himalayas where, after
climbing Broad Peak, they turned to the ascent of
Chogolisa.*

June 27th dawned clear, fine and calm, a veritable gift of
the Gods. We were happy beyond words. Our rest-day
had done us good, and we felt brimming over with
fitness, and a burning zeal to bag the summit.

We were off at about a quarter to five. It was still very
cold, but we knew it couldn't be for very long. The sky grew
lighter and lighter above Baltoro Kangri. To the south lay a
sea of summits, peaks about 20,000 to 23,000 ft high, and
hardly even explored. To the north the sun was already
touching K2. Between us and it, Broad Peak displayed only
its main summit, masking the other two.

Almost as soon as we had got our legs moving, the
warmth of the sun reached us. We tramped happily up
over the glittering snow. Free of our loads, we made
unbelievably easy progress. The going was excellent on
the very crest of the ridge, but the snow was deep and trying
on either side; besides which, the wind had formed dangerous wind-slabs on the slope. One of them broke away
quite close to us and went thundering down in a fair-sized

avalanche to the level plateau of the Kaberi Saddle below. It made quite an impression on us and we stuck carefully to the crest of the ridge, which was so far uncorniced. But how would things go up there on Ridge Peak, where we could see cornices several yards wide projecting unpleasantly in a continuous hem? No doubt the storm of the previous day had notably increased their size.

At 23,000 ft we left the ridge, by now corniced, and traversed a little way across a smooth ice-slope to reach a projection farther up. There were actually a few rocks here, quite a curiosity on this mountain. And what about the route above? Ye Gods! There was the summit, just over there! It couldn't be any great distance and it certainly didn't look difficult. We ought to be up on it by midday, we thought.

Indeed, the next bit was easy; the slope flattened out appreciably and all we had to do was to keep along it to the deep notch beyond Ridge Peak. We made light of turning the huge cornices which towered over us to the right. Chogolisa's immense roof drew rapidly nearer, but after a quarter of an hour we had to admit it wasn't going to be easy. The slope grew steeper and the sector of ridge rising behind it had a distinctly airy look. Then suddenly we could see the whole route, and there was nothing about it to be lightly dismissed. The ridge down to the notch was as sharp as a knife-blade, its left-hand side a giddily steep precipice of rock and ice, to its right great cornices hanging far out over the North Face. We should have to be very careful there. The rock precipices below us kept on forcing us farther up towards the jagged white crest. We belayed carefully with the rope, watching for avalanches. A small wind-slab did in fact break away and went sliding away into the abyss. The snow conditions were really a curse. Just as we got to the rocks, Hermann went through to his waist, and hardly had he scrambled out when he was sitting in another hole. Damn it, the slope was a positive honeycomb! Hermann balanced his way forward as if walking on egg-shells – lucky man, he didn't weigh much. He reached ice-plastered rocks and moved from foot-hold to foot-hold with incredible delicacy of balance, hardly touching the holds as he moved. A moment later he disappeared over a rib. "Up you come!" I could hear him calling.

Rope's length by rope's length, we worked our way along the ridge, sometimes on the slope, sometimes right up at the edge of the cornices. Steadily, the wind passed over the crest; glittering snow rose towards the deep blue dome of the sky. Down in the south there were huge clouds now. But they did not move.

We had made good time in spite of the unexpected difficulties. It was only 9 o'clock when we reached the saddle at 23,000 ft. And there, only 2,000 ft above us, was the sharp tip of the turret on the long crest of the summit-ridge. A steep, but for the most part broad, ridge of snow led up to it.

We sat down in a sheltered hollow, in glorious warm sunshine, and took off the rope. We were ravenous; what about a drop of tea and those delicacies we had saved up for our trip to the top? "This is the best day for me since I came out with the expedition," mused Hermann. How well I understood him. Climbing a seven-thousander in three days . . . not in three weeks! This was just his pigeon – very different from what he went through on Broad Peak. I shared his obvious delight.

We didn't move on for a whole long hour. When we did, we took alternate leads in deep snow. We were unroped now. It was enough to carry the rope with us in the rucksack, Hermann said, so I did not think much about it. A steep pitch with a short ice-cliff called for work with the axe; after that it was easy again. Occasional cracks in the slope spelled avalanche-danger. They pushed us out farther on to the brink of the precipice than we had intended.

Ridge Peak was gradually sinking below and behind us. To the south, the great mountainous banks of cloud were moving very slowly nearer. The sky was calm and of a deep, deep blue. The banner of snow blowing from Ridge Peak seemed to have grown a little. To the north lay a tremendous prospect: all the giants of the Baltoro lined up in a row, a whole chain of peaks 26,000 ft high or only just less. We let our gaze range in wonderment from K2 to Hidden Peak. We took photographs and then moved on again.

How quickly the clouds were coming towards us now! We hoped they wouldn't interfere with our view from the top. We quickened our pace. The last steep pitch began a little way up there, and close above it we could see the tower that was the summit – 1,500 feet at the most – *that* couldn't take so very long.

Presently a little cloud came climbing up the slope below us. It grew larger, enveloping us, enveloping the peak. Without any warning, all hell broke loose. Grey veils of mist scurried across the ridge. Unnatural darkness swamped us. We fought our way forward through clouds of blown snow, bending double to meet the fury of the gale. On the crest of the ridge it flung itself upon us in full blast, snatching at our clothes, trying to claw us from our footing. It was terribly cold and the needles of ice blowing down into our faces hurt savagely. We could only see the next yard or two ahead. We kept on changing the lead, struggling grimly upwards.

It didn't seem possible. I thought of the blue sky such a short time back. It had all been so quick. I had an uncanny feeling – hadn't exactly the same thing happened to the Duke of the Abruzzi, quite close to the summit? Were we going to be robbed, too? Away with such stupid thoughts; it was only a few hundred feet, and we had *got* to do it.

It grew lighter for a moment, as the wind parted the driving clouds. We stood rooted, looking up to where the summit must be. There it was, near enough to touch, looming darkly above us. An instant later the wrack had swallowed it up again.

The storm continued its horrific din. Laboriously we moved up, with a steep, bottomless precipice below us, keeping close to the ridge crest. Everything was white now and we could hardly see.

We were at about 24,000 ft. Only another thousand to the summit-tower. Suddenly Hermann spoke: "We've got to turn back at once, or the wind will cover our tracks up, and then we shall stray out on to the cornices!" He was quite right. We hadn't given a thought to it; and now visibility was almost nil.

We should have to hurry. We turned then and there. Hermann had been leading, so I was in front now. He followed at a safe distance of ten to fifteen yards, which was all that visibility would permit.

Bent double, I felt my way downwards. It was incredible – only 150 ft down, there was no trace to be seen of our upward trail, except the deep holes made by our axes. Very soon there wouldn't be very many of *them*. And still the tempest kept up its infernal din.

I reckoned we must be at about 23,600 ft, and that we must be near the steep avalanche slope which had pushed us so close to the cornices. If only one could see a bit more! I turned and saw Hermann coming after me, keeping the distance unaltered, following in my actual steps. As I moved down, I kept on looking across to the left, trying to see through the mist. All I could see was that it was getting a bit darker overhead and a bit lighter below. That must be the edge of the cornices. It seemed a safe distance away, but in mist distances can be deceptive. Perhaps it would be better to keep a bit to the right, but then I should have to look out for the precipice. It ought to be here by now. Ah, there's another axe-hole . . .

I looked anxiously to the left and then down to the surface at my feet. I was at a loss; it was almost impossible to see anything at all. *Crack!* Something shot through me like a shock. Everything shook, and for a second the surface of the snow seemed to shrink. Blindly, I jumped sideways to the right – an instantaneous reflex action – two, three great strides, and followed the steep slope downwards a little way, shattered by what I had seen at my feet – the rim of the cornice, with little jagged bits breaking away from it. My luck had been in, all right! I had been clean out on the cornice. What would Hermann have to say about that, I wondered? I stopped and turned, but the curve of the slope prevented my seeing over the crest as I looked up. The light was improving a little. Hermann must bob up any moment up there. I still couldn't fathom that extraordinary shaking sensation; had the snow really settled under my weight?

Still no Hermann. "Hermann!" I shouted. "For God's

sake, what's up? Hermann!" I rushed, gasping up the slope.
There it was, the crest . . . and beyond it, smooth snow . . .
and it was empty . . . Hermann . . . You! . . .

Done for . . .

I dragged myself up a little farther. I could see his last
footmarks in the snow, then the jagged edge of the broken
cornice, yawning. Then the black depths.

The broken cornice – that had been the quaking beneath
my feet, then.

I couldn't get a sight of the North Face from anywhere
near. I should have to get down to Ridge Peak for that. As I
went down, the storm gradually abated, and the mists lifted
from time to time. I was utterly stunned. How could that
have happened just behind me? I had the greatest difficulty
in getting up the short rise to Ridge Peak, but even before I
got there it had cleared up. I hurried out to the farthest edge
of the cliffs.

The storm was hunting the clouds high into the heavens.
Above the veils of mist and through them a ridge loomed up
– a tower – a great roof with tremendous banners of blown
snow streaming from it. Chogolisa, the horrible. I could see
the spot where we had turned at about 24,000 ft. Our trail
down the broad snow-field below was crystal clear. Then
that fearsome drop to the north – into the clouds. And
there, even closer to our tracks as they ran straight downwards, the encroaching precipice. And then I could see it all
with stark and terrible clarity. Just at that point, Hermann
had left my tracks at a slight bend, where I was hugging the
rim of the precipice, and gone straight on ahead, only three
or four yards – straight out on to the tottering rim of the
cornice – straight out into nothingness. Of the foot of the
wall I could see nothing. Stupidly, I stared upwards again.

If we had been roped . . .

I looked down along the face, shuddering . . .

No, I should never have been able to hold him there; at
the moment of his fall I myself was too far out on the
overhanging snow.[1]

At last I could see clearly down below, where the broad

1 Though, perhaps, the pull of the rope would have kept him in my tracks, and he
   might never have strayed from the right line of descent. – K.D.

snow-masses of an avalanche fanned out. The crashing cornice had set it off and it had swept the face clean. Hermann was nowhere to be seen. He must have fallen at least 1,000, maybe 2,000 ft and was lying there buried under the piled-up snow. Could he have survived that? There was no answer to my shouts and I had no way of getting down there. I should have to fetch the others and we should have to come from below. That was the only faint possibility. I strained my eyes, searching every cranny, searching for a rucksack, a ski-stick, a dark blob. But there was nothing to be seen – absolutely nothing. Only our tracks – up there . . .

Clouds blotted the mountain out again. I was alone.

Mists and a high wind were sweeping the corniced ridge as I tried to find the way down. At times I could see nothing at all and could only tell from rifts in the snow that I had strayed too far down the slope. After what seemed an age, I found our tent. It was a horror of emptiness. I took the absolute essentials for the descent and went on down. At the Kaberi Saddle there was knee-deep fresh snow, through which only a tiny corner of the marker-pennants showed. I probed with my feet under that smooth expanse of white to find out from which side our ascent-route had come, then went straight on into the whiteness . . . to the next pennant. I wandered vaguely down endless hollows, over crevasses, through fog, then into the darkness of night. For long, indescribable hours of horror – during which I at times had a feeling that Hermann was still with me – I managed, by some miracle, to find my way, onwards, downwards. Then, just before the great ice-falls, my pocket-lamp failed; so I had to bivouac at 18,000 ft. In the first pale light of dawn I made my way down the ice-falls. On and on . . . endlessly on . . . till, 27 hours after Hermann's fall, I tottered into Base Camp.

The search which followed found absolutely nothing.

Once again, the monstrous rubble-covered river of ice lay freed of all human presence. The sun burned down on it with scorching intensity. The snow was rapidly vanishing, melting into the waters of gurgling glacier-streams. Chogolisa's white roof-tree seemed to lift into the very sky itself. The great peaks stood silently all around. Were they, too, mourning? Or was this only the great healing silence which eternally enfolds all living and dying?

The Hard Way

Doug Scott and Dougal Haston

The British climbers Doug Scott (1941–) and Dougal Haston (1940–77) made the first ascent of Everest's difficult South-West face. The expedition, which took place in 1975, was led by Chris Bonington.

Dougal Haston

I hauled onto the proposed site of Camp VI. Straight away my energy and upward urges came rushing back – there ahead in reality was the way we'd been hypothetically tracing for so long with fingers on photographs and making us forget everything else was the fact it looked feasible. There was a steepish-looking rock pitch just ahead, but after it seemed like unbroken snow slopes to the couloir. It looked as if progress was inevitable as long as the others were successful in their carry. Ang Phurba kept muttering about a campsite further up under some rocks, but this looked like wasted effort to us, as the traverse line started logically from where we were at the moment. Diplomatically we told him that we were staying there, it being mainly Doug's and my concern, as we were going to have to occupy the camp, and he started off down, leaving his valuable load. We began digging in spells, without oxygen, but using some to regain strength during the rests.

Mike Thompson, Chris Bonington and Mick Burke arrived one after the other, looking tired, as well they should be. Carrying heavy loads at over 27,000 ft is no easy occupation.

Doug Scott

Theirs had been a magnificent carry, especially Chris, who had now been at Camp V and above for eight days, and also Mick, who was carrying a dead weight of cine equipment. He had been at Camp V for five days, and Pertemba had worked hard practically every day of the expedition carrying heavy loads and encouraging his Sherpas, while Mike Thompson, who had never been above 23,000 ft before, had arrived carrying a heavy sack with apparent ease at 27,300 ft. We sat there talking confidently in the late afternoon. There was a strong bond of companionship as there had been all the way up the Face. One by one they departed for Camp V and they left us with the bare essentials to make this last step to the top of our route and perhaps the summit itself. I yelled our thanks down to Mike as they were sliding back down the rope. He must have known his chances of making a summit bid were slim, yet he replied, "Just you get up, that's all the reward I need." And that's how it had been from start to finish with all members of the team. It had taken the combined effort of forty Sherpas, and sixteen climbers, together with Chris's planning, to get the two of us into this position. We knew how lucky we were being the representatives of such a team and to be given the chance to put the finishing touches to all our efforts. Finally Mick left, having run all the film he had through the cameras. Dougal and I were left alone to dig out a more substantial platform and to erect the two-man summit tent. We were working without oxygen and took frequent rests to recover, but also to look across the Upper Snow Field leading up to the South Summit couloir. After the tent was up, Dougal got inside to prepare the evening meal, whilst I pottered about outside stowing away equipment in a little ice cave and tying empty oxygen bottles around the tent to weight it down. They hung in festoons on either side of the snow arête. Finally I bundled rope and oxygen bottles into our sacks for the following morning and dived into the tent to join Dougal.

Dougal Haston

Inside, we worked on plans for the next day. We had 500 metres of rope for fixing along the traverse and hoped to do that, then come back to [Camp] VI and make our big push the day after.

I was higher on Everest than I'd ever been before, yet thoughts of the summit were still far away in the thinking and hoping process. It had all seemed so near before in 1971 and 1972: euphoric nights at Camps V and VI when progress had seemed good and one tended to skip the difficult parts with visions of oneself standing at the top of the South West Face, then reality shattering the dreams in progressive phases as realization of certain failure burst the bubble. There had been an inevitability about both previous failures, but still carrying a lot of disappointment. Failure you must accept, but that does not make it any easier, especially on a project like the South West Face, where so much thinking, willpower and straight physical effort are necessary to get to the higher points. This time it seemed better. We were above the Rock Band and the ground ahead looked climbable, but I kept a rigid limit on my thoughts, contemplating possible progress along the traverse to the exit couloir, nothing more. If that proved possible then I would allow for further up-type thinking.

Our physical situation felt comfortable. Maybe that is a reflection of the degree of progress that we have made in our adaptation to altitude. Many the story we had read or been told about assault camps on the world's highest peak. No one ever seemed to spend a comfortable night at Camp VI on the South Col route. Their nights seemed to be compounded of sleeplessness, discomfort and thirst. Here there was none of that. The situation was very bearable. We weren't stretched personally, didn't even feel tired or uncomfortable, despite a long day. The stove brewed the hours away – tea, lemon drinks and even a full-scale meal with meat and mashed potatoes. Each was deep into his own thoughts with only one slightly urgent communal reaction as a change of oxygen cylinder went wrong and the gas stove roared into white heat. Order was restored before an explosion, with Doug fixing the leak at the same time as I turned off the stove. Emergency over, we laughed, conjuring visions of the reaction at Camp II as Camp VI exploded like a successfully attacked missile target. It would have been a new reason for failure!

Thereafter sleep claimed its way, and I moved gently into another world of tangled dreams, eased by a gentle flow of oxygen. The night was only disturbed by a light wind rocking our box and a changing of sleeping cylinders. One would need to be a good or very exhausted sleeper to sleep through a cylinder running out. From a gentle warm comfort one suddenly feels cold, uneasy and very awake. Just after midnight and the changeover, we gave up sleeping and started the long task of preparing for the morning's work.

Shortly after first light I moved out into blue and white dawn to continue the upward way, leaving Doug wrapped in all the down in the tent mouth, cameras and belays set up for action. There was a rock step lurking ahead that had seemed reasonably close in the setting afternoon sun of the previous day. Now in the clear first light, a truer perspective was established as I kept on thrusting into the deep-powdered fifty-degree slope, sliding sideways like a crab out of its element reaching for an object that didn't seem to come any closer. One hundred metres of this progress it was, before I could finally fix a piton and eye the rock step. It wasn't long, seven or eight metres, but looked difficult enough. Downward-sloping, steep slabs with a layer of powder. Interesting work. Grade 5 at this height. Much concentration and three more pitons saw a delicate rightwards exit and back, temporarily thankful, into deep snow to finish the rope length and finally give Doug the signal to move.

Doug Scott

I traversed across on his rope and up the difficult rocks to his stance. I led out another 400 ft over much easier ground, parallel with the top of the Rock Band. We gradually armed to the task and began to enjoy our position. After all the months of dreaming, here we were cutting across that Upper Snow Field. Dougal led out the next reel of rope.

Dougal Haston

The conditions and climbing difficulty began to change again. Kicking through with crampons I found there was no ice beneath. Rock slabs only, which have never been renowned for their adherence to front points. A few tentative movements up, down, sideways proved it existed all around. It seemed the time for a tension traverse. But on what? The rock was shattered loose and worse – no cracks. After I had scraped away a large area a small moveable flake appeared. It would have to do. Tapping in the beginnings of an angle, which seemed to be okay to pull on but not for a fall, I started tensioning across to an inviting-looking snow lump. Thoughts flashed through my mind of a similar traverse nine years before, near the top of the Eiger Direct. There it would have been all over with a slip, and suddenly, as I worked it out, things didn't look too good here, if you cared to think in those directions. Not only didn't I care to, I also didn't dare to think of full consequences, and chasing the dangerous thoughts away, I concentrated on tiptoeing progress. Slowly the limit of tension was reached and my feet were on some vaguely adhering snow. This will have to do for the present, were my thoughts as I let go the rope and looked around. A couple of probes with the axe brought nothing but a sense of commitment.

"No man is an island," it is said. I felt very close to a realization of the contrary of this, standing on that semi-secure snow step in the midst of a sea of insecurity. But there was no racing adrenalin, only the cold clinical thought of years of experience. About five metres away the snow appeared to deepen. It would have to be another tension traverse. Long periods of excavation found no cracks. Tugs on the rope and impatient shouting from Doug. Communication at altitude is bad in awkward situations. One has to take off the oxygen mask to shout. Then when one tries to do this, one's throat is so dry and painful that nothing comes out. Hoping that Doug would keep his cool, I carried on, looking for a piton placement. A reasonable-looking crack came to light and two pitons linked up meant the game could go on. This time I felt I could put more bearing weight on the anchor. Just as well. Twice the tension limit

failed, and there was the skidding movement backwards on
the scraping slabs. But a third try and a long reach saw me
in deep good snow, sucking oxygen violently. The way
ahead relented, looking reasonable. My voice gained enough momentum to shout to Doug, and soon he was on his
way. Following is usually monotone – sliding along on
jumars. This one was not so. I could almost see the gleam
in Doug's eyes shining through his layers of glasses as he
pulled out the first tension piton with his fingers.

"Nasty stuff, youth."

I had to agree as he passed on through.

Doug Scott

I continued across further, using up one of our two climbing ropes, before dropping down slightly to belay. We had
probably come too high, for there was easier snow below the
rocks that led right up towards the South Summit couloir.
However, avalanches were still cascading down the mountain, so we climbed up to the rocks in an effort to find good
peg anchors for the fixed ropes. We didn't want to return
the next day to find them hanging over the Rock Band.
Dougal led a short section on easy snow, then all the rope
was run out and we turned back for camp.

I sat in the snow to take photographs and watched the sun
go down over Gaurishankar. What a place to be! I could look
straight down and see Camp II 6,000 ft down. There were
people moving about between tents, obviously preparing to
camp for the night. Mounds of equipment were being covered
with tarpaulins, one or two wandered out to the crevasse
toilet, others stood about in small groups before diving into
their tents for the night. A line of shadow crept up the face to
Camp IV by the time I was back to our tent. I again sorted out
loads and pushed in oxygen bottles for the night, whilst
Dougal melted down snow for the evening meal.

We discovered over the radio that only Lhakpa Dorje had
made the carry to Camp VI that day. He had managed to
bring up vital supplies of oxygen, but unfortunately the
food, cine camera and still film we needed had not arrived.
Anyway they were not essential, so we could still make our
bid for the summit next day. There was also no more rope

in camp, but I think we were both secretly relieved about this. Chris had always insisted that whoever made the first summit bid should lay down as much fixed rope as possible so that if that first attempt failed the effort would not be wasted. This made good sense, but it did take a lot of effort up there and we all longed for the time when we could cut loose from the fixed ropes. It was a perfect evening with no wind at all as we sat looking out of the tent doorway sipping mugs of tea. Finally the sun was gone from our tent and lit up only the upper snows, golden turning red, before all the mountain was in shadow. We zipped up the tent door and built up quite a fug of warm air heating up water for corned beef hash.

Dougal Haston
Five hundred metres of committing ground was a good day's work on any point of the mountain. The fact that it was all above 27,000 ft made our performance level high and, more to the point, we hadn't exhausted ourselves in doing it. This was crucial because deterioration is rapid at such altitudes. Over tea we discussed what to take next day. I still reckoned deep down on the possibility of a bivouac. Doug seemed reluctant to admit to the straight fact, but didn't disagree when I mentioned packing a tent sac and stove. The packs weren't going to be light. Two oxygen cylinders each would be needed for the undoubtedly long day, plus three fifty-metre ropes, also various pitons and karabiners. Even if a bivouac was contemplated we couldn't pack a sleeping bag. This would have been pushing weight too much. The bivouac idea was only for an emergency and we would have hastened that emergency by slowing ourselves down through too much weight – so we tried to avoid the possibility by going as lightly as possible. The only extra I allowed myself was a pair of down socks, reckoning they could be invaluable for warming very cold or even frostbitten feet and hands. There was no sense of drama that evening. Not even any unusual conversation. We radioed down and told those at Camp II what we were doing, ate the rest of our food and fell asleep.

Doug Scott

About one in the morning we awoke to a rising wind. It was buffeting the tent, shaking it about and pelting it with spindrift, snow and ice chips. I lay there wondering what the morning would bring, for if the wind increased in violence we should surely not be able to move. At about 2:30 we began slowly to wind ourselves up for the climb. We put a brew on and heated up the remains of the corned beef hash for breakfast. The wind speed was decreasing slightly as we put on our frozen boots and zipped up our suits. Dougal chose his down-filled suit, whilst I took only my windproofs, hoping to move faster and easier without the restriction of tightly packed feathers around my legs. I had never got round to sorting out a down-filled suit that fitted me properly.

Because of the intense cold it was essential to put on crampons, harnesses, even the rucksack and oxygen system in the warmth of the tent. Just after 3:30 we emerged to get straight on to the ropes and away to the end. It was a blustery morning, difficult in the dark and miserable in the cold. It was one of those mornings when you keep going because he does and he, no doubt, because you do. By the time we had passed the end of the fixed ropes the sun popped up from behind the South Summit and we awoke to the new day. It was exhilarating to part company with our safety line, for that is after all what fixed ropes are. They facilitate troop movements, but at the same time they do detract from the adventure of the climb. Now at last we were committed and it felt good to be out on our own.

Dougal Haston

There's something surrealistic about being alone high on Everest at this hour. No end to the strange beauty of the experience. Alone, enclosed in a mask with the harsh rattle of your breathing echoing in your ears. Already far in the west behind Cho Oyu a few pale strands of the day and ahead and all around a deep midnight blue with the South Summit sharply, whitely, defined in my line of vision and the always predawn wind picking up stray runners of spindrift and swirling them gently, but not malignantly, around me. Movement was relaxed and easy. As I passed by yesterday's tension points only a brief flash of them came into memory. They were stored for future remembrances, but the today mind was geared for more to come. Not geared with any sense of nervousness or foreboding, just happily relaxed, waiting – anticipating. Signs of life on the rope behind indicated that Doug was following apace and I waited at yesterday's abandoned oxygen cylinders as he came up with the sun, almost haloed in silhouette, uncountable peaks as his background. But no saint this.

"All right, youth?" in a flat Nottingham accent.

"Yeah, yourself?"

A nod and the appearance of a camera for sunrise pictures answered this question, so I tied on the rope and started breaking new ground. The entrance to the couloir wasn't particularly good, but there again it was not outstandingly bad by Himalayan standards, merely knee-deep powder snow with the occasional make-you-think hard patch where there was no snow base on the rock. On the last part before entering the couloir proper there was a longish section of this where we just climbed together relying on each other's ability, rope trailing in between, there being no belays to speak of.

The rope length before the rock step changed into beautiful, hard front-pointing snow ice but the pleasure suddenly seemed to diminish. Leading, my progress started to get slower. By now the signs were well known. I knew it wasn't me. One just doesn't degenerate so quickly. Oxygen again. It seemed early for a cylinder to run out. Forcing it, I reached a stance beneath the rock step. Rucksack off. Check cylinder gauge first. Still plenty left. That's got to be bad. It must be the system. Doug comes up. We both start investigating. Over an hour we played with it. No avail. Strangely enough I felt quite calm and resigned about everything. I say strangely because if the system had proved irrepairable then our summit chance would have been ruined. There was only a quiet cloud of disappointment creeping over our heads. Doug decided to try extreme unction. "Let's take it apart piece by piece, kid. There's nothing to lose." I merely nodded as he started prising apart the jubilee clip which held the tube onto the mouth-piece. At last something positive – a lump of ice was securely blocked in the junction. Carving it out with a knife, we tentatively stuck the two points together again, then shut off the flow so we could register oxygen being used. A couple of hard sucks on the mask – that was it. I could breathe freely again.

Doug started out on the rock step, leaving me contemplating the escape we'd just had. I was still thinking very calmly about it, but could just about start to imagine what my feelings of disgust would have been like down below if we'd been turned back by mechanical failure. Self-failure you have to accept, bitter though it can be. Defeat by bad weather also, but to be turned back by failure of a humanly constructed system would have left a mental scar. But now it was upward thinking again. Idly, but carefully, I watched Doug. He was climbing well. Slowly, relaxed, putting in the odd piton for protection. Only his strange masked and hump-backed appearance gave any indication that he was climbing hard rock at 28,000 ft.

Doug Scott
At first I worked my way across from Dougal's stance easily in deep soft snow, but then it steepened and thinned out until it was all a veneer covering the yellow amorphous rock underneath. I went up quite steeply for thirty feet, hoping the front points of my crampons were dug well into the sandy rock underneath the snow. I managed to get in three pegs in a cluster, hoping that one of them might hold, should I fall off. However, the next thirty feet were less steep and the snow lay thicker, which was fortunate seeing as I had run out of oxygen. I reached a stance about a hundred feet above Dougal, and with heaving lungs, I started to anchor off the rope. I pounded in the last of our rock pegs and yelled down to Dougal to come up. Whilst he was jumaring up the rope I took photographs and changed over to my remaining full bottle of oxygen. I left the empty bottle tied on the pegs.

We were now into the South Summit couloir and a way seemed clear to the top of the South West Face. We led another rope length each and stopped for a chat about the route. Dougal's sporting instincts came to the fore – he fancied a direct gully straight up to the Hillary Step. I wasn't keen on account of the soft snow, so he shrugged his shoulders and continued off towards the South Summit. I don't know whether the direct way would have been any less strenuous, but from now on the route to the South Summit became increasingly difficult.

Dougal Haston

The South West Face wasn't going to relax its opposition one little bit. That became very evident as I ploughed into the first rope length above the rock step. I had met many bad types of snow conditions in eighteen years of climbing. Chris and I had once been shoulder-deep retreating from a winter attempt on a new line on the North Face of the Grandes Jorasses. The snow in the couloir wasn't that deep, but it seemed much worse to handle. In the Alps we had been retreating, but now we were trying to make progress. Progress? The word seemed almost laughable as I moved more and more slowly. A first step and in up to the waist. Attempts to move upward only resulted in a deeper sinking motion. Time for new techniques: steps up, sink in, then start clearing away the slope in front like some breast-stroking snow plough and eventually you pack enough together to be able to move a little further and sink in only to your knees. Two work-loaded rope lengths like this brought us to the choice of going leftwards on the more direct line I had suggested to Doug in an earlier moment of somewhat undisciplined thinking. By now my head was in control again and I scarcely gave it a glance, thinking that at the current rate of progress we'd be lucky to make even the South Summit.

It seemed that conditions would have to improve but they didn't. The slope steepened to sixty degrees and I swung rightwards, heading for a rock step in an attempt to get out of this treadmill of nature. No relief for us. The snow stayed the same, but not only was it steeper, we were now on open wind-blown slopes and there was a hard breakable crust. Classic wind slab avalanche conditions.

In some kind of maniacal cold anger I ploughed on. There was no point in stopping for belays. There weren't any possibilities. I had a rhythm, so kept the evil stroking upwards with Doug tight on my heels. Two feet in a hole, I'd bang the slope to shatter the crust, push away the debris, move up, sink in. Thigh. Sweep away. Knees. Gain a metre. Then repeat the process. It was useful having Doug right behind, as sometimes, when it was particularly difficult to make progress, he was able to stick two hands in my back to stop me sliding backwards. Hours were flashing like minutes, but it was still upward gain.

Doug Scott
I took over the awful work just as it was beginning to ease off. I clambered over some rocks poking out of the snow and noticed that there was a cave between the rocks and the névé ice – a good bivvy for later perhaps. Just before the South Summit I rested whilst Dougal came up. I continued round the South Summit rock whilst Dougal got his breath. I was crawling on all fours with the wind blowing up spindrift snow all around. I collapsed into a belay position just below the frontier ridge and took in the rope as Dougal came up my tracks. After a few minutes' rest we both stood up and climbed onto the ridge, and there before us was Tibet.

After all those months spent in the Western Cwm over this and two other expeditions now at last we could look out of the Cwm to the world beyond – the rolling brown lands of Tibet in the north and north east, to Kangchenjunga and just below us Makalu and Chomo Lonzo. Neither of us said much, we just stood there absorbed in the scene.

Dougal Haston
The wind was going round the South Summit like a mad maypole. The Face was finished, successfully climbed but there was no calm to give much thought to rejoicing. It should have been a moment for elation but wasn't. Certainly we'd climbed the Face but neither of us wanted to stop there. The summit was beckoning.

Often in the Alps it seems fine to complete one's route and not go to the summit, but in the Himalayas it's somewhat different. An expedition is not regarded as being totally successful unless the top is reached. Everything was known to us about the way ahead. This was the South East ridge, the original Hillary/Tenzing route of 1953. It was reckoned to be mainly snow, without too much technical difficulty. But snow on the ridge similar to the snow in the couloir would provide a greater obstacle to progress than any technical difficulties. There were dilemmas hanging around and question marks on all plans.

My head was considering sitting in the tent sac until sunset or later, then climbing the ridge when it would be, theoretically, frozen hard. Doug saw the logic of this thinking but obviously wasn't too happy about it. No other suggestions were forthcoming from his direction, however, so I got into the tent sac, got the stove going to give our thinking power a boost with some hot water. Doug began scooping a shallow snow cave in the side of the cornice, showing that he hadn't totally rejected the idea. The hot water passing over our raw, damaged throat linings brought our slide into lethargic pessimism to a sharp halt.

Swinging his pack onto his back Doug croaked, "Look after the rope. I'm going to at least try a rope length to sample conditions. If it's too bad we'll bivouac. If not we carry on as far as possible."

I couldn't find any fault with this reasoning, so grabbed the rope as he disappeared back into Nepal. The way it was going quickly through my hands augured well. Reaching the end Doug gave a "come on" signal. Following quickly, I realized that there were now summit possibilities in the wind. Conditions were by no means excellent, but relative to those in the couloir they merited the title reasonable. There was no need to say anything as I reached Doug. He just stepped aside, changed the rope around and I continued. Savage, wonderful country. On the left the South-West Face dropped away steeply, to the right wild curving cornices pointed the way to Tibet. Much care was needed, but there was a certain elation in our movements. The Hillary Step[1] appeared, unlike any photograph we had

1 A vertical step of about eighty feet which is the final serious obstacle to the summit of Everest.

seen. No rock step this year, just a break in the continuity of the snow ridge. Seventy degrees of steepness and eighty feet of length. It was my turn to explore again. Conditions reverted to bad, but by now I'd become so inured to the technique that even the extra ten degrees didn't present too much problem.

Doug Scott
As I belayed Dougal up the Hillary Step it gradually dawned upon me that we were going to reach the summit of Big E. I took another photograph of Dougal and wound on the film to find that it was finished. I didn't think I had any more film in my rucksack, for I had left film and spare gloves with the bivvy sheet and stove at the South Summit. I took off my oxygen mask and rucksack and put them on the ridge in front of me. I was seated astride it, one leg in Nepal, the other in Tibet. I hoped Dougal's steps would hold, for I could think of no other place to put his rope than between my teeth as I rummaged around in my sack. I found a cassette of colour film, that had somehow got left behind several days before. The cold was intense and the brittle film kept breaking off. The wind was strong and blew the snow Dougal was sending down the Nepalese side right back into the air and over into Tibet. I fitted the film into the camera and followed him up. This was the place where Ed Hillary had chimneyed his way up the crevasse between the rock and the ice. Now with all the monsoon snow on the mountain it was well banked up, but with snow the consistency of sugar it looked decidedly difficult.

A wide whaleback ridge ran up the last 300 yards. It was just a matter of trial-breaking. Sometimes the crust would hold for a few steps and then suddenly we would be stumbling around as it broke through to our knees. All the way along we were fully aware of the enormous monsoon cornices, overhanging the 10,000 ft East Face of Everest. We therefore kept well to the left.

It was whilst trail-breaking on this last section that I noticed my mind seemed to be operating in two parts, one external to my head. It warned me somewhere over my left shoulder about not going too far right in the area of the cornice, and it would urge me to keep well to the left. Whenever I stumbled through the crust it suggested that I slow down and pick my way through more carefully. In general it seemed to give me confidence and seemed such a natural phenomenon that I hardly gave it a second thought at the time. Dougal took over the trail-breaking and headed up the final slope to the top – and a red flag flying there. The snow improved and he slackened his pace to let me come alongside. We then walked up side by side the last few paces to the top, arriving there together.

All the world lay before us. That summit was everything and more that a summit should be. My usually reticent partner became expansive, his face broke out into a broad happy smile and we stood there hugging each other and thumping each other's backs. The implications of reaching the top of the highest mountain in the world surely had some bearings on our feelings, I'm sure they did on mine, but I can't say that it was that strong. I can't say either that I felt any relief that the struggle was over. In fact, in some ways it seemed a shame that it was, for we had been fully programmed and now we had to switch off and go back into reverse. But not yet, for the view was so staggering, the disappearing sun so full of colour that the setting held us in awe. I was absorbed by the brown hills of Tibet. They only looked like hills from our lofty summit. They were really high mountains, some of them 24,000 ft high, but with hardly any snow to indicate their importance. I could see silver threads of rivers meandering down between them, flowing north and west to bigger rivers which might have included the Tsangpo. Towards the east, Kangchenjunga caught the setting sun, although around to the south clouds boiled down in the Nepalese valleys and far down behind a vast front of black cloud was advancing towards us from the plains of India. It flickered lightning ominously. There was no rush, though, for it would be a long time coming over Everest – time to pick out the north side route – the Rongphu Glacier, the East Rongphu Glacier and Changtse in between. There was the North Col, and the place where, in 1924, Odell, who had climbed to 28,000 feet on the North Face, was standing when he last saw Mallory and Irvine climbing up toward the summit of Everest. Wonder if they made it? Their route was hidden by the convex slope – no sign of them, edge out a bit further – no nothing. Not with all the monsoon snow, my external mind pointed out.

The only sign of anyone was the flag; it was some time before I got round to looking at it. It was an unwelcome intrusion and there had been more to do than look at manmade objects. Still, you couldn't help but look at it, seeing as how it was a tripod and pole nearly five feet high with a rosary of red ribbons attached to the top. Take a photograph. Ah, yes! Dougal ought to get some of me. He hadn't taken a single photograph on the whole trip. "Here you are, youth. Take a snap for my mother." I passed him my camera. "Better take another one, your glove's in front of the lens. Now a black and white one." He's never been keen on photography, but he obliged.

Dougal Haston
We were sampling a unique moment in our lives. Down and over into the brown plains of Tibet a purple shadow of Everest was projected for what must have been something like 200 miles. On these north and east sides there was a sense of wildness and remoteness, almost untouchability. Miraculous events seemed to be taking place in the region of the sun. One moment it seemed to dip behind a cloud layer lying a little above the horizon. End Game – thought we. But then the cloud dropped faster than the sun and out it came again. Three times in all. I began to feel like Saul on the road to Tarsus. More materially, right in front of me was an aluminum survey pole with a strip of red canvas attached. The Japanese ladies in the spring hadn't mentioned leaving or seeing anything. Puzzlement for a moment. Then the only answer. There had been a Chinese ascent of the North East Ridge claimed, just after the Japanese ascent. Some doubt, however, had been cast on the validity of this, due to the summit pictures lacking the detail associated with previous summit shots. It was good to have the ultimate proof in front of us. Having to play the doubt game in climbing is never a pleasant experience.

Slowly creeping into the euphoria came one very insistent thought as the sun finally won its race with the clouds and slid over the edge. The thought? Well; we were after all on the top of the world, but it was still a long way back to Camp VI and it was going to be dark very soon and then what would we do? We knew we could get back to the South Summit in the half light. On the previous nights there had been a very bright moon, and it seemed reasonable to assume we could retrace our steps down the Face if this came out. If it didn't, as a last resort we could bivouac. That, after all, was the reason for bringing the tent sac. I'd always reckoned a bivouac possible at such altitude, but that doesn't mean to say I looked upon the project with a great degree of enthusiasm. We finally turned our backs to the summit and set off down.

Our tracks were already freezing up, making the going reasonable. An abseil got rid of the Hillary Step with the rope left in place. Moving together we were soon back at our little cave. Much cloud activity didn't bode well for the appearance of a moon. The oxygen cylinders dribbled out their last drops of usefulness and became mere burdens. Standing vaguely waiting for some light to happen it was good to take off the tanks and mask. Lighter feeling but not lighter-headed. Slowly, as it clouded over, the choices were gradually cut down. We decided to have a look at the possibility of a descent in the dark, knowing the up-trail to be deep and maybe now frozen, but a tentative fifty-foot grope on the South-West Face side of the ridge into the strong night wind with finger and toes going solid finally slammed all the alternative choices to a bivouac out of mind. Dropping back to the sheltered side I told Doug the news. There was nothing really to say. He started enlarging the hole.

Doug Scott

Dougal melted snow on the stove once again whilst I continued digging into the hillside. After we had had a few sips of warm water, Dougal joined me and we quickly enlarged the snow cave, digging away with our ice-axes, pushing the loose snow out through the entrance. By nine o'clock it was big enough to lie down in; we pushed out more snow against the entrance and reduced it to a narrow slit. We were now out of the wind, which was fortunate, as already our oxygen bottles were empty, or our sets had refused to function. The little stove, too, was soon used up. So there we lay on top of our rucksacks and the bivvy sheet, wishing perhaps we had given more thought to the possibility of bivouacking, for we had no food and no sleeping bags. I was wearing only the clothes that I had climbed up in, a silk vest, a wool jumper, a nylon pile suit and my wind suit. I don't think we were ever worried about surviving, for we had read of other climbers who had spent the night out on Everest without much gear, although lower down. However, they had all subsequently had some fingers and toes cut off. What worried us was the quality of survival, and we brought all the strength of our dulled listless minds to bear upon that. I shivered uncontrollably and took off my gloves, boots and socks to rub life back into my extremities for hours at a time. We were so wrapped up in our own personal miseries that we hardly noticed each other, though at one point Dougal unzipped the front of his duvet suit and kindly allowed me to put my bare left foot under his right armpit and my other at his crotch, which seemed to help. Without oxygen there didn't seem to be any internal heat being created, so I mostly sat and rubbed and rubbed my fingers and toes. This was no time for sleep. It needed the utmost vigilance to concentrate on survival, keeping my boots upright out of the snow, keeping the snow off my bare hands and feet, warming my socks against my stomach, keeping my head from brushing snow off the roof of the cave. The temperature was probably – thirty degrees Centigrade. It was so cold that at first when I left a sock on my rucksack the foot of the sock went as stiff as a board. Most of the night I dug away at the cave just to keep warm, hacking away at the back with the ice-axe into the hard snow and pushing it out through the doorway. By the dawn it was to be big enough to sleep five people lying down!

Our minds started to wander with the stress and the lack of sleep and oxygen. Dougal quite clearly spoke out to Dave Clarke. He had quite a long and involved conversation with him. I found myself talking to my feet. I personalized them to such an extent that they were two separate beings needing help. The left one was very slow to warm up, and after conversations with the right one, we decided I had better concentrate on rubbing it hard. And all the time my external mind was putting its spoke in as well.

Dougal Haston
I was locked in suffering silence except for the occasional quiet conversation with Dave Clarke. Hallucination or dream? It seemed comforting and occasionally directed my mind away from the cold. That stopped, and then it was a retreat so far into silence that I seemed to be going to sleep. Shaking awake, I decided to stay this way. We'd heard too many tales of people in survival situations falling asleep and not waking up. It seemed as if we'd both come to this conclusion and Doug's incoherent speech served to keep both awake. There was no escaping the cold. Every position was tried. Holding together, feet in each other's armpits, rubbing, moving around the hole constantly, exercising arms. Just no way to catch a vestige of warmth. But during all this the hours were passing. I don't think anything we did or said that night was very rational or planned. We were suffering from lack of oxygen, cold, and tiredness but we had a terrible will to get through the night; all our survival instincts came right up front. These and our wills saw the night to a successful end.

First light came, and we were able to start the process of preparing for downward movement. Checks showed an ability to stand up and move. Extremities had slight numbness, but no frostbite. Kidney pains were locking us in an almost bent-in-two position. Boots were difficult to get on. I gave up my frozen inner boots and used downfilled boots as a replacement. The sun came up, but with no hope of getting any warmth to our bodies. Movement was the only way, and soon we were across the cornice, saying adieu to Tibet and starting off back down the Face. The warmth of movement was almost orgasmic in its intensity as the blood started recirculating. Aware of the possibilities of lack-of-oxygen hallucinations and their potentially dire effects, we kept a wary eye on each other as we belayed down the first few pitches.

Doug Scott

We had not slept or eaten for nearly thirty hours, we had actually spent the night out in China, and we had done it at 28,700 ft without oxygen. Eventually we made the fixed rope and at 9 a.m. fell into our sleeping bags at Camp VI. I put the stove on and looked around for something to eat and came across the radio. We had been so absorbed in surviving the night and the descent that at times it had all seemed so much like a dream, just the two of us and no one else in the world to share the cold swirling snow. The radio brought us back to reality; it crackled into life. Answering voices – Chris concerned, relieved – happy with the success. Put on a good voice, I thought, don't want to sound slurred, although I felt it. "No, I don't think we are frostbitten," I said, for by then our fingers and toes were tingling.

The quality of survival had been good.

Attack on Kangchenjunga

F.S. Smythe

Frank Smythe was a British mountaineer and the first to climb the Himalayan peak of Kalmet. He was a member of three Everest expeditions (1933, 1936 and 1938) and during the Second World War led the Commando Mountain Warfare School. Here Smythe (1900–49) recalls his part in the dogged German ascent of the avalanche-stricken Kangchenjunga peak of the Sikkim Himalaya in 1930.

On May 10, the day after the accident, Professor Dyhrenfurth, Kurz and Dr Richter arrived from Base Camp, and a conference was held on the situation. "Conference" is perhaps a little misleading. It is a word conjuring up a picture of frock-coated gentlemen seated round a long mahogany table, the highly polished surface of which reflects waistcoats ornamented with gold watch-chains, and earnest countenances on which responsibility and a heavy lunch sit heavily. In the present instance I must ask the reader to imagine the sombre interior of the large porters' tent, the thick canvas of which reduces the light within to a faint depressing green, whilst a pungent reek of smoke struggles with a faint, yet perceptible odour of unwashed bodies that have lain there during the previous night. In the middle a heterogeneous collection of packing cases do duty as a table. Seated on other packing cases are a number of unsavoury looking ragamuffins with unkempt hair, frowsy beards, cracked sun-scorched countenances, and eyes bleared by the snow glare.

The first suggestion made by those who had remained at
the Base Camp was that the attack on the ice wall should be
renewed, but this was very properly rejected by all those
who had shared in the attack. The sole remaining alternative was to attempt the North-West Ridge which rises
from the western tributary of the Kangchenjunga Glacier.
This ridge ends in a snow and ice terrace beneath the
Kangbachen summit, 25,782 ft, of Kangchenjunga. Even
supposing the terrace to be reached, however, the most we
could hope for was to ascend the Kangbachen summit, as
there was no possibility of traversing to the highest summit,
as both distance and difficulty were too great. Personally, I
must confess to a longing to flee from the mountain altogether, and be able to lie in a sleeping bag at nights and
sleep undisturbed by the fear of annihilation from ice
avalanches. I suggested, therefore, that we should retire,
cross the Jonsong La, and attempt the Jonsong Peak, 24,344
ft high. This idea met with no support, and it was decided
to attempt the North-West Ridge. Should we fail, as it
seemed certain we must do, judging from appearance, at all
events we could ascend the Western Tributary Glacier,
explore its head, and possibly climb the Ramthang Peak.

In order to do this, it was decided to move Camp I across
the glacier to the foot of the rocky spur separating the
Western Tributary Glacier from the glacier falling between
the Wedge Peak and the Ramthang Peak. This new site
would have the advantage of being considerably safer than
the present one, for it was by no means certain that we were
safe in the event of an exceptionally large ice avalanche
falling from Kangchenjunga or the Twins. This uncertainty was emphasized the same afternoon in a startling
fashion.

We were aroused from an after-lunch siesta by the
thunder-clap of a great avalanche. We issued from our
tents in alarm. Thousands of feet above us on the face of
Kangchenjunga masses of hanging glacier were collapsing.
Sweeping the precipices with appalling violence, the avalanche crashed down to the glacier, and roared straight
across at us.

Huge clouds of snow were raised by the wind blast from

the surface of the glacier, and came rushing down upon the camp. They concealed the falling ice, and it was hard to tell whether the camp was safe or not. My own inclination was to run for it, and I was about to bolt precipitately when I saw Duval calmly turning the handle of his cine camera with that sang-froid peculiar to his calling, the tradition of which demands that the handle of a cine camera shall be turned in the face of charging elephants, and at shipwrecks, fires, explosions, earthquakes and other catastrophies. Fired by his example, I pulled out my own folding camera and took a hurried snap. The avalanche resembled the white clouds of some new and deadly form of gas attack. The God of Kangchenjunga is evidently well up in the technique of modern warfare. The roar of the avalanche subsided. We knew that we were safe from ice debris, but the clouds of snow continued to pour down the glacier towards the camp with extraordinary velocity. The next moment a wind blast struck the camp, and a blizzard of snow sent us scuttling into shelter.

The blizzard lasted some minutes, and when it had cleared the upper part of the glacier was seen to be covered in nearly an inch of wind-blown snow. The actual ice debris of the avalanche had stopped well short of the camp, but it had swept quite half a mile down the glacier. This was not the only avalanche; other lesser ones fell, but none of such terrifying dimensions. It was obvious, however, that it was a mere question of volume and momentum whether or not the camp was to be swept away by a future avalanche. If it was a rest day for tired bodies, it was scarcely so for nerve-racked minds.

It was a simple matter moving camp the next day, and the new site on the other side of the glacier was safer than any we had yet discovered. We had not been able to bring down all our equipment from Camp II, so some porters under the charge of Kurz went up to fetch it. Schneider and Duvanel, meanwhile, descended to the Base Camp, the former in order to make a new track up the glacier to our new camp, the latter to develop some cine film. I was left in charge of the evacuation of the old camp, and took the opportunity of donning a pair of skis, and making short runs on the glacier.

The snow was excellent and similar to late spring Alpine snow.

The new Camp I was pitched in a fine situation. There was a delightful view northwards up the moraine-stacked Jonsong Glacier winding sinuously up towards the little notch of the Jonsong La. The background was dominated by the rocky mass of the Jonsong Peak. Farther to the east, rose a ridge of icy peaks running northwards from Kangchenjunga and the Twins, from which the Tent Peak, 24,089 ft, rose head and shoulders above everything else. It is as aptly named as the Wedge Peak, for its horizontal summit ridge with its small points at either end resembles a tent, the ridge of which sags between its supporting poles.

Some useful stores arrived from the Base Camp that day, among them being synthetic rubber ground-sheets for the tents. Though light and spongy, and weighing but a pound or so each, the difference they made to our comfort was amazing, and we were able to sleep then and afterwards far more warmly and comfortably than we would have done otherwise, insulated as we were from the snow. There is no question that they are far superior to any ground-sheet, and form an item of equipment that no future Himalayan expedition can afford to leave out, for they induce the sleep which is so essential if climbers are to keep fit.

Relieved by the thought that we were tolerably safe from avalanches, we slept well that night. It would have been wise to have started early the next morning while the snow was still hard from the overnight frost, but we did not get away until the sun had thawed its crust sufficiently to let it break beneath our weight. The obvious route up the Western Tributary Glacier was a trough between the glacier and the rock ridge forming its northern containing wall. The trough was snow-filled for most of its distance, except for one section where a scree slope interposed. These troughs, which form such a convenient line of least resistance up the glaciers of this district are perhaps the only thing vouchsafed by Kangchenjunga which seems to have been intended for the benefit of the long-suffering mountaineer.

Wieland and I, with some porters, were the first to set off. Hoerlin, Kurz, and some more porters were to follow, but at the last moment Kurz, who was again not feeling well, decided to return to the Base Camp.

The snow in the trough was in the worst possible condition. We floundered waist-deep into holes between concealed snow-covered boulders, and wallowed in hollows where the snow was soft and watery. An hour passed; we had made but little progress. I suggested to Wieland that we should leave the trough in favour of the ice-fall of the glacier. In making this suggestion I was actuated by the fact that at one place the trough seemed likely to be swept by falling stones from the cliffs above. Hoerlin, was of a different mind; he would stick to the trough. As things transpired, he was right; the danger was more apparent than real.

Ascending the ice-fall was fatiguing work on account of the soft snow. Snow-shoes eased the porters' labours to some extent, but there were not enough pairs to go round. Considering how broken was the ice, it was remarkable how few crevasses there were, but these few were dangerous ones, subtly concealed. We toiled up and down over hummocks, or threaded our way between pinnacles. The devil of doubt began to gnaw at our hearts; would we be able to get through the ice-fall? The sun beat down upon us mercilessly, and glacier lassitude sapped the strength of sahib and porter alike. At last we saw a sort of corridor leading from the ice-fall into the upper part of the trough. We could see that the trough was perfectly safe, but had it been dangerous, we should still have preferred it to the sweltering gullies and hollows of the ice-fall, for glacier lassitude tends to undermine the judgment and warp the conscience of the mountaineer.

A crevasse barred the way. We stepped gingerly on to a fragile snow bridge. Icicles were dislodged and went tinkling down into the green depths with a noise like the banging together of small chandeliers. The corridor stretched ahead; its smooth, snow floor looked innocuous, but Wieland suddenly disappeared up to his waist in a concealed crevasse: it was merely one of Kangchenjunga's little jokes.

At the top of the trough, where it debouches on to the

glacier, above the worst of the ice-fall, there is a short section liable to be swept by ice avalanches from a hanging glacier forming the edge of a snow plateau on the Ramthang Peak. While still within the danger area we were startled by a sudden crash, but all that came down were a few boulders and blocks of ice.

The porters were by now very tired, and they begged us to camp as soon as possible. We promised to do so as soon as we were out of range of ice avalanches. The sun was declining, and evening mists gathering around us as we reached the smooth slopes above the ice-fall, where stretched Hoerlin's straggling track, man's first score on these snow-fields. Here we decided to camp, while Wieland went on with ski to bring down Hoerlin, who had camped some distance farther up the glacier.

The evening was strangely still save for an undercurrent of sound, as though the goblins and witches who haunt the cliffs of Kangchenjunga above were murmuring at our coming. As usual, it was the wind. An upward glance disclosed the snow eddying and swirling from the polished ice cliffs defending the snowy terraces. The sun set calmly. Barely had its last rays faded when they were replaced by silver moon sheen behind the North Ridge of Kangchenjunga. The snow blown off the ridge by the wind was illumined from behind, and Kangchenjunga took to itself a glowing aureole of light. Imperceptibly the upper snowslopes were resolved from the darkness; ghostlike, unreal, they shimmered far above the world. Mindless of the cold, we stood outside our tents entranced by the glorious spectacle. At long last the laggardly moon peered over the ridge in a shy, self-deprecating sort of way. It seemed to wither and shrivel as it mounted into the frosty sky and its radiance, at first soft and wan, became a hard, cold electric blue. Details stood forth as clearly as in daylight. Only the shadows were black, and in these lurked the darkness of a pit.

The cold gripped us. We crawled into our tents, and with numbed fingers laced-to the flaps. As Sir Leslie Stephen wrote: "Bodily fatigue and an appreciation of natural scenery are simply incompatible." He might have added cold and discomfort.

The sun reached us early the next morning, and we were off betimes. Our first business was to move camp farther up the glacier to a site that would form a convenient upper base for operations against the North-West Ridge. As we marched up the glacier we were able to examine the latter. First impressions are not always accurate and it is never easy to assess the difficulties of a mountainside or ridge at their true worth. As that great mountaineer, Captain J. P. Farrar used to remark: "You can never tell what rocks are like until you have rubbed your nose against them." Yet, even bearing these things in mind, no ridge I have examined affected me with the same feeling of utter and complete hopelessness as that of the North-West Ridge of Kangchenjunga. Picture a ridge rising 4,000 ft. Thin, trim and whittle down its edges until they are as keen as a Gurkha's *kukri*; then hack deep gaps into these edges and perch rocky towers hundreds of feet high on them. Armour every smooth bit with ice, and mask every ledge with snow, and you will perhaps obtain a faint glimmering of an idea of the North-West Ridge of Kangchenjunga. The ridge attempted by the Munich party is formidable, but it cannot compare to the North-West Ridge. Ice pinnacles alone had to be surmounted on the former; spiky rock pinnacles bar the way on the latter, and between these are some of those extraordinary ice ridges peculiar to the Himalayas. In appearance and sensationalism they are comparable to those on the Wedge Peak. There are the same tottering masses, the same biscuit-like flakes through which the sun gleams, the same extravagant forms, hacked and torn by the wind, lurching and tottering at the behest of gravity, and the same ice flutings to emphasize by their graceful lines the appalling steepness of the slopes they decorate. If we had been forced to attack the ridge from its base, I think we would have relinquished any idea of attempting it at the outset, for the lowest rock towers are hopeless from a climbing point of view. It looked possible, however, to gain the crest of the ridge above these initial pinnacles, by a steep snow-filled couloir about 600 ft high, leading upwards from the glacier to one of the gaps in the crest of the ridge.

Camp was pitched on the glacier, and leaving the porters

to make it comfortable we set off to climb the couloir. The lower half was simple; then the angle steepened. It was not difficult, but care had to be taken that the footsteps kicked in the floury snow that masked rock slabs and ice did not collapse. The last hundred feet was very steep. The angle must have exceeded sixty degrees, but we were comforted by the thought that we could fix a rope to facilitate the descent. A small cornice leaned over the summit. The leader, Hoerlin, hacked and flogged it down, and squirmed through and over to the gap, Wieland and I following one by one. The ascent had taken only forty-five minutes, indicating that we had become well acclimatized to altitude.

My first impression was probably somewhat similar to that experienced by a house-breaker, not a burglar, but one of those phlegmatic gentlemen who stands on the dizzy edges of aged and tottering walls knocking bricks off into space with a pick-axe. But surely no house-breaker has ever stood on top of such an unstable wall as we found ourselves on. A modern £25 down and balance in rent villa could scarcely be more "jerrybuilt" than the place on which we stood. On either side of us the rocks were piled in loose masses needing but a touch to send them crashing down on either side of the ridge below us. On the opposite side of the ridge to that which we had ascended loose yellowish pre-cipices dropped to the head of the Ramthang Glacier. From our gap it appeared possible to descend to the glacier down another steep gully, scarred with falling debris. Such a descent would, however, involve unavoidable dangers. And far above this scene of perpetual decay rose the great ice slopes and ice walls of Kangchenjunga.

Is there any hope of ascending Kangchenjunga from the Ramthang Glacier? The answer must be, no, unless the climber is prepared to take his life, *and* the lives of his porters in his hand. Like the face above the Kangchenjunga Glacier, that above the Ramthang Glacier is defended by enormous walls of ice running across the mountainside. At one point only is there any hope of climbing the *lowest* of these ice walls, and this point is also liable to be swept at any moment by ice avalanches from another and tottering ice wall above. Kang-chenjunga was not built for the mountaineer.

Leaving rucksacks and spare rope, we commenced to climb along the unstable ridge. Almost immediately, we were forced off the crest to avoid a decrepit rocky tower. A traverse had to be made on the southern side of the ridge over steep, loose rocks, here and there treacherously covered in snow. It was a place not so much difficult as dangerous. There was not a reliable rock round which a rope could be placed to secure the party, and had a slip occurred, it would in all probability have been attended by the worst results.

From the traverse, an upward ascent brought us into the mouth of a loose gully, the head of which consisted of slippery slabs disagreeably covered by a few inches of unstable scree.

It is curious how on any climb the mental equilibrium of the mountaineer is liable to be upset by bad rock. Difficulty is one thing, danger another. The nerve-stressed mountaineer needing a safety valve for his feelings frequently finds an outlet for them in forceful language. I make no excuses, therefore, for certain improper remarks when clambering up these rocks. I cannot remember what Hoerlin and Wieland said, I had not yet learned the English translation of the German epithets that they held in reserve for such occasions, but once, Hoerlin turned and remarked to me in perfect English, "These rocks are ——!" sentiments which, happily, I was able to return with interest.

The principal advantage of taking photographs on a mountain is that the mountaineer is thus enabled to stop at frequent intervals and recover his breath. That is why most elderly mountaineers carry cameras. Taking a photograph is a much more convincing excuse for a halt than a boot-lace or braces that need adjusting. All those liable to be touched in the wind should take a camera. With what the reader will no doubt consider admirable foresight, I had brought up my camera with me, and not left it at the gap. I was not blown, but the ridge beyond the top of the little gully appeared so uninviting that I decided to stop there and photograph Hoerlin and Wieland doing it.

Seated in a sheltered place, with the sun glancing warmly down upon me, I was able to appreciate the situation to the full. For a short distance the ridge appeared possible, and although extremely loose, not excessively difficult. But beyond the next tower it was very different. It rose abruptly in a huge pinnacle, quite 300 ft high, and above this pinnacle, connecting it to the next pinnacle, was the first of those appalling ice ridges. As I sat there I tried to think of an Alpine ridge comparable to it, but I could think of none. The Pétéret, the Brenva, the East Ridge of the Jungfrau, none would fit.

How were porters to be got up? Even supposing ropes were to be fixed the whole way up the smooth slabs of the first great pinnacle, they would not be able to climb with anything but a light load; also we had lost so much rope in the avalanche that we certainly had not enough to spare for even this first pinnacle. There was, however, no necessity for experiencing renewed pessimism. What we were now seeing simply confirmed the opinion that some of us had formed when gazing from the glacier below.

Hoerlin and Wieland were moving slowly and carefully, but even so they could not avoid dislodging many rocks which thundered down the precipices of the Ramthang Glacier. They turned a corner, and disappeared from view, but presently I saw them on the top of another minor pinnacle. There they remained, and I formed the conclusion that they could not advance farther.

The usual mists gathered, but without threatening anything beyond desultory snow flurries. Occasionally, they rolled aside to disclose a beautiful snow mountain, unknown and unnamed in a south-westerly direction, apparently on the ridge separating the Yalung and Ramthang Glaciers. This peak was in shape something like the Ober Gabelhorn, and possessed the same sweeping lines as the graceful Zermatt peak. Jannu should have been visible beyond, but mists obscured it. Almost immediately beneath us was the camp we had just established. We seemed to be looking almost vertically down upon it so steep were the precipices below. It seemed that a jump would have landed us on our tents. Above the camp, the Western Tributary Glacier swept up serenely to the col separating the Ramthang Peak from the first rock towers of the ridge we were on. The Ramthang Peak itself was playing hide-and-seek in a fitful mist but what was visible of it reminded me forcibly of the Mönch seen from the Jungfrau Glacier. There were the same graceful lines, the same flowing yet defiant massiveness.

It was late when we returned to camp, where we found Professor Dyhrenfurth, Schneider and Duvanel, who had come up that day from Camp I. I fear none of us was particularly optimistic over the day's work, and it was refreshing to find that Professor Dyhrenfurth did not agree with an opinion that the ridge was hopelessly inaccessible and considered that we should continue with the attack towards the terrace above.

For once, the afternoon clouds, instead of thickening for a snowstorm, dissolved. The evening was a calm and beautiful one, sky and world were unsullied by a single speck of cloud, a profound silence brooded over the sanc-tuaries of the snows, and only an occasional streamer of wind-blown snow sallied into space from the upper reaches of Kangchenjunga. Slowly night's floods filled the valleys, and the peaks became steeped in gaudy hues, like waxen deities covering their countenances with rouge and lipstick. Imperceptibly, the aerial pageantry died, but its riot of colourings was superseded by an afterglow which released the peaks from night's bonds for a few instants revealing them as cold statues of purest alabaster against a sky of deepest indigo. It was of such a day's end that Mr G. Winthrop Young once wrote:

> When in the hour of mountain peace
> The tumult and the passion cease,
> As the red sunfloods sink,
> And the pale lords of sovereign height,
> Watch the cold armies of the night
> Mustering their first assault.

Who would suspect evil to lurk in such a sunset? Yet, somehow, its superlative colourings put me in mind of a sunset I had once watched from a tiny ledge 12,000 ft up on the south face of Mont Maudit. *That* had been a sunset preceding a heavy snowstorm in which retreat had been no easy matter.

I awoke some hours later to hear the pattering of snow on my tent. In the quietude it sounded like the light tread of fairy feet. Presently I became aware of a faint under-current of sound like the far-off throb of a train down some pastoral valley. The train approached, its distant murmurings rising gradually to a booming crescendo of sound. A gust of wind struck the tent, hurling the snowflakes against it with rude fierce spatterings. The gust passed, but soon came another and stronger gust. In a few minutes the blizzard burst, furiously sweeping upon our encampment. I snuggled more closely into my sleeping bag, for strong though the tent fabric was, it was not entirely proof against this bitter onslaught at a height of 20,000 ft. We had thought to be sheltered by the North-West Ridge, but it afforded no protection, for the wind seemed to pour over it like a cataract, and descend almost vertically upon the camp.

The gusts grew stronger, they wailed and shrilled, rising to a roaring sort of boom like an express train racing through a tunnel. I could feel the tent floor rise as though malicious wind devils were undermining it with the object of my abode flying upwards into space. The wind dug viciously at the sides, or strove with strong fingers to tear apart the flaps, and burst the tent asunder. I prayed that Nemu had driven the pegs firmly and deeply into the snow, and then I recollected that the guy ropes were pitifully thin, no thicker than a sashline. There seemed every possibility of the tent carrying away; if it did, there would be little fun in being overtaken by such a disaster clad only in under-clothes, so I struggled out of my sleeping bag, pulled on my climbing clothes, and packed my rucksack with some necessaries.

The storm had now reached a pitch of intensity I had never before experienced when camping, and the night was filled with thunderous volleyings. Sometimes the wind would sink to a mysterious calm, during which it was possible to hear the storm snarling and worrying on the North-West Ridge as a preliminary before gathering its forces for a fresh charge on the camp. It was during one of these temporary lulls that I heard a sort of wailing outside, a wailing more human than storm-like. Peering through the flaps, I could just perceive a figure crawling through the snow. It approached my tent. In the light of my electric torch I saw the white, frightened face of Nagpa, the cook. "Sahib! Sahib!" he cried, "Tent go! Tent go!" Opening the flaps wider, I glanced out, the porters' tent was intact; the cook had merely lost his head. I was unwilling to have him for a bedfellow, and told him to go back. The cook, however, was completely demoralized, and shielding his face from the blast, he crawled down the line of tents with his constant wailing of "Sahib! Sahib! Tent go! Tent go!" Eventually, he found sanctuary with Wieland and Schneider, but as they explained later, they took him in not for love or charity, but simply as additional ballast for their own tent! It was the solitary untoward incident of the storm. Well and truly had our tents been pitched.

An hour or two later the wind began to subside, and ere dawn it withdrew with some last mutters and snarls, leaving a clean sky picked out with stars against which the windy banners of Kangchenjunga softly lit by moonlight streamed in ghostly rivalry to the starry constellations.

We awoke to a warm sun glancing benevolently over the Twins. The North-West Ridge was plastered with new snow, and our steps in the couloir had been obliterated. As there was a possibility of avalanches occurring, we decided not to renew the attempt that day, and devoted the morning to building a wall of snow blocks on the windward side of the camp. Hoerlin was not feeling well; somehow he had contracted a severe chill. Duvanel was also by no means fit, and only his devotion to his cinematographic duties had torn him away from the Base Camp.

At the head of the glacier on the ridge separating the Ramthang Peak from the North-West Ridge of Kangchenjunga is a small point about 20,800 ft high. This Wieland climbed by himself, using ski most of the way, and returned reporting that he had had a splendid view of the Ramthang Glacier and the North-West Ridge. It was decided, therefore, that the whole party should ascend to this point the following day, and carefully examine the latter to see whether it was worth while persisting in the attempt to climb it.

The following morning, May 15, dawned fine. Unfortunately, Hoerlin was so ill that there was no option but for him to return to the Base Camp. This was a serious loss to the climbing party; at the same time, the prospect of getting any distance up the North-West Ridge was so utterly hopeless that it did not really matter.

After the experiences of the past fortnight, it was with something more than relief that we set out to climb something that could be climbed. It has been said that on Everest the climbing party were so heartily "fed up" with the mountain, its weather, and the effects of altitude that their sole wish was to get the job over and done with, no matter who did it. Our attitude towards Kangchenjunga was the same. I do not think there was one of us who was not sick to death of work on the mountain. At exactly what height mountaineering ceases to be pleasurable is not easily defined, the matter is rather one of individual temperament, but I do not think there is one mountaineer who has climbed on Everest or Kangchenjunga who can honestly say that he enjoyed the work. Achievement may be good for the soul, but it is not necessarily enjoyable. It was a relief to turn away from our exacting opponent for a day and *enjoy* ourselves.

The 20,800 ft point is easily reached along the ridge connecting it to the Ramthang Peak, but from sheer exuberance we chose to ascend by a little rock face rising from the glacier. We raced each other up by various routes, and subsided puffing and blowing on the summit. What a summit it is – one of the most extraordinary that I have ever stood upon. From the Western Tributary Glacier it appears a mere knob, an insignificant excrescence, but had we stood on the Ramthang Glacier we should have seen an "impossible" peak. Seldom have I gazed down such abysmal precipices as those falling to the Ramthang Glacier. They were as long as the south-eastern face of the Finsteraahorn, and as steep as the Dolomite wall of the Winklerthurm. The seamed and wrinkled surface of the Ramthang Glacier was spread out beneath us like a relief map, and we gazed down upon it like pilots from the nose of a bombing aeroplane. The upper portion of the Ramthang Glacier rises very steeply in an almost continuous ice-fall. From the col we had reached in the North-West Ridge we had been separated by but a few hundred feet from it, but the drop from Point 20,800 must be at least 4,000 ft and as this point is separated from the col by only about a mile, the inclination of the glacier is a steep one.

At its extreme head the Ramthang Glacier forms a snowy plain beneath the west face of the Kangbachen summit of Kangchenjunga Glacier. This face resembles closely the north face above the Kangchenjunga Glacier. There are the same impregnable ice walls stretching across it from which ice avalanches fall at least as big as those that fall from the north face. At the southern end of the face where it abuts against the main West Ridge of Kangchenjunga, which separates the head of the Ramthang Glacier from the Yalung Glacier, there appeared to be a remote possibility of ascending between the ice walls and gaining the West Ridge. But, like the route we had already tried to the North Ridge, the possibility of success was more than counter-balanced by the possibility of annihilation, for the whole of the route was liable to be swept at any moment by ice avalanches. Even if the West Ridge was gained, what then? At the best it could only lead to the Kangbachen summit. To traverse the ridge between the Kangbachen summit and the highest summit, over the third highest summit, would be beyond the powers of any party. Therefore, it can be said without hesitation that Kangchenjunga is definitely unassailable from the Ramthang Glacier.

But if this side of Kangchenjunga is disappointing as regards its climbing potentialities it is hardly so otherwise. Great tiers of ice, gleaming steeps, and terrific red granite precipices combine to form a mountain face of a magnificence and grandeur worthy of the high summits it defends.

We had looked upon the last portion of Kangchenjunga to be properly seen by man, and what we had seen but confirmed our opinion that there are no groups of mountain tops defended so impregnably as the "Five Treasures of the Snows". We tore our eyes away from those terrible ice walls and glanced for relief along the winding trench down which flows the Ramthang Glacier, and up over the sea of peaks to the west. Woolly clouds were rising from the valleys and draping themselves about the shoulders of the peaks. Once the cloudy waves rolled back; in a distant trough a great peak rose in noble solitude above the world. Someone said, "Everest". Then the mists closed in, and we saw it no more.

We turned to the North-West Ridge. Our view of it was an end-on one, but if it was impossible to gauge its length, its height and difficulty were apparent. Below us on the glacier was the camp, a mere smudge on the immaculate expanse of snow. The terrace we must gain was 4,000 ft higher. The North-West Ridge was the connecting link. I have already described its knife-like edges of ice and its rocky towers. Seen thus, end on, they were jumbled one against the other, and one gained but little idea of the real length of the ridge. Perhaps it was this that deceived Professor Dyhrenfurth into deciding to continue with the attack. To those used only to Alpine scale, it is easy to be misled by the length of these Himalayan ridges. But if the length was not apparent, the difficulties were, and one could not but wonder how porters were to be got up, and camps established along that tremendous crest. There was no answer to this question. Even supposing the upper ice wall, against which the ridge abutted, to be climbed, and the terrace gained, what next? There was no possibility whatever of reaching any of Kangchenjunga's summits. The terrace did not extend right across the mountain to the North Ridge, there was a cut-off of impassable precipices. At the best, we could only hope to reach the Kangbachen summit, and that was separated from the terrace by 1,500 ft at least of formidable granite precipices. The most we could do was to climb as high as possible, perhaps even as high as the Bavarians, but what was the practical use of that? I fear my companions thought me a pessimist, but what else could one be taking everything into consideration? Anyway, the decision was made. We were to go on. This settled, we sat and lazed two or three hours away in the warm sun, happy hours, but trammelled by the thought of the morrow. The evening mists saw us jogging down the glacier to the camp.

The party that left the next morning consisted of Professor Dyhrenfurth, Schneider, Wieland and myself, with two porters, Lewa and Nima, the last named not to be confused with Nemu, my servant, both experienced Everest men. The couloir was in bad condition, and steps had to be kicked or cut through an upper layer of powdery snow a foot deep. The porters were not happy; neither of them had experienced similar climbing before. Lewa stuck gamely to the task, but Nima was constantly slipping from his steps. I was next to him on the rope, and had several times to hold him. The ridge itself was also in a worse condition than it was during our reconnaissance.

We climbed on two ropes, Schneider, Wieland, and Lewa on the first, and Professor Dyhrenfurth, Nima, and myself on the second. The duty of the second party was to drive in pitons and fix ropes to the rocks. Nima caused us some anxious moments. It made one shudder to see the way he climbed on the loose rocks, hauling himself up on his hands without testing loose holds. So poor a show did he put up that we decided to leave him on a broad and safe part of the ridge, a decision that relieved him as much as it did us. Lewa was, however, an excellent rock climber, and followed Schneider and Wieland without difficulty to the top of the pinnacle, which had been the farthest point reached during the reconnaissance.

From the top of the pinnacle a vertical and holdless slice of granite drops to a gap. The climber must descend the granite slice on the rope, and alight on a sharp edge of snow. A piton was driven into a crack on the pinnacle, and a double rope fixed to it. Schneider and Wieland then descended hand over hand down the fixed rope, while being held at the same time from above on another rope by the remainder of the party. It was the sort of place fiction writers would make much of. Their descriptions would bristle with "unfathomable abysses", "like a fly on a wall", "beetling precipices", and so forth. The mountaineering guide-book writer would, however, describe it simply as "a twenty feet absail"[1] and as a grudging compliment to the

---

1 A German term for double roping.

place add "sensational". In this case, however, the fiction writer would convey a better picture to the mind of even the most sophisticated reader than the guide-book writer. To add to the sensationalism might be added the fact that the cracked and disintegrating pinnacle on which we stood exhibited a distinct tremor if rudely handled. I distinctly remember thinking, a trifle morosely, what a grand finale it would make to the expedition if the thing collapsed, and toppled into the "unfathomable abyss" with its human load.

As Wieland swung over the edge, the dirty and battered topi he was accustomed to affect looked strangely incongruous in these surroundings of rock, snow and ice, and, as he bumped and rasped down the rough granite, I half hoped that it would be knocked from his head and go spinning down the precipices, arriving at the camp below a pulped and shapeless mass. No such diversion occurred, and soon he had joined Schneider in the gap on the snow ridge.

Professor Dyhrenfurth and I remained on the pinnacle for an hour or two. We were privileged in witnessing one of the finest feats of climbing we had ever seen. Immediately above the gap rose a semi-detached mass of rock; beyond was another small gap, above which rose the great pinnacle in 300 ft of slabs set at an angle not far removed from the vertical. Ice in the interstices of these slabs had forced them apart in many places and dangerously unstable flakes rested against the face. Every ledge was loaded with snow or ice. On an Alpine climb of exceptional severity the ascent of this pinnacle would be a formidable task; at 20,000 ft it seemed impossible.

Wieland ensconced himself on top of the semi-detached mass, and Schneider descended, without much difficulty, into the secondary gap, and began the ascent of the slabs. Methodically he worked his way upwards. The exertion of hard rock climbing at such an altitude was obviously severe, and after each upward heave he was forced to halt and rest. At length he reached a small stance, a tiny triangular recess, where Wieland joined him. Above this rose a slanting crack formed by the edge of a projecting flake the upper part of which bulged out unpleasantly. It was not a place to linger over, and Schneider did not linger. A foot scrape on the wall, a hand wedged in the crack, a quick upward caterpillar-like movement with naught but tiny hand-holds to prevent a backward topple, and the hardest part had been accomplished. In the silence, unbroken save by an occasional whisper of wind, I could hear the sibilant sucking in of breath by sorely stressed lungs. A few feet more of difficult, but not such exacting climbing brought him to a sloping shelf. Wieland followed, and although burdened by both ice-axes and a rucksack, he came up without relying on the rope.

So far, so good. For a few feet the work was easier; then the slopes steepened once more. In places they were dangerously ice glazed, and their sloping icy shelves were masked by snow. Ice-axes were called into play to clear holds. Now and again loose flakes of rock were dislodged. Hurtling madly down the cliffs they loosed other rocks and sent the echoes thundering.

Two hours' work, 200 ft of ascent, such was the climbing on the great pinnacle. Professor Dyhrenfurth and I watched the struggle with intense interest. It was, probably, the finest piece of rock climbing ever done at such an altitude. We forgot for the moment that the real problem was not the ascent of the ridge by the Europeans but the establishing of camps and the getting up of porters over this gaunt backbone of rock and ice.

The weather restored pessimism, grey mists came flying up from the west, a chill wind sobbed over the ridge, driving before it small moths of snow. Schneider and Wieland were out of sight now. Occasionally we could hear their voices, whilst an occasional stone crashed out news of their advance. We rose, stretched our cramped limbs, tied on Lewa, and started to descend.

We had collected Nima but were still above the col when we were startled by an enormous roar. Millions of tons of ice had broken away from the ice wall and were thundering down to the Ramthang Glacier. Instantly, the whole upper basin of the glacier was filled with a writhing hurricane of snow. Whirling up at us, it enveloped us in a blizzard, that whitened and sheeted our clothes in snow. The sky was darkened; the whole district seemed filled with wind-blown snow dislodged by this monstrous avalanche.

Such an avalanche, had it occurred in the Alps would command widespread attention, newspapers would refer to it as a "Cataclysm of Nature", and questions would be asked in the Swiss Parliament about it. But on Kangchenjunga, such avalanches are not the exception, but the rule – almost an everyday occurrence.

Kangchenjunga is by no means the only Himalayan peak to discharge avalanches of such magnitude, but it is probably safe to say that there is no other Himalayan peak that discharges them with such frequency. This is due, of course, to its great snowfall, the quick downward movement of its glaciers. A good instance of the size of a Himalayan avalanche is that which occurred during the late A. F. Mummery's attempt on Nanga Parbat. The party had bivouacked on a rock rib which projected some 500 ft from the mountainside, but when they returned to their bivouac site after an unsuccessful attempt on the mountain, they found that their gear had been swept away by an ice avalanche. The avalanche had fallen diagonally and taken the 500 ft rib in its stride! The size and destructive power of Himalayan avalanches is the first thing that should be studied when climbing in the Himalayas. A purely Alpine-trained mountaineer finds it difficult to appreciate the scale on which such avalanches occur. Mummery paid the penalty of not realizing this when he made his final and disastrous attempt on Nanga Parbat. No trace of him and his two Gurkha followers was ever discovered. We narrowly missed paying the same penalty too, and had we been wiped out during our attempt to reach the North Ridge of Kangchenjunga, we should have received our just deserts.

It must be remembered that Himalayan ice avalanches *habitually* sweep the whole breadth of glaciers. To illustrate this I can but add that were the peaks in the vicinity of the well-known Concordia Hut in the Bernese Oberland enlarged to Himalayan scale, the mountaineer staying at the hut would not be safe from ice avalanches falling from the peaks on the opposite side of the Aletsch Glacier.

It was a relief to leave the rotten rocks, and to stand once more in the col; and it was pleasant to escape from the cutting wind, and seizing the fixed rope that hung down the steep upper part of the couloir step blithely down the ladder of holds to the camp.

We glissaded down the lower part of the couloir, and for the first time that day Nima's worried expression gave place to a broad grin of delight. The porters are children at heart, and they have all the enthusiasm for a glissade down snow that a child has for a toboggan. For the benefit of the uninitiated I should explain that there are two methods of glissading. One is to stand upright, and the other is to sit down. The former is best employed on hard snow, the latter on soft snow. A certain degree of expertness is necessary for the stand-up glissade. Many commence in elegant style. With ever increasing speed, they slide down the slope. Presently, as the speed becomes faster and faster, they become flustered. From stability, they are reduced to instability; their elegance, their dignified deportment is lost, their balance is upset, they struggle wildly to regain it, then the snow comes up and hits them on the nose. They go head over heels, their ice-axes are snatched from their hands, their hats torn from their heads, their rucksacks wind themselves round their necks, endeavouring to strangle them, snow is forced down their collars, up their sleeves, and into their pockets and trousers. Over and over they go in a series of somersaults, to subside finally at the bottom where they rise to their feet vowing it was good fun.

There is one other variety of glissade worthy of mention, and that is glissading on a rope. This is one degree worse than skiing on a rope. What usually happens is this: the leader, without troubling to enquire whether the second man is ready, shoots off with great velocity, despite the agonized cries of the latter. In a moment or two, the rope tightens on the second man who has barely had time to start, snatching him forward on to his head, and squeezing the breath out of him. The jerk arrests the leader, who hurls an uncomplimentary remark over his shoulder at the unfortunate second man, who meanwhile slides, or somersaults pell-mell past the leader. Then, before the leader has time to continue, he is in his turn dragged in the wake of the second man. And so it goes on, a vicious cycle, until they have reached the bottom, where they sit in the snow roundly abusing one another.

We reached camp in desultory snow squalls. Mists concealed the North-West Ridge, but now and again they blew aside and we scanned the rocks a little anxiously for signs of Schneider and Wieland. It was not until evening that we saw them descending, mere dots silhouetted against the jagged skyline. Dusk was falling when they returned. They reported immense difficulties, difficulties both of rocks and ice. Short of roping the great tower up from top to bottom, there was no possibility of getting the porters up it, and even with ropes, it would most likely prove impossible for laden men. The prospect of farther advance beyond the tower was doubtful in the extreme. The whole crest of the first knife-like ice ridge would have to be hacked away before a passage could be won. At the end of this ridge, there was another tower, not so high as the first, but more difficult, in fact, probably impassable. Its summit was capped by a boss of ice which flowed down its sides like icing on a cake. There was no avoiding this tower, for the precipices on either side were sheer and offered no hope of a traverse. Above this tower, other ice ridges rose, a whole series of them, up to the terrace. Nowhere, said Schneider, was there a place on which a camp might be pitched. There were not even any ice pinnacles of a type suitable for bivouac caves. And the weather? What would be the position of a party caught high up on this great ridge in bad weather or high winds? The storm on the glacier three nights previously had been bad enough, but what would it have been like on the ridge? Retreat would be impossible. It would probably mean two weeks hard work to reach the terrace, even supposing camps could be established, and porters brought up, and by then the monsoon would most likely have broken. Each of these facts taken separately was sufficiently weighty to militate against any attempt.

There was no alternative but to abandon the project, and the following day Wieland and I accomplished the dreary task of collecting and bringing down the fixed ropes. Kangchenjunga had beaten us, beaten us not by bad weather, so much as by sheer difficulty. We had examined every portion of the faces above the Kangchenjunga and Ramthang Glaciers. Nowhere was there a chink in the armour of the giant; nowhere was there a route at which the mountaineer might look and say, "Well, it *might* go." Others sceptical as to the truth of these assertions may follow in our footsteps, but they too will return disappointed, and tremble, even as the ground trembles, at the roar of the great ice avalanches that seek their destruction, and like us, their hope and optimism will be ruthlessly crushed beneath the icy heel of Kangchenjunga.

The Ridge

Tom Hornbein

An American physician and mountaineer, Hornbein was born in 1930. Together, with Willi Unsoeld he summitted Everest via the unclimbed West Ridge. They then traversed Everest (another first), to descend the South Ridge. To cap one of mountaineering's greatest exploits, they also survived – like Herman Buhl before them (see pp 286–294) – an emergency bivouac at 8,000 m (26,000 ft). The year was 1963.

At four the oxygen ran out, a most effective alarm clock. Two well-incubated butane stoves were fished from inside our sleeping bags and soon bouillon was brewing in the kitchen. Climbing into boots was a breathless challenge to balance in our close quarters. Then overboots, and crampons.

"Crampons, in the tent?"

"Sure," I replied, "It's a hell of a lot colder out there."

"But our air mattresses!"

"Just be careful. We may not be back here again, anyway. I hope."

We were clothed in multilayer warmth. The fishnet underwear next to our skin provided tiny air pockets to hold our body heat. It also kept the outer layers at a distance which, considering our weeks without a bath, was respectful. Next came Duofold underwear, a wool shirt, down underwear tops and bottoms, wool climbing pants, and a lightweight wind parka. In spite of the cold our down parkas would be too bulky for difficult climbing, so we used them to insulate two quarts of hot lemonade, hoping they might remain unfrozen long enough to drink during the climb. Inside the felt inner liners of our reindeer-hair boots were innersoles and two pairs of heavy wool socks. Down shells covered a pair of wool mittens. Over our oxygen helmets we wore wool balaclavas and our parka hoods. The down parka-lemonade muff was stuffed into our packs as padding between the two oxygen bottles. With camera, radio, flashlight, and sundry mementos (including the pages from Emerson's diary), our loads came close to 40 lb. For all the prior evening's planning it was more than two hours before we emerged.

I snugged a bowline about my waist, feeling satisfaction at the ease with which the knot fell together beneath heavily mittened hands. This was part of the ritual, experienced innumerable times before. With it came a feeling of security, not from the protection provided by the rope joining Willi and me, but from my being able to relegate those grey brooding forbidding walls, so high in such an unknown world, to common reality – to all those times I had ever tied into a rope before: with warm hands while I stood at the base of sun-baked granite walls in the Tetons, with cold hands on a winter night while I prepared to tackle my first steep ice on Longs Peak. This knot tied me to the past, to experience known, with that which man might do. To weave the knot so smoothly with clumsily mittened hands was to assert my confidence, to assert some competence in the face of the waiting rock, to accept the challenge.

Hooking our masks in place we bade a slightly regretful goodbye to our tent, sleeping bags, and the extra supply of food we hadn't been able to eat. Willi was at the edge of the ledge looking up the narrow gully when I joined him.

"My oxygen's hissing, Tom, even with the regulator turned off."

For the next twenty minutes we screwed and unscrewed regulators, checked valves for ice, to no avail. The hiss continued. We guessed it must be in the valve, and thought of going back to the tent for the spare bottle, but the impatient feeling that time was more important kept us from retracing those forty feet.

"It doesn't sound too bad," I said. "Let's just keep an eye on the pressure. Besides if you run out you can hook up the sleeping T and extra tubing and both climb on one bottle." Willi envisioned the two of us climbing Everest in lockstep, wed by six feet of rubber hose.

We turned to the climb. It was ten minutes to seven. Willi led off. Three years before in a tent high on Masherbrum he had expounded on the importance of knee-to-toe distance for step-kicking up steep snow. Now his anatomical advantage determined the order of things as he put his theory to the test. Right away we found it was going to be difficult. The Couloir, as it cut through the Yellow Band, narrowed to ten or fifteen feet and steepened to fifty degrees. The snow was hard, too hard to kick steps in, but not hard enough to hold crampons; they slid disconcertingly down through this wind-sheltered, granular stuff. There was nothing for it but to cut steps, zigzagging back and forth across the gully, occasionally finding a bit of rock along the side up which we could scramble. We were forced to climb one at a time with psychological belays from axes thrust a few inches into the snow. Our regulators were set to deliver two litres of oxygen per minute, half the optimal flow for this altitude. We turned them off when we were belaying to conserve the precious gas, though we knew that the belayer should always be kept at peak alertness in case of a fall.

We crept along. My God, I thought, we'll never get there at this rate. But that's as far as the thought ever got. Willi's leads were meticulous, painstakingly slow and steady. He plugged tirelessly on, deluging me with showers of ice as his axe carved each step. When he ran out the hundred feet of rope he jammed his axe into the snow to belay me. I turned my oxygen on to "2" and moved up as far as I could, hoping to save a few moments of critical time. By the time I joined him I was completely winded, gasping for air, and sorely puzzled about why. Only late in the afternoon, when my first oxygen bottle was still going strong, did I realize what a low flow of gas my regulator was actually delivering.

Up the tongue of snow we climbed, squeezing through a passage where the walls of the Yellow Band closed in, narrowing the Couloir to shoulder width.

In four hours we had climbed only 400 ft. It was 11 a.m. A rotten bit of vertical wall forced us to the right onto the open face. To regain the Couloir it would be necessary to climb this sixty-foot cliff, composed of two pitches split by a broken snow-covered step.

"You like to lead this one?" Willi asked.

With my oxygen off I failed to think before I replied, "Sure, I'll try it."

The rock sloped malevolently outward like shingles on a roof – rotten shingles. The covering of snow was no better than the rock. It would pretend to hold for a moment, then suddenly shatter and peel, cascading down on Willi. He sank a piton into the base of the step to anchor his belay.

I started up around the corner to the left, crampon points grating on rusty limestone. Then it became a snowplowing procedure as I searched for some sort of purchase beneath. The pick of my axe found a crack. Using the shaft for gentle leverage, I moved carefully onto the broken strata of the step. I went left again, loose debris rolling under my crampons, to the base of the final vertical rise, about eight feet high. For all its steepness, this was a singularly poor plastering job, nothing but wobbly rubble. I searched about for a crack, unclipped a big angle piton from my sling, and whomped it in with the hammer. It sank smoothly, as if penetrating soft butter. A gentle lift easily extracted it.

"Hmmm. Not so good," I mumbled through my mask. On the fourth try the piton gripped a bit more solidly. Deciding not to loosen it by testing, I turned to the final wall. Its steepness threw my weight out from the rock, and my pack became a downright hindrance. There was an unlimited selection of handholds, mostly portable. I shed my mittens. For a few seconds the rock felt comfortably reassuring, but cold. Then not cold anymore. My eyes tried to direct sensationless fingers. Flakes peeled out beneath my crampons. I leaned out from the rock to move upward, panting like a steam engine. Damn it, it'll go; I know it will,

T, I thought. My grip was gone. I hadn't thought to turn my oxygen up.

"No soap," I called down. "Can't make it now. Too pooped."

"Come on down. There may be a way to the right."

I descended, half rappeling from the piton, which held. I had spent the better part of an hour up there. A hundred feet out we looked back. Clearly we had been on the right route, for above the last little step the gully opened out. A hundred feet higher the Yellow Band met the grey of the summit limestone. It had to get easier.

"You'd better take it, Willi. I've wasted enough time already."

"Hell, if you couldn't make it, I'm not going to be able to do it any better."

"Yes you will. It's really not that hard. I was just worn out from putting that piton in. Turn your regulator clear open, though."

Willi headed up around the corner, moving well. In ten minutes his rope was snapped through the high piton. Discarding a few unsavoury holds, he gripped the rotten edge with his unmittened hands. He leaned out for the final move. His pack pulled. Crampons scraped, loosing a shower of rock from beneath his feet. He was over. He leaned against the rock, fighting for his breath.

"Man, that's work. But it looks better above."

Belayed, I followed, retrieved the first piton, moved up, and went to work on the second. It wouldn't come. "Guess it's better than I thought," I shouted. "I'm going to leave it." I turned my oxygen to four litres, leaned out from the wall, and scrambled up. The extra oxygen helped, but it was surprising how breathless such a brief effort left me.

"Good lead," I panted. "That wasn't easy."

"Thanks. Let's roll."

Another rope length and we stopped. After six hours of hiss Willi's first bottle was empty. There was still a long way to go, but at least he could travel ten pounds lighter without the extra cylinder. Our altimeter read 27,900. We called Base on the walkie-talkie.

Willi: West Ridge to Base. West Ridge to Base. Over.

Base (Jim Whittaker, excitedly): This is Base here, Willi. How are you? How are things going? What's the word up there? Over.

Willi: Man, this is a real bearcat! We are nearing the top of the Yellow Band and it's mighty tough. It's too damned tough to try to go back. It would be too dangerous.

Base (Jim): I'm sure you're considering all about your exits. Why don't you leave yourself an opening? If it's not going to pan out, you can always start your way down. I think there is always a way to come back.

Willi: Roger, Jim. We're counting on a further consultation in about two or three hundred feet. It should ease up by then! Goddammit, if we can't start moving together, we'll have to move back down. But it should be easier once the Yellow Band is passed. Over.

Base (Jim): Don't work yourself up into a bottleneck, Willi. How about rappeling? Is that possible, or don't you have any *reepschnur* or anything? Over.

Willi: There are no rappel points, Jim, absolutely no rappel points. There's nothing to secure a rope to. So it's up and over for us today . . .

While the import of his words settled upon those listening 10,000 ft below, Willi went right on:

Willi (continuing): . . . and we'll probably be getting in pretty late, maybe as late as seven or eight o'clock tonight.

As Willi talked, I looked at the mountain above. The slopes looked reasonable, as far as I could see, which wasn't very far. We sat at the base of a big, wide-open amphitheatre. It looked like summits all over the place. I looked down. Descent was totally unappetizing. The rotten rock, the softening snow, the absence of even tolerable piton cracks only added to our desire to go on. Too much labour, too many sleepless nights, and too many dreams had been invested to bring us this far. We couldn't come back for another try next weekend. To go down now, even if we could have, would be descending to a future marked by one huge question: what might have been? It would not be a matter of living with our fellow man, but simply living with ourselves, with the knowledge that we had had more to give.

I listened, only mildly absorbed in Willi's conversation

with Base, and looked past him at the convexity of rock cutting off our view of the gully we had ascended. Above – a snowfield, grey walls, then blue-black sky. We were committed. An invisible barrier sliced through the mountain beneath our feet, cutting us from the world below. Though we could see through, all we saw was infinitely remote. The ethereal link provided by our radio only intensified our separation. My wife and children seemed suddenly close. Yet home, life itself, lay only over the top of Everest and down the other side. Suppose we fail? The thought brought no remorse, no fear. Once entertained, it hardly seemed even interesting. What now mattered most was right here: Willi and I, tied together on a rope, and the mountain, its summit not inaccessibly far above. The reason we had come was within our grasp. We belonged to the mountain and it to us. There was anxiety, to be sure, but it was all but lost in a feeling of calm, of pleasure at the joy of climbing. That we couldn't go down only made easier that which we really wanted to do. That we might not get there was scarcely conceivable.

Willi was still talking.

Willi: Any news of Barrel and Lute? Over.

Jim: I haven't heard a word from them. Over.

Willi: How about Dingman?

Jim: No word from Dingman. We've heard nothing at all.

Willi: Well listen, if you do get hold of Dingman, tell him to put a light in the window because we're headed for the summit, Jim. We can't possibly get back to our camp now. Over.

I stuffed the radio back in Willi's pack. It was 1 p.m. From here we could both climb at the same time, moving across the last of the yellow slabs. Another 100 ft and the Yellow Band was below us. A steep tongue of snow flared wide, penetrating the grey strata that capped the mountain. The snow was hard, almost ice-hard in places. We had only to bend our ankles, firmly plant all twelve crampon points, and walk uphill. At last, we were moving, though it would have appeared painfully slow to a distant bystander.

As we climbed out of the Couloir the pieces of the puzzle fell into place. That snow rib ahead on the left skyline should lead us to the Summit Snowfield, a patch of perpetual white clinging to the North Face at the base of Everest's final pyramid. By three we were on the Snowfield. We had been climbing for eight hours and knew we needed to take time to refuel. At a shaly outcrop of rock we stopped for lunch. There was a decision to be made. We could either cut straight up the north-east ridge and follow it west to the summit, or we could traverse the face and regain the West Ridge. From where we sat, the Ridge looked easier. Besides, it was the route we'd intended in the first place.

We split a quart of lemonade that was slushy with ice. In spite of its down parka wrapping, the other bottle was already frozen solid, as were the kippered snacks. They were almost tasteless but we downed them more with dutiful thoughts of calories than with pleasure.

To save time we moved together, diagonalling upward across downsloping slabs of rotten shale. There were no possible stances from which to belay each other. Then snow again, and Willi kicked steps, fastidiously picking a route between the outcropping of rocks. Though still carting my full load of oxygen bottles, I was beginning to feel quite strong. With this excess energy came impatience, and an unconscious anxiety over the high stakes for which we were playing and the lateness of the day. Why the hell is Willi going so damned slow? I thought. And a little later: He should cut over to the Ridge now; it'll be a lot easier.

I shouted into the wind, "Hold up, Willi!" He pretended not to hear me as he started up the rock. It seemed terribly important to tell him to go to the right. I tugged on the rope. "Damn it, wait up, Willi!" Stopped by a taut rope and an unyielding Hornbein, he turned, and with some irritation anchored his axe while I hastened to join him. He was perched, through no choice of his own, in rather cramped, precarious quarters. I sheepishly apologized.

We were on rock now. One rope length, crampons scraping, brought us to the crest of the West Ridge for the first time since we'd left Camp 4W yesterday morning. The South Face fell 8,000 ft to the tiny tents of Advanced Base. Lhotse, straight across the face, was below us now. And near at hand 150 feet higher, the South Summit of

Everest shone in the afternoon sun. We were within 400 ft of the top! The wind whipped across the ridge from the north at nearly sixty miles an hour. Far below, peak shadows reached long across the cloud-filled valleys. Above, the Ridge rose, a twisting, rocky spine.

We shed crampons and overboots to tackle this next rocky bit with the comforting grip of cleated rubber soles. Here I unloaded my first oxygen bottle though it was not quite empty. It had lasted ten hours, which obviously meant I'd be getting a lower flow than indicated by the regulator. Resisting Willi's suggestion to drop the cylinder off the South Face, I left it for some unknown posterity. When I resaddled 10 lb lighter, I felt I could float to the top.

The rock was firm, at least in comparison with our fare thus far. Climbing one at a time, we experienced the joy of delicate moves on tiny holds. The going was a wonderful pleasure, almost like a day in the Rockies. With the sheer drop to the Cwm beneath us, we measured off another four rope lengths. Solid rock gave way to crud, then snow. A thin, firm, knife-edge of white pointed gently toward the sky. Buffeted by the wind, we laced our crampons on, racing each other with rapidly numbing fingers. It took nearly twenty minutes. Then we were off again, squandering oxygen at three litres per minute since time seemed the shorter commodity at the moment. We moved together, Willi in front. It seemed almost as if we were cheating, using oxygen; we could nearly run this final bit.

Ahead the North and South ridges converged to a point. Surely the summit wasn't that near? It must be off behind. Willi stopped. What's he waiting for, I wondered as I moved to join him. With a feeling of disbelief I looked up. Forty feet ahead tattered and whipped by the wind was the flag Jim had left three weeks before. It was 6.15. The sun's rays sheered horizontally across the summit. We hugged each other as tears welled up, ran down across our oxygen masks, and turned to ice.

Just rock, a dome of snow, the deep blue sky, and a hunk of orange-painted metal from which a shredded American flag cracked in the wind. Nothing more. Except two tiny figures walking together those last few feet to the top of the earth.

For twenty minutes we stayed there. The last brilliance of the day cast the shadow of our summit on the cloud . . . plain a hundred miles . . . to the east. Valleys were filled with the indistinct purple haze of evening, concealing the dwellings of man we knew were there. The chill roar of wind made speaking difficult, heightened our feeling of remoteness. The flag left there seemed a feeble gesture of man that had no purpose but to accentuate the isolation. The two of us who had dreamed months before of sharing this moment were linked by a thin line of rope, joined in the intensity of companionship to those inaccessibly far below, Al and Barry and Dick – and Jake.

From a pitch of intense emotional and physical drive it was only partly possible to become suddenly, completely the philosopher of a balmy afternoon. The head of steam was too great, and the demands on it still remained. We have a long way to go to get down, I thought. But the prospect of descent of an unknown side of the mountain in the dark caused me less anxiety than many other occasions had. I had a blind, fatalistic faith that, having succeeded in coming this far, we could not fail to get down. The moment became an end in itself.

There were many things savoured in this brief time. Even with our oxygen turned off we had no problem performing those summit obeisances, photographing the fading day (it's a wonderful place to be for sunset photographs), smiling behind our masks for the inevitable "I was there" picture. Willi wrapped the kata given him by Ang Dorje about the flag pole and planted Andy Bakewell's crucifix alongside it in the snow; Lhotse and Makalu, below us, were a contrast of sun-blazed snow etched against the darkness of evening shadow. We felt the lonely beauty of the evening, the immense roaring silence of the wind, the tenuousness of our tie to all below. There was a hint of fear, not for our lives, but of a vast unknown which pressed upon us. A fleeting disappointment – that after all those dreams and questions this was only a mountaintop – gave way to the suspicion that maybe there was something more, something beyond the three-dimensional form of the moment. If only it could be perceived.

But it was late. The memories had to be stored, the meaning taken down. The question of why we had come was not now to be answered, yet something up here must yield an answer, something only dimly felt, comprehended by senses reaching farther yet than the point on which we stood; reaching for understanding, which hovered but a few steps higher. The answers lay not on the summit of Everest, nor in the sky above it, but in the world to which we belonged and must now return.

Footprints in the snow told that Lute and Barrel had been here. We'd have a path to follow as long as light remained.

"Want to go first?" Willi asked. He began to coil the rope.

Looking down the corniced edge, I thought of the added protection of a rope from above. "Doesn't matter, Willi. Either way."

"OK. Why don't I go first then?" he said, handing me the coil. Paying out the rope as he disappeared below me I wondered, Is Unsoeld tired? It was hard to believe. Still he'd worked hard; he had a right to be weary. Starting sluggishly, I'd felt stronger as we climbed. So now we would reverse roles. Going up had been pretty much Willi's show; going down would be mine. I dropped the last coil and started after him.

Fifty feet from the top we stopped at a patch of exposed rock. Only the summit of Everest, shining pink, remained above the shadow sea. Willi radioed to Maynard Miller at Advance Base that we were headed for the South Col. It was 6.35 p.m.

We almost ran along the crest, trusting Lute and Barrel's track to keep us a safe distance from the cornice edge. Have to reach the South Summit before dark, I thought, or we'll never find our way. The sun dropped below the jagged horizon. We didn't need goggles any more. There was a loud hiss as I banged against the ice wall. Damn! Something's broken. I reached back and turned off the valve. Without oxygen, I tried to keep pace with the rope disappearing over the edge ahead. Vision dimmed, the ground began to move. I stopped till things cleared, waved my arms and shouted into the wind for Willi to hold up. The taut rope finally stopped him. I tightened the regulator, then turned the oxygen on. No hiss! To my relief it had only been jarred loose. On oxygen again, I could move rapidly. Up twenty feet, and we were on the South Summit. It was 7.15.

Thank God for the footprints. Without them, we'd have had a tough time deciding which way to go. We hurried on, facing outward, driving our heels into the steep snow. By 7.30 it was dark. We took out the flash-light and resumed the descent. The batteries, dregs of the Expedition, had not been helped by our session with Emerson's diary the night before; they quickly faded. There was pitiful humour as Willi probed, holding the light a few inches off the snow to catch some sign of tracks. You could order your eyes to see, but nothing in the blackness complied.

We moved slowly now. Willi was only a voice and an occasional faint flicker of light to point the way. No fear, no worry, no strangeness, just complete absorption. The drive which had carried us to a nebulous goal was replaced by simple desire for survival. There was no time to dwell on the uniqueness of our situation. We climbed carefully, from years of habit. At a rock outcrop we paused. Which way? Willi groped to the right along a corniced edge. In my imagination, I filled in the void.

"No tracks over here." Willi called

"Maybe we should dig in for the night."

"I don't know. Dave and Girmi should be at six."

We shouted into the night, and the wind engulfed our call. A lull. Again we shouted. "Helloooo," the wind answered. Or was it the wind?

"Hellooo," we called once more.

"Hellooo," came back faintly. That wasn't the wind!

"To the left, Willi."

"OK, go ahead."

In the blackness I couldn't see my feet. Each foot groped cautiously, feeling its way down, trusting to the pattern set by its predecessor. Slowly left, right, left, crampons biting into the snow, right, left . . .

"*Willeeee!*" I yelled as I somersaulted into space. The rope came taut, and with a soft thud I landed.

"Seems to be a cornice there," I called from beneath the wall. "I'll belay you from here."

Willi sleepwalked down the edge. The dim outline of his foot wavered until it met my guiding hand. His arrival lacked the flair of my descent. It was well that the one of lighter weight had gone first.

Gusts buffeted from all directions, threatening to dislodge us from the slope. Above a cliff we paused, untied, cut the rope in half, and tied in again. It didn't help; even five feet behind I couldn't see Willi. Sometimes the snow was good, sometimes it was soft, sometimes it lay shallow over rocks so we could only drive our axes in an inch or two. With these psychological belays, we wandered slowly down, closer to the answering shouts. The wind was dying, and so was the flashlight, now no more than an orange glow illuminating nothing. The stars, brilliant above, cast no light on the snow. Willi's oxygen ran out. He slowed, suddenly feeling much wearier.

The voices were close now. Were they coming from those two black shapes in the snow? Or were those rocks?

"Shine your lights down here," a voice called.

"Where? Shine yours up here," I answered.

"Don't have one," came the reply.

Then we were with them – not Dave and Girmi, but Lute and Barrel. They were near exhaustion, shivering lumps curled on the snow. Barrel in particular was far gone. Anxious hungering for air through the previous night, and the near catastrophe when their tent caught fire in the morning, had left him tired before they even started. Determination got him to the top, but now he no longer cared. He only wanted to be left alone. Lute was also tired. Because of Barrel's condition he'd had to bear the brunt of the climbing labour. His eyes were painfully burned, perhaps by the fire, perhaps by the sun and wind. From sheer fatigue they had stopped thinking. Their oxygen was gone, except for a bit Lute had saved for Barrel; but they were too weak to make the change.

At 9.30 we were still 1,000 ft above Camp VI. Willi sat

down in the snow, and I walked over to get Lute's oxygen for Barrel. As I unscrewed Lute's regulator from the bottle, he explained why they were still there. Because of the stove fire that had sent them diving from the tent, they were an hour late in starting. It was 3.30 p.m. when they reached the summit. Seeing no sign of movement down the west side, they figured no one would be any later than they were. At 4.15 they started down. Fatigue slowed their descent. Just after dark they stopped to rest and were preparing to move when they heard shouts. Dave and Girmi, they thought. No – the sounds seemed to be coming from above. Willi and Tom! So they waited, shivering.

I removed Barrel's regulator from his empty bottle and screwed it into Lute's. We were together now, sharing the support so vigorously debated a week before. Lute would know the way back to their camp, even in the dark. All we had to do was help them down. Fumbling with unfeeling fingers, I tried to attach Barrel's oxygen hose to the regulator. Damn! Can't make the connection. My fingers scraped uncoordinatedly against the cold metal. Try again. There it goes. Then, quickly, numb fingers clumsy, back into mittens. Feeling slowly returned, and pain. Then, the pain went and the fingers were warm again.

Willi remembered the Dexedrine I had dropped into my shirt pocket the evening before. I fished out two pills – one for Barrel and one for Lute. Barrel was better with oxygen, but why I had balked at his communal use of Lute's regulator, I cannot say. Lack of oxygen? Fatigue? it was fifteen hours since we'd started the climb. Or was it that my thoughts were too busy with another problem? We had to keep moving or freeze.

I led off. Lute followed in my footsteps to point out the route. Lost in the darkness sixty feet back on our ropes, Willi and Barrel followed. The track was more sensed than seen, but it was easier now, not so steep. My eyes watered from searching for the black holes punched in the snow by Lute's and Barrel's axes during their ascent. We walked to the left of the crest, three feet down, ramming our axes into the narrow edge. Thirty feet, and the rope came taut as Barrel collapsed in the snow, bringing the entire caravan to a halt. Lute sat down behind me. Got to keep moving. We'll never get there.

We had almost no contact with the back of the line. When the rope came taut, we stopped, when it loosened we moved on. Somewhere my oxygen ran out, but we were going too slow for me to notice the difference. Ought to dump the empty bottle, I thought, but it was too much trouble to take off my pack.

Heat lightning flashed along the plains to the east, too distant to light our way. Rocks that showed in the snow below seemed to get no closer as the hours passed. Follow the axe holes. Where'd they go? Not sure. There's another.

"Now where, Lute?"

"Can't see, Tom," Lute said. "Can't see a damn thing. We've got to turn down a gully between some rocks."

"Which gully. There's two or three."

"Don't know, Tom."

"Think, Lute. Try to remember. We've got to get to six."

"I don't know. I just can't see."

Again and again I questioned, badgering, trying to extract some hint. But half blind and weary, Lute had no answer. We plodded on. The rocks came closer.

Once the rope jerked tight, nearly pulling me off balance. Damn! What's going on? I turned and looked at Lute's dim form lying on the snow a few feet further down the Kangshung Face. His fall had been effectively if uncomfortably arrested when his neck snagged the rope between Willi and me.

We turned off the crest, toward the rocks. Tongues of snow pierced the cliffs below. But which one? It was too dangerous to plunge on. After midnight we reached the rocks. It had taken nearly three hours to descend 400 ft, maybe fifteen minutes' worth by daylight.

Tired. No hope of finding camp in the darkness. No choice but to wait for day. Packs off. Willi and I slipped into our down parkas. In the dark, numb fingers couldn't start the zippers. We settled to the ground, curled as small as possible atop our pack frames. Lute and Barrel were somewhere behind, apart, each alone. Willi and I tried hugging each other to salvage warmth, but my uncontrollable shivering made it impossible.

The oxygen was gone, but the mask helped a little for warmth. Feet, cooling, began to hurt. I withdrew my hands from the warmth of my crotch and loosened crampon binding and boot laces, but my feet stayed cold. Willi offered to rub them. We removed boots and socks and planted both my feet against his stomach. No sensation returned.

Tired by the awkward position, and frustrated by the result, we gave up. I slid my feet back into socks and boots, but couldn't tie them. I offered to warm Willi's feet. Thinking that his freedom from pain was due to high tolerance of cold, he declined. We were too weary to realize the reason for his comfort.

The night was overpoweringly empty. Stars shed cold unshimmering light. The heat lightning dancing along the plains spoke of a world of warmth and flatness. The black silhouette of Lhotse lurked half sensed, half seen, still below. Only the ridge on which we were rose higher, disappearing into the night, a last lonely outpost of the world.

Mostly there was nothing. We hung suspended in a timeless void. The wind died, and there was silence. Even without wind it was cold. I could reach back and touch Lute or Barrel lying head to toe above me. They seemed miles away.

Unsignalled, unembellished, the hours passed. Intense cold penetrated, carrying with it the realization that each of us was completely alone. Nothing Willi could do for me or I for him. No team now, just each of us, imprisoned with his own discomfort, his own thoughts, his own will to survive.

Yet for me, survival was hardly a conscious thought. Nothing to plan, nothing to push for, nothing to do but shiver and wait for the sun to rise. I floated in a dreamlike eternity, devoid of plans, fears, regrets. The heat lightning, Lhotse, my companions, discomfort, all were there – yet not there. Death had no meaning, nor, for that matter, did life. Survival was no concern, no issue. Only a dulled impatience for the sun to rise tied my formless thoughts to the future.

About 4.00 the sky began to lighten along the eastern rim, baring the bulk of Kangchenjunga. The sun was slow in following, interminably slow. Not till after 5.00 did it finally come, its light streaming through the South Col, blazing yellow across the Nuptse Wall, then onto the white wave crest of peaks far below. We watched as if our own life was being born again. Then as the cold yellow light touched us, we rose. There were still miles to go.

The rest is like a photograph with little depth of field, the focused moments crystal sharp against a blurred background of fatigue. We descended the gully I had been unable to find in the dark. Round the corner, Dave and Girmi were coming toward us. They thought they heard shouts in the night and had started up, but their own calls were followed only by silence. Now as they came in search of the bodies of Lute and Barry they saw people coming down – not just two, but four. Dave puzzled a moment before he understood.

The tents at Camp VI – and we were home from the mountain. Nima Dorje brought tea. We shed boots. I started blankly at the marble-white soles of Willi's feet. They were cold and hard as ice. We filled in Emerson's diary for the last time, then started down.

With wind tearing snow from its rocky plain, the South Col was as desolate and uninviting as it had always been described. We sought shelter in the tents at Camp V for lunch, then emerged into the gale. Across the Geneva Spur, out of the wind, onto the open sweep of the Lhotse Face we plodded in sombre procession. Dave led gently, patiently; the four behind rocked along, feet apart to keep from falling. Only for Willi and me was this side of the mountain new. Like tourists we looked around, forgetting fatigue for a moment.

At Camp IV we stopped to melt water, then continued with the setting sun, walking through dusk into darkness as Dave guided us among crevasses, down the Cwm. It was a mystery to me how he found the way. I walked along at the back, following the flashlight. Sometimes Willi stopped and I would nearly bump into him. We waited while Dave searched, then moved on. No one complained.

At 10.30 p.m. we arrived at Advance Base. Dick, Barry, and Al were down from the Ridge, waiting. Frozen feet and Barrel's hands were thawed in warm water. Finally to bed, after almost two days. Short a sleeping bag, Willi and I shared one as best we could.

May 24 we were late starting, tired. Lute, Willi, and Barrel walked on thawed feet. It was too dangerous to carry them down through the Icefall. Willi, ahead of me on the rope, heeled down like an awkward clown. The codeine wasn't enough to prevent cries of pain when he stubbed his toes against the snow. I cried as I walked behind, unharmed.

At Camp I Maynard nursed us like a mother hen, serving us water laboriously melted from ice samples drilled from the glacier for analysis. Then down through the Icefall, past Jake's grave – and a feeling of finality. It's all done. The dream's finished.

No rest. The next day, a grim grey one, we departed Base. From low-hanging clouds wet snow fell. Willi, Barrel, and Lute were loaded aboard porters to be carried down over the rocky moraine. It was easier walking.

At Gorak Shep we paused. On a huge boulder a Sherpa craftsman had patiently carved:

IN MEMORY OF JOHN E. BREITENBACH,
AMERICAN MOUNT EVEREST EXPEDITION, 1963.

Clouds concealed the mountain that was Jake's grave.

As we descended, the falling snow gave way to a fine drizzle. There was nothing to see; just one foot, then another. But slowly a change came, something that no matter how many times experienced, is always new, like life. It was life. From ice and snow and rock, we descended to a world of living things, of green – grass and trees and bushes. There was no taking it for granted. Spring had come, and even the grey drizzle imparted a wet sheen to all that grew. At Pheriche flowers bloomed in the meadows.

Lying in bed, Willi and I listened to a sound that wasn't identifiable, so foreign was it to the place – the chopping whir as a helicopter circled, searching for a place to light. In a flurry of activity Willi and Barrel were loaded aboard. The helicopter rose from the hilltop above the village and dipped into the distance. The chop-chop-chop of the blades faded, until finally the craft itself was lost in the massive backdrop. The departure was too unreal, too much a part of another world, to be really comprehended. Less than five days after they had stood on the summit of Everest, Barrel and Willi were back in Kathmandu. For them the Expedition was ended. Now all that remained was weeks in bed, sitting, rocking in pain, waiting for toes to mummify to the time for amputation.

Up over barren passes made forbidding by mist and a chill wind, we travelled. Hard work. Then down through forests of rain-drenched rhododendrons, blossoming pastels of pink and lavender. Toes hurt. Two weeks to Kathmandu. Feet slipped on the muddy path. Everything was wet.

We were finished. Everest was climbed; nothing to push for now. Existence knew only the instant, counting steps, falling asleep each time we stopped to rest beside the trail. Lester, Emerson, and I talked about motivation; for me it was all gone. It was a time of relaxation, a time when senses were turned to perceive, but nothing was left to give.

Pleasure lay half-hidden beneath discomfort, fatigue, loneliness. Willi was gone. The gap where he had been was filled with question: Why hadn't I known that his feet were numb? Surely I could have done something, if only . . . I was too weary to know the question couldn't be resolved. Half of me seemed to have gone with him; the other half was isolated from my companion by an experience I couldn't share and by the feeling that something was ending that had come to mean too much. Talk of home, of the first evening in the Yak and Yeti Bar, of the reception that waited, was it really so important? Did it warrant the rush?

We'd climbed Everest. What good was it to Jake? To Willi, to Barrel? To Norman, with Everest all done now? And to the rest of us? What waits? What price less tangible than toes? There must be something more to it than toiling over the top of another, albeit expensive, mountain. Perhaps there was something of the nobility-that-is-man in it somewhere, but it was hard to be sure.

Yes, it satisfied in a way. Not just climbing the mountain, but the entire effort – the creating something, the few of us moulding it from the beginning. With a lot of luck we'd succeeded. But what had we proved?

Existence on a mountain is simple. Seldom in life does it come any simpler: survival, plus the striving toward the summit. The goal is solidly, three-dimensionally there – you can see it, touch it, stand upon it – the way to reach it well defined, the energy of all directed toward its achievement. It is this simplicity that strips the veneer off civilization and makes that which is meaningful easier to come by – the pleasure of deep companionship, moments of uninhibited humour, the tasting of hardship, sorrow, beauty, joy. But it is this very simplicity that may prevent finding answers to the questions I had asked as we approached the mountain.

Then I had been unsure that I could survive and function in a world so foreign to my normal existence. Now I felt at home here, no longer overly afraid. Each step toward Kathmandu carried me back toward the known, yet toward many things terribly unknown, toward goals unclear, to be reached by paths undefined.

Beneath fatigue lurked the suspicion that the answers I sought were not to be found on a mountain. What possible difference could climbing Everest make? Certainly the mountain hadn't been changed. Even now wind and falling snow would have obliterated most signs of our having been there. Was I any greater for having stood on the highest place on earth? Within the wasted figure that stumbled weary and fearful back toward home there was no question about the answer to that one.

It had been a wonderful dream, but now all that lingered was the memory. The dream was ended.

The Upper Tower

Peter Boardman

The British climbers Peter Boardman and Joe Tasker formed one of the most dynamic climbing partnerships of the late 1970s. Below Boardman recounts their negotiation of the Upper Tower during their ascent (the first) of the awesome 6,844 m (22,462 ft) Changabang West Wall of Kumaon Himalaya in 1976. Six years later Boardman and Tasker disappeared whilst attempting the unclimbed North-East Ridge of Everest.

9th–13th October

Camp I shrank below me, a blue dot on the curve of the ridge that swept from far beneath my feet towards Bagini Peak and Dunagiri. The only sounds were the wind whipping the corners of my down hood, and my own heavy panting as I pushed and pulled myself up the rope with the jumars. I was returning to the problem, feeling strong. Everything around me was pure in the light of receding dawn. The fresh powder snow, the harsh crystalline granite, the air itself, seemed newly created. There was even a terrible cleanliness about the danger to which I was exposed.

Two hundred feet below me, Joe was fixing a few short lengths of the rope from Shipton's Col, over the rock steps above Camp I. He had agreed to continue up behind and do the finger work of dismantling the fixed ropes beneath the Balcony and bringing them up with him. To compensate his extra burden, I was carrying all the down equipment.

It had been the earliest start we had ever made on the mountain. I had not slept well. I had kept on waking up and thinking about the route. At three in the morning I had decided I was certainly not going to get any more sleep. Silently resenting Joe's peaceful doze, I had leant out of the door in the darkness and smashed some snow off the ever-retreating section of the cornice outside the tent and put the brew on. "Typical!" I had thought. "I bet he hardly stirs for another three hours." And he did not. Nevertheless, we had moved off by half past six, at first light.

The plan was to pull up all the six terylene ropes hanging below the spike beneath the Balcony, where we had spent our first hammock bivouac. These, combined with the ropes on the icefield, ought to be enough to fix the Upper Tower. In this way we could still leave two ropes tied through the overhangs. We knew that if we retrieved these, we could never get back again. We had mused morbidly that it was retrieving the rope after the first crossing of the Hinterstoisser traverse on the Eiger that had cut off the retreat and precipitated the tragic deaths of the four climbers in 1936, including Toni Kurz. Joe and I were not prepared to cut off our retreat completely. If the hammock plan had worked, then we would have moved slowly up the mountain, stopping whenever we finished the day's climbing. But now, if we could establish the tent on the icefield, we would have to work every day from there, and take all the risks of jumaring and prusiking that it entailed.

I was astonished how smoothly the jumaring went. I was carrying two long sticks of bamboo that we had rescued from one of the Japanese expedition camps. I had pushed them as far as possible to the bottom of my sack. Now their ends wavered in the air above my head like bizarre antennae, as if they were rendering mysterious aid to my progress. I was wearing my one-piece down suit, yet even when the sun came out I was not too hot. The weather was steadily becoming colder. As I negotiated the vertical jumaring onto the foot of the icefield above the Toni Kurz pitch,[1] I was

1 Mordantly named by Boardman and Tasker after Toni Kurz, the German climber who died of exposure hanging on the end of a rope on Eiger Nordwand in 1936.

bouncing about as usual when I ripped a large tear in the suit. For the rest of the journey up the ropes, I was accompanied by a trail of down, which rose, hovered and plummeted on the up-and-down draughts of air that sailed around the West Wall. Now, instead of staring glumly at the ice as I recovered between bursts of effort, I watched feathers soar hundreds of feet, with the intensity of a child at a balloon competition at a fair. Yet this was a more expensive game. I decided, and determined to wear my oversuit on top of my down suit in the future.

I reached the high point at half past two in the afternoon, thankfully to find that all the equipment, food and fuel we had left there was still intact. Combined with the food and fuel we were bringing up with us, we had a week's provisions – or ten days in an uncomfortable emergency. We were still feeling fit and fresh. I knew that I had lost a lot of weight, and that my body had become hardened and sinews become wiry with the effort of the previous few weeks. And I knew, also, that this feeling might not last for long. However, for the moment my mind and body felt in perfect accord, as if my will could force my limbs into any situation, as long as it entailed reaching the summit of the mountain.

The critical problem then was to find a site for us to pitch Camp II. I unclipped from the rope and started soloing around the mixed ground above the fixed rope. After climbing about fifteen feet, I came to my senses and decided to clip back on. It was stupidity to deny myself some sort of chance if I were to slip. Joe was still a long way behind me on the icefield, so I pulled through fifty feet of the spare rope we had left up there and tied on to it. Then, with more confidence, I started climbing. I ran half the rope out, by which time Joe had arrived. Joe belayed me and I looked at all the area within seventy feet above our high point. Every time a line of rock promised a ledge, on inspection I always found its top stacked steeply with hard water ice. I crept back to Joe. I could not talk to him because of the wind, until I had reached him.

"Well, there aren't any good ledges. We might as well try and hack a platform out of this bit of ice as any other."

We tied off to fifteen-foot lengths of rope and started slicing into the ice with our axes.

We set about the work with enthusiasm. This was mountaineering at its most basic; serious play. As a child I had loved building tree-top dens and digging dug-outs. This was similar elemental home building, except the difference was the situation and the materials. Now we had the threat of bad weather and avalanche hanging over our heads if we did not do a good job. Secure shelter would make the difference between success and failure.

The ice-cutting was exhausting work. We hacked furiously until stopped by shortness of breath or cramp in the forearms. We soon hit the rock of the slab under the ice, and this forced the limit on the width of the ledge. By the time the sun was sinking into the cloud beyond Dunagiri, we had enlarged a ledge six feet long, two feet six inches wide at one end and tapering to two feet at the other. Whilst I tensioned the tent off from a system of nuts, spikes and rock and ice pegs I had fixed above, Joe lashed two sticks of the Japanese bamboo together and bent them across the entrance like a hoop. He improvised guylines from little stones knotted into the walls of the tent and hammered our hammock spacer bars into the ice for tent pegs.

Before the afternoon sun disappeared, I finished off the pitch I had started leading earlier. The climbing was quite awkward, but it was mere scrambling compared to that beneath the icefield. My thoughts raced ahead with the hope that the Upper Tower would be quickly climbed if it were all like that.

The last rays of the sun had moved off the Wall high above us and "home" was ready.

"There doesn't seem to be much room in there," I commented.

"We'll have to tie on well," said Joe.

"Yeah, that's a drag, we'll have to leave part of the tent open to let the line through. And we'll have to keep our harnesses on inside our sleeping bags."

We had left our full body harnesses at Camp I, and put on our sit harnesses, hoping to save weight and also because the full body harnesses got in the way of the pockets of our

oversuits. Now we regretted having made this decision, for
the point of attachment of the sit harnesses was so low
down. Outside the tent there was a chaos of equipment,
slings and ropes, and after we had sorted them out the
question that had been in the backs of our minds came out
into the open. "Who's going to sleep on the outside then?"
If Joe was still insisting that I cooked breakfast, then I was
not going to give in on this question. To my surprise, he
agreed to sleep on the side of the tent overhanging the edge.

"Only for a couple of nights, mind you," he said.

The tent was so cramped there was only room for one of
us to sort himself out at a time. I went in and laid the
insulating mats and the hammocks down, took off my boots
and got into my sleeping bags. Joe squeezed in and did the
same.

"Christ, my knees protrude over the edge," he said.

"Isn't it cosy?" I said.

"Good job we've got our pee bottles with us," said Joe.
"I wouldn't fancy getting up in the middle of the night for a
piss!"

"Make sure you pour it out on the left-hand side, we
don't want our cooking ice polluted," I said.

We wedged the stove in between the soles of my boots in
the tent entrance and put a brew on. The wind did not seem
to be penetrating the thin fabric.

"You taking Dalmane or Valium tonight?" asked Joe.

"Dalmane, Dalmane, all around my brain, please."

Saturday, October 9th. I had missed the BMC Peak Area
Meeting!

The improvised tent was protecting us – the problem of
shelter had been solved, and my heart warmed to the action
to come.

We had decided that on the Upper Tower we would do
two leads each in succession. We expected to go just as
slowly on the Upper Tower as we had done below and had
found that leading four rope lengths each was too much –
two days' consecutive leading had been exhausting, and if
you were seconding, you lost a feel for the action. The next
day I was intending to run out another rope length before
Joe took over.

It was an exciting change to start climbing in the cold of the morning, straight from the camp and without any jumaring. But the optimism of the previous afternoon was short lived.

The only line that offered any feasibility of progress was a bottomless groove that was guarded from me by a bulge of ice. As I moved up to the bulge I started feeling tired. The climbing became hard and the wind and cold were sapping my strength. I was now wearing both down and nylon Ventile oversuits – far more than I had ever found it necessary to wear on Everest the year before. With my overmitts off and dangling from my wrists, and wearing only the pairs of gloves underneath, my fingers quickly became cold. I wanted to avoid making them colder by trying to put my crampons on. I traversed left on the rock to below where a bulge turned into a rock overhang. This was slit by a ramp, which I managed to step onto, and I traversed across to the side of the ice that filled the back of a hanging groove. Rather than put crampons on, I tapped a drive-in ice peg into the ice. It went in a couple of inches before stopping against the rock underneath. I tied a nylon rope sling around it where it came out of the ice, and stepped into it. Then I repeated the same movement further up the groove twice, before I could bridge out with my feet on either side on to rock. A few feet of climbing and I had reached the top of the groove.

The groove was capped by a six-foot overhang. I saw one ledge eighteen inches wide over on the left that ran around the corner onto the North Face and, after shouting a few warning words to Joe, I crawled along it. The wall above me bulged out and I was virtually on all fours. The ledge was in a horrifying position, without the icefield to soften the view downwards. Below me was a sheer drop of 4,000 ft onto the Bagini Glacier. By curling my fingers around narrow side-holds, I braced myself sideways and peered round the corner. We had seen, through our binoculars from the glacier, a long slanting groove line high on the edge of the Upper Tower between the West and North Walls. It had been the only obvious feature on the Upper Tower and we had hoped it would offer some straightforward crack

climbing. We had called it "the Niche". Looking upwards
now I could see it, and it scared me even to look at it! The
corner was vertical, ice-smeared and 200 ft high. I shouted
down to Joe.

"I've seen the Niche. It's around the corner. It overhangs
the North Face and looks bloody impossible – to reach it,
climb it, or get upwards from the top of it. We'll only get up
if we climb the right side of the Upper Tower for the next
few pitches!"

It was a measure of our trust in each other's climbing
judgment that Joe accepted all this immediately, without
demanding a look of his own.

The right-handed exit offered the only option – a fifteen-
foot leaning crack. I tried to climb it by artificial aid, but
none of the pegs or nuts I had with me would fit the crack.
"Don't be such a chicken," I told myself inside. "If this was
on gritstone you'd bomb up it. It's obviously a lay back
crack and doesn't look as if it'll play any tricks. Just take a
few deep breaths and fight up it."

I felt as if I had lead in my boots and my weight had
doubled as soon as I swung my weight onto my arms. Half-
way up the lay back, my fingers started to unfold from the
edge of the crack so I rammed my fist round and into the
back of the crack and squeezed it in a hand jam. I locked my
arm straight from the jam and hung there until my breathing returned to normal. Then I returned to the lay back
position and fought, with continually draining strength,
upwards. My fingers curled over the edge of the arête that
bounded the top of the crack. The arête rocked a little – it
was a granite block of dubious quality. But I was past caring
about that. One last heave and I swung up onto some
footholds and gasped for air. A momentary feeling of
nausea welled up from my stomach; I thought I was going
to vomit. I managed to bang a peg in, tied the rope off and
shouted down into the wind to Joe that he could start
jumaring.

"That would have been quite a respectable grade on
gritstone," I thought, and resolved to avoid such strenuous
climbing in the future. I looked down past Joe at the buff-
coloured tent of Camp II, now two hundred steep feet

below. Beyond that was the sweep of the icefield and then nothing. The Wall seemed to breathe in under that. There was only the Rhamani Glacier, and the tiny dot of the Ridge Camp I was just visible. Joe was dangling beneath me, all arms and legs, braced across the groove, hanging from a thread. He was unscrewing the ice pegs.

"A pity you'll miss the lay back," I said.

It was an uncharitable sentiment which back home on rock I used to relish when I watched seconds struggling up something difficult that I had led. Joe heard me from beneath his layers of balaclava, helmet and hood.

"It looked quite hard," he muttered. With a few upward strokes of his jumars, he had joined me. Now it was his turn.

With confident balance, Joe moved up a few feet above my head and then traversed diagonally rightwards under a line of overhangs, placing his feet carefully on a narrow sloping granite shelf. He placed a runner around a spike and looked around, obviously enjoying himself:

> The climbing was delicate and thrilling, tip-toeing up the edge with stupendous exposure below. At the end of the shelf was a magnificent groove, steep and reminiscent of a Scottish climb. I put on my crampons. I found it hard, but on the right side of the borderline. Rocks frozen in place provided welcome holds and, when loose, added an extra thrill to the climbing. I was bridged across the icy runnel for most of the way. It was just the kind of pitch I enjoyed most, varied, intricate, uncertain.

I was watching the progress of the sun. The shadow crept back towards me imperceptibly, but inexorably. It had long since moved down the Bagini Peak and past Camp I. As the Wall steepened, so its speed increased. For a few moments I could see the icefield crystals shimmering in the sun's halo above the windswept South-West Ridge. Then the sun came out and the shadow ran away up the Wall. But the wind and the altitude were fighting away the warmth that should have come with the light.

The rope stopped moving, and there was not much of it

left. The restless wind swept our shouts aside and threw
them around the mountain. I decided that Joe must have
tied on. I pulled on the terylene rope. Yes, it seemed
secured. I shouldered the sack and moved off.

I was tense with concentration as I crossed the shelf that
Joe had appeared to stroll across with such ease. "Perhaps
my boots are too big. Perhaps it's the weight of the sack.
Perhaps I'm having an off day. I wish he'd put more
runners in, I might swing off," I thought. The thought
that Joe was climbing well, was not allowed. I swallowed
my moans.

The groove up which he had disappeared looked as if it
had been fun to climb, with a succession of spikes to haul up
on – held on to the mountain by hard water ice. But now I
had swung into the line of the rope and was jumaring past
them. Above the groove there was some easier angled rock
and the rope whipped back left around the edge of the
Upper Tower. I followed it and found Joe standing at the
bottom of an overhanging groove that split the edge of the
mountain for about 300 ft. We both hoped it would not be
necessary to climb that, and called it the "Big Groove".
However, the alternative over on the right did not look
much more attractive – massive blank walls stepped by
overhangs looming upwards for over 500 ft confronted us.

"There might be some easier angled ground on the left
between us and the top of the Niche," said Joe. And he
disappeared round the corner, leaving me standing at the
foot of the Big Groove.

For two hours, Joe fought a hard and cunning battle with
the rock and ice of the North Face on the left of the Big
Groove:

> I came to a long, slightly overhanging crack. I chose to
> look further left. The crack was feasible but would
> have been very strenuous. Another corner had a ton-
> gue of ice running up into it – this seemed a better
> proposition. The ice was steep, a lot steeper than it had
> looked from below and, as I gained height, the tongue
> of ice became narrower and thinner. I had difficulty in
> maintaining my balance. I hammered a thin blade

piton into a crack above. It only went in an inch, but gave me a little more support. I wondered whether to come down and try the other corner. It would be time-wasting to start again; I could see nothing of Pete. He would be wondering at the slow movement of the rope. I hoped he had secure hold of it. The next few moves would depend on everything working together just right.

I hammered the pick of an axe into the ice; carefully, I balanced up and stood on the head of the axe protruding from the ice. Gently I reached down and undid my crampons. With my boots free of the crampons I stepped up onto small footholds on the rock, feeling strangely naked. I bent down and yanked out the axe.

There were some delicate moves to make on the rock, but the friction of the rope pulled me back. I had to strain furiously to pull sufficient rope through to allow me to move up a few feet.

Above was another ice slope. It seemed like a haven of security. On the rock I had been exposed and vulnerable. I drove the pick of my axe into the ice and went through the procedure of refixing my cram-pons.

With my crampons on, I climbed up the ice to a grotto where I could see some boulders to which I attached the rope, and relaxed.

It was obvious that this lead had been desperately hard and, for Joe, the most demanding of the climb so far. I found it very difficult leaving Joe's last runner without swinging off further over the North Face like a pendulum – a sixty-foot swing could do a lot of damage and I would have difficulty getting back. I felt mentally and physically tired when I reached Joe. "It's getting late," I said.

Joe, full of accounts of sliding feet and frightening hops with ice hammers, was obviously thirsting for more action. It was 4.30. We had not far to descend back to the tent, but we knew it would start getting dark at five. There were seventy feet of steep ice above us on the North Face. It was my turn to lead but Joe was obviously more in tune than I. He set off up it, after agreeing to stop at five. He climbed it carefully but quickly and hammered in two pegs. The shadow that had climbed upwards six hours before was now returning. It was good to have snatched those extra feet at the end of the day. We swung quickly down the ropes to Camp II, feeling happy. Things were going well.

Back in the tent, we peered at our photographs of the Face, trying to calculate our latest high point. We knew that we could not continue up the North Face any further, for we wanted to reach a feature which we had named "the Ramp" – a thin line of snow that appeared from our photographs to stretch down from the summit snowfield, through an area of steep rock to the top of the Upper Tower. If we became committed to the upper section of the North Face, we would inevitably miss that exit. We only had five lengths of rope left which we could fix in place. After that we would have to climb away from our lifeline, and the Ramp seemed to be the only feature that would not trap us on the Wall or dangerously slow us down, but would offer us a slim chance of success. So the next day we would have to try and regain the crest of the Upper Tower above the Big Groove. And that would be my task.

It was morning.

"Bloody hell, no lumps of ice left." I swore violently.

Joe's eyes shuttered open briefly. "What's up, hasn't it been delivered?"

All my pent-up fears and frustrations were being released in curses into the morning wind. I had forgotten to break any ice the night before for the breakfast cooking and, in the darkness, was having to stretch out and claw at the ice hanging above the tent. Slowly, I accumulated a pile of ice chips on the side of the level patch outside, shouting loudly and angrily at the fragments that splintered off into the air and bounced down the mountainside. Back inside the tent, I tried to warm myself up again and started melting the ice, chip by chip. "I'll be glad when we've got up this mountain!" I mumbled, as it started becoming lighter. "I'm fed up with this view, I hope we can see Nanda Devi from the top."

The reality that soon I was going to have to do two hours of frightening jumaring was gnawing at me and I was irritable. I crushed thoughts that Joe, lying snoozing peacefully, was deliberately obstructing my cooking, and felt embarrassed about my morning moaning. I had not been shouting at him; I wanted to say I wasn't blaming him for suggesting this climb, for not cooking breakfasts. I was just exploding with the tension and shouting at everything – it did not mean anything and I was all right now. But our conversation had died to a basic minimum. I tried to rouse him with some talk about how settled the weather was. I felt that we ought to talk about something. But Joe hated small talk and platitudes, and felt as if I were treating him as if he were on one of the BMC Committees. He preferred to keep his brain ticking over in neutral.

It was the lonely hour of dawn. Joe went down to the icefield to pick up three ropes which we would need for climbing on and fixing on the Upper Tower. We had done a lot of diagonal climbing backwards and forwards the previous day, and I went up to straighten out the first three rope lengths. By removing the first two anchors, I hoped to be able to save a hundred and fifty feet of rope for higher up. It all seemed feasible in theory. On reaching the second anchor, I wanted to swing the rope into line below Joe's shelf pitch. I took the peg out and leaned sideways on the rope. But I had miscalculated the distance I was going to swing. Time closed up before me, like the progression of incidents in a split-second dream. I was soon hurtling through the air with a momentum that would not have been out of place on an Outward Bound ropes course. Too late I tried to spin my legs round to take the impact, but was not fast enough and I crashed into a wall, vertically below the next anchor, with a sickening thud that squeezed all the wind out of me. I had swung forty feet – half a pendulum, stopped abruptly by a rock wall.

I wriggled as much as I was able, whilst suspended from my jumars. No, nothing seemed to be broken. My mind shrugged grimly, "Well, I'm still here." I looked down at Joe, a tiny dot on the icefield. He probably had not seen my mishap, and why should he bother about it anyway? There

was nothing he could do. We were further apart than we
had been for a long time.

It was strange deciding the line of the ropes, by myself,
after days of deciding all tactics by consultation. I laughed
at how dependent I was becoming, and moved on. I chose
to keep the line of the rope going through Joe's groove in
the overhangs, so as to avoid any overhanging jumaring.
Soon after eleven, I was established at the previous day's
highpoint and waiting for Joe, feeling determined to maintain the momentum he had set in his lead the previous day.

The problem was to try and move back right to the edge
of the Upper Tower. There was a line of cracks stretching
across a steep wall in between us and the sky line. Guarding
any entrance to them was an enormous flake. It was angular
and about ten feet across, and it was possible to see light
behind it in places. It seemed to be glued to the side of the
mountain by a few patches of ice. Wearing my crampons, I
front-pointed up to it and thumped it hard with my hammer. "BOOMM!" it replied threateningly.

"What do you think to this, Joe, do you think it'll be safe?
It might skate off with me riding it."

"Oh, it'll be all right," he replied. "It must have been
there long enough. Anyway," he added reassuringly, "it's
not my lead, is it?"

Nervously, I draped a sling over the top of the spike, as if
I were conferring a holy order. I curled my fingers around
the edge of this spike and swung my weight onto it. Nothing
moved, except my mind, which was whirring with thoughts
of the sweeping action this great tonnage of rock would have
on us if it decided to detach itself. What would Joe do with
me if I broke my back up here?

I slotted the front points of my crampons into a tiny lip of
granite on the block and edged across. Leaning across the
wall I could just reach a crack about two inches wide. At full
stretch, I managed to prod a large bong peg into it, and this
I patted in until it seemed to stay there by itself. Using this
as a hand hold, I traversed out a little further. I reached
high above my head with my hammer pick and hooked it
into a little niche in the rock, then, pulling myself up onto
this, made a lunge with my feet for a foothold on the edge of

the buttress. Gently, I eased my weight over my feet until I was in balance. The foothold was a good one and I relaxed, detachedly amused at myself for reaching such an extra-ordinary position.

The sun had moved onto us whilst I had been climbing and I could see my shadow silhouetted on the rock above Joe. Beyond his self-absorbed form hanging in slings, I could see the forbidding sweep of the North Face and the brown lines of moraine on the Bagini Glacier, far below. I was directly above the Big Groove, and could now see parts of the West Wall again. I leant across and screwed a good hand jam into the top of the crack at the back of the Big Groove, and bridged across. A few feet above, the Big Groove reached an apex, like a pea pod, and I swarmed up to it. Above this, there was a ten-foot-high iceslope and I planted my ice-axe and hammer into this and pulled up until I was teetering on the ice with my front points. My calves were quivering with the strain and I battered the ice with my axe until a foothold splintered into existence and I could rest my foot sideways. Above me, the Wall reared up again, split by a thin crack. Longing for security, I pounded three pegs into it, a blade, a soft steel blade and a leeper. These three pegs provided a welcome refuge after the sixty feet of instability beneath me.

Joe jumared up to me and we quickly discussed the situation. We had generated such unified intensity of pur-pose that whatever Joe said I had been thinking at the same time. Yes, we would straighten the fixed ropes the next morning. Yes, the next pitch should bring the Ramp into view. Yes, the crack looks the best line to follow until I can tension around the corner. The wind and the sunshine were forgotten.

The crack line became continually thinner, but there were no other features to use to climb this blank wall. After twenty feet, it faded out among the granite crystals. I leant down and sideways until it seemed every muscle in my body was taut. My balance was wobbling on the point of swing-ing me round and off the rock like an unfastened barn door in a draught. I was able to place a one-inch long knife blade peg in upside down, and this enabled me to reach another crack line which took me around an arête into a groove. For twenty feet I was able to establish a pattern of movement as the pegging became straightforward, and there was no hope of free climbing, since the rock was either vertical or overhanging. However, soon I was running out of equipment and above a short overhang I could see the back of the upper part of the groove gleaming with bulging ice. "Nothing's ever simple," I thought. I took out two pegs I had used below me and placed them, and then knocked two ice pegs into the ice-filled crack. As I moved my weight onto them, I was not quite sure if it was the rock, ice or just a lot of luck that held them there. Now I only had small angle pegs left, and there were no ledges in sight.

Our route seemed to be forcing us up into ever more bleakly exposed fly-on-the-wall situations. However careful we always were at retrieving pegs, there were always some that were dropped or were left behind, and now we were running short of many sizes. The three angles that I had hammered in did not inspire my confidence, but I convinced myself that, on the law of averages, one of them would stay in, and I tied the rope off. "Joe can sort it out from here in the morning," I decided.

"Can you see the start of the Ramp?" shouted Joe.

"Yes, I think so." I returned to him, de-pegging as I descended and it was nearly dark when I reached him. We were late and, for the first time, I realized the full consequences of the loss of my descendeur as I struggled down with my complicated karabiner brake, past pegs and knots. The difficulty of this descent was a harbinger of the nightmare descents to come.

Dawn, the following morning, was the time of reckoning. I was going to have to go to the loo. I had been fighting this moment off all the previous day. Crawling out of the tent was a problem in itself, there were so many things I could knock over, including Joe and the tent. Only one person could move at a time and it was my turn. I imagined that I was at the fairground, trying one of those games where you have a circle of wire in your hand which you have to thread along another meandering piece of thicker wire without touching it. If you do touch it, a buzzer rings and you lose your money. Joe, the tent door, the pan on the stove, I thought, would all buzz loudly if I touched them as I threaded myself past them. Once outside the tent the game was just as delicate. On the third night, in Camp, II, we had not bothered to tie ourselves on whilst we slept, because the criss-crossed ropes inside the tent made the simplest movement too complicated. Once outside, however, to move anywhere you had to climb, and it was important to tie on. We had cut a line of steps underneath the tent and these I followed until I reached the back of the ledge. There, leaning out on the rope, I wrestled with the specially-designed zips of the oversuit, down suit and polar fibre undersuit. As soon as they were undone, my trousers started flapping agitatedly upwards, like medieval streamers in the bitter wind that was rolling up the Wall. Occasionally, my face or backside was lashed by a volley of spindrift or a flailing zip. The whole bizarre procedure took half an hour and, at the end of it, the word "masochism" had taken on a new meaning.

We had decided it was Joe's turn to go up the fixed ropes first that morning, and this gave me a feeling of relief – we were sharing the risk. Joe was to go up and straighten the fixed rope and sort himself out at the high point of the previous day. The first one up always took the risk that the wind might have frayed the rope against a sharp edge of rock somewhere. Nevertheless, following him I was still apprehensive, even though he had tested the rope and anchors like the jester sampling the king's food for poison. When we had climbed the rock below the icefield we had thought it steep, but it seemed that now the Wall was rearing even steeper. The jumaring was correspondingly more exhausting. My thoughts, refreshed by the night's sleep, were alert to all the dangers. I was delayed by still having some rearranging of the anchors to do on the ropes above Camp II, and when I arrived at the foot of the Big Groove a shock was awaiting me. Joe had de-pegged the anchors from the three rope lengths above me and, on reaching the three peg crack, he had swung all the rope round in a great loop like a 400-ft skipping rope until he had lodged them in the Big Groove. Then he pulled them up tight. As a result I was confronted by nearly 200 ft of eight-millimetre terylene rope hanging out from the rock down towards me.

"Joe's put it there, so he must be prepared to jumar it," I thought as I started up, the competitive urge the only motivation. All the instances I had ever known of ropes snapping flashed through my mind like slides on a projector on autochange, interspersed with pictures of me spread out in the air in the apparent standstill of a free fall. "Still, at least terylene doesn't saw up and down," I thought. But as I got higher, this rope started to shudder sideways on an edge of rock at the top of the Big Groove. The apex was far away. I moved very stealthily, trying not to jerk the rope, looking at my jumars, eyes focused only on the umbilical cord that held me. The uncanny double-take, a constant companion at altitude, moved in. Was my mind here? My body seemed to be, but my mind felt free and uninvolved. Suddenly it was the top of the apex – there was the short ice slope, Joe, and the three peg crack. Joe was preparing to jumar up the last pitch to our high point.

"That last bit was exciting – it's in a good position," I said.

"It's saved a lot of rope," said Joe.

I knew that we could not afford to go up and down that length of rope many times without it wearing through, but did not mention it. Joe could see it as well as I, and he would find out all about what it was like to jumar the Big Groove when we next came back up! But did he worry as much as I did? I was filled with envy – I was seeing his existence from my separateness, and it seemed to possess a coherence and unity that mine did not.

I followed Joe up to the high point I had reached the previous day. It was a tangled procedure, interlocking me onto the hanging belay. I noticed he had only clipped into two of the three angle pegs I had placed so apprehensively before.

"Why have you only clipped onto two, Joe?"

"They look all right. Two should be enough," he said.

I hastily clipped into the third one. Pegs always give an illusion of safety if you have not put them in yourself.

The sun was filtering around on to us, as Joe set off in the lead. At first the climbing was almost identical to that of the pitch before. Joe did a few feet of pegging until the crack disappeared. He drove a blade peg until it stopped half way, and then passed the climbing rope through a karabiner on the peg. As I held the rope taut he leaned across rightwards, his weight supported by the tension in the rope. Using tiny flakes on the slab, he pulled himself across to the arête. Soon all that I could see were his left hand and foot, scything the arête. It was a fascinating puppet show. The hand and the foot jerked up and then scuttled down. Up, and then down. Up, and then down. Then suddenly they disappeared.

Around the corner, Joe was having a grim struggle:

From the arête I could see a groove with a crack in the back about six feet away. The groove continued up-wards towards the corners above.

I pulled myself round the arête. The rope was horizontal between my waist and the peg; it was still holding my weight. I tried to reach the groove but as I stretched further right I tended to swing away from the rock. There were no holds big enough to hang onto; I relied on friction to keep me in place. Moving further rightwards round the arête was to move be-yond the balance of friction maintained by the rope taking much of my weight and the rugosities of granite beneath my boots and hands. If I parted company, I would swing back twenty feet and the peg would probably come out.

I juggled with the precarious balance for a while, stretching slightly further each time by clinging to tiny flakes discovered by my groping fingers. My body was almost horizontal and still I could not reach the groove. I glanced at the rope – it was rubbing, every time I moved, up and down the sharp edge of the arête. There was a sense of detachment about this observa-tion; I wondered if I would reach the safety of the groove before the rope was cut through.

I was quite exhausted by now and as a final resort took a nylon sling from around my neck. It had an aluminium chockstone on it, which I threw towards the crack. It lodged there first time, and I pulled myself to the crack on the nylon tape. The groove was overhanging; I didn't look down to soak in the atmosphere, but hammered in a peg immediately, fastened myself to it and rested.

A few feet of free climbing took him to a large granite block, which he flopped his arm around and rested again. From the block Joe could see on his right an enormous hanging corner, 200 ft high. Above that hung tendrils of ice, signifying the start of the Ramp. Towards the middle of this corner, across an overhanging wall, ran a two-foot wide sloping ledge, thirty feet long and banked high with ice. Joe gingerly put his crampons on and kicked his way across it until he was barred by an overhang. This he pegged over. Then he hammered two pegs in to hang from, and waited:

I shouted for Pete to follow. When I remembered to examine the rope which had been wearing away on the arête I saw that it had been half cut through. I felt a lot more frightened now that I was safe and just thinking about what could have happened, than what I had actually been when involved with the situation. I cut away the frayed part and re-fastened the good rope to my waist.

Joe's tension traverse was difficult to follow, and I moved the diagonal line of his ropes by a series of swings as I knocked pegs out. It was acrobatic, and I felt like Tarzan swinging on a long vine that kept on snagging amongst twigs and branches. When I reached the big block, I peered around the corner and could see Joe, roosting forlornly above the overhang, like a big black hooded bird.

"Where are you going from there?" I shouted.

It looked like a dead end to me. The corner above him that stretched up to the Ramp would take a whole day to climb, if it was possible at all.

"Don't worry," came the habitual reassurance, with its over-emphasized, patronising tone. "I can see a way."

Feeling thankful that he did not sound frightened, I tightened up the rope along the ledge like a handrail on a catwalk, and set off along it. I had decided not to waste time putting my crampons on and my feet felt very insecure in the footholds Joe had hacked in the ice. Most of my weight was on the rope, which felt even thinner than normal, since it was stretched sideways. I remembered that the breaking strain of the rope was even lower when it was stretched horizontally. It had started to snow, and Joe was busily recording the dramatic situation and the snow and cloud effects with his camera.

Joe was right, there was a way out. Between the over-hangs, and out of sight from below, a stepped corner reached up leftwards for sixty feet back to the crest of the Upper Tower. "Good route-finding," I complimented him, wondering if he had been led there by his sixth sense, blind luck or just because he could not climb up anywhere else. At first the crack in the corner was blind and he reached another crack on the left wall by a tension traverse. This crack he followed into the corner, and proceeded to climb it by a series of delicate free moves. After an hour he reached the crest. "Can you see the Ramp? Will it go?"

"Yes, it only looks one rope length away. Hurry up, it's a hell of a way down and it will be dark in a minute."

The snow shower had passed and rock was turning red around us. But I felt relaxed. I took some pictures of Joe, varying the exposures so as to catch the lighting.

"Hurry up, there's no time for taking photographs." It was the first time Joe had sounded angrily impatient.

"Don't worry," I shouted back. "You'll be glad of them when you are an old man!"

It was another diagonal swinging pitch to follow. I retrieved all the pegs and nuts so that we could fix the edge out straight down the over-hanging wall to the big block. Joe was perched on one foothold and I hung off the slings of his spike belay whilst he sorted the equipment out for his descent. I had taken half an hour longer than he did the day before to descend back to Camp II, because I had to use a karabiner brake.

"Don't forget to put the brew on," I reminded him.

"See you soon," he said as he reeled off down the rope and out of sight.

Irrationally, I did not share Joe's sense of urgency. I looked up and saw an overhanging groove reaching up to the Ramp. For me it was a golden line of promise through an area of turmoil, as if parted by the rod of Moses. At the top it was crowned by an enormous block of granite bridging across the walls of the groove like a beam across the corner of a roofless house. Perhaps we could peep beneath the crown? Nothing could stop us now.

The rope that had been my tormentor in the harsh light of early morning awareness, had now become a friend. I was descending in a trance. The swooping slides, the dancing traverses and swings, were part of the pattern deeply hidden within the game of the descent. The complicated procedures for passing knots and pitons were factual procedures to be mastered as part of the choreography. The consequences of a mistake were forgotten. The emphasis of progress and the numbness induced by the cold, altitude and fatigue had put me in a state of reverie. A fantasy world had grown around me assuming nonsensical names and nationalities. The knots in the rope I called "cows", the pegs became "Americans", the karabiners at my waist all took the names of different girls. I was a big spider scuttling down.

There was a blue light inside the tent, telling me that the stove was purring. The brew was on. I crouched in the darkness, sorting and clipping my equipment to the slings outside, ready to crawl in for shelter.

"I nearly left you to finish the climb on your own, whilst I was up there," said Joe. He was shaken and unnerved.

At the point where there were three pegs together, the rope was criss-crossed between them. Whilst Joe had been passing this section, he had realized something was amiss, and had noticed that his jumar had become unclipped from his waist, his descendeur was in his right hand and all his weight was hanging from his left hand on the jumar.

It was really weird, odd thoughts kept on spinning round like "Is this it?" and "Is Pete going to have to finish the climb on his own?" and "I don't want to drop my descendeur." Eventually I fumbled a nylon sling from my neck, wrapped that round the rope and put my arm through it, so that I could get myself clipped in.

Joe said little as we ate our evening meal. It was the usual Oxo with freeze-dried meat and mashed potato and a cup of tea, followed by a nibble of chocolate. I dozed out of his way, as he cooked. What a day it had been – from doubt and fear to resolution. Then from intense effort to joy – all the emotions of a lifetime had been carried to my heart with extraordinary power. Yet our conversation reflected no more than a quiet, calculated hopefulness. In the morning we would move away as early as possible, pack food for two days, and push, alpine style, for the summit.

It was as if our subconscious was plugged into the same internal clock. We both woke late, having already made the decision whilst we were asleep to have a rest day. Now we were waiting for the other one to suggest it. Eventually I asked Joe what he thought about the idea since I had to decide whether to start cooking or not.

"I'm glad you suggested that," he said. And we laughed and slid back onto our imaginations, comforted by the thought that we could wait for the sunshine before starting the cooking or venturing outside into the wind to go to the toilet. That morning at least our internal clock could rest unwound.

During the afternoon, I started to feel claustrophobic inside the tent. When crawling out I accidentally knelt on some of Joe's camera equipment. He snapped at my clumsiness. I had not understood until that point his enthusiasm as a photographer. He had brought his lens tissues and brush up with him and was fastidiously cleaning his equipment.

"I had to buy my cameras," he said. "They weren't given to me, you know."

I had been given an Olympus OMi camera for the Everest climb, which I had brought up with me, fitted with a wide-angle lens. But I wasn't lavishing it with the attention that Joe thought it deserved. As usual, Joe's precise, orderly approach to bivouacking and equipment made me feel muddled and clumsy, like a small boy told off for touching in a china shop. Some people judge mountaineers by their speed, and by the difficulty of the rock they can climb. But on Changabang the real test was more how efficiently you could put a brew on, warm your fingers or take your boots off.

Outside I drank in the view in the afternoon sunshine. All the mountain shapes nearby were so familiar. Was that the Holy Kailas I could see, I wondered, looking at a solitary white-topped mountain above the distant brown plains of Tibet? Kailas – the throne of Shiva, the precious ice mountain, the crystal one, the centre of the universe. The waters of Kailas fed some of the greatest rivers of Asia and before politics and a war changed borders and religions, thousands of pilgrims travelled to walk or crawl around it. To me it was a white signpost to a forbidden land. Soon, I thought, I would see Nanda Devi from the Summit Ridge, and we would have worked hard for that view. It was now the 13th October, and soon the winter would come. We had not much time.

As I began to squirm back inside the tent I noticed some dark stains on the snow just outside the door, where Joe had been coughing. He had been spitting blood. Since he had not talked about it to me, I decided not to mention it. Inside the tent he was lying in his sleeping bag with an ecstatic look on his face.

"What's making you look so pleased with yourself?" I asked.

"Ooh," he said, "have you felt the tent fabric? It's sort of billowing down over my face, and when you touch it it sort of bulges in soft round yielding curves. Ultimate Bill says that it's the same material used for making women's underwear."

The rest of the day floated past in idle banter. Changabang did not worry us any more.

White Spider

Heinrich Harrer

Harrer was an Austrian climber, born in 1812, who was a member of the team which made the first ascent of the notorious Eigerwand. This 1938 epic is described below. During the Second World War Harrer was detained by the British in India, from whence he escaped to Tibet, where he became a friend of the Dalai Lama. His internationally famous memoir Seven Years in Tibet *(1953) details this time.*

The summer of 1938 began sadly enough, with the death of two young Italian climbers. Bartolo Sandri and Mario Menti, employees in a wool factory at Valdagno in the Province of Vicenza, were both respected members of the Italian Alpine Club though only 23 years old. Sandri, especially, was known to be an unusually fine rock-climber, who had done a number of super-severe climbs ranking as "Grade VI", among them some first ascents. True they had hardly any experience of ice-climbing in the Western Alps. Like all true mountaineers, they came to Alpiglen and the Scheidegg quietly, without any fuss, indeed almost secretly. They studied the Face, tried themselves out by a reconnaissance of its lower structure and came down again. They decided that the direct route, followed three years before by Sedlmayer and Mehringer, was easier than that discovered by Hinterstoisser. But it wasn't any easier. The fact is that the Face was not yet fit for climbing at all.

None the less Bartolo and Mario started up it early on

June 21st. They reached a greater height than Sedlmayer and Mehringer had on their first day. Their courage and enthusiasm ran high, and they were driven on by a burning urge to succeed. They just couldn't wait. Nature, however, followed her own laws, heedless of courage, enthusiasm or ambition. Late in the evening one of the Eiger's notorious thunderstorms set in . . .

The very next day a search-party of Grindelwald guides, led by Fritz Steuri Senior, found Sandri lying dead on a patch of snow at the foot of the Face. Menti's body was only recovered with some difficulty a few days later from a deep crevasse.

That was a bad enough start to operations on the Eiger in the summer of 1938, but it could not hold up the developments which were due. The memory of the successful retreat of Rebitsch and Vörg, which had been the turning point in men's minds, was still vivid. So was the lesson that it was impossible to capture the Face by surprise. *Veni, vidi, vici* wouldn't work on the Eiger. Endless patience was required and long waiting . . . for days, even weeks.

Meanwhile, Fritz Kasparek was waiting impatiently for my arrival. That tremendous climber from Vienna, bursting with life, blessed with an optimism nothing could destroy, had already been in Grindelwald for some time, skiing around the Bernese Oberland, keeping a constant watch on the Eiger's mighty Face. Though, so far, there hadn't been much to watch except continual avalanches, sufficient in themselves to nip in the bud even the thought of an attempt. All the same, Fritz would have liked by now to have had with him his partner on the big climb they had planned to do together; for one never knows what may happen to interrupt one's plans. Sepp Brunnhuber, too, with whom Fritz had done the first winter ascent of the North Face of the Grosse Zinne as long ago as February – to some extent as a training climb for the Eiger project – could still not get away. I had promised Fritz to arrive at Grindelwald by July 10; but at the bottom of his heart he had good grounds for mistrusting students' promises.

Actually I was no longer a student by the time I got to Grindelwald. My tutors at the University of Graz were greatly astonished at the speed with which I suddenly attacked my Finals. I could hardly explain to them that I wanted my studies out of the way before I climbed the North Face of the Eiger. They would certainly have shaken their heads and – not without some justification – reminded me that it was quite in order to "come off" that climb without having graduated first. I told nobody of our plan, not a fellow-student, not a mountaineering or sporting acquaintance. The only person I let into the secret was that wise, practical and plucky woman, my future mother-in-law, Frau Else Wegener. In 1930 her husband Professor Alfred Wegener had given his life for his companions on Greenland's inscrutable inland ice, when he perished in a blizzard; so she might well have had strong grounds for being fiercely opposed to ventures involving a risk to life. She, however, uttered no warning word; on the contrary, she encouraged me, though well acquainted with the reputation of the Eiger's North Face.

My last paper was on the morning of July 9th. At lunch-time I mounted my heavily laden motor-bicycle; and I arrived at Grindelwald punctually on July 10th, as promised. Fritz Kasparek, burnt brown by the glacier sun, his fair mop almost bleached white, greeted me in unmistakable Viennese.

He was blessed with the gift of the gab. His was a positively original gift for inventing expletives when faced with apparently insurmountable difficulties of the kind he was never in the habit of giving in to – both in the mountains and in ordinary life. However, he never used to parade his feelings; nor did he waffle about companionship and friendship. But his nature was such that, at times of crisis, he would not only share his last crust of bread or crumb of chocolate with his companions, but would give the whole of it away to them. And then not as a pathetic gesture, but to the accompaniment of some good nervous Viennese expression or other.

With friends of that kind one could go horse-rustling, invite the Devil to a picnic or – attempt the North Face of the Eiger.

Fraissl and Brankowski, those two old Eiger-hands, were

also in Grindelwald. We strolled up to a pasture above Alpiglen together and there set up house. It was our firm intention to avoid the errors which had proved fatal to previous parties. The most important thing was to get to know our mountain as a whole, before attempting its most interesting and difficult face. So we first of all climbed from the "Hoheneis" diagonally across the (north-east) flank to the Mittellegi Ridge, then up it to the summit and down again by the normal route. In addition we climbed the Mönch by the "Nollen".

Meanwhile cows had been driven up on to our idyllic pasture. Fritz and I decided to move our abode, and pitched our little tent in a small meadow close under the Face. Fraissl and Brankowsky stayed on the pasture. It was a fine day when Fritz and I started up the lower part of the Face and after climbing about 2,300 ft, to the so-called "Bivouac Cave" above the "Shattered Pillar", parked a rucksack full of provisions and equipment there. We attached a label to it, which read: "The property of Kasparek and Harrer. Don't move."

This notice did not indicate any particular mistrust of other North Face climbers. It was simply that, thanks to the many attempts and frequent rescue- and recovery-operations, the Face was littered with pieces of equipment, ropes and pitons, which served as very welcome aids and additions to the equipment of subsequent parties. This made it absolutely necessary to mark clearly any rucksack intentionally parked on the Face like this one of ours.

We climbed down again to our tent. Conditions would not yet allow of an attempt with the slightest prospect of success. We had taken a firm stand not to let ourselves be pushed, driven or goaded. Past tragedies and particularly the deaths of the two Italians earlier in the summer had taught us that unseemly haste can ruin every sober consideration and lead to the direst results. We could wait and we meant to wait.

Days of fine weather set in; and still we waited, watching how the snow which had fallen during storms and been whipped against the rocks altered in consistency, melted away, settled and bound firmly with the old underlying layer. It now seemed reasonable to hope that conditions up on the higher, unknown sector of the Face too would be bearable.

By July 21st we decided that everything was in order. At about 2 a.m. on that day we started up the Face, crossing the edge-crevasse in the dark, climbing independently, unroped, up towards the "Shattered Pillar". We moved in silence, each of us picking his own line, each of us thinking his own thoughts.

Those hours between night and day are always a keen challenge to one's courage. One's body goes mechanically through the correct movements essential to gaining height; but the spirit is not yet awake nor full of the joy of climbing, the heart is shrouded in a cloak of doubt and diffidence. My friend Kurt Maix once described this diffidence as Fear's friendly sister, the right and necessary counterweight to that courage which urges men skywards, and protects them from self-destruction. It is certainly not fear which besets the climber; but doubts and questionings and "butterflies" are human failings. And climbers are after all only human beings.

They have to reconcile themselves with their own short-comings and with constraining feelings; they have to subject themselves to the will-power already geared to the enterprise in hand. And so the first hour, the hour of the grey, shapeless, colourless dusk before dawn, is an hour of silence.

Sheer thrustfulness is false, indeed fallacious, at times when a man is struggling to achieve a balance and is busy trying to reconcile subtle *nuances* of feeling with his will-power. And the glorious thing about mountains is that they will endure no lies. Among them, we must be true to ourselves, too.

Fritz and I climbed on up, in the darkness before dawn, to the right of the "Shattered Pillar". From time to time we heard voices behind us, could distinguish individual words. It was Fraissl and Brankowsky, who like ourselves had waited for the fine weather, and had started up the Face behind us. We would get on well enough with them. Two parties on that great precipice are no hindrance to one another; indeed, they can help each other in a variety of ways.

The rocks looked grey, even the snow looked grey in the first livid light of dawn. And there was something else grey moving in front of us. Not rocks this time, but people, peeling out of their tent-sacks in front of the bivouac-cave.

In an instant all thought, doubts and self-questionings which had risen up out of the secret depths of our *ego* had sunk back again. We did not talk about them, least of all in front of strange fellow-climbers who were at one and the same time comrades and competitors.

Strangers? Climbers are never really strangers, least of all on this Face. We introduced ourselves to these two who had only just woken up from their night's sleep. Then they told us who they were: Andreas Heckmair and Ludwig Vörg. It was a unique place for such an introduction. The light of an unborn day was strong enough for each of us to be able to see the faces of our opposite numbers clearly, to sample their features, to assess their characteristics.

So this was the famous Andreas Heckmair. At 32 he was the oldest of us four. His face was limned by the hills themselves, spare, deeply lined, with a sharp, jutting nose. It was a stern, bold face, the face of a fighter, of a man who would demand much of his companions and the last ounce of himself.

The other man, Ludwig Vörg, seemed to be exactly the opposite type; a well-rounded, athletic type, not in the least sinewy or spare, nor were his features as prominent as Heckmair's. They radiated amiable relaxation; his whole being personified latent strength and an inner peace. His friends with whom he had been to the Caucasus two years before had nicknamed him the "Bivouac King". Even those nights in the open on the 7,000 ft ice-face of Ushba, the "Terrible Mountain", had failed to rob him of his sleep. On a snap judgment one would attribute the dynamic force to Heckmair, the stamina to Vörg. In any case two such diverse and complementary characters couldn't help making up a rope of quite extraordinary climbing ability and strength.

We couldn't tell if the two men were disappointed at our

all being on the Face at the same time. If they were, they certainly didn't show it. Heckmair said: "We knew you were trying the Face too. We saw your rucksack and read the label." We couldn't quite grasp why we had been in the dark about the presence of these two men, who hadn't been living in a tent either at Alpiglen or Kleine Scheidegg, nor in the hay on any of the pastures. We only found out later that this time they had completely covered their traces. They had come to Grindelwald with luggage and taken a room in one of the hotels at Kleine Scheidegg. Who ever heard of a candidate for the North Face of the Eiger sleeping in a hotel bedroom? The ruse had worked perfectly.

Heckmair and Vörg had with them the best, most up-to-date equipment. They were in fact just as poor as we were, but had raised a sponsor for their climb in advance and had therefore found themselves for the first time in their lives in a position to buy to their hearts' desire at Munich's best sports shop, and even to order gear which had to be specially manufactured. Of course they both had the twelve-pointer crampons which had just become fashionable. Fritz had ten-pointers, but I hadn't any at all. Admittedly this was a mistake, but it wasn't the result of carelessness, but rather of over-careful consideration. We had taken the view that the North Face was a rock-wall with aprons of snow and ice embedded in it. A pair of crampons weighs a good deal, and we felt that if we did without it, we could take more equipment or provisions along. My boots were nailed with the well-known claw system popular in Graz, a lay-out providing an equally good grip on rock and ice. Our plan was for Fritz to lead on the ice pitches and me to take over on the rocks. We also hoped to avoid the irksome and time-wasting necessity of strapping crampons on and taking them off again all the time. We were quite wrong, and it was a mistake; but it did not prove disastrous, for all it did was to lose us time and provide me with extra exertion. But we hadn't yet discovered that as we stood talking to Heckmair and Vörg outside the bivouac-cave.

· Vörg, used to bivouacking in all sorts of conditions and places, was grousing about the night they had just spent. "It was cold and uncomfortable," he complained. "Falling stones wouldn't allow us to stay outside the cave, and the cave itself was narrow and wet. It dripped steadily on our tent-sack all night long."

Heckmair studied his altimeter and shook his head dubiously. "It has risen about sixty metres." he announced, "which means the barometer has fallen about three points. I don't like the look of the weather."

Just at that moment Fraissl and Brankowsky came up with us. Introductions and friendly greetings followed, but by now there was a note of real concern detectable in Heckmair's voice. Like a good trouper he concealed his disappointment. He just pointed to a fish-shaped cloud on the horizon and said: "I'm sure the weather's breaking. We're not climbing any further."

We ourselves felt certain that the weather would hold, and Fritz put forward that viewpoint in his optimistic way: "Oh, sure, the weather'll hold all right. And someone's got to climb the Face sometime, after all!"

Heckmair and Vörg were getting ready to go down, as we moved on up. I kept on thinking about the retreat of those two superb climbers and remembering the look of utter disappointment on Vörg's face. And what about Heckmair? I soon realized that his fishy cloud and the "rise in the altimeter" were only excuses. He knew that the presence of three ropes on the Face could mean serious delays, but he was too good a sport to stand on his rights of "first come, first served" and ask one of our parties to turn back. So he turned back himself: instead of saying "you're in the wrong", he remarked that he didn't like the look of the weather. It was a decision dictated by a true sense of mountaineering responsibility.

Time and again climbers on the North Face had got into difficulties, through allowing themselves to be hurried not only by the state of the Face or by weather conditions, but by the competition of others. Vörg, one of the finest climbers ever to attempt the climb, was not going to let himself be hurried.

At the moment there was little time for psychological studies or similar problems. The Face itself was providing our immediate problems, as we reached the "Difficult Crack". Twilight had at last been forced to yield to the first full light of morning. We roped up, and Fritz tackled the first severe pitch with his own personal craftsmanship. The heavy Eiger-pack on his shoulders brought his first swift upward drive to a halt. Down he had to come and leave his rucksack at my feet. Then he began his second assault. It was a pleasure to watch him. Higher and higher he went, stylishly, using every projecting wrinkle, never breaking his rhythm, never struggling. And in a staggeringly short time he had mastered this first great defence-work on the Face.

The job of roping Fritz's rucksack up after him was difficult and time-wasting; it kept on jamming under overhangs. However, the first one got up there in the end; the second, weighing 55 lb, followed, but on my shoulders. We just hadn't time to indulge in another bout of roping-up. Fritz hauled on my rope; his assistance at least offset the weight of my pack, and I too was soon at the top of the crack. The pitch gave me a gentle foretaste of what the Face had in store; but the fact that I hadn't lost my breath coming up the crack strengthened my confidence that I was up to the work in hand. There is, of course, a huge difference between balancing upwards like a gymnast totally unencumbered on even the hardest Dolomite wall and climbing heavily-laden up the Face of the Eiger. But then isn't the ability to hump heavy loads a requisite for every successful major climb?

Many climbers still to come will use rope slings on the "Difficult Crack". We preferred to climb it free. A rock-climber of Kasparek's supreme skill only resorts to slings where they are absolutely unavoidable.

By now we were just below the Rote Fluh, that sheer wall, hundreds of feet high, which goes winging up to the sky in a sweep of incomparable smoothness. According to the book of the rules, based on man's experience, the mountain walls sleep quietly in the early morning, blanketed by the night frost. Even the stones are supposed to be frozen into inactivity. But the Eiger's Face doesn't go by any Queensberry rules; this was just another instance of the

way it tips human experience overboard. Down came the
stones. We could see them taking off over the top edge of
the Rote Fluh and whizzing out through empty space in a
wide arc. The Face was raking us with defensive fire. We
hurried on upwards, for the nearer we got to the foot of the
Rote Fluh, the safer we should be.

We could hear another heavy block coming. It landed
below us, splintering into a thousand pieces.

Then we heard Fraissl's voice, Not a call for help or an
SOS, just a communication; one of them had been hit on
the head and hurt.

"How bad is it? Do you need help?" we asked.

"No, but I'm pretty giddy. I think we've had it. We'll
have to turn back."

"Can you manage it alone?"

"Yes, we can."

We were sorry that our two Viennese friends couldn't
keep us company, but we didn't try to dissuade them. So
Fraissl and Brankowski started to climb down again.

Now, before sunrise, we two were alone on the Face
again. Only a little while ago there had been six of us; now
Fritz and I had only each other to rely on. We didn't discuss
it, but subconsciously it strengthened our feeling of mutual
dependence and comradeship. We made rapid progress
over easier ground; and then, suddenly, we were at the
passage which Rebitsch and Vörg had christened the "Hinterstoisser Traverse" the year before.

The rocks across which we now had to traverse to the left
were almost vertical, plunging away beneath into thin air.
We were full of admiration for Hinterstoisser's brave
achievement when he opened up this rope-assisted traverse
across to the First Ice-field for the first time, feeling his
perilous way from hold to hold. We were full of gratitude
too to Vörg and Rebitsch for having left a traversing-rope –
shouting a welcome to us, it seemed – in place here. We
tested it and found it firmly anchored and secure against
any strain, although it had been exposed for twelve months
to storms and showers, to the wet and the cold.

We knew from reports, descriptions and photographs
how to effect the traverse. Nobody, however, had described

the pitch when heavily iced over. The rock was absolutely glazed, offering no hold whatever to a frictioning foot. None the less, Fritz led off into the traverse with that tremendous skill of his, fighting for his balance on smooth holdless film, winning his way, inch by inch, yard by yard, across that difficult and treacherous cliff. In places he had to knock away snow or a crust of ice from the rock with his ice-hammer; the ice-splinters swept down the slabs with a high whirring sound, to disappear into the abyss. But Fritz held on, pushing, feeling his way over to the left, climbing, hanging right away from the rock on the rope, from hold to hold, till he reached the far end of the traverse. Then I followed, shoving Fritz's rucksack along ahead of me on a snap-link in the traversing-rope, and soon joined him at the other end.

Soon after the traverse we came to the "Swallow's Nest", the bivouac place already made famous by Rebitsch and Vörg, and there we halted for a rest and some breakfast. The weather was holding, and a fine dawn had turned into a lovely day. The light was so good that it had already been possible to take pictures down on the traverse, a traverse which is certainly one of the most photogenic pitches in all the Alps. That one prosaic epithet tells the whole story – the extreme difficulty, the exposure, the daring of the traverse. And I should at once like to take the opportunity of correcting a misapprehension: the Hinterstoisser Traverse is one of the key pitches to the climb, not the only one. There are numerous critical places on this incredibly huge Face, which – thanks to the safe return of Rebitsch and Vörg – had by now been reconnoitred as far as Sedlmayer and Mehringer's "Death Bivouac". As yet we didn't know what key-pitches lurked up there on the final precipice. All we knew was that, wherever it might rise in the Alps, it would by itself have been an object of wonder to the beholder and a highly-prized objective for the best rock-climbers alive.

We were going splendidly, the weather was fine, and we had no doubt that we stood a good chance of success; but we also knew that the very best of climbers had had to beat a retreat. So we equipped the "Swallow's Nest" as a strong point in case of a withdrawal. The old rope left by the 1937 party on the traverse was not enough. We proposed to assure the direct line of descent, which in 1936 had proved fatal to the party of four, a tragedy which only reached its appalling end with the ghastly death of Toni Kurz. At the "Swallow's Nest" we left behind us 330 ft of rope, pitons, snap-links, rope-slings and provisions.

It was July 21st 1938. Exactly two years ago to a day Hinterstoisser had spent hour upon hour in desperate attempts to climb back along the traverse he himself had been the first to discover. All in vain. He, and with him Angerer and Rainer, died on that same day. We were tremendously impressed by that memory. If those four men had only left their traversing-rope in place at the Traverse, if they had only had a long enough rope at the "Swallow's Nest", if only . . . We had to thank the dead for our knowledge. The memory made us both proud and said, but it did not scare us. Life has its laws, which we unconsciously obey. They pointed to the way up.

Fritz had strapped on his crampons; soon he was on his way up the First Ice-field. Here was no névé, but hard, brittle somewhat watery ice. I assessed the angle at from fifty to fifty-five degrees, that is, somewhat steeper than the average slope of the Grossglockner's Pallavicini Couloir. After the first rope's-length, Fritz cut a big stance and drove in an ice-piton, to protect me on my ascent. We were already beginning to realize that our calculations had gone astray when we decided to leave my crampons behind. I now had to make up for lack of equipment by a considerable increase in muscular energy. Never mind, my training in several forms of sport would be a great asset . . .

We were aiming for a vertical cliff, which leads from the First to the Second Ice-field. The only possible way seemed to be through an icy groove, later to be known as the "Ice-Hose". This barrier between the two shields of ice is one of the many snares and delusions on this Face. Optically, a wall in the Dolomites is far more impressive than any single pitch on the Eiger's Face. When I recall the great Dolomite faces, there is much which seems more difficult, steeper, more inaccessible than it really is. But when you lay your hand on the Dolomite rock, you immediately delight in the rough surface, the horizontal stratification, the resulting proliferation of holds and of the never-failing crannies and cracks into which pitons may safely be driven.

But here? The first illusion – the ice-covered rock-barrier doesn't look particularly difficult. All you have to do is to hammer in a belaying-piton below it . . . but it doesn't offer a belay. In fact there isn't a cranny anywhere for a reliable piton, and there aren't any natural holds. Moreover, the rock is scoured smooth by falling stones, bread-crumbled with snow, ice and rubble. It isn't an invitation to cheerful climbing, it offers no spur to one's courage; it simply threatens hard work and danger. All the same, it is a part of the Eiger's North Face, which we are trying to climb . . .

The "Ice-Hose" does justice to its name. The rock was thickly plastered with the stuff; but even the hose part couldn't have been more accurate. Water was pouring down under the frozen layer, between the ice and the rock. The only way was up through it. The water poured into our sleeves, flowing right down our bodies, building up for a short time above the gaiters, which were supposed to separate our trousers from our boots, before finding its way out. There were practically no holds in this crack consisting of ice, rock and water. It is severe, calls for the best climbing technique and demands the most ingenious balancing manoeuvres. Here too Fritz showed his supreme skill; but it took hours to reach the Second Ice-field. We were wet to the skin when we got there.

It was still early in the afternoon. High and wide above us loomed the Second Ice-field. Our way led diagonally up to the left towards the arête of the "Flatiron", in the direction of the last bivouac of Sedlmayer and Mehringer. The huge ice-apron was greatly foreshortened from where we stood; but even allowing for the optical illusion and remembering that it had taken first-class ice-exponents like Rebitsch and Vörg five hours – twenty rope's-lengths – to reach its upper rim, we still had plenty of time to do it and probably even to reach the "Death Bivouac". For there would still be at least six hours of daylight.

In spite of all that, we decided to climb not to the left but to the right, to a little knob of rock sticking out of the snow above the upper edge of the Rote Fluh. The fine afternoon was letting the sun beat diagonally down on the upper part of the Face – up there where the "little icicles blow their noses". That was what started the avalanches; and stones, once released from the imprisoning ice up there, were in the habit of following the laws of gravity.

And further over to the west – for one has to traverse diagonally across the Face for hundreds of feet on those ice-shields – snow-slides, stone-falls and cascades of water were coming down in their vertical, unhampered course from the "Spider".

Admittedly, every stone doesn't find a target. But we hadn't carefully built a strong-point for a retreat down at the "Swallow's Nest" in order to be knocked out by stones or wiped off the Face by avalanches up here. Falling stones are numbered among the "objective" dangers of climbing or in other words as circumstances over which man has no control; but to venture with one's eyes open into the line of fire of falling stones is no longer an objective but a sub-jective exposure to danger, the outcome of sheer careless-ness or stupidity. This huge ice-apron was a place to be climbed during the morning. Even then the danger from stones wouldn't be entirely eliminated, but it would be considerably less.

We reached our knob and were able to fix two belaying-pitons; then we spent hours in digging a small seat out of the ice below it. It was still daylight when we began to make the final preparations for our bivouac. We tied ourselves and our belongings to the pitons for security's sake, furnished our seat with coils of rope, and started to cook our meal. The knob of rock afforded us complete protection from stones; the view from our perch was magnificent. All the conditions for a happy bivouac were present; but we hadn't a dry stitch on us. Yet, although we had warm clothing and a change of underwear in our rucksacks, we dared not risk getting it, too, damp by putting it on under soaking clothes. We didn't know what the weather might do, or how often, where and under what conditions we should have to bi-vouac. So we would have to keep our spares dry against nights yet to come; but it needed some strength of mind not to fetch them out of the packs and put them on, even though we knew better.

The night was long, cold and uncomfortable. The bivouac was not a good one. We were only to know later on that it was the worst on the whole Face, in spite of its comparatively good sitting-space. Our wet clothes made us doubly susceptible to the cold; our minds and spirits were as busy as our bodies trying to cope with the discomfort. No training in the world is proof against that.

Every night has to come to an end sometime. In the grey light of dawn we got up with chattering teeth and prepared the ropes for the day's climbing. The weather was still good and the frost had anchored all the stones, as we started on the diagonal climb across the Second Ice-field. It was only now that we realized to the full what a mistake we had made in leaving my crampons behind. Fritz counteracted the error by a tremendous output of energy, as he built a positive ladder of steps. It was amazing to see how expert with his ice-axe was this best of all Vienna's rock-climbers. For hours on end he swung it rhythmically to cut step upon step, resting only when he stopped to safeguard me up them. And the steps were so good that my claw-nails gave me excellent holds in them.

From down below, the Ice-field looks like a smooth surface; but that is pure illusion. Huge waves in the ice constantly gave the impression that we were quite close to the safety of the rocks above; but we soon realized that we had only reached another bulge in the ice and that there was yet another ice-valley to be crossed. It was the phenomenon the climber so often experiences in the Western Alps, when he mistakes one of many subsidiary excrescences for the main summit.

The fully-equipped modern mountaineer handles his ice-axe like a guide of the classical Alpine era. Speed is the essence of modern climbing; steady, slow progress that of the classic past. We were naturally taking longer because we were using the technique of the past. Even Rebitsch and Vörg had taken five hours the year before to cross this huge patch of ice. We took exactly the same time.

Just before the rocks separating the Second from the Third Ice-field, I looked back, down our endless ladder of steps. Up it I saw the New Era coming at express speed; there were two men running – and I mean running, not climbing – up it. Admittedly, practised climbers can move quickly in good steps; but for these two to have reached this point quite early in the morning was positively amazing. They must have bivouacked last night on the lower part of the wall; it hardly seemed possible that they had only started up it today. But it was, in fact, the case.

These two were the best of all the "Eiger Candidates" – Heckman and Vörg – wearing their twelve-pointer crampons. I felt quite outmoded in my old claws. We exchanged a brief greeting; then they went on up to Fritz. I knew my friend and his highly developed set of alpine etiquette pretty well; I knew he preferred to find his own way, and that, though he wore the honourable badge of the Mountain Rescue Service, he himself didn't like assistance. Even Heckmair's obviously joking enquiry whether he wouldn't prefer to turn back only brought a good strong Viennese reply from Fritz.

But Anderl didn't mean to start a squabble. His is a character with no touch of malice in it; moreover, Kasparek and Heckmair had far too great a respect for one another, and so the result of the encounter was neither discord nor rivalry, but a teaming-up such as has rarely been seen on this mighty Face. We naturally continued to climb as two separate ropes, with Heckmair and Vörg now taking over the lead. They told us later how they had seen Fraissl and Brankowsky turn back; after that there had been no holding them. They had started up the Face early in the morning and now they had already caught us up. And now, too, we would be staying together . . .

We moved on up the steep ridge towards the "Death Bivouac" at a uniform pace. During our extended midday rest at that point we felt completely united. Not a word was spoken indicative of any sense of disappointment. It was just as if we had always intended to climb together and now we were glad to have joined up at long last.

There could be no difference of opinion as to the con-

tinuation of the route. It led from our resting place diagonally downwards across the Third Ice-field towards the
foot of the "Ramp", the rock-feature rising steeply towards
the ridge up which lies the Lauper Route; then from the
"Ramp" a right-hand traverse to the "Spider"; across the
"Spider" and then up the adjacent exit-cracks to the
summit-névé, crowning the final wall. It all sounds so easy.
Yet each of the pitches named has its own big question-
mark. But when I looked at my companions, Fritz, Anderl
and Wiggerl, I felt quite certain that any pitch which
offered the faintest possibility of a route up it would be
climbed by our party of four.

It might perhaps have been possible to climb straight up
the cliff from the "Death Bivouac" to the "Spider", but we
could not see very far as we looked up the precipice. Mists
were closing in on the mountain, and beginning to drift
gently down to us. These were the mists which are known
"out there" as the Eiger's "Wad of cotton-wool" and hug
every contour of its ice and rock. That didn't upset us very
much. It is one of the Eiger's regular features to put on a
skull-cap for its after-lunch nap, much to the fury of the
inquisitive people milling round the telescopes. We, of
course, couldn't know the intensity of that fury, stemming
from the fact that queue-tickets were being issued and that
their purchasers had to pay for three minutes' viewing,
whether they saw anything or not. Meanwhile, unobserved
by the great world outside, we were traversing across an ice-
slope, whose inclination exceeds sixty degrees, to the start
of the "Ramp".

The "Ramp" – well, it fits that Face, on which everything is more difficult than it looks. You cannot run up it,
for there are no rough slabs, no good foot- or hand-holds.
Here too the rock-strata slope outwards and downwards,
and the crannies into which a piton can be driven can be
counted on one hand. At all events, I had a good belaying-
piton at the foot of the "Ramp". I stood watching Fritz as
he moved upwards with even, rhythmic movements, to a
point some eighty feet above me.

Suddenly he slipped. I couldn't tell whether a hold had
come away in his hand or whether he had failed to find a

foot-hold. Everything went so quickly – he was already out of sight. I took in as much slack as I could and stood there waiting for the shock. I knew the piton was firmly in and would hold. And the rope, cushioned by the belay round my shoulders, ought with any luck to take the strain. Anybody coming off unbelayed at this point would go winging straight down to the outcrops at the bottom of the Face . . .

Luck was with us. The rope ran out over a little ridge of snow, cutting into the surface névé. This checked the velocity of Fritz's fall to such an extent that the shock I had to withstand was perfectly bearable. But was Fritz hurt?

My mind was soon at rest. Up from below came a couple of words only intelligible to one who knows Viennese slang inside out – a good aggressive oath. Then Fritz was climbing again. Soon he was at the top of the "Ramp", moving on above it, just as if nothing had happened, till presently I shouted up to him that there was no more rope. On my way up, I took a look at the place where he had come off. Fritz had fallen sixty feet through thin air straight down from the diagonal "Ramp" and had then calmly climbed back again by a difficult crack. We didn't mention the mishap again. Fritz carried it off as quietly as a player whom the dice condemn to go back to the start at "Snakes and Ladders". We weren't in the least upset: we just laughed because we were enjoying life. No sentimental handshakes either. Back to the start – and then six forward up the next waterfall – that was the way we looked at it. It was quite natural for Fritz to have climbed straight up again after his fall, for he hadn't hurt himself. And it was quite natural for me to have held the rope because that was what I was there for. Fritz was just the right companion for this great Face. He treated irrelevancies as such, never burdening his friends with "if" and "suppose", nor with the thought "what might have happened", or the question "why did it happen?" What really mattered was that nothing *had* happened.

Late in the afternoon the four of us were all together again. Above us the "Ramp" had contracted to a narrow gulley with a crack blasted out of it. Water was running down the crack. None of us wanted to bivouac in wet clothes – our own had dried out during the morning, while we were traversing the Second Ice-field; moreover, we were beginning to find the day's labours sufficient. The crack would be a good prelude to the next day's work; so we prepared to bivouac.

That sounds easy enough. And we had thought it would be easy enough when we were looking at the "Ramp" in photographs or through a telescope. We even thought we could pick our seats. Actually there were no seats, in fact not a single seat. Indeed, good stances were a rarity.

We arranged our bivouac about 8 feet below that of Heckmair and Vörg. We managed to drive a single piton into a tiny crevice in the rock. It was a thin square-shafted piton. It held after only a centimetre, but it was just jammed. Obviously, once we hung our whole weight on it, it would very likely work loose with the leverage. So we bent it downwards in a hoop, till the ring was touching the rock. In this way we did away with any question of leverage and knew we could rely on our little grey steely friend. First we hung all our belongings on to it and, after that, ourselves.

There was no room to sit down. The "Ramp" was very narrow and very steep at this point; but we managed to manufacture a sort of seat with the aid of rope-slings, and hung out some more to prevent our legs dangling over the gulf. Next to me there was a tiny level spot, just big enough for our cooker, so we were able to brew tea, coffee and cocoa. We were all very much in need of liquids.

Heckmair and Vörg were no more comfortably lodged. The relaxed attitude of Vörg, the "Bivouac King" was quite remarkable; even in a place like this he had no intention of doing without every possible comfort. He even put on his soft fleece-lined bivouac-slippers, and the expression on his face was that of a genuine connoisseur of such mattters. It is absolutely no exaggeration to say that we all felt quite well and indeed comfortable. Experienced climbers will understand that statement, and laymen must simply believe it. A famous philosopher, when asked what true happiness was, replied; "If you have some broth, a place to sleep in and no bodily pains, you are well on the way." We can improve on that definition. "Dry clothes, a reliable piton and precious revivifying drinks – that is true happiness where the North Face of the Eiger is concerned."

Yes, we were quite happy. This huge mountain-face had brought our lives down to the lowest common denominator. After cooking for hours we pulled the Zdarsky-sack over us and tried to find as comfortable a position as possible, so that we could at least doze off occasinally. It was great to be able to look forward to a night in dry clothes. Our perch was about 4,000 feet above the snow-fields at the base of the precipice; if one of us fell off now, that was where he would certainly finish up. But who was thinking about falling off?

It was a good bivouac. Bodily aches and discomfort made no disturbing intrusion on the train of our thoughts. As I fell asleep, I saw a picture, a happy, sunny picture of something that happened when I was very young; no mirage of a sheltering roof over my head or a warm bed, but a memory of one of my first experiences in the mountains.

It happened when I was only 15. I had climbed all alone to the top of the Mangart, that proud summit in the Julian Alps, and was coming down, very impressed by my great experience. I reached a huge scree-slope, of the kind one so often finds in the Julians, miles long. Down it I went, through the bleak hanging-valley, taking long bounding strides. The sun was scorching and my tongue was sticking to my gums. There in the middle of the rubble, I saw two eagles tearing huge lumps of flesh from the carcass of a chamois. The birds of prey only flew away reluctantly as I came by. I was so fascinated by the sight that I momentarily forgot my thirst. Young as I was, the knowledge that the death of one thing can mean the life of another was borne in on me ineradicably. Was that an immutable law of Nature, I wondered? Was it true for people as well as for animals? Every fibre of my being protested against the notion.

I came down to the shore of the Weissenfelser See. There, by the lake, stood a shepherd's hut, next to a spring, from which fell a glittering column of water. I bent down and let the water run down over my wrists. Then I drank and drank and drank. . . .

Suddenly I felt a sharp box on my ears. The tall, white-haired herdsman was standing there, his sharp-etched face burnt mahogany by the sun.

"Boy, why are you drinking water?" he asked. "There in my hut I have cool milk and sour cream. You can quench your thirst and drink your fill indoors."

I shall never forget that old man, who allowed his tongue to grow sharp in order to do me a good turn. I remained for days as his guest, eating and drinking everything the little farm produced, milk and cream and cream-cheese. He was a proud, hospitable man and, what is more, educated and much-travelled, who could speak eight languages fluently. For many years he had been a ship's cook over the face of the seven seas; and all his life's experiences added up to kindness towards his fellow men. I remembered the horrible picture of the eagles and the dead chamois. And instantly I realized, with the receptive idealism of early youth, that Nature's cruelty didn't hold among men. Men must be kindly . . .

With that memory of the old man by the Weissenfelser See I nodded off, into a deep and dreamless sleep. I don't know how long I slept like that. Suddenly, dreaming now, I saw the old man there again in front of me. His face was no longer kind; he was angry as he tugged at my breast. I tried to shake him off, wanting to go on sleeping, but I could not, he was so strong. He tugged at me and shook me harder still.

I only half woke up, but could still feel the fierce pressure on my chest. It was the rope. I had slid off my perch as I slept, and was hanging on it with my full weight. I knew then that I was on the "Ramp", on the Eiger's North Face, and that I really ought to straighten myself out, raise myself and resume a proper sitting posture; but I was too lethargic and only wanted to go on sleeping. Vaguely I recognized that one shouldn't for a moment longer than necessary weigh down a piton which is only a centimetre deep into the rock; but it was so pleasant to snatch just a few more minutes before straightening everything out. So I fell asleep again.

The moment I nodded off, there was the dream, back again. This time the old man shook me properly awake. I stood up in the slings, resumed my sedentary posture on that vertiginous little stance. Fritz mumbled something in his sleep.

Then I heard Andreas and Ludwig talking overhead. Vörg's voice sounded worried, so I asked what was the matter.

"Anderl feels sick," came the answer. "The sardines he ate last night have upset his tummy."

I was wide awake by now and fully restored. I could hardly feel the cold any more. There, close by me, on its little level spot, stood the cooker.

"I'll brew you some tea, Anderl," I said. "It always helps."

Tea is surely the king of all drinks. It helps against cold, it helps against the heat, against discomfort and sickness, against weariness and weakness. And it helped on this occasion too. The sardines quietened down in Anderl's tummy. We dozed and slept till the stars began to pale and the light of a new day crept through the twilight before dawn. Night was over; it had not been a bad one.

Vörg began cooking at about four o'clock. Like everything else, he did it thoughtfully, unhurriedly and thoroughly. He cooked porridge and coffee in large quantities. That cheered us up and drove away the cold. It was seven o'clock before we finally started to climb again. To have to cope with the crack in the gully as early morning physical training was quite a big demand on bodies still stiff from a bivouac. It didn't look any easier this morning than it had yesterday evening, except that the waterfall had stopped. In its place there was a thin armouring of ice on the rocks. Even Anderl, leading up it, looked a little doubtful.

He seemed to think straight on up was the best way and took the gully direct, knocking in a piton wherever he could. One of them actually held safe. He worked his way higher and higher with supreme technical skill, trying to get off the ice by climbing into the overhanging cliffs on the Face. He was nearly up the overhang, trying out a hold from which to get a final pull-up; but it wasn't a hold, it was a loose block, and it broke away bringing him down with it. A second or two later our friend was hanging safely from the good piton below the overhang. That wouldn't do at all for Andreas Heckmair: overhangs can't behave like that. He was very cross indeed. If it wouldn't go on the ice-free stuff, then it had better go right up the middle of the ice itself. So he put on his famous twelve-pointer crampons.

Then he treated us to an acrobatic *tour de force*, an exhibition exercise, such as we had rarely witnessed before. It was half superb rock-technique, half a toe-dance on the ice – a toe-dance above a perpendicular drop. He got a hold on the rock, a hold on the ice, bent himself double, uncoiled himself, the front points of his crampons moving ever upwards, boring into the ice. They only got a few milli-metres' purchase, but that was enough. Heckmair defeated that difficult pitch, cut foot-holds and banged pitons into the ice slope which began above it, then safeguarded Vörg up it after him.

We were still climbing as two separate ropes. It was now Kasparek's turn to tackle the crack in the gully. Not only had he no twelve-pointer crampons, he had a completely different conception of the pitch. He took it direct, avoiding entanglements with the icy and the ice-free containing walls alike. By a masterly piece of climbing he got up the crack as if climbing in the Gesäuse[1] at home rather than on the great Face of the Eiger.

I came up last. Then we were all four together again on the ice, looking up in incredulous astonishment at the menacing bulge of ice which here threatens finally to bar all progress up the "Ramp". Could anybody climb that?

The cliff was more than thirty feet high. I had never seen anything to match it; even the others at first seemed flabbergasted. Would it go on the left? No. On the right? No. Straight up seemed to be the best bet: but was this "best" a possible one? Heckmair had a go. He began by banging pitons into the ice below the bulge. One of them went in and held like a vice. Then he balanced his way delicately upwards. There were icicles hanging from the bulge; to one of these he fastened a sling and pushed himself up a bit in it. It looked terrifying, but he didn't seem in the least impressed by the danger; inch by inch he moved

1 The famous Austrian rock-climbing area in Upper Styria, with limestone faces of more than 3,000 ft. – Translator's note.

upwards, but as soon as he trusted his weight to the icicle, the pretty glittering thing broke away and off he came . . .

The piton held.

Once again we saw the same reaction as before. A rebuff as thorough-going as a fall rouses Heckmair to a cold fury. He immediately tackled the bulge again. This time he didn't trust to the icicles with which the Architect of our mighty prison had decorated it. Was it really a prison? Was this where we were going to have to give in and turn back?

No, our Andreas climbed up and out of our prison, having found an "ice-handle". An icicle hanging down had coagulated with an ice-stump pushing upwards – a stalagmite and a stalactite, both of ice, had grown into one. And this object, carpentered by some freak of nature, proved to be the key to our prison door. Heckmair threaded another sling through the handle, leaned outwards almost horizontally, banged some notches with his ice-hammer in the ice above the bulge, felt around with one hand, took a firm hold.

I had never seen a pitch that looked so hazardous, dangerous and utterly extraordinary. Fritz, who knows many of the famous key-pitches in the Alps, thought that the famous overhanging roof on the Pillar of the Marmolata looked child's play in comparison with this bulge. We were all pretty tense. Vörg had a tight hold on the rope, ready at any moment to hold Heckmair if he came off again.

But he didn't come off. We couldn't imagine how, but in some masterly fashion or other he had managed to drive an ice-piton deep into the ice above the bulge and thread the rope through a snap-link. Then he gave the order: "Pull!"

Vörg pulled him up on the rope, over the bulge, up to the piton.

Heckmair used his axe a few more times. Then "Let her go!" he said.

Vörg let the rope go loose, so that Heckmair could stand up; at the same time he was still keeping a careful watch in case of another fall. But Heckmair was soon in firm holds; he hurried a few feet up on to the ice-slope above the bulge, cut a roomy stance in the ice and drove a belaying-piton deep into firm ice. Then as the curtain-cue to an unusually dramatic scene we heard the welcome words: "Up you come!"

Our prison gate was open. Vörg followed through it. The North Face of the Eiger is so vast, so difficult and so serious that any display of human vanity would be out of place. No doubt Fritz and I could have climbed the bulge without any assistance from above, but it would have taken precious hours we would later have begrudged. So Fritz didn't hesitate a moment to take the rope Vörg let down to us. We who followed were robbed of the thrill and the adventure of this, the hardest pitch till now on the Face; we only tasted the toil it involves. And I, as last on the rope, had to knock out and retrieve all the pitons. I was decorated with them like a Christmas tree and the clank of the iron-mongery drowned my gasps as I struggled up over the bulge.

The ice-slope above was easy compared with what we had just done. We went straight up the ice for a short way only, then traversed out to the right at once.

It is of course easy enough for anyone who has made a successful first ascent to shake his head about the mistakes of those who follow. I do not propose to do it. But I am surprised that so many parties which climbed the Face after us went straight on up the ice-slope towards the Mittellegi Ridge and only tried to traverse across to the "Spider" much too high up. This was the cause of many delays and also brought about the disaster of 1957. It was perfectly clear to the four of us that the right-hand traverse must be attempted as soon as possible.

So we were traversing out to the right from the ice-slope, all four roped together, along a brittle belt of rock below an overhanging cliff. It was midday by now, and we could hear the hissing of the avalanches and the tattoo of the stones, but we were protected from both by the overhang.

While we were traversing these broken rocks – Heckmair was about 200 ft ahead of me at the time – we suddenly heard a fearful humming and whining sound. It was neither a stone-fall nor an avalanche, but an aeroplane flying past quite close to us. We could see the faces of its passengers quite plainly. They waved and we waved back. Hans

Steiner, the Bernese photographer managed to take some photographs of unique documentary value at that moment. His pictures showed three of us on the traverse while Heckmair has already started up a crack beyond it.

That crack is the only possible line of ascent from where the brittle belt peters out to a level on which the traverse to the "Spider" can be completed. Heckmair thought he could climb it by the usual methods; but every pitch on the Eiger's Face is harder than it looks and tricky with ledges on which the snow is only pressed against the rocks, with hand- and foot-holds that let you down. So he had to leave his rucksack behind to have a second go at the pitch, unencumbered. For this he kept his crampons on, in view of the icing one continually meets on the Face. It was an entirely new type of rock-climbing, this ascent of severe, often super-severe rock, overhanging in places – on crampons. Heckmair frequently stood in imminent danger of a fall, but somehow his fingers held him when he thought his strength was used up. The scrape of his climbing irons on the hard rock sounded like a furious gritting of teeth, which only stopped when he disappeared from sight overhead.

We three followed without crampons.

It took ages before we had all got up that 100 ft vertical rock-pitch. But surely not so long that it was dusk already? It had suddenly grown very dark; but a glance at the watch showed that, in spite of the darkness, it was still early afternoon. Heavy clouds bulked up into the sky; and this time the thundering roar caught up by the rocks and thrown back in a hundred reverberations was not the sound of an aeroplane, flying past dangerously near. This was genuine thunder.

By the time I reached Fritz's stance, the other two had gone ahead. They had untied from the communal rope again, so as to reach the "Spider" before the storm broke.

The thunderstorm provided a gloomy, menacing, but magnificent setting. A few minutes before, the sun had been shining, at least for the people down in Grindelwald. This sudden change was typical of the North Face; but we were already so familiar with its caprices that the oncoming storm caused us no alarm. Indeed, I was even sorry that there was no time to linger on the stance where Fritz had been waiting for me. That stance had all the elements of the miraculous; it was the first place, indeed the only one in the whole 6,000-ft Face where you could make yourself comfortable. It would have been grand to sit and rest there, looking down the great wall, into the valley, out over the surrounding hills. But the weather was hunting us on, and we followed the others.

The rock-traverse to the "Spider" is no promenade. But at least the rocks at this point are horizontal and the stratification consequently favourable. And the patches of ice which link them were firm enough to allow us to bite deeply into them with our ice-pitons. Not only is the traverse indescribably fine from the scenic angle, but it is so exciting and technically safe that we almost forgot the approaching storm. I cannot remember who first gave it the name of "the Traverse of the Gods", but it is comprehensively descriptive.

We reached the "Spider", the great sheet of ice set in the Face, quickly and without encountering any great difficulties. We hadn't time to examine the scene and the terrain more closely, and now even the possibility of so doing was withdrawn, for the sky had meanwhile taken on a blue-black tinge; then it disappeared altogether, as tattered mists chased across the Face, closing in on us, then lifting again to give a glimpse of things, then settling into a thick blanket of cloud. As the storm set in it began to sleet, mixed with snow; lightning began to flash and thunder to grumble and roar.

We could still see Heckmair and Vörg, already on the way up the ice-slope of the "Spider", about a rope's length and a half ahead of us; so we followed them up.

As I have already explained, the name "Spider" has been given to this steep patch of névé or ice high up in the almost vertical Face because of the white streaks spreading out from it in every direction like legs and clutching arms. These run more especially upwards – in cracks and gullies up towards the summit snow-cap – and down towards the "Death Bivouac". But nobody had discovered how apt the appellation was before we got there; nor had we, as yet, while we went up the first rope's length. We hadn't yet discovered that this "Spider" of snow, ice and rock can become a fearful trap; that when hail or snow falls, ice particles and snow, coming sliding down from the steep summit-névé, get canalised in the cracks and gullies, shoot out on to the "Spider" under pressure, there join up in a flood of annihilating fury and then sweep across the "Spider's" body, finally to fling themselves outwards and downwards, obliterating and taking with them everything which isn't part of the living rock. Nor is there any escape from the "Spider" for anyone caught on it by bad weather and avalanches.

We didn't know it then, but we very soon found out. Very soon. Immediately . . .

I was already on the "Spider's" ice and had hacked out a reasonable stance in which I was able to stand quite well without crampons. I felt very safe on account of a deeply-embedded ice-piton. The rope ran through a snap-link hung on the piton-ring to Fritz, working his way up about sixty feet above me. I could see him vaguely through the mist and the driven snow.

Presently he disappeared from my sight, swallowed up in the mist. The screaming of the storm, the rattle of the hail, were alarming. I tried to penetrate the grey veils to catch a glimpse of him, but in vain. Only a greyness within a greyness . . .

The howling of the wind increased, gathering a very strange note – a banging and swishing, a whistling hiss. This wasn't the voice of the storm any more coming down out of wild dance of ice-particles and snowflakes, but something quite different. It was an avalanche and as its harbingers, rocks and fragmented ice!

I snatched my rucksack up over my head, holding it firmly with one hand, while the other gripped the rope which ran up to my companion. I jammed myself against the ice-cliff, just as the whole weight of the avalanche struck me. The rattle and hammering of stones on my pack was swallowed up by the clatter and roar of the avalanche. It snatched and clutched at me with fearful strength. Could I possibly survive such pressure? Hardly . . . I was fighting for air, trying above all to prevent my rucksack being torn away and also to stop the endless stream of rushing snow from building up between me and the ice-slope and forcing me out of my foot-holds.

I hardly knew whether I was still standing, or was sliding down with it. Had the ice-piton come adrift? No, I was still standing, and the peg was still firm; but the pressure was growing unbearable. And Fritz must be coming off any moment. Standing out there in the open he couldn't possibly withstand the fury of the avalanche . . . it must sweep him away . . .

My thoughts were quite clear and logical, although I felt certain that this avalanche must hurl us all off the "Spider" and down to the bottom of the mighty wall. I was only resisting because one tries to resist so long as there is life in one. I was still gripping the rope with one hand, determined to do all I could to hold Fritz. At the same time I began to wonder whether we were already so high on the "Spider" that he wouldn't hit the rocks below, but would remain hanging on the ice-slope if he came off, slid past me and fetched up on the full run of the rope sixty feet below? And could I stand the shock if he hit me in passing?

All these thoughts were calm, without any sense of fear or desperation. I had no time for things like that. When would Fritz come off? I seemed to have been standing in this crushing, sliding Hell for endless ages. Had stones cut the rope and Fritz fallen alone, deprived of its protection? No, if that had happened the loose rope would have come sliding down to me. It was still stretching upwards, so Fritz must somehow or other still be holding on . . .

The pressure decreased, but I got no time to draw new breath or to shout before the next avalanche arrived. Its fury exceeded that of the first; it must bring the end for us. Even that realization was almost objective. It was odd that no important thoughts moved me, such as one might expect on reaching the very frontier of existence itself. Nor did scenes from my whole life go chasing past in front of my eyes. My thoughts were almost banal, ridiculous, unimportant. I felt a little cross that the critics and wiseacres, and also the Grindelwald gravedigger, who had already numbered us, like all those who try the North Face, as belonging to his parish had been justified. Then I remembered my accident on the West Face of the Sturzhahn in the Totengebirge, years ago. I was trying to climb that difficult wall in the winter and fell 150 ft. On that occasion, too, I hadn't lived all my life over again, nor had I felt any great sense of despair, much as I loved life. Is everything different when one really crosses that border, then?

And now, I was still alive; my rucksack was still protecting my head; the rope was still threaded through the snaplink; and Fritz had still not fallen.

Then a new, unbelievable, and this time shattering realization came over me. The pressure of the avalanche had ceased. The snow and the ice-granules were tinkling away into the gulf. Even the raging of the storm seemed gentle to me, now that the crashing of the avalanche was stilled.

Then, tremulously, through the grey mists, came the first shouts, to be caught up by the cliffs framing the "Spider" and thrown back to the human beings, scarcely able to grasp the incredible truth. Names were being called, voices were answering: "Fritz! Heini! Anderl! Wiggerl!" I told myself that we were all alive. The others were all alive, and so was I. The greatest Eiger-miracle had happened. The "White Spider" had not claimed a victim.

But was it really a miracle? Had the mountain been kind? Would it be true to say that the "Spider" had spared the lives of her victims?

Climbers are not only men of action, they are also matter-of-fact people. Such reflections are only to be explained by the first upsurge of joy at one's recaptured life; they won't stand up to sober judgment. The miracle and the mercy were none of nature's fashioning nor the mountain's, but were the result of man's will to do the right thing even in moments of direst peril. Who can say we were merely lucky?

A famous man once said: "In the long run only the efficient man has luck." I am not so presumptuous as to claim that we mountaineers are always efficient. It seems to me that one of Alfred Wegener's remarks fits our situation on the Eiger's "Spider" better. He said: "Luck is the output of one's last reserves."

We had put out our last reserves.

Kasparek was standing sixty feet above me on the ice-slope. When he heard the avalanche coming, he tried, with an instantaneous reaction, to drive in an ice-piton. He had no time to be frightened even for a split second. The piton was only a few centimetres into the ice, and quite loose, when the first avalanche arrived. In spite of the danger, even while the avalanche was roaring down on him in all its fury, he thought of the loose piton. It would have to stay firm, it simply mustn't be torn out by the shock of the cascading masses of snow and ice, nor by a falling stone; so Kasparek kept one protecting arm over the piton. Stones hit him on the hand, tearing the skin away. He was in great pain, but his will to keep the piton firm was greater. And during the short respite between the first and second avalanche, he drove the piton into the ice up to its ring, hooked a snap-link in and attached himself to it. And that is why Fritz didn't come off . . .

It was only afterwards, when the tension of the moment had passed, that I remembered having fastened myself by a rope-sling to my own piton for greater protection during that same interval.

The avalanche took Heckmair and Vörg by surprise, on a projection about sixty feet below the rock-rim above the "Spider". Owing to the configuration of the Face, it divided close above them into two separate streams; but the snow and ice-granules pouring down over each of them were quite strong enough to sweep even men of their build away. Neither of them could obtain protection by driving in a piton, not only because there was no time, but because they hadn't one between them. I had the whole collection by then: owing to being last on the rope, I was carrying about 20 lb of ironmongery which I had retrieved.

Heckmair only had his axe to hold him. The river of ice came up to his hips and threatened to whirl him away like a dead leaf; but he managed to resist the apparently irresistible pressure. At the same time he proved himself as an outstanding climbing partner as well as an outstanding leader of a climb. In spite of his own terrible distress, he had time to think of his number two, standing below him and still more exposed on the top of the knob. Holding his axe with one hand as an anchorage, he grabbed Vörg by the collar and held him tight. And so they both survived the assaults of the avalanches.

It was only now, when the danger was over, that Fritz felt the burning pain in his "scalped" hand. Only then did he shout up to Heckmair and Vörg. "Send a rope down, I'm hurt."

It took a long time to splice the ropes and send them down towards where Fritz was standing. And then they were still thirty feet short, so that Kasparek had to climb that distance unprotected.

How right Wegener is! Luck is certainly the output of one's last reserves.

This is how Heckmair described the end of the avalanche and his joy at finding that we were all still alive:

> Slowly it grew lighter and the pressure eased. We knew then, but still could hardly believe, that we had come through safely. And how had the others fared? The mists were thinning now – and there –
>
> "Wiggerl," I cried. "They're still on!"
>
> It seemed impossible, an outright miracle. We started to shout, and there they were, actually answering. An indescribable joy swept over us. One only discovers how strong a thing team-spirit can be when one sees the friends again whom one has counted for dead . . .

We all joined up again at the upper rim of the "Spider". Our feeling of delight at seeing the faces of our comrades again was overwhelming. As the outward sign of our friendship we decided to tie up again in a single rope of four – all the way to the top. And our leader should be Anderl. The "Spider's" avalanches hadn't been able to wipe us off the Face, but they had succeeded in sweeping away with them the last petty remnants of personal niggardliness and selfish ambition. The only answer to this mighty wall was the enduring bond of friendship, the will and the knowledge

that each of us would give of his very best. Each of us was
responsible for the lives of the others, and we refused to be
separated any more. We were all filled with a great joy.
From it stemmed the certainty that we would climb out of
the Face on to the summit and find our way back to the
valley where men live. It was in a mood of almost cheerful
relaxation that we resumed the climb.

Our climb was in the full glare of public interest, though
we neither knew nor cared about that; but it is interesting to
note how the doings on the North Face were being interpreted by the watching eyes below. This is how Ulrich
Link, the well-known Munich journalist, reported it from
his observation post on the Kleine Scheidegg:

On Saturday at about 12.30 p.m., a break in the
weather announced itself on the Eiger. A slate-grey
menacingly dark cloud covered the Lauterbrunnen
Valley. At that time the four climbers had, after five
hours of tremendous labour, scaled the "Diagonal
Gully", perhaps the hardest sector on the whole Face
. . . At one o'clock all four were one behind the other at
the left-hand edge of the snow field. Heckmair, himself a guide and probably the hardest-trained and most
proficient on ice, was leading.

For half an hour a cloud hid the climbers from our
view. At about 1.30 the Face was clear again. By then
they had traversed the snow-ledge and the leader had
already reached the crossing to the snow-field called
the "Spider". Heckmair led in splendid style – he had
been in the lead all day – across to the "Spider".
Kasparek and Harrer had meanwhile rested at the
end of the snow-ledge. From 3 to 3.30 p.m. the Face
was once again enveloped in cloud. Then it cleared
again and everyone rushed to the telescopes. The
leader of the second rope was just traversing from
the rocks on to the "Spider". At the same moment
Heckmair reached the rock outcrop in the upper snow-
couloir. The second party was moving more slowly,
but with the same steadiness and caution as the first.
Heckmair and Vörg had now reached a height of

11,800 ft and it was ten minutes past four. Mist came down on the Face again, and we were left cut-off with our fears and our hopes. The summit was still more than a thousand feet above the four men.

And now the weather was looking very bad again. Hour by hour it was impossible to tell whether it was going to finish up better or worse. The Lauterbrunnen Valley lay under a dirty grey pall; the Jungfrau and the Mönch were wrapped in cloud. The ice-falls glimmered pale blue and bluish green in the lurid light. There was a patch of blue sky between the rain clouds. The Grosse Scheidegg over yonder was still quite clear, but the weather was making up relentlessly. Meanwhile the second party must be in the Funnel on the "Spider".

At 4.25 it began to rain gently, and exactly five minutes later a violent, noisy downpour set in, as if the clouds had been torn apart. It must be hitting the Face and the four climbers on it like a tidal wave. One could hear many voices raised in a confused gasp of alarm. The whole breadth of the North Face had become one fearsome waterfall. Water was pouring down the cliffs in ten, twelve, fifteen wide columns of white foam. A marvellous rainbow stood arched widely over Alpiglen; but who had any eyes for its miraculous play of colour? Up there, two of the men must be on the snow-slope, exposed to the full force of the flood pouring down on them. Would they be able to hang on?

At last the cloud lifted. The telescope was clear at last. There lay the great snow-slope . . . and there were the climbers, both moving up quietly and calmly. They had survived the deluge, then. Vörg and Heckmair had probably had a much easier passage, for they had managed to escape into the rocks at the edge of the couloir. Then the clouds closed down again . . .

At 6.45 all four men were re-united and moving towards the upper end of the belt of snow. At 7 o'clock they reached it; at 8 they were still moving on up, either because they had not yet found a bivouac-site or else having decided to go ahead as long as daylight allowed, to get as near the summit as possible. They had now reached 12,150 ft, high above the "Spider", a wonderful performance in fourteen hours. At 8.20 it began to rain again. During short intervals when the clouds permitted, we could see them climbing on and on. At 9 o'clock they were still moving, probably preparing their perch for the night; Kasparek and Harrer's third, Vörg and Heckmair's second bivouac. It will certainly be an ordeal, in wet clothes on an inadequate resting place most likely. But all four are tough as steel . . .

Ten o'clock and pitch dark now. From now on the four men have to endure the long hours of darkness; they have enough food for six days. They will probably find little sleep during the night and will probably crouch over their cooker making hot tea and warming food. There can be no retreat now . . .

That report from a knowledgeable and experienced journalist makes pleasant reading even for a climber; for it is written in a manner which would also grip a layman, but without any uncalled-for dramatisation, and without cheap sensations thought up at a writer's desk. The mere facts, the keen observation of nature, the bare description of the Face are quite sensational enough by themselves.

But Ulrich Link was wrong about one thing. We couldn't crouch over our cooker. There was no room for that, though cooking still played its important part.

As to our bivouac-site, with the exception of the site above the crack leading to the "Traverse of the Gods", there is no single tiny spot where one can sit or where one can bivouac without thorough preparation.

After we had climbed an ice-bulge, we came upon a rock-ledge protected by overhangs from falling stones and avalanches. When I say a ledge, I do not mean a smooth comfortable feature on which it is possible to sit; it was far too narrow and precipitous for that. Heckmair found a place where he could drive in a rock-piton firmly, and with great patience fixed enough hooks on which to hang all the stuff, as well as securing himself and Vörg. There was no

room there for us. Fritz and I arranged our overnight abode
about ten feet away. The ledge was scarcely as broad as a
boot, and only just allowed us to stand erect, pressed close
against the rock; but we contrived to knock in a piton to
which we could tie ourselves. Even then we still couldn't
sit, not even on the outer rim of the ledge.

However, we found a solution. We emptied our rucksacks and tried fastening them too to the piton, in such a
way that we could put our feet in them and so find a hold.
We were sure it would work all right, and so it did.

Between us and our friends we had fixed a traversing
rope, along which a cookery-pot went shuttling back and
forth hanging from a snaplink. Vörg had taken on the
important post of expedition-cook. So, even if we couldn't
crouch over it, as Link had imagined us doing, the bubbling
of Vörg's cookery-pot produced a comfortable feeling.
None of us wanted any solid food; all we needed was drink.
So Ludwig brewed coffee, for hours on end. As soon as a
bowl was ready, he would have a taste and then pass it to us
others in turn. Fritz, being Viennese, is a coffee connoisseur, and praised Ludwig's concoction.

But good coffee calls for a cigarette, if one is a smoker;
and Fritz was the only real addict amongst us four. Unfortunately, his cigarettes hadn't stood the deluge of rain,
hail, snow and avalanches at all well; they were soaked and
pulpy. Fritz, who hadn't uttered a word or complaint about
the considerable pain in his damaged hand, grew feeble at
the thought of his cigarettes: "If only I could light a dry
cigarette with a dry match . . ."

I don't know what I would not have given to be able to
fulfil Fritz's wish, but I hadn't any cigarettes.

Then I remembered how I had come to know Fritz
Kasparek in the first place. It was at the beginning of
the thirties, when I was a young student with a great
enthusiasm for climbing but precious little money. Those
were the days when one somehow contrived the miracle of
spending weeks on end in the Dolomites with but thirty
shillings in one's pocket. A bicycle was one's only means of
transport and as one needed a licence for it in Italy at that
time, and since that cost money, we used to tramp the roads

for endless hours on foot, in order to reach one mountain group from another.

One day I left my bike at the frontier at Sillian and walked across into Italy, on my way to Innichen in the South Tyrol. There is an old wayfarers' song of Hermann Löns' which goes: "I never, never get my fill of dust." I was hungry, and thirstier still, but I was compelled by the thought of my slender purse to pass by inns and shops displaying the most glorious fruit and delicacies.

Then I saw another wayfarer coming towards me. He too had a huge pack, a typical climber's rucksack; he also had a mop of fair hair, two amused-looking eyes and a sun-tanned face. We summed each other up, mutually recognized a kindred soul in one another, nodded. Then the fair-haired one, marching towards the Austrian frontier, called out: "Hi, who are you? Where from? Where to?"

"I'm Heini Harrer from Graz," I told him, "on my way to the Sexten Dolomites."

"I'm Fritz Kasparek from Vienna."

Fritz Kasparek . . . I knew that name already. He was one of Vienna's most daring and experienced climbers. This young Viennese had done the Pillar of the Marmolata, the North Face of the Western Zinne, the North Buttress of the Admonter Reichenstein, innumerable other superseveres and new routes. He was only a year or two older than I was, but I addressed him as "Sir" out of respect for his great reputation. "Nonsense," said he, shaking his head. "I'm Fritzl and you're Heini and that's that." And then straight out: "Hungry? Thirsty? No money, eh?"

I nodded.

Kasparek disencumbered his shoulders of his rucksack, waved invitingly towards the bank of grass at the edge of the road, sat down and produced a huge bag of glorious pears and peaches out of his pack.

"Eat!" he commanded.

I didn't wait for a second order. We ate all the fruit, lock, stock and barrel, and I must admit that Fritz only consumed half the amount I did. He laughed, got up, shook my hand. "So long," he said. "I'll be seeing you."

Then he strolled off towards the Austrian frontier, and I

stood watching him for a long time. I didn't know then – it wouldn't have been Fritz Kasparek if he had breathed a word of it – that he had bought that fruit as his provisions for the journey to Vienna with his last penny. As a result he had to pedal his pushbike 300 miles from Sillian to Vienna without a coin in his pocket and no food to eat. Maybe he used his unblushing Viennese charm to cadge an invitation from one or two farmers to a glass of milk; I couldn't say. But the reader will understand how sorry I was up there on the North Face not to be able to hand Fritz a dry packet of fags and say: "Smoke!" – just as he had once held out a bag of fruit to me on a red-hot high-road and said: "Eat!"

It was now 11 p.m. Ludwig had given over cookery and "retired to rest". Even here, on this tiny perch 12,300 ft up, and 5,000 ft sheer above the nearest level ground, he hadn't foregone the comfort of those bivouac-slippers. Andreas had to keep his crampons on, so as to get some kind of a stance in the ice for him to maintain a hold; but his head rested on Vörg's broad back. Next morning we discovered that Vörg had sat motionless, without a single movement of a muscle, so that Heckmair's sleep might be undisturbed. Fritz and I had pulled the Zdarsky-sack over us; our rucksack architecture served splendidly as support for our legs, and very soon I could hear the deep, regular breathing of my friend as he slept by my side. Through the little window in the tent sack I could see that there were no stars in the sky and the weather was still bad; it looked as if it were snowing. There was an occasional small snow-slide from above, but they only slid over the skin of the tent, with a gentle swishing sound, like a hand stroking it . . . I wasn't worried about the weather. I was possessed by a great feeling of peace; not the resignation to our fate, but a certainty that, whatever the weather might be, we would reach the summit tomorrow and after that regain the safety of the valley. This sense of peace increased to a conscious glow of happiness. We humans often experience happiness without recognizing it; later we realize that at such and such a moment we were happy. But here, in that bivouac of ours, I was not only genuinely happy; I knew I was.

This, the third bivouac for Fritz and me on the North

Face, was the smallest in terms of room; in spite of that it was the best. And if you ask why, the reason was the rest, the peace, the joy, the great satisfaction we all four enjoyed there.

If, during the hours just past, while we were being tried to the utmost, one of us had given in or lost his nerve for a second; if driven by the instinct of self-preservation, one of us had thought of trying to save his own life by leaving the party – no one would have blamed him. His companions would not have cut him, even if they might perhaps have greeted him a little less warmly ever after. If, down in the valley, people had honoured and cheered him, his friends would not have said a word. But that particular happiness which is born of absorption in a common endeavour would have passed him by and he would not have tasted its joy. We four in that bivouac on the Face of the Eiger were all happy. It might snow, and the little slides might come swishing over our covering tent-sack; but our sense of happiness was deeply rooted in us. It allowed us to think pleasant thoughts; and we were able to sleep . . .

Putting oneself to the supreme test – the expression is in itself an exaggerated description of a healthy, honest experience, and a contradiction of the quiet account one renders to oneself. But a far greater mistake is to suggest that this extreme testing of oneself is the mainspring of mountaineering. It is a suggestion initiated by the incurable complex-fiends, because no better explanation of what was to them inexplicable has occurred to them. I really cannot help smiling when I imagine Fritz Kasparek's face if one of these know-it-alls asked him whether he climbed in order to prove himself. The questioner would no doubt retire discomfited, routed by a caustic reply couched in those well-known Viennese terms which are so hard to translate into good classical German.

Of course no climber embarks on a difficult climb in order to test himself. If during moments of extreme danger on the mountain he thinks first of his rope-mates, if he subordinates personal well-being to the common weal, then he has automatically passed the test; and so he probably would in any of the everyday disasters, flood or fire. Nor would such a man go whizzing past injured people on the Autobahn; but he would bring aid where he could. For him the knowledge that he has done his best is enough. A passion to prove his mettle can never be the mainspring which makes him tick.

It makes me very angry to think of the many critics who categorize climbers of the "extreme" school as mentally abnormal. I can think of no more normal men than my three Eiger companions. True, the position in which we were situated was quite out of the ordinary; but my friends' reaction to that element of extraordinariness was perfectly normal. Fritz longed for dry cigarettes; Ludwig changed into cosy, lined boots for the bivouac; and Andreas, an-chored upright in the ice by his crampons, protected by Ludwig's broad back, slept the sleep of the just.

The peace and harmony of that night in the open allowed me to drift off into a twilight state between waking and sleeping. My body, almost bereft of being, was at rest. The cold did not plague; it only served to remind me that I was on a great mountain-face, as indeed did the somewhat cramped posture imposed by our rucksack bivouac. But that didn't plague me either. Here, as elsewhere in life, bliss was born of contrast. For, after the drubbing we had gone through a few hours before at the hands of the avalanches on the "Spider", our bivouac-perch seemed a very Heaven.

I was awakened by a considerable snow-slide over our tent. Dawn was glimmering through the little window; a new morning was at hand. Unfortunately it was not her-alded by the gorgeous play of colour of sunrise, nor by a clear pale-blue sky in which the stars were being dimmed by the new light of day; its approach was a greyness coming out of a grey fog. When we pulled the tent-sack away, we looked out on a winter landscape. It was still snowing; everything sharp or edgy had been fined away by the snow. Even our ledge had disappeared. Our friends, a few yards from us, appeared to be stuck on to the vertical rocks. The very idea that in this landscape, savage beyond the wildest dreams of imagination, people were alive, and actually planning to escape, this very day, from this prison of perpendicular rock, glassy with ice and plastered with snow, was ludicrous. But we were indeed alive; and we were not only planning to climb up out of it, we felt certain that we would manage to do so.

We could hear the gale shrieking across the ridges overhead. Where we were not a breath was stirring. Only the avalanches coming down and sweeping out over us generated a wind. We studied their timetable and planned how to use the knowledge. It was sombre to reflect in what poor case we would have been, had we been further down the Face, with the ice-slope of the "Spider" still to be climbed. The little slides which came down upon us from the gully were only a fraction of the great avalanches which get fed by the many diverse channels above to sweep over the slope of the "Spider". We were lucky indeed to be as high up as we were. But we soon realized that our cramped bivouac would seem a light trial compared with what we would still have to cope with today.

We were in good shape. The pain in Kasparek's hand seemed to have diminished. Thanks to Vörg's broad back, Heckmair had enjoyed a splendid sleep. Vörg was already busy in his capacity as chef. He brewed pots-full of coffee, melted chocolate in condensed milk, and altogether prepared a fine and plentiful breakfast. And while we consumed it, we held a council of war. The weather had done all the changing it was likely to do – for the worse. It was as bad as it always was when men had to stay on the Face for days on end. We had enough food and fuel to bivouac there for several more days. What good would that do us? Even if it cleared up tomorrow or the day after or in three days' time, the conditions on the Face could not improve, nor the rocks be fit to climb, for several days after that. Were we to let ourselves be worn down by sitting and waiting?

"It is better to fall off than to freeze." This remark came from Michel Innerkofler, the oldest of a famous dynasty of Dolomite guides. We were not thinking of falling off, but still less of surrendering just because the Face had put on its winter raiment. We decided to move on.

As soon as the decision had been taken, I lightened our rucksacks, by throwing down the precipice that part of the equipment and provisions which had become superfluous. Among it was a whole loaf of bread, which disappeared at a great pace in the mists below us. I had grown up in hard circumstances and had never before thrown away a piece of bread; but now the act almost seemed symbolic to me – we were moving on. "Forward" was the only way now; no more turning back. The past was wiped out, all that mattered was the future; and the future lay over the snow-plastered, ice-glazed summit-wall. I believe no man can be completely able to summon all his strength, all his will, all his energy, for the last desperate move, till he is convinced that the last bridge is down behind him and that there is nowhere to go but on.

We moved on. Anderl would lead us out at the top of the Face; this was to be Heckmair's great day.

It is my considered opinion today, as I sit writing these lines, that we would all have escaped safely from the Face, even without his protection from in front; Fritz too would have done it solo, in spite of his injured hand. But we would never have done it so well, without Anderl's leadership; and we might in all probability have had to bivouac again. That probably wouldn't have killed us either; I think we were all good enough, strong enough and in high enough spirits to survive even that. But are we one whit the worse, do we lose one jewel out of our crown, by recognizing with all due admiration that one of us was the best of us all?

We roped up again as a single, united rope of four. The order was now: Heckmair, Vörg, myself and Kasparek, who was coming up last today so as not to have to haul on the rope with his damaged hand.

Heckmair ran into problems from the very start. The first decision to be made was which of two routes to take? The icy overhanging, crack-like chimney which looked damnably difficult, but seemed safe from snow-slides; or up the steep, icy gully to its left, down which little avalanches seemed to descend from time to time? He chose the chimney and Vörg belayed him; but it proved necessary to drive a piton straight away. The chimney proved so difficult that even Heckmair's skill was of no avail.

So back he had to come and try the gully, having first studied the time-table of the avalanches. It kept on snowing, and now that day had come, it was damp snow, the kind that slides and adds to the fury of avalanches. But even without an avalanche the couloir was so difficult that even Heckmair slipped down it twice and it was only at the third attempt that his well-known powers of attack succeeded in taking him up to a small rock-crest to the left of the gully. There he knocked the snow and ice away with his axe and so managed to fashion usable foot-holds.

"Up you come," he said.

Vörg went up, and we two followed. Then Heckmair went on climbing on stuff that made the utmost demands on us all. He could not afford to waste time, for he had to reach the next safe stance in the pauses between avalanches, before the next snow-slide arrived. Not that there were any safe stances; a step in the ice, a piton, on to which to belay oneself, were the best we could hope for up here. But the higher we got, the thinner grew the film of ice in the gully; so thin that it would not bear the strokes of an axe, nor offer a reliable hold for a piton. The steel shafts went clean through the ice, impinged on the rock beneath and simply bent over.

We were all on a single rope. If the leader came off and number two couldn't hold him, it would be up to me to try to arrest the fall. And if I should be pulled off, the whole force would come on Fritz. We knew that one man could not hold three on this terrain. No one knew it better than Heckmair, who was often moving, and was forced to move, at the very limit of safety, if he was to force a way up to freedom for us. And once we were very close to annihilation. I was standing on a small knob, seeing Fritz up to me. One hundred feet above me stood Vörg, safeguarding Heckmair, as he grappled with icy rock, treacherous ice gullies and snow-slides high above us in the mists and driving snow. We couldn't see either of them.

Fritz joined me on my stance.

Still no order from Vörg to come up. We could hear voices and short, muffled cries. What could have gone wrong up there?

Then we could only hear a murmur of voices. At the same time a snow-slide came down on us. That was nothing unusual and we were quite used to it by now; but this wasn't white snow. It was stained red with blood. Definitely blood, because the next thing to come down was an empty bandage cover and this was followed by a small empty medicine bottle.

"Hallo!" we yelled. "What's happened?"

No reply. We waited for what seemed an age, racked with doubt and anxiety. Then, according to schedule, another avalanche came down with savage force. Not till it had passed did we obtain relief in the shape of an invitation to move on up.

Vörg was hauling on the rope so hard that it took my breath away. But I understood what this man-handling meant. No longer was there time to climb pitches neatly according to the rules. Time was now the watchword, if we were to escape from the Face. And evidently something had happened up there to cause great delay. What could it be?

When I reached Vörg's stance, a great weight fell from me. They were both alive and not even seriously hurt. Vörg had a blood-soaked bandage on one hand, but Heckmair was already a whole rope higher up, on a tiny, exposed, rickety stance.

Later on, he reported in his dry but lively way how Vörg came by his injury:

Wet snow was coming down heavily. There hadn't been an avalanche for a long time. So – quick, up the overhang! Curse it . . . the ice on the rock had thinned out, and the pitons wouldn't hold any more. At the second stroke they went clean through and bent themselves on the rock. On the overhang itself I could only cross my crampons, because there was only a narrow strip of old ice in the gully and the new ice overlaying the rock was too hard, smooth and thin. The point of the ice-piton on to which I was clinging for dear life only went a little way in and so did the pick of my ice-axe. Suddenly the piton came out, and at the same moment my axe gave way. If I could only have straddled, I could have kept my balance. But with my legs crossed, there wasn't a hope.

I shouted, "Look out, Wiggerl!"

Then I came off.

Wiggerl was looking out all right. He took in as much rope as he could, but I bore straight down on him – not through thin air, for the gully was inclined, but in a lightning-swift slide. Just as I fell, I turned face outwards so as not to go head over heels.

Wiggerl let the rope drop and caught me with his hands, and one of the points of my crampons went through his palm. I did turn head over heels, but in a split second I grabbed the rope-piton, which gave me such a jerk that I came up feet first again. I dug all twelve points of my irons into the ice – and found myself standing.

The force with which I had come down on Wiggerl had knocked him out of his holds but he, too, had been able to save himself and there we were, standing about four feet below our stance on steep ice without any footholds. One stride and we were back on it again. Naturally, the pitons had come out and I immediately knocked new ones in.

All this took only a matter of seconds. It was a purely reflex action which saved us; our friends, standing a rope's length below and linked to us by the same rope, hadn't even noticed that anything had happened. If we hadn't checked our fall we would have hurled them out from the face with us in a wide arc.

Meanwhile Wiggerl had taken his gauntlet off. Though blood spurted out, it was quite dark in colour, so it couldn't be a severed artery.

I looked quickly up the wall; thank goodness, there was as yet no avalanche on its way down. Off with my pack, out with the bandage, and I had Wiggerl's hand tied up. He was very pale; in fact if he had any colour at all, it was green.

"Do you feel bad?" I asked.

"I'm not very sure," he answered.

I placed myself in such a way that he could in no circumstances fall, and urged him to pull himself together, because it was now or never.

Just then a little phial of heart drops came to hand in

the first-aid bag. That devoted woman Dr Belart of
Grindelwald had made me take it along in case of
emergency, remarking: "If Toni Kurz had only had
them along, he might even have survived *his* ordeal."

We were only supposed to use them in the direst
need, though.

On the bottle it said . . . "ten drops". I simply
poured half of it into Wiggerl's mouth and drank
the rest, as I happened to be thirsty. We followed it
up with a couple of glucose lozenges, and were soon in
proper order again.

An avalanche was due, but I couldn't see any signs
of it.

"Look, I'm going to have another whack at the
overhang," I told him.

"All right," he said, "but please" – and his voice
was still quite weak – "no more using me as a mattress."

I braced myself, and managed the difficult pitch
absolutely safely this time, doing entirely without
pitons so as to get as quickly as I possibly could across
the really tricky bit it turned out to be. I went up
nearly 100 ft – almost the whole run of the rope –
without finding a stance; but I was at least able to put
in one of the small rock-pitons up there.

And just at that spot and at that moment, when Heckmair
had anchored himself to that kindly little piton, down came
the avalanche which shook us so severely down below, as
already described.

It failed to carry away Heckmair or Vörg, or either of us;
but it was many hours after our start before I was up
alongside Vörg and in a position to see Fritz safely up.
Vörg, freely assisted by the rope, hurried on to join Heckmair. I too hauled Fritz up. In fact we all pulled on the rope,
for time was racing away and the sector still to be climbed
was high, steep and difficult; nor had we any idea what it
would be like. I had never been on a face-climb where there
was so much chasing and racing with time as on this Eiger
thing. And yet this final cliff, in its ice-armoured snowed-

up state, called for an inch by inch struggle on the leader's part.

On we went. It snowed without respite. Visibility was hardly more than a rope's length upwards or sideways. Then through the cloud and the whirling flakes we heard shouts coming down to us, though we couldn't say exactly where from. They might come from the summit, or again from the West Ridge. Anyway they were reaching us. We agreed, on the spot, not to answer. Whoever was calling to us was too far from us to understand exactly what we might say in reply. Our answer might well launch a rescue operation which, once in motion, could not be called off; there might be a long descent for someone from the summit to the valley, a drumming up of the rescuers, a renewed ascent . . . one shout from us might well precipitate all that, if they misunderstood us . . . even if we only yodelled up a greeting . . .

So we climbed on with Anderl in the lead. Minutes passed into hours. Up we went, yard by yard, rope by rope.

Then we heard more shouts, this time clearer and nearer. We could even recognize that these were different voices from the earlier ones. Once again we refused to answer. We learned later that the first voices were those of Fraissl and Brankowsky, shouting down the Face, deep in their concern for our fate. The second time it was Hans Schlunegger, that great Oberland guide, shouting down to ask if we wanted help. True, he and the two Vienna boys were equally convinced that at the moment the foul conditions on the snow-laden Face made it quite impossible to lend us any aid; but he and our friends were equally ready to help us, or rescue us, as soon as the weather improved. At this point I must stress again the self-sacrificing readiness of the local guides. The two parties had reached the summit independently by the relatively easy normal route up the North-West Face, but had turned back immediately on receiving no answer from us. Obviously, after the hopeless reports brought back by those who had climbed to the summit to search for us, nobody rated the value of our lives very highly.

All the same, we were still alive, and still climbing. The

steepness of the gully eased off. The avalanches were harmless now, too; up here they had as yet no strength. And then we emerged from the gully on to an ice-slope.

It was the Summit Ice-field. If we hadn't just come off the Eiger's Face we would have said it was steep; now it seemed flat. The final gully was behind us; we had escaped from the clutch of the "Spider's" last arm. It was noon when Heckmair reached the lower rim of the ice-slope. An hour later the last of us four was safely up.

Only the ice-slope now separated us from the summit ridge. We didn't traverse to the left towards the Mittellegi Ridge, but climbed diagonally to the right, somewhere in the direction of the summit.

Only the summit ice-slope. Only . . .

Even this last rampart of the Eiger is no joke. The wet snow had not cohered firmly with the névé and ice beneath; it kept on sliding away. This is the very source of the Eiger's avalanches. We couldn't hasten our assault. We all had it firmly anchored in our minds that the Face had not yet given us leave to feel indifferent and stroll away in a carefree manner. Anderl was still leading, as coolly and carefully as ever. He knew that a change of the lead would mean manoeuvring with the rope and the loss of time; added to which he could get his breath back while seeing us up on the rope, while we arrived completely out of breath. These explanations, too, sprang from the modesty of his nature.

At this point I was particularly conscious of the absence of my crampons. Even though Heckmair was cutting huge steps for me where necessary, even though Vörg was carefully watching the rope which ran down to me, I couldn't and wouldn't risk any sign of weakness. I dared not slip; but it called for a great output of strength to hang on with nothing but the claw-nails in my boots.

It was snowing harder than ever now. Nor were the flakes falling vertically any more but almost horizontally, whipped by the wind. The ice-slope seemed interminable. Two more hours had slipped away.

Then something happened which would have been amusing, if it had not meant a moment of extreme danger.

Heckmair was climbing up the slope in the mist and the wild pother of snow. The slope was less steep now but, fighting his way against the wind and unable to see anything, he had not noticed it. Vörg, following him, suddenly saw dark patches in front of him. No – not in front – *below* him. Far, far below him . . .

They were the rocks on the South Side of the Eiger, which was not so thickly veiled in cloud and driven snow. The first two men ever to climb out of the North Face had almost fallen straight over the summit cornice down the South Face. If they had, I doubt whether we would have been able to hold them. As it was, they stepped back from the cornice in the nick of time.

We followed, gained a lodging on the wind-battered ridge, plodded our way over it to the summit of the Eiger. It was 3.30 p.m. on July 24th 1938. We were the first people to climb the North Face of the Eiger from its base to its top.

Joy, relief, tumultuous triumph? Not a bit of it. Our release had come too suddenly, our minds and nerves were too dulled, our bodies too utterly weary to permit of any violent emotion. Fritz and I had been on the Face eighty-five hours, Heckmair and Vörg sixty-one. We had not had a hair's-breadth escape from disaster; on the contrary, our bond of friendship had throughout given us a firm sense of mutual reliance. And hard as the climb had been, we had never doubted its successful outcome.

The storm was raging so fiercely on the summit that we had to bend double. Thick crusts of ice had formed around our eyes, noses and mouths; we had to scratch them away before we could see each other, speak or even breathe. We probably looked like legendary monsters of the Arctic, but we felt in no mood for the humour of such a reflection. Indeed, this was no place in which to turn handsprings or shriek with joy and happiness. We just shook hands without a word.

Then we started down at once. I remember another remark of Innerkofler's: "Downhill's easy! You've got all the little angels with you . . ."

But it wasn't easy. The descent was full of spite and malice. The wind hadn't blown the snow away here; it had fallen wet and heavy on the western slope, covering the icy slabs to a depth of nearly three feet. We kept on slipping and recovering ourselves. We suddenly felt tired, terribly tired. I had been given the job of finding and leading the way down because I already knew the route; but when I had traversed the Eiger on that previous occasion, visibility had been good. Now I didn't always find the correct route immediately; then, my companions hauled me over the coals. I didn't argue, for they were quite right. Particularly Anderl, who had led like an absolute hero all the way up the climb – a real hero, quietly doing the job and serving his friends. He wasn't the sort who needed drums and bugles or the cheers of the crowd to spur him on to a great performance. The urge sprang from within him, from his nature, from his true character as a man.

But now we could see how he was collapsing, not in a physical but in a spiritual sense. Uncomplainingly, mechanically, he moved forward; but by now he had given up the leadership. The fantastic nervous tension under which he had lived for days and nights on that mighty Face just had to induce a reaction. During those endless hours of danger he had excelled himself; now he could afford to be an ordinary man again, with all an ordinary man's weakness, susceptible and exposed to all the caprices of normal life.

For instance, take the matter of Anderl's trousers. The elastic band of his overalls had broken. Anderl kept on pulling his trousers up and they kept on falling down again. This man, who had reacted with the speed of lightning when he fell in the icy gully and so saved us all from disaster, the man who had so often withstood the pressure of the deadly avalanches, who had climbed ice-bulges in a blizzard and, with unexampled endurance, fought a way to freedom for himself and his three team-mates – this same man was almost driven to desperation by a broken elastic.

So Andreas had given up the lead. He had every right to expect to be led down on the descent just as surely and safely as he had led up that appalling Face; and he had every right to swear now when, racked by the exhaustion of a body exerted to the uttermost, he was asked to climb up a few hundred feet again because, in the mirk and the blown snow, I had led the wrong way down. I could see nothing amusing in this internal collapse of Anderl's. On the contrary, the very human nature of his reaction endeared him all the more to me.

We found the right route again and climbed on down it. We slipped, slid, stumbled, all securing one another. Gradually we lost height, and at last we were below the clouds. The snow turned into rain. But close down there now was the safe world of people.

For that multitude of dark dots down there, moving about on the glacier, were people. They were coming slowly up to meet us. We wondered what they were looking for on the glacier. Once we had seen people, we suddenly craved for the comforts of human civilization, about which we had not even dared to think during our bivouac nights. You mustn't long for a bed when you are hanging from a piton on a snowed-up precipice.

But now as we saw people coming up towards us we were gripped by an overwhelming desire for a hot bath, for a bed, for comfort. True, down there at the bottom of the wall stood our tent, a luxury home compared with our bivouac above the "Spider"; but we hadn't a dry stitch of clothing on us, and oh how we wanted to sleep in a bed! Would a hotel on the Kleine Scheidegg give us credit? How much money had we got left? Anderl was the richest; he still had a franc and a half, but that wouldn't go very far. Yet we still hankered after a bath and a bed.

Suddenly there was a young boy in front of us, staring at us as if we were ghosts. His face expressed embarrassed, incredulous astonishment. Then he summoned up his courage to ask:

"Have you come off the Face?"

"Yes," we admitted. "Off the Face."

Then the lad turned downhill again and ran away, screeching in a high treble: "They're coming! Here they are! They are coming!"

Soon we were encircled by people. Guides, our Viennese friends, the men from Munich, members of the Rescue Service, journalists, rubbernecks – all united in their great joy at seeing alive four men they had believed dead.

They took our rucksacks off for us, they wanted to carry us, and they would have, if we hadn't suddenly felt as fresh and gay as if we were back from a walk and not from the North Face of the Eiger. Someone gave Fritz his first dry cigarette. Rudi Fraissl held out a small flask of cognac to Andreas.

"Drink some," he said. "It'll warm you up."

Anderl emptied the flask at one pull. It didn't make him drunk. We were all drunk with the general joy around us. And then, for the first time, we felt the intense satisfaction, the relaxation, the relief from every care, and the indescribable delight at having climbed the North Face. Suddenly, too, all our problems were solved. Beds, baths? Everyone was showering invitations on us, simply everyone, just because they were human beings and we had come back safely to humanity.

Yes, we had made an excursion into another world and we had come back, but we had brought the joy of life and of humanity back with us. In the rush and whirl of everyday things, we so often live alongside one another without making any mutual contact. We had learned on the North Face of the Eiger that men are good and the earth on which we were born is good.

And now that earth was welcoming us home . . .

Mischabel

Geoffrey Winthrop Young

Born in 1876, the son of a mountaineer, Young began his climbing career on the spires of Trinity College, Oxford. One of the great mountaineers of the Edwardian era, particularly when teamed with the guide Josef Knubel, Winthrop Young lost a leg in action during the First World War but, undeterred he invented an artificial limb and carried on climbing. He died in 1958. Below he recounts the first ascent of the South-West face of the Taschhorn in the Alps, made in 1906 with V. J. E. Ryan and the guides Franz and Josef Lochmatter, Little J, and Josef Knubel.

The day was still bright and young, and the men obviously in fine climbing form. It was, therefore, no effort to telephone hearty remarks up and down the rope, or to emerge at Franz' feet after each struggle with a breathless but honest grin. But still the cliffs leaned out at us; still the unchancy upward and sideways traversing was forced upon us. A little cloud of anxiety crept upon the edge of my mind. My eye glanced unwillingly up or down: it was beginning to dodge, instinctively, the questions that the sight suggested. Our hands and feet grew gradually numb with the uninterrupted clinging to rounded, cold and slippery ledges.

At last – and how vividly the scene starts to mind – I stood on such a shelf, looking up at Franz' head and shoulders as he poised over a sheer wall above me, his prehensile feet balancing him erect upon a gutter-slope whose gracelessness I was yet to discover. The wall up to him bothered me a little; and as I got one arm over the coping and felt only the comfortless incline of the narrow band, I called out in joking patois, "Watch out, Franz, for my rope!" He looked down at me and out beyond me thoughtfully, almost abstractedly, without the customary flash of big brown eyes and big white teeth: "You must do what you can; here we can no longer help one another!" And then he turned away, dropping my rope symbolically from his hand and watching his brother, whose struggles, invisible to me, were audible far up round a black repulsive corner.

From such a man the words had the effect of an icy douche. The detachment of mind which a leader may never lose whatever his occupation with his own struggles returned upon the instant. I looked down over my arm: to see the deadly continuity of descending precipice with its narrow snowy eavelets leaning out one above another, and still one above another, dizzily; and seeming to shrug even the glance of my eye off into space. And I realized in a flash what a return down them must mean. I looked up: to discover that worse lay before us, if we failed to force a way up the chimney into which we were traversing for an escape. For hours already, deceived by our spacing from each other up a seeming ladder of terraces that were no terraces, we must have been climbing in reality at our several risks: each of us unprotected by the man above: the slip of any one imperilling the rest. For how many more hours would this, or could we, continue?

A slight, pricking snow began to drift across us. From the exposed height of our great pyramidal wall, surging above other ranges, we looked out across a frozen and unheeding stillness of white peak and glacier, disappearing under the darker clouds to the south. We seemed very much removed from the earth, and very much alone. As I turned back to the rock I could see nothing but antagonism in the ice-wrinkled face of the crags upon which we were venturing; and I had the feeling – it was too formless at the time to take the definite shape I must now give to it – as if somewhere low down beyond the horizon behind me a great grey bird was just lifting on its wings into heavy flight. As the hours wore on, this shadow at our backs seemed to be approaching soundlessly and covering more and more of the sky. Gradually it was enclosing us within its spread of cold wings, and isolating us from all the world of life and movement in our contest with the frigid wall of grey precipice.

Precariously we crawled up to and along, and up to and along, the sloping ribbons, silky with chill snow, and leading interruptedly upward towards the projecting corner which shut us off from the big couloir. On the decrepit mantelpiece by which we turned the corner itself, we could use a rock "hitch" for the rope, one of the only three we found on all this upper face! We edged round into the couloir, a forbidding chasm; and found ourselves on a slim, shattered ledge, that continued inwards at a high level across the sheer wall of rock forming our side of the rift.

We were more or less together now; and no one could any longer pretend that some one above saw a gleam of hope denied to himself. Forty feet below, the slabby back of the chasm slanted steeply outward, and down into space. Past us, the same backing of slabs mounted precipitously, to splay out in an amphitheatre of over-leaning walls far above. And every hopeless curve of slab was glassy with ice and glitter-film. The couloir, as an upward escape, needed no second glance. Josef was already clinging down our wall into the chasm below. His object was plain. The same belt or flaw by which we had entered the rift appeared again, at a lower level, upon the wall opposite to us, and disappeared round the profile of the further containing buttress. What could be seen of its re-start was no more than a sloping shelf, that wound steeply upwards and out of sight round the all but vertical corner. But Josef had evidently made up his mind that our only chance, now the couloir had failed, was to resume our perilous ribbon-traverses along the bands; in the hope – if they continued far enough – of finding the second, smaller chimney, the branch which forked out on to the south-east ridge, accessible; and if accessible, less icy-hearted. It appeared to me, and probably to him, a very faint and rather fearsome chance. Even the slabs below us, which gave difficult access to the crazy re-start of the traverse, looked villainous enough.

Josef moved tentatively about on the smooth shoot of the slabs, steadied by Ryan with the rope from our ledge. He never looked like crossing them; and I think that the nearer view of the re-start of the traverse was weakening his resolution. The dark chilly depths of the chasm gave muffled answer to his agitated comments. Franz, beside me on the ledge, watched him, hissing a gay little French song between his teeth, the only sign of excitement I have ever known him show. Then – "It won't go!" came in a hollow shout from below; and – "But it must go!" echoed from Franz, who at once leaped into action. I untied my rope to him. He was down and out on to the slabs in a breath, still singing to himself. He caterpillared his way across the ice-bosses above Josef. Josef, and other great guides, on slabs moved with the free poise of an athlete and the footcling of a chamois. Franz, in such case, had the habit and something of the appearance of a spider or crustacean. His curled head disappeared altogether. His body and square shoulders split and elongated into four steely tentacles, radiating from a small central core or hub of intelligence, which transmitted the messages between his tiny hands and boots as they clung attached and writhing at phenomenal angles and distances.

At the far side of the slabs he crawled on to and up the sloping shelf of the disappearing traverse, only keeping himself on it, so far as could be seen, by thrusting one foot firmly out against the aether. Presently Ryan followed, out of sight; and then Josef. Even with little J playing my rope from high up on the wall behind me, I found the crossing of the iced slabs of the couloir upon a descending diagonal nasty enough. More especially towards the farther side, when the rope, sagging across from above, began to pull me back with a heavy draw. But the start of the traverse looked unspeakable. A downward and outward leaning shelf, with nothing below and an over-hanging wall above it, screwed steeply upward out of sight round the buttress. From far up along it came Josef's voice, thinly crying caution. How was

I to keep on the shelf – and, much more, wriggle up it?

Little J joined me on the ice-nicks in the slabs; and after many attempts the end of Josef's rope, slung from above and weighted with a stone, was lassoed back and round to a point on the slabs from which we could recover it. I tied on, and started. Once up on the shelf, I found that there was nothing to keep me on it against the urgency of the slant into space. A hailing match between little J and Josef only produced the information that while he was "good" to hold – but not to pull – along the diagonal upward line of the shelf, he would be helpless against any direct downward strain, such as must result if I fell off the shelf. There was nothing for it but to thrust myself desperately upward, relying only upon the friction of my outer knee on the hem of the sloping ribbon to resist an outward drag to which the weight of the world seemed to be added. Of service, also, were two or three painful finger-tip pinches on the down-sloping prickles of the wall above my head.

When I reached Josef, I found him sprawled over rugosities on the buttress. His "hitch" – the second of our dauntless three – was no more than a prong of rock sticking downward like a tusk from the overhang above him, and of course useless against a pull from any but the one, sideways, direction. Little J, who had by now begun his assorted collection of all our sacks and axes, followed up magnificently.

The next clear memory is of finding ourselves inside the second, smaller, chimney, a precipitous narrow cleft up the face, of worn, skull-smooth rock. It was all dirty white and boneblue in the gloomy afternoon light, with blurred ice-nubbles bulking through the adhesive snow. But at least there was the singular rest for eye and nerves which the feeling of enclosing walls gives us after long hours on an exposed cliff. We even found a nominal stance or two, in ice-pockets on chockstones, where we could *almost* hold on without help from the hands. Franz, who was back again above me resting from the lead, could spare me a few partial hoists with the rope. I began to feel my muscles slackening with the relief, and I became conscious of the cold. I had time to notice that I was climbing less precisely, a symptom

of relaxed tension: time, too, to admit ungrudgingly that
nothing in the universe but Franz' rope could have got me
up to and over some of the expulsive ice bulges in the
chimney. Ignorant in my remote position of what the front
men saw awaiting us above, I even thawed into a congra-
tulatory remark or so: but I drew no response.

And then, it all ended! The chimney simply petered out:
not under the south-east ridge, as we might have hoped, but
in the very hard heart of the diamond precipice some 600 ft
below the final and still invisible summit. The vague exit
from the chimney faded out against the base of a blank cliff.
One of its side walls led on for a little, and up to the left.
There it too vanished, under the lower rim of a big snowy
slab, sloping up, and slightly conical, like a dish-cover. I
have reason to remember that slab. It formed the repellent
floor of a lofty, triangular recess. On its left side, and in
front, there was space and ourselves. On its right, and at the
back, a smooth leap of colossal cliff towered up for a
hundred feet of crystallized shadow, and then arched out
above our heads in a curve like the dark underside of a
cathedral dome. A more appalling-looking finish to our
grim battle of ascent could hardly have been dreamed in a
"falling" nightmare; and we had not even standing room to
appreciate it worthily! As I looked up and down, I had an
overpowering sense of the great grey wings behind us,
shadowing suddenly close across the whole breadth of
precipice, and folding us off finally from the world.

But our long apprenticeship to discouragement stood us
in good stead. Muscles braced anew obstinately; determination quickened resentfully. The recess on whose lip we
hung had been formed by the sliding of a great wedge of
rock off the inclined, dish-cover slab, once its bed. But on
our right the cliff continued the original line. My impression of this, therefore, was as of a high building viewed from
under one corner. Its sheer front wall stretched away to the
right, flush with the sill of our slab. The end wall of the
building formed the right side of our recess, and overhung
the slab. The rectangular house-corner, where the two walls
joined, rose immediately above us, vertical and iced, but a
little chipped by the rending out of the wedge. Again, the

front wall of this projecting house did not rise to the same height as the cliff that backed our recess. Forty feet up – my measures are merely impressions – the wall slanted steeply back in a roof, receding out of sight. Presumably another huge wedge had here slid from its bed, on a higher plane. Above and beyond this roof the precipices rose again into sight, in the same line and of the same height as the cliffs which backed our recess. Only, the cliff vertically above us was crowned by the great dome or overhang. There must be, therefore, invisible above, some rough junction or flaw where the line of cliffs above the receding house-roof linked on to the forward jut of our dome. Four vital questions suggested themselves: Could the house-corner be climbed? Was the roof, if attainable, too steep to crawl up? Might there be a flawed connection where the precipice upon which the roof abutted joined on to the side of the dome? If there was such a flaw, would this yield us a passage out on to the face of the convex dome above its circle of largest dimension, on its retreating upper curve, or below it, under its hopeless arch? These details are tiresome, perhaps unintelligible. But they may help other climbers to a better understanding of Franz' remarkable feat.

Right up in the angle of the recess there was a rotund blister of rock modelled in low relief on the face of the slab; and round this a man, hunched on small nicks in the steep surface, could just belay the rope. Josef and Franz were crouching at this blister up in the recess. The rest of us were dispersed over freezing clingholds along the lower rim of the slab. And the debate proceeded, broken by gusts of snow. The man to lead had clearly to run out 100 to a 150 ft of rope. He could be given no protection. His most doubtful link would come some eighty feet up above the roof. If he found a flaw there, and it served him favourably, he would be out on the convex of the dome fully a hundred feet above us, and outside us in a direct line above our heads. If, at this point, he could not proceed – well, it was equally unlikely that he could return!

Franz showed no hesitation. The hampered preparations for the attempt went on hurriedly. We had all to unrope as best we could, so as to arrange for the 200 ft of possible run-out, and we hooked on to our holds with difficulty, while the snow-frozen rope kinked and banged venomously about us. In the end little J and I had to remain off the rope, to leave enough free.

Franz started up the corner, climbing with extraordinary nerve but advancing almost imperceptibly. It was much like swarming up the angle of a tower, rough-cast with ice. Ryan and little J crept up near the blister; but as there was no more room I remained hanging on to the fractured sill of the slab. In this position I was farther out; and I could just see Franz' two feet scratting desperately for hold to propel him up the tilt of the roof above the corner. The rest of him was now out of sight. The minutes crawled like hours, and the rope hanging down to us over the gable-end hardly seemed to stir upwards. The snow gusts distracted us cruelly. A precipice in sunshine seems at least interested in our microscopic efforts. Its tranquillity even helps our movement by giving to it a conspicuous importance. But when the stable and unstable forces of nature join in one of their ferocious, inconclusive conflicts, the little human struggle is carelessly swallowed up in uproar, and tosses unregarded and morally deflated, like a wet straw on a volcanic wave.

Suddenly I heard that unmistakable scrape and grit of sliding boot-nails and clothes. Above my head, over the edge of the roof to the right, I saw Franz' legs shoot out into space. Time stopped. A shiver, like expectancy, trembled across the feeling of unseen grey wings behind me from end to end of the cliff. I realized impassively that the swirl of the rope must sweep me from my holds before it tightened on the doubtful belay of the blister. But fate was playing out the game in regions curiously remote. My mind watched the moves, itself absorbed into the same remote, dispassionate atmosphere. It seemed unwilling to disturb the issue by formulating a thought, or even a fear. The fact of the body seemed negligible; it had no part in the observant aloofness into which all consciousness had withdrawn. Something of the same feeling of separation between the body and the watching mind is the experience of men actually falling or drowning, when action is at an end and there is not even pain to reunite bodily and mental sensation. But during the crises of this day the condition lasted, with me certainly, for spaces that could only be measured by hours.

Franz' boots again disappeared above the edge. No one in the recess had known of the slip, out of their sight and lost in the gusts. He had stopped himself miraculously on the rim by crushing his hands on to ice-dimples in the slab. The hanging rope began again to travel up along the slanting gable-end of the roof. There was a long interval, and now and then the sound of a scratting boot or the scrabble of loose surface. Then the rope began, jerkily, to work out and across far above our heads. Franz had found a flaw in the join of the cliffs above the roof, and he was creeping out on to the projection of the dome. The lengthening rope now hung down well outside the men in the recess, and it might have hung outside me on the lower rim, had they not held in its end. Its weight upon Franz, as it swayed down through the snow, must have added to his immense difficulties. He was well out of sight, clinging somewhere above on the upper curve of the overhang.

An indistinct exchange of shouts began, half swallowed by echo, wind, and snow. Franz, it appeared, was still quite uncertain if he could get up any further. For the time he could hold on well enough to help one man with the rope; but he had not two hands free to pull. I could hear his little spurt of laughter at the question – "Could he return?" He suggested that Josef should join him, and the rest wait until they two might return with a rescue-party. Wait, there! – for at best fifteen hours, hanging on to the icy holds, in a snow wind!

At that hour of the day and upon those treacherous cliffs, now doubly dangerous under accumulating snow, all the odds were against any of us who turned back getting down alive. Franz in any case could not get back to us, and he might not be able to advance. We were committed, there-fore, to the attempt to join him, however gloomy its out-look. As many as possible must be got up to him – and the rest must be left to chance.

Josef started his attempts on the corner. This left room for me to move up to Ryan on the slab. He asked me, I remember, what I thought were the chances of our escape. I remember, too, considering it seriously, and I can hear myself answering – "About one in five."

The end of the long rope hooted down past me. It hung outside the recess, dangling in air; and I could only recover it by climbing down again over the rim of the slab and reaching out for it one-handed with my axe. I passed it up; and then I stayed there, hanging on, because I could no longer trust my hands or feet to get me up the slope again. Ryan began the corner; but if I have described the position at all intelligibly, it will be seen that while the corner rose vertically on our right, the long rope hung down on a parallel line from the dome directly above our heads. So it came that the higher we climbed up the corner the more horizontal became the slanting pull of the rope, and the more it tended to drag us sideways off the corner and back under the overhang. Very coolly, Ryan shouted a warning before he started of the insufficient power left in frozen hands. Some twenty feet up, the rope tore him from his inadequate, snowy holds. He swung across above our heads and hung suspended in mid-air. The rope was fixed round his chest. In a minute it began to suffocate him. He shouted once or twice to the men above to hurry. Then a fainter call, "I'm done," and he dangled to all appearance unconscious on the rope. Franz and Josef could only lift him half-inch by half-inch. For all this hour – probably it was longer – they were clamped one above the other on to the steep face of the dome, their feet on shallow but sound nicks, one hand clinging on, and only the other free to pull in. Any inch the one lifted, the other held. The rough curve of the rock, over which the higher portion of the rope descended, diminished by friction the effectiveness of each tug. The more one considers their situation, the more superhuman do the cooperation and power the two men displayed during this time, at the end of all those hours of effort, appear. Little J and I had only the deadly anxiety of watching helplessly, staring upward into the dizzy snow and shadow: and that was enough. J had followed silently and unselfishly the whole day; and even now he said nothing: crouching in unquestioning endurance beside the freezing blister on the slab.

Ryan was up at last, somehow, to the overhang; and being dragged up the rough curve above. A few small splinters were loosened, and fell, piping, past me and on to me. I remember calculating apathetically whether it was a greater risk to try and climb up again into the recess, unroped and without any feel in fingers and toes, or to stay where I was, hanging on to the sill, and chance being knocked off by a stone. It is significant of the condition of body and mind that I decided to stay where I was, where at least stiffened muscles and joints still availed to hold me mechanically fixed on to my group of rounded nicks.

Ryan was now out of sight and with the others. When the constriction of the rope was removed he must have recovered amazingly toughly, and at once; for down once more, after a short but anxious pause, whistled the snow-stiffened rope, so narrowly missing me that little J cried out in alarm. I could not for a time hook it in with the axe; and while I stretched, frigidly and nervously, Josef hailed me from seemingly infinite height, his shouts travelling out on the snow eddies. They could not possibly pull up my greater weight. Unless I felt sure I could stick on to the corner and manage to climb round to them by Franz' route, it was useless my trying! At last I had fished in the rope, with a thrill of relief, and I set mental teeth. With those two tied on to the rope above, and myself tied on – in the way I meant to tie myself on – to the rope below, there were going to be no more single options. We were all in it together; and if I had still some faith in myself I had yet more in that margin of desperation strength which extends the possible indefinitely for such men as I knew to be linked on to me above. And if I were once up, well there would be no question after that about little J coming up too!

I gave hands and feet a last blue-beating against the rock to restore some feeling to them. Then I knotted the rope round my chest, made the loose end into a triple-bowline "chair" round my thighs, and began scratching rather futilely up the icy rectangular corner. For the first twenty-five feet – or was it much less? – I could just force upward. Then the rope began to drag me off inexorably. I clutched furiously up a few feet more; and then I felt I must let go, the drag was too strong for frozen fingers. As I had already resolved, at the last second I kicked off from the rock with all my strength. This sent me flying out on the rope, and across under the overhang, as if attached to a crazy pendulum. I could see J crouching in the recess far below, instinctively protecting his head. The impetus jumped the upper part of the rope off its cling to the rock face of the dome above, and enabled the men to snatch in a foot or two. The return-swing brought me back, as I had half hoped, against the corner, a little higher up. I gripped it with fingers and teeth, and scrambled up another few feet. But the draw was now irresistible. I kicked off again; gained a foot or so, and spun back.

I was now up the corner proper, and I should have been by rights scrambling up the roof on the far side of my gable edge. But the rope, if nothing else, prevented any chance of my forcing myself over it and farther to the right. Another cling and scratch up the gable end, and I was not far below the level of the dome overhanging above and to my left. For the last time I fell off. This time the free length of the rope, below its hold upon the curve of the dome, was too short to allow of any return swing. So I shot out passively, to hang, revolving slowly, under the dome, with the feeling that my part was at an end. When I spun round inward, I looked up at the reddish, scarred wall freckled with snow, and at the tense rope, looking thin as a grey cobweb and disappearing fraily over the forespring of rock that arched greedily over my head. When I spun outward, I looked down – no matter how many thousand feet – to the dim, shifting lines of the glacier at the foot of the peak, hazy through the snowfall; and I could see, well inside my feet, upon the dark face of the precipice the little blanched triangle of the recess and the duller white dot of J's face as he crouched by the blister. It flashed across me, absurdly, that he ought to be more anxious about the effect of my gymnastics upon the fragile thread of alpine rope, his one link with hope, than about me!

I was quite comfortable in the chair; but the spinning had to be stopped. I reached out the axe at full stretch, and succeeded in touching the cliff, back under the overhang.

This stopped me, face inward. I heard inarticulate shouting above, and guessed its meaning, although I was now too close under the dome to catch the words: "They could not lift my dead weight!" I bethought me, and stretched out the axe again; got its point against a wrinkle of the wall, and pushed out. This started me swinging straight out and in below the dome. After two pokes I swung in near enough to be able to give a violent, short-armed thrust against the cliff. It carried me out far enough to jump quite a number of feet of rope clear of its cling down the rock above. The guides took advantage of the easing to haul in, and I pendulum'd back a good foot higher. The cliff facing me was now beginning to spring out in the Gothic arch of the overhang; so it could be reached more easily. I repeated the shove-out more desperately. Again they hauled in on the released rope. This time I came back close under the arch; and choosing a spot as I swung in, I lifted both feet, struck them at the wall, and gave a convulsive upward and outward spring. The rope shortened up; and as I banged back the cornice of the arch loomed very near above my head. But the free length of rope below it was now too short to let me again reach to the back of the arch with leg or axe. I hung, trying in vain to touch the lowest moulding of the cornice above with my hands. I heard gasps and grunts above quite distinctly now. The rope strained and creaked, gritting over the edge of the rock above me. I felt the tremor of the sinews heaving on it. But for all that, I did not move up. I reached up with the axe in both hands, just hooked the pick into a lucky chink of the under-moulding, and pulled, with a frantic wriggle of the whole body. It was a feeble lift, but enough for the sons of Anak above to convert into a valuable gain. The axe slipped down on to my shoulder, held there by its sling. I reached up and back with both arms, got hold of a finger-grip and gained another inch. Infinitesimal inches they seemed, each a supreme effort, until my nose and chin scratched up against a fillet of the cornice. Then the arms gave out completely, so much at the end of their strength that they dropped lifeless. But the teeth of the upper jaw held on a broken spillikin and, with the stronger succour of the rope, supported me for the seconds while the blood was running back into my arms.

Wrestle by wrestle it went on. Every reserve of force seemed exhausted, but the impulse was now supplied by a flicker of hope. Until, at last, I felt my knee catch over a moulding on the edge, and I could sink for an instant's rest, with rucked clothes clinging over the rough, steep, upward but *backward* curving of the dome. It is impossible to suggest the relief of that feeling, the proof that the only solid surface which still kept me in touch with existence had ceased to thrust itself out for ever as a barrier overhead, and was actually giving back below me in semi-support.

But there was no time, or inclination, to indulge panting humanity with a rest or a realization. I crept up a few feet, on to small, brittle, but sufficient crinkles. The dark figures of the three men above were visible now, clinging crab-like and exhausted on to similar nicks, indistinct in the snow dusk, but still human company. I had to stay where I was, and untie my rope, knotting up a coil at the end of the heavy length so that I could swing it inward to little J back and out of sight beneath me in the recess. The second cast was true: I felt him handle it, and then I let it go for those in the more direct line above to hold. Presently I saw it writhing away from me across the few visible feet of stooping crag, as J below moved away to start the icy corner. He had, I think, two sacks beside his own and at least three extra axes slung on to him; but he grappled up the corner masterfully and forced his way out on to the roof. Hopeless of lifting him as they had lifted us, the men above had learned, from pure fatigue, to leave him more free upon the rope. But he was naturally a very long time; and there was all too much leisure in which to realize how irrevocably our descent was now cut off, and how improbably our ascent could be continued.

The first flare of blinding relief died down. The obscure future settled round again like a fog. The precipice receding into murky uncertainty above looked more than ever dark with discouragement for a vitality ebbing on the tide of reaction. The shadowy, humping figures above were silent; there was none of that heartening talk which greets us over a difficult edge, giving us assurance that the worst is past.

With no longer even the rope about me as a reminder of companionship, the sense that others were near me and in like case passed out of mind. My thoughts wandered drowsily, and all life in the limbs seemed suspended, as we feel it to be sometimes in the moments just preceding sleep.

The snow began to fall in large, soft flakes; not the tingling darts that assail us with the crisp hostility of intruders upon our alien earth, but flakes like wings, instinct with life, surrounding and welcoming a visitor to their own region of air with vague but insistent friendliness. A few of them settled inquisitively, to gleam and fade for a second like fallen starlight, on the short arc of brown crag racing into shadow between my feet. The rest drifted lightly and recklessly down past my heels, to disappear over the rim of void: suggesting how easy and restful might be my own descent could tired muscles but be persuaded to relax their tenacious hold upon the few remaining feet of inhospitable rock. Far below and to the right, a brow of bending and frosted precipice frowned into sight; and against and round its more familiar obstruction, lit by a pale glare diffused through the low clouds, the white flakes twirled and circled intimately, already forgetful of their more timid flight past the stranger above. When they sank from it, it was into an immensity of grey haze, featureless but for the black ribbons of moraine which floated high and distinct above their unseen glaciers, as reeds seem to sway and float high over the reflecting depths of a transparent stream. Into these immeasurably grey depths everything seemed to be descending, unresistingly and as of choice – the long lines of ice-fast crag, the shifting eddies of snow, the rays of darkness under the storm-clouds, even the eye and the tired mind. Some rebellious instinct of hand and foot alone appeared to defy a universal law.

The appearance of little J as he clambered, a clattering brown goblin of sack-humps and axe-points, over a boss on the shadowy dome beside me brought me back to the world of human company, and struggle. The day was darkening steadily – or is my memory of darkness only the shadow of our circumstance? for it was not yet four o'clock: but the snow stopped, having done its worst where it could most impede us. We roped up patiently, and began again our age-long crawl and halt up icy slabs as little kindly as before; and every fifty feet above us loomed still the threat of a total interruption. If it came now – it must just come! We had none of us, I think, any apprehension left: or for that matter, any comprehension of much more than hanging on and forcing up. In my own case – and a truthful record of sensation limits me to thinking only of myself – the capacity to feel or to remark was exhausted. Franz must have been more nervously alert, for he ground out a devious upward line through the upheaving of giant slabs without a halt or a false attempt. I can recall nothing but obscurity, steepness, and an endless driving of the muscles to their task. Still no message of hope reached us from above; and yet we must have left another 400 ft of rib and crack, snow-ice and equivocal holds below us. Even fancy dared not whisper to itself of the summit: the next five feet, and still the next five feet were the end of all effort and expectation.

And then, something was happening! There came a mutter of talk from the dusk above. Surely two shadows were actually moving at one time? I was at the foot of a long icy shelf, slanting up to the right. It was overhung by cliff on the left, as usual; and it had the usual absence of any holds to keep me on it. I began the eternal knee-friction crawl. The rope tightened on my waist. "Shall I pull?" – called Josef's voice, sounding strange after the hours of silence, and subdued to an undertone as if he feared that the peak might still hear and wake up to contrive some new devilment. "Why not? – if you really can!" – I echoed, full of surprise and hope; and I skimmered up the trough, to find Josef yoked to a royal rock hitch, the third and the best of the day! And, surely, we were standing on the crest of a great ridge, materialized as if by magic out of the continuous darkness of cliff and sky? And the big, sullen shadow just above must be the summit! It was indeed the mounting edge of the south-east ridge upon which we had arrived; and sixty feet above us it curled over against the top of the final pyramid. Josef unroped from me, while I brought up little J; and as we started to finish the ascent together in our old-time partnership, I saw the silhouettes of the other three pass in succession over the pointed skyline of the peak.

We found them, relaxed in spent attitudes on the summit-slabs, swallowing sardines and snow, our first food since half-past seven in the morning. It was now close upon six o'clock. Franz came across to meet me, and we shook hands. "You will never do anything harder than that, Franz!" "No," he said reflectively, "man could not do much more."

Avalanche

George Leigh Mallory

Born in Cheshire, England, in 1886, Mallory was the golden boy of early-twentieth century mountaineering. Originator of the cliche "Because it's there", he was a member of the first three Everest expeditions (the episode below is taken from the 1922 attempt). The mountain took his life on 8 June 1924 when he, and the very inexperienced Andrew Irvine, departed Camp VI to climb the last 600 m (1,900 ft) to the summit. They were briefly spotted below the peak but never seen again. Almost a decade later an ice-axe belonging to Irvine was found at 8,400 m (27,500 ft), suggesting that an accident happened at that height and that they did not reach the summit still more than 400 m (1,300 ft) above them. Mallory's body was discovered in 1999, perfectly preserved. He lay face-down with his arms outstretched.

The project of making a third attempt this season was mooted immediately on the return of Finch and Geoffrey Bruce to the Base Camp. There in hours of idleness we had discussed their prospects and wondered what they would be doing as we gazed at the mountain to make out the weather on the great ridge. We were not surprised to learn when they came down that the summit was still unconquered, and we were not yet prepared to accept defeat. The difficulty was to find a party. Of the six who had been already engaged only one was obviously fit for another great effort. Somervell had shown a recuperative capacity beyond the rest of us. After one day at the Base he had insisted on going up again to Camp III in case he might be of use to the others. The rest were more or less knocked out. Morshead's frost-bitten fingers and toes, from which he was now suffering constant pain, caused grave anxiety of most serious consequences, and the only plan for him was to go down to a lower elevation as soon as possible. Norton's feet had also been affected; he complained at first only of bruises, but the cold had come through the soles of his boots; his trouble too was frost-bite. In any case he could not have come up again, for the strain had told on his heart and he now found himself left without energy or strength.

Geoffrey Bruce's feet also were so badly frost-bitten that he could not walk. Finch, however, was not yet to be counted out. He was evidently very much exhausted, but an examination of his heart revealed no disorder; it was hoped that in five or six days he would be able to start again. My own case was doubtful. Of my frost-bitten finger-tips only one was giving trouble; the extremity above the first joint was black, but the injury was not very deep. Longstaff, who took an interest which we all appreciated in preventing us from doing ourselves permanent injury, pointed out the probability that fingers already touched and highly susceptible to cold would be much more severely injured next time, and was inclined to turn me down, from his medical point of view, on account of my fingers alone. A much more serious matter was the condition of my heart. I felt weak and lazy when it was a question of the least physical exertion, and the heart was found to have a "thrill". Though I was prepared to take risks with my fingers I was prepared to take none with my heart, even had General Bruce allowed me. However, I did not abandon hope. My heart was examined again on June 3rd, no thrill was heard, and though my pulse was rapid and accelerated quickly with exertion it was capable of satisfactory recovery. We at once arranged that Somervell, Finch and I, together with Wakefield and Crawford, should set forth the same day.

It was already evident that whatever we were to do would now have to wait for the weather. Though the Lama at the Rongbuk Monastery had told us that the monsoon was usually to be expected about June 10th, and we knew that it was late last year, the signs of its approach were gathering every day. Mount Everest could rarely be seen after 9 or 10 a.m. until the clouds cleared away in the evening; and a storm approaching from the West Rongbuk Glacier would generally sweep down the valley in the afternoon. Though we came to despise this blustering phenomenon – for nothing worse came of it than light hail or snow, either at our camp or higher – we should want much fairer days for climbing, and each storm threatened to be the beginning of something far more serious. However, we planned to be on the spot to take any chance that offered. The signs were even more ominous than usual as Finch and I walked up to Camp I on the afternoon of June 3rd; we could hardly feel optimistic; and it was soon apparent that, far from having recovered his strength, my companion was quite unfit for another big expedition. We walked slowly and frequently halted; it was painful to see what efforts it cost him to make any progress. However, he persisted in coming on.

We had not long disposed ourselves comfortably within the four square walls of our "sangar", always a pleasant change from the sloping sides of a tent, when snow began to fall. Released at last by the west wind which had held it back, the monsoon was free to work its will, and we soon understood that the great change of weather had now come. Fine, glistening particles were driven by the wind through the chinks in our walls, to be drifted on the floor or on our coverings where we lay during the night; and as morning grew the snow still fell as thickly as ever. Finch wisely decided to go back, and we charged him with a message to General Bruce, saying that we saw no reason at present to alter our plans. With the whole day to spend confined and inactive we had plenty of time to consider what we ought to do under these conditions. We went over well-worn arguments once more. It would have been an obvious and easy course, for which no one could reproach us, to have said simply: The monsoon has come; this is the end of the climbing season; it is time to go home. But the case, we felt, was not yet hopeless. The monsoon is too variable and uncertain to be so easily admitted as the final arbiter. There might yet be good prospects ahead of us. It was not unreasonable to expect an interval of fine weather after the first heavy snow, and with eight or ten fair days a third attempt might still be made. In any case, to retire now if the smallest chance remained to us would be an unworthy end to the expedition. We need not run our heads into obvious danger; but rather than be stopped by a general estimate of conditions we would prefer to retire before some definite risk that we were not prepared to take or simply failed to overcome the difficulties.

After a second night of unremitting snowfall the weather on the morning of June 5th improved and we decided to go on. Low and heavy clouds were still flowing down the East Rongbuk Glacier, but precipitation ceased at an early hour and the sky brightened to the west. It was surprising, after all we had seen of the flakes passing our door, that no great amount of snow was lying on the stones about our camp. But the snow had come on a warm current and melted or evaporated, so that after all the depth was no more than 6 inches at this elevation (17,500 ft). Even on the glacier we went up a long way before noticing a perceptible increase of depth. We passed Camp II, not requiring to halt at this stage, and were well up towards Camp III before the fresh snow became a serious impediment. It was still snowing up here, though not very heavily; there was nothing to cheer the grey scene; the clinging snow about our feet was so wet that even the best of our boots were soaked through, and the last two hours up to Camp III were tiresome enough. Nor was it a cheering camp when we reached it. The tents had been struck for the safety of the poles, but not packed up. We found them now half-full of snow and ice. The stores were all buried; everything that we wanted had first to be dug out.

The snow up here was so much deeper that we anxiously discussed the possibility of going farther. With 15 to 18 inches of snow to contend with, not counting drifts, the labour would be excessive, and until the snow solidified there would be considerable danger at several points. But the next morning broke fine; we had soon a clear sky and glorious sunshine; it was the warmest day that any of us remembered at Camp III; and as we watched the amazing rapidity with which the snow solidified and the rocks began to appear about our camp, our spirits rose. The side of Everest facing us looked white and cold; but we observed a cloud of snow blown from the North Ridge; it would not be long at this rate before it was fit to climb. We had already resolved to use oxygen on the third attempt. It was improbable that we should beat our own record without it, for the strain of previous efforts would count against us, and we had not the time to improve on our organization by putting a second camp above the North Col. Somervell, after Finch's explanation of the mechanical details, felt perfectly confident that he could manage the oxygen apparatus, and all those who had used oxygen were convinced that they went up more easily with its help than they could expect to go without it. Somervell and I intended to profit by the experience. They had discovered that the increased combustion in the body required a larger supply of food; we must arrange for a bountiful provision. Their camp at 25,000 ft had been too low; we would try to establish one now, as we had intended before, at 26,000 ft. And we hoped for a further advantage in going higher than Finch and Bruce had done before using oxygen; whereas they had started using it at 21,000 ft, we intended to go up to our old camp at 25,000 ft without it, perhaps use a cylinder each up to 26,000 ft, and at all events start from that height for the summit with a full supply of four cylinders. If this was not the correct policy as laid down by Professor Dryer, it would at least be a valuable experiment.

Our chief anxiety under these new conditions was to provide for the safety of our porters. We hoped that after fixing our fifth camp at 26,000 ft, at the earliest three days hence, on the fourth day of fine weather the porters might be able to go down by themselves to the North Col in easy conditions; to guard against the danger of concealed crevasses there Crawford would meet them at the foot of the North Ridge to conduct them properly roped to Camp IV. As the supply officer at this camp he would also be able to superintend the descent over the first steep slope of certain

porters who would go down from Camp IV without sleeping after carrying up their loads.

But the North Col had first to be reached. With so much
new snow to contend with we should hardly get there in one
day. If we were to make the most of our chance in the
interval of fair weather, we should lose no time in carrying
up the loads for some part of the distance. It was decided
therefore to begin this work on the following day, June 7th.

In the ascent to the North Col after the recent snowfall
we considered that an avalanche was to be feared only in one
place, the steep final slope below the shelf. There we could
afford to run no risk; we must test the snow and be certain
that it was safe before we could cross this slope. Probably
we should be obliged to leave our loads below it, having
gained, as a result of our day's work, the great advantage of
a track. An avalanche might also come down, we thought,
on the first steep slope where the ascent began. Here it
could do us no harm, and the behaviour of the snow on this
slope would be a test of its condition.

The party, Somervell, Crawford and I, with fourteen
porters (Wakefield was to be supply officer at Camp III),
set out at 8 a.m. In spite of the hard frost of the previous
night, the crust was far from bearing our weight; we sank up
to our knees in almost every step, and two hours were taken
in traversing the snowfield. At 10.15 a.m. Somervell, I, a
porter, and Crawford, roped up in that order, began to work
up the steep ice-slope, now covered with snow. It was clear
that the three of us without loads must take the lead in turns
stamping out the tracks for our porters. These men, after
their immense efforts on the first and second attempts, had
all volunteered to "go high", as they said once more, and
everything must be done to ease the terrible work of
carrying the loads over the soft snow. No trace was found
of our previous tracks, and we were soon arguing as to
where exactly they might be as we slanted across the slope.
It was remarkable that the snow adhered so well to the ice
that we were able to get up without cutting steps. Everything was done by trenching the snow to induce it to come
down if it would; every test gave a satisfactory result. Once
this crucial place was passed, we plodded on without

hesitation. If the snow would not come down where we had formerly encountered steep bare ice, *a fortiori*, above, on the gentler slopes, we had nothing to fear. The thought of an avalanche was dismissed from our minds.

It was necessarily slow work forging our way through the deep snow, but the party was going extraordinarily well, and the porters were evidently determined to get on. Somervell gave us a long lead, and Crawford next, in spite of the handicap of shorter legs, struggled upwards in some of the worst snow we met until I relieved him. I found the effort at each step so great that no method of breathing I had formerly employed was adequate; it was necessary to pause after each lifting movement for a whole series of breaths, rapid at first and gradually slower, before the weight was transferred again to the other foot. About 1.30 p.m. I halted, and the porters, following on three separate ropes, soon came up with the leading party. We should have been glad to stay where we were for a long rest. But the hour was already late, and as Somervell was ready to take the lead again, we decided to push on. We were now about 400 ft below a conspicuous block of ice and 600 ft below Camp IV, still on the gentle slopes of the corridor. Somervell had advanced only 100 ft, rather up the slope than across it, and the last party of porters had barely begun to move up in the steps. The scene was peculiarly bright and windless, and as we rarely spoke, nothing was to be heard but the laboured panting of our lungs. This stillness was suddenly disturbed. We were startled by an ominous sound, sharp, arresting, violent, and yet somehow soft like an explosion of untamped gunpowder. I had never before on a mountainside heard such a sound; but all of us, I imagine, knew instinctively what it meant, as though we had been accustomed to hear it every day of our lives. In a moment I observed the surface of the snow broken and puckered where it had been even for a few yards to the right of me. I took two steps convulsively in this direction with some quick thought of getting nearer to the edge of the danger that threatened us. And then I began to move slowly downwards, inevitably carried on the whole moving surface by a force I was utterly powerless to resist. Somehow I managed to turn out from the slope so as to avoid being pushed headlong and backwards down it. For a second or two I seemed hardly to be in danger as I went quietly sliding down with the snow. Then the rope at my waist tightened and held me back. A wave of snow came over me and I was buried. I supposed that the matter was settled. However, I called to mind experiences related by other parties; and it had been suggested that the best chance of escape in this situation lay in swimming. I thrust out my arms above my head and actually went through some sort of motions of swimming on my back. Beneath the surface of the snow, with nothing to inform the senses of the world outside it, I had no impression of speed after the first acceleration – I struggled in the tumbling snow, unconscious of everything else – until, perhaps only a few seconds later, I knew the pace was easing up. I felt an increasing pressure about my body. I wondered how tightly I should be squeezed, and then the avalanche came to rest.

My arms were free; my legs were near the surface. After a brief struggle, I was standing again, surprised and breathless, in the motionless snow. But the rope was tight at my waist; the porter tied on next me, I supposed, must be deeply buried. To my further surprise, he quickly emerged, unharmed as myself. Somervell and Crawford too, though they had been above me by the rope's length, were now quite close, and soon extricated themselves. We subsequently made out that their experiences had been very similar to mine. But where were the rest? Looking down over the foam of snow, we saw one group of porters some little distance, perhaps 150 ft, below us. Presumably the others must be buried somewhere between us and them, and though no sign of these missing men appeared, we at once prepared to find and dig them out. The porters we saw still stood their ground instead of coming up to help. We soon made out that they were the party who had been immediately behind us, and they were pointing below them. They had travelled farther than us in the avalanche, presumably because they were nearer the centre, where it was moving more rapidly. The other two parties, one of four and one of five men roped together, must have been carried even farther. We could still hope that they were safe. But as we hurried down we soon saw that beneath the place where the four porters were standing was a formidable drop; it was only too plain that the missing men had been swept over it. We had no difficulty in finding a way round this obstacle; in a very short time we were standing under its shadow. The ice-cliff was from forty to sixty feet high in different places; the crevasse at its foot was more or less filled up with avalanche snow. Our fears were soon confirmed. One man was quickly uncovered and found to be still breathing; before long we were certain that he would live. Another whom we dug out near him had been killed by the fall. He and his party appeared to have struck the hard lower lip of the crevasse, and were lying under the snow on or near the edge of it. The four porters who had escaped soon pulled themselves together after the first shock of the accident, and now worked here with Crawford and did everything they could to extricate the other bodies, while Somervell and I went down into the crevasse. A loop of rope which we pulled up convinced us that the other party must be here. It was slow work loosening the snow with the pick or adze of an ice-axe and shovelling it with the hands. But we were able to follow the rope to the bodies. One was dug up lifeless; another was found upside down, and when we uncovered his face Somervell thought he was still breathing. We had the greatest difficulty in extricating this man, so tightly was the snow packed about his limbs; his load, four oxygen cylinders on a steel frame, had to be cut from his back, and eventually he was dragged out. Though buried for about forty minutes, he had survived the fall and the suffocation, and suffered no serious harm. Of the two others in this party of four, we found only one. We had at length to give up a hopeless search with the certain knowledge that the first of them to be swept over the cliff, and the most deeply buried, must long ago be dead. Of the other five, all the bodies were recovered, but only one was alive. The two who had so marvellously escaped were able to walk down to Camp III, and were almost perfectly well next day. The other seven were killed.

The Void

Kees Egeler

A Dutch mountaineer and professor of geology, Egeler, accompanied by Tom De Booy and the French guide Lionel Terray (a member of Herzog's Annapurna expedition) sought, in 1950, the untrodden summit of Nevada Huantsan, 6,395 m (20, 981 ft) in the Andes. Although the expedition met with eventual success, the first assault involved a catastrophic accident.

At long last, all was ready. A few curt final instructions, and Terray slid down. About 200 ft below, at the end of the rope, he cut out a broad step in the ice-wall. Then I followed – first over a bulge, then a short distance dangling through the air, and finally down the steep ice-pitch of which the lower portion of the flank consisted. By the time I arrived, Terray had already hammered in a long ice-piton for the next rappel. We waited side by side, with our faces to the wall, until De Booy could join us. He had a most ticklish job. Whilst Terray during his descent had been secured by me at the end of the rope, and I, in turn, had been safeguarded by De Booy, the latter now had to lower himself down by the double rope unsecured. He naturally went to work with the utmost caution, particularly when tackling the first stage over the bulge.

Terray and I looked at each other. Up above, when it looked as though we were caught like rats in a trap, he had been definitely apprehensive. Now he was back again to true form. He grinned at me and said:

"What a game! Ever been up against anything like this, Kees? Who would have guessed, this morning . . .?"

I smiled back. His magnificent self-assurance was infectious. I no longer doubted that, under his skilful guidance, we should extricate ourselves from this ugly situation. Nevertheless, we were not happy about the next rappel. The steep ice-wall (about sixty degrees) on which we were poised went down another 100 ft or so and then abruptly ended in a void. Apparently the wall over-hung at that point, but how far it projected and what came underneath were imponderables. We could only assume that it would be exceptionally steep. We were, we thought, about 300 ft above the glacier at the moment. But the foot of the wall was not visible.

To our great relief De Booy joined us safe and sound on our little artificial shelf. We could now restart roping down from the lower piton. But would the rope be long enough to reach over the bulging overhang and enable us to gain a foothold lower down? Again Lionel went first so that he could make preparations as quickly as possible for the succeeding stage. About 100 ft down, he reached the edge of the bulge and could see what lay below.

"Ca touche nettement!" he called up. This was great news, for visibility was fading fast and we had not a moment to spare. A second later he disappeared from view, whilst De Booy and I waited in suspense. Then a vague reverberating shout came from below. To us above, it was completely incomprehensible. The words were lost under the overhang. Yet it was essential for me to know what awaited me down below, so I bellowed out to Terray that I could not catch what he was shouting. De Booy and I waited anxiously, debating what to do next. Then we felt the tension on the rope slacken, indicating that Terray had found a foothold somewhere and had released the rope. Once again several precious minutes were lost. Then, further hesitation being out of the question, I let myself down the rope as quickly as possible until I reached the edge of the overhang. Peering warily over, I saw Terray about eighty feet directly below, clinging to the rock face. The situation was unpleasant. The overhang projected so far out that the whole of the next eighty feet down had to be descended through space. Never before had I been faced with such a manoeuvre. Thank goodness I was being secured from above by my companion. There was not much time to dally. De Booy had asked me to give him a shout as to the position so I called out that the rappel went fairly deep and that everything seemed all right. Then cautiously turning over on my stomach, I let my legs dangle into nothing, slid over the edge, and in the failing light began to descend the thin rope. This swaying through space made an unforgettable impression on my mind. The upper crust of the overhang was fringed with enormous icicles, one of which broke off as I accidentally came in contact with it and went tinkling past me down into the void. It was eerie.

If it had not been for the pressing time factor this would have been a thrilling adventure; but, suspended there, I was all too conscious that the occasion was not just another interesting descent. It was grim reality. A desperate race against time.

Farther down, the wall receded sharply away. I lowered myself, feeling very much like a spider on its thread, until my foot touched the ice-wall below. What a relief! As always, after a long descent by rope, it was wonderful to find one's feet again. Actually I had quite a job to get a footing, for the flank on which I landed was pitched at a gradient of at least sixty-five degrees and I was almost at the end of the rope. There was little scope for manoeuvring. Luckily Terray came to my assistance and cut out a few steps for me. He himself had had the greatest difficulty in arriving safely. What was worse, he found himself suddenly hampered by stubborn cramp in the arm.

I simply could not manage to get any more favourable stance than one with holds for one foot and one hand. I waited quietly for the next move, hoping that it would not take too long. It was De Booy's turn to come down. As experience had shown that it was useless to call out from below, I untied myself and gave three hard tugs at the rope, that being the agreed signal for him to follow down. He understood, for immediately there was a movement in the rope. Two minutes later his dim shadow appeared above on the edge of the overhang. In the meantime darkness had descended apace. A last spark of light seemed to linger on the spot where De Booy stood, but below the bulge, where we were, everything was shrouded in dusk. We exchanged a few words. De Booy asked what the position was like, and I shouted to him to try and land as high up the slope as possible because the rope was too short to allow of much playing about for position. I implored him to take the utmost care. One end of the rope was longer than the other, I bawled, but he ought to be able to manage.

Like some dim ghost De Booy slid down the thin nylon rope. Everything was going so swimmingly that I jocularly complimented him on his style. But, as he tried to get a foothold on the ice just above me, the treacherous light misled him. The slope was far steeper than he thought. His feet slid away. His hands found no hold on the slippery rock, covered with verglas. The heavy weight of his ruck-sack pulled him down and over backwards, and . . .

He fell.

To my horror he fell past me. Several yards lower, however, he was brought up with a jerk, hanging head downward, his feet tangled in the rope. I frantically con-centrated on ways and means of rescuing him. My own delicate position prevented me from getting nearer. The wall, where I was precariously poised, was terribly steep, and the rocks at my side were covered with ice. Somehow or other I managed to grasp the looped end of the longer rope which was hanging loosely down and gave it a turn round my hand. Then, by grabbing the other rope, I formed, as it were, a continuous ring of rope, from a part of which De Booy hung upside-down. This action, I thought, would at least reduce the possibility of his slipping away. My brain worked feverishly, taking in every detail, trying to straight-en out things, wondering whether De Booy's hands were also still clinging to the rope. If his feet did not untangle, he might be able to hold out until Terray came to his aid. I saw the latter some ten yards to our right on the slope, busily unearthing his torch from his ruck-sack. It had all hap-pened in a matter of seconds, and as yet he had noticed nothing amiss. Only when I lustily yelled for help did he realise what was up. Then, without even giving himself time to grasp his axe, he sped across the wall towards us. And once again my heart stood still! He, too, missed his footing.

Some forty feet or so farther down he managed, in his own inimitable way, to save himself. Thank God! For a moment he was completely dazed: he had wrenched his arm. I cried out to him to do his utmost, for De Booy's life was in peril. He could not possibly hang on the rope much longer.

De Booy was aware of this, too, for he said in a remarkably quiet voice:

"This is it, Kees! It's all over with us."

But I still had hope. I called out that it wasn't all over! He must do everything to hang on! Then, I focused my attention again on Terray who, on my other side, was laboriously climbing up the steep slope. It was slow, agonisingly slow. I spurred him on: "Quicker, Lionel, much quicker!"

Then I heard a rending noise. I turned instantly to the other side, only to see De Booy plunging down towards the glacier. For a dramatic second or two I followed his fall as his crampons scraped the rock and sent up showers of sparks. Then he vanished in the void. A terrible silence followed.

Terray and I clung, petrified, to the face. Black despair for our comrade choked us. I saw no reason to call out. De Booy could hardly have escaped being killed.

Staring into the darkness below, I thought I could distinguish a vague dark blob against the white snow. From his greater distance Lionel had secured a rather better view. He had the feeling that, if De Booy had not bashed his head against projecting rocks and had avoided falling into the bergschrund, he might possibly be alive. He called at the top of his voice: "Tom! Tom!" The dead silence seemed to confirm our worst fears; but Terray kept on calling and suddenly there came an answer – an unmistakable answer!

What a wonderful moment that was! To hear a voice, as it were, from the dead! For a time we were almost too

astounded to react. Then we realized that the incredible had
happened. An excited babble of Dutch and French went
up. Anxiously we yelled to ask what he had broken. From
the depths came the laconic reply: "Nothing!"

A few moments later we saw a tiny light appear some
hundreds of feet below. We had brought out with us special
"forehead" lamps in case we ever had to climb in the dark.
The light was fastened on an elastic band which went round
the forehead, thus enabling one to have the hands free. De
Booy had obviously put his on to show us where he was.
Seeing his light was our signal to get into action. Terray
climbed up towards me and pulled at the end of the rope,
but it wouldn't budge. This was the worst that could
possibly happen at such a critical time. The nightmare
thought of a jammed rope after a rappel over an overhang
is always enough to give any climber grey hairs. Terray
pulled with increasing force. He raged and swore – and,
curiously enough, it seemed as though this helped, for
suddenly the rope freed itself and was easily pulled
through. Terray worked with might and main to prepare
a new rappel. Once it had been rigged up, I was able to leave
my awkward position and slide downwards, feeling my way
in the dark. The rope reached to about sixty-five feet above
the bergschrund. I cut a big step with my axe and then
waited for Terray to join me.

Meanwhile I could talk more easily with De Booy. My
disquiet lessened considerably when he called out: "Why
the devil are you two taking so long? I showed you the quick
way down, didn't I?" This was an encouraging sign. That
he could still wise-crack cheered me up no end. I saw his
light going to and fro and assumed that he was moving
about to keep warm. He even climbed a little way up the
slope to give me some light when, a little later, I came, via
the bergschrund, on to the glacier. Terray followed closely
behind. The three of us stood united again at the foot of the
slope.

In the dark it was naturally impossible to trace the line of
De Booy's fall. Not until next day were we able to assess its
length and direction. But even in the dark one could tell that
he had fallen at least 300 ft. He had been hanging upside

down when he started falling and must have turned a somersault. His feet had struck the rock face some yards lower down and had taken the first brunt of his fall.

This probably saved his life. The steep ice-wall down which he had slithered with ever-increasing velocity was actually fraught with much less danger. We reckoned that he cleared the gaping mouth of the bergschrund which, at this point, was several yards wide, by sailing right over it. Landing on the sloping glacier, he had gradually lost speed because it was thickly covered with snow.

At that time all this did not interest us so much as finding out if he really were uninjured. It was almost unbelievable. He was examined in the light of our torches and prodded all over. A first glance only revealed a skinned nose. He complained of pains in the back. How could it be otherwise after a fall of some 300 ft? He was also chilled to the marrow, a poor condition to be in with the prospect of an ice-cold bivouac at a height of 18,000 ft without tent or sleeping-bag. It was clear now that we should have to spend the night on the glacier, for De Booy was in no fit state to cope with a descent lasting several hours.

As soon as we found a more or less suitable spot we levelled it off as far as possible and laid down the ropes to insulate us a little from the rising glacial cold and to keep us as dry as possible. We then put on everything that we could find in the shape of clothing. We took off our boots and put on dry socks. Then we got into our nylon bivouac-sets, consisting of a long anorak and a narrow bag in which to place the legs, the so-called *pied d'éléphant*. Both parts fastened together with press studs.

We also drew our rucksacks over our feet to help keep them warm, and thus installed ourselves for the night. For extra security we belayed ourselves with ropes attached by a turn or two to axes rammed in the ice – a necessary precaution, as several yards away down the slope an enormous crevasse gaped open and we had no desire to slide into this in our sleep.

Actually we hardly snatched any sleep. The air was crystal clear and the pitiless cold cut us to the bone. Terray and I had De Booy between us, and were continually rubbing and massaging him, but we found it difficult to keep him at all warm. We ourselves had to keep on piano-playing with our fingers and toes. Blood circulation had to be maintained at all costs to prevent frost-bite. If we dozed off, it was only to wake a moment later, disturbed by some movement of the others or tormented by the terrible thirst from which we now all suffered.

I unearthed a lemon from my rucksack and squeezed some of its juice on lumps of sugar, which I tried to get to De Booy. But it was no good. The acid lemon-juice caused him acute agony, owing to split lips. Then I tried to obtain some water to drink by filling my field-flask with snow and putting it under my clothes against the bare flesh. Apparently I, too, must have been near freezing-point, because the snow did not melt.

There is no comparison between a bivouac in the Cordillera Blanca and one in the Alps. In Europe a bivouac lasts only about seven hours and one can get going again towards four in the morning. In the Andes it gets dark about six and the night lasts a full twelve hours. Even when dawn breaks, no start is possible because it is still too freezingly cold and the risk of frost-bite is too great.

It seemed that the wretched night would never end. We tried to divert our thoughts. Amongst other titbits, Terray told us of the many bivouacs he had endured in his career. He spoke of that terrible night on the Annapurna when, at an altitude of 23,000 ft, he had huddled in a crevasse with his companions, two of whom, Lachenal and Herzog, were suffering horribly from frost-bitten extremities. His last bivouac had occurred the previous winter on the vertical face of the Fitz Roy in Patagonia.

None of us had much heart for talk. Our thoughts were too taken up by our recent nerve-racking experiences and by the miraculous turn of events. What would have happened if De Booy had broken an arm or a leg? He could not possibly have survived this bleak icy bivouac. Yet there he was between us, apparently unscathed. We wondered if and when we should ever to able to renew the attack.

Thinking of the past eventful hours, I realized that it was not only De Booy who had enjoyed fantastic luck. Terray, too, might have hurtled precipitously down that face. And, if both of them had been seriously injured, what chance should I have had, without a light, to grope my way down that wall in the dark? Yes, we were all lucky to be still alive and kicking.

Act of Folly

Christian Klucker

*Christian Klucker (1853–1928) was one of the greatest of
Alpine guides, making no less that 44 new ascents of peaks.
His greatest season was 1890 when, with Ludwig Norman-
Neruda, he climbed the virgin North East face of Piz
Bernina (Bernina Alps) and North East Face of Lyskamm
(Pennine Alps). Klucker's autobiography,* Adventures of
an Alpine Guide *was published posthumously in 1932.*

W hen we took leave of the guests at the Roseg inn on
July 17th [1890], it did not occur to us that our
Bernina climb, planned for July 18th, would end up in the
Roseg valley again insted of at Boval. We went to Pontre-
sina, and reached the old Boval Hut at 8 p.m., our object
being to open up a new route to Piz Bernina (13,304 ft.) on
the following day. Although I could not see any practical
value in this, I refrained from saying so to my companion,
since the proposal had come from him and I did not wish to
hurt his feelings.

In those days things were quieter up in Boval. Except for
numerous darting mice we two were the only inhabitants of
the hut that evening.

Before sketching our heroic exploit of July 18th, I consider it essential to rectify my companion's description of
this climb in several particulars.

Norman-Neruda knew the environment of the Morteratsch Glacier only from the map and from Alpine literature.
When in his writings he presents it as my opinion that the

long snow corridor, leading up to the west of the Labyrinth by the rocks, was the route of Dr. Ludwig in October 1879, he bases this on a misunderstanding. Since I had in the early 'eighties spoken not only with Dr. Ludwig, but also with Hans Grass about their ascent of the Bernina, I knew perfectly well where the lower part of their ascent had taken place, starting from the Morteratsch Glacier. The ascent of Dr. Ludwig and Grass was made to the west of Point 2,749, while ours was to the east of it. Ludwig's entry into the so-called "Gurgel" took place at a level of about 9,650 feet, as against ours at 8,950 feet. Our snow gorge is a good 1,300 feet high and is nowhere threatened by falling ice throughout its length. On the other hand, the "Gurgel" of Ludwig-Grass (which by the way has a length of 650 feet) led up all the way amidst débris from the glaciers above. I had already made it clear to my companion on the evening of July 17th in the hut that I would under no circumstances attempt the "Gurgel" of Dr. Ludwig. Therefore we chose to make our start through the long gorge described above.

Regarding our ascent through the gorge, which lasted about three hours, my companion writes the following words: "We had, however, been in an almost continuous hail of stones and fragments of ice for 3 hours and 8 minutes." I do not understand how Norman-Neruda came to make such a statement. On the lower level, before we entered the snow gorge, I had called his attentions to the fact that this couloir showed no evidence of danger from stones, since there were none lying about which had fallen from above. Three or four times during our ascent there was a fall of ice fragments which came from the rocky rim of the couloir on our right. This was easily explained, because ice had formed on the rocks during the night; and since by sunrise we had put hardly a third of the couloir behind us, we had this bother thrown in. If we had started from the hut at 2 a.m., as I had proposed the evening before, instead of as late as 3.15, we could have conquered the whole gorge before the sun overtook us. Rising and starting early were, however, not always our strong point.

After hard step-cutting work we stood at 7.10 at the upper end of the snow gorge, and after a short halt we turned to the right, mounting over rocks in an easy climb up to Point 3,208 on the map, just where the snow slope begins that leads up in a south-westerly direction to the lower end of the Bernina east ridge. This point Norman-Neruda and others mistakenly call "Sass del repos" (rock of rest). The "Sass del repos" lies south-eastward from here and lower down – about by the "e" of the word "repos." Bernina climbers, who use the Labyrinth for their ascent, reach this halting-place shortly after leaving the Labyrinth.

We set forth on the further ascent at 9 a.m., after an ample rest. It led us in a south-westerly direction in a gentle curve to the bergschrund below the north-east wall of Piz Bernina and the Scharte, which we reached about where the "P" of the name "P. Bernina" stands. It was already past ten o'clock, and the steep snow wall rising from the bergschrund did not inspire us with great confidence. And from where we stood it was hard to tell whether the rocks which crowned the ice slope were scaleable or not. My comrade's idea of ascending direct to the Berninascharte had to be dropped at the outset, because a huge snow corniche occupied it, stretching out many feet above our wall. What made us somewhat uneasy was the threatening change in the weather. Still, we stubbornly continued the ascent and went on undismayed with our task, which consisted first of all in getting across the difficult bergschrund. This we finally succeeded in doing. What followed from here upwards was hard, heavy labour. The thin snow on the ice-wall was soft and unstable. So I had to remove the snow at every step to make a good, safe foothold. After long and toilsome work we arrived at the rocks and found them anything but easy to climb. The fresh snow of July 12th and 13th had not entirely disappeared, and our climbing was much hindered by the underlying ice. And to make matters worse, the weather was changing rapidly. We worked in feverish haste. Leaving the awkward rocks to the left below the Berninascharte and crossing further to the right, we mounted upwards and finally reached the foot of the so-called "Schartenkopf" (to the right of the corniche). The hour was 2.20 p.m.

A powerful south-west wind drove the mist from the Tschierva side across our ridge; and from the direction of

Maloja and the Julier we already heard thunder. It was my first acquaintance with the Berninacharte, but its welcome to the stranger was far from friendly. It was clear, of course, that under such weather conditions the ascent from the Scharte to Piz Bernina must be given up, and this was decided without discussion. Rapidly we clambered up to the Schartenkopf, noting by the way that this terrible drop near the Scharte had nothing so very terrible about it after all.[1]

Without a pause we traversed the ridge northward towards Pizzo Bianco, but seeing in advance that the Bianco could offer us no shelter from the thunderstorm, we sought and found, about ten or fifteen feet below the crest of the ridge on the Morteratsch side – therefore out of the wind – a tiny place where we could anchor ourselves. But it was high time, for our axes were humming omniously, which moved me to unrope myself and carry them across to Pizzo Bianco and to ram them deep into the summit corniche. It was probably about three o'clock in the afternoon by the time we sat side by side again in the little niche, tied fast to the rock with the rope. The thunderstorm had begun in all its fury. And the next three hours were without a doubt the most disagreeable I have ever experienced.

The concert that was given, up near the 13,000-feet level between Pizzo Bianco and the Berninascharte, was a gruesome one! The wild battle for storm, hail and snow, the glaring flashes of lightning, and the mighty thunderclaps, threatened to confound our senses. Uncanny was the play of the lightning just a few feet above our heads, and there was no end to the howling and hissing on the Bianco ridge. In silence we cowered against the rock directly above the precipice, overwhelmed by hail and snow. There was a roaring vibration round my hat all the while, such as a strong wind makes passing through a feather, and sparks were sometimes hanging from its brim, though the hat was loaded with a quantity of snow and hail.

We expected confidently that the storm would have spent its rage in half an hour, but unfortunately this was not so.

---

1 Klucker refers to the exaggerated account of Paul Güssfeldt, "Die Ueberwindung der Berninascharte," S.A.C. Year Book, 1879.

One hour grew into two, and still the fearful electrical discharges would not come to an end. Soon after five, my companion began to complain that he could stand the cold no longer, and thought it would surely be better to attempt the descent over the Bianco ridge at once. I refused emphatically and declared that I was not going to leave our niche so long as there was any lightning coming over the ridge from the west.

Towards 5.30 a north-west wind set in and the electric tension quickly relaxed. We decided at once to be off on our difficult way. It is remarkable, but nevertheless true, that as soon as the uncomfortable lightning flashes stopped, I recovered my self-confidence.

The situation called for vigorous action; to make use of the time we had until eight o'clock so as to reach the lower regions by nightfall. What did I care for the raging wind which drove continuous snow and hail into our faces! We were surely not to be stopped by this handicap nor yet by the long Bianco ridge, though the latter was an unknown quantity to both of us.

The short stretch from our niche to Pizzo Bianco proved very bad, as the rock ridge was completely buried in snow, and wind and driving snow made things worse. Regardless of all this we got to our ice-axes on Pizzo Bianco by 6 p.m. A glance down the ridge told me that we should not be dealing with a nice city pavement. "If there is only no ice on the crest, we shall certainly get down."

The strong wind and heavy driving snow were very hard on my companion, who declared that he could not descend this steep snow ridge without steps. "Nonsense!" I replied, "no steps unless we strike bare ice! Turn round the climb down backwards! You'll find me like a rock; you'll not drag me off the ridge this evening! Let's get on with it, and reach the Prievlusa saddle before nightfall!" With this very strong wind, sweeping in gusts over the ridge, the six-foot-two Norman-Neruda could hardly have cut steps without being swept from the ridge; and since he had had little practice in step-cutting, anything that might lose us time must be avoided. Anything to get down!

Those who have traversed the Bianco Ridge will have

some grasp of what our situation was just then. At the steepest places, where one had to keep entirely to the crest, we were certainly not able to do any double-quick march. And my companion had to halt very frequently and cling to the ridge, because the gale and driving snow took his breath away. By good fortune, no bare ice was encountered, and as soon as we had overcome the bad places on the ridge I was much relieved to note that my comrade also was regaining his self-confidence and vigour. We came further and further down, and the cruel wind gradually abated, or at least could no longer do its utmost, because the ridge widened out considerably at its lower end.

At 8 p.m. we came to the rock ridge which, as continuation of the Bianco ridge, descends to the Fuorcla Prievlusa. Unfortunately we found it under heavy snow. Clambering over it under such conditions did not appeal to me, since I had learned from previous climbers that the rocks by the Fuorcla Prievlusa were very trying. A glance to the left over the wall down to the Tschierva Glacier and a short calculation told me that this way, though very steep, would bring us quicker to the bergschrund than the route via the Fuorcla Prievlusa. The steep rock-drops below us, I judged to be manageable; and on the ice-wall just under them I had noticed a rib of snow leading down toward the bergschrund, which seemed likely to facilitate our descent. I may say that this wall as marked on sheet "Bernina" of the Siegfried map is much too high, some 1,000 feet. Actually, it should be 500 feet at most.

Any doubts on the part of my companion were ignored: "That is the shortest way down! And we can count on reaching the bergschrund before dark, and perhaps before the second thunderstorm overtakes us, which is now approaching from the west." And we did get down, and safely crossed the bergschrund. The rock portion required the utmost caution and securing of the rope, while on the ice-slope, contrary to all expectation, we found conditions favourable.

It might have been about 8.45 p.m. when we lit our lanterns and hastened onward. But our trials were not yet at an end. Scarcely a quarter of an hour had passed before we were caught in another thunderstorm of unusual severity. Lightning and thunder followed each other in rapid succession, and the quantity of hail and rain which the heavens poured down upon our heads in one hour baffles description. It was all we could do to hold on to our axes and lanterns, and we would gladly have drawn closer to the rocks of Piz Morteratsch but dared not risk it on account of falling stones. Hence we were forced into the maze of crevasses of the Tschierva Glacier, which forms a kind of ice-fall at Point 2,771. It proved a toilsome passage indeed.

About ten o'clock, we finally reached the right moraine of the Tschierva Glacier, took off the rope which had bound us together for eighteen hours, and staggered on in pouring rain. At 11.40, two dead-tired comrades entered the Roseg Restaurant. A servant-boy with a lantern was expecting us, as he had already espied our light above Margun Misaun.

Neither of us demanded a complete rest. It is true we had sat down in the guest-room, but were obliged to get out again, because the surplus water ran from our clothes and boots on to the floor and threatened to flood it. The end of that unhappy yet memorable 18th of July was, that the boy ushered my companion Norman-Neruda into the room which he had occupied three days before, and offered me a wooden platform above the empty horse-stall, which would have done honour to a galley slave. There was no straw nor hay; only a thin layer of musty, crumbling litter for my bed; and according to the boy there was no blanket available for me! This thoughtless treatment depressed and pained me, for besides Norman-Neruda's there were three unoccupied beds at the inn. To argue the matter with a servant-boy was not to my liking, and finally I thought to myself, "What do you care for wet clothes and a wretched hard sleeping-place? Be glad that you are down in the Roseg valley with a roof to your head, and don't have to make the best of a complulsory bivouac on the Bianco ridge in the midst of a storm!" I took my wet coat for a blanket, and the rucksack served as a pillow. Five minutes later I was so fast asleep that all the thunderclaps of the Berninascharte and the Bianco ridge could not have wakened me.

A little before 7 a.m. I woke up shivering. The sky was clear, and as the slope to the west of the inn was already in sunlight, I made for it without breakfast, found myself a nice warm place on a big smooth rock, took off my wet clothes, spread them out in the sun, and basked in its warmth till even my underclothing was dry.

Our "new Bernina route," to which I had been unable to attach any practical value from the outset, was an enterprise which brought us pretty close to destruction; and it was certainly a mere chance that we came off with whole skins. The greatest mistake was that we had set out from Boval far too late for an undertaking of this kind. An earlier start would have got us over Piz Bernina before the storm broke. Every time I think about that grim Bianco ridge traverse I come to the same conclusion: without a comrade of the stamina of Norman-Neruda, our expedition would very probably have come to a tragic end.

We left the Engadine on July 21st 1890, and travelling by *dilgence* over the Flüela came to Davos, where we met Dr. Tauscher and his wife. Our plan had been to visit the Gross Litzner in the Silvretta group by the ordinary way before our journey to the Valais, but we modified it in favour of first attacking the Gross Seehorn by a new route and combining with it a traverse of the Gross Litzner.

On July 24th this undertaking was carried out from Alp Sardasca in fine weather, and was successful in every respect: the ascent of the Gross Seehorn from the shout-west direct to the lower summit, and then the first traverse of the Gross Litzner from west to east.[1]

On both summits we admired the wonderful clear view. In the foreground, the beautiful pyramid of the Linard and the north face of the Verstanklahorn most often attracted our gaze. I called my companion's attention repeatedly to the latter. My telescopic observations showed that a direct ascent from the Verstankla Glacier, while probably not easy, would at any rate be possible. And when I wandered in 1894 with Captain J. P. Farrar from the Silvretta Hut

---

1 See the description in *The Climbs of Norman-Neruda*, pages 28–39.

over the Verstanklator, this assumption was strengthened. Of course at that time this north face did not look so black as thirty years later.

My representations carried no weight with Norman-Neruda. "To-morrow we are off to the Valais. I don't want to sacrifice two days to this Verstankla north face," was his response.

After a very comfortable journey via Zürich-Berne-Lausanne, we reached Zermatt on the evening of July 27th. At that time the stretch from Vispach to St. Niklaus had to be covered on foot.

On July 29th we two alone traversed the Triftjoch to the Mountet Hut. On the next day it was raining, and when it cleared about midday we used this interval for making telescopic observations of the north face of the Dent Blanche, which rises very steeply from the western basin of the Zinal Glacier almost 3,500 feet to the summit. The result was not very promising.

Nevertheless, at 1.30 a.m. on July 31st we started from the Mountet Hut for a reconnaissance of this north face. We went to the right of the Roc Noir by lantern light across the heavily crevassed glacier to the north foot of Dent Blanche. A few minutes before 4 a.m. we attacked the forbidding wall at a point somewhere near the letter "h" in the word "Blanche" on the map. Then followed 7½ laborious hours across smooth, heavily-glazed rock slopes. Nowhere was there any *névé* or winter snow. At a level of fully 13,000 feet we gave up any further exploration. At 11.30 we climbed down a little, and then crossed eastward to the Zinal arête – also known as Viereselgrat – descended it, and reached the Zinal Glacier at 4.15. After passing to the east of Roc Noir, we were back at the Mountet Hut by 5.20 p.m.[1]

1 Concerning this expedition Norman-Neruda notes: "There is no doubt that the route we chose on this attempt is the right way up given the right weather and the right conditions of snow and ice, which were not present in 1890 or '91; and Klucker would not risk the dangerous upper part of the climb under such bad conditions. Up to our highest point, that I reckoned by aneroid as about 13,000 feet, Klucker never hesitated for a moment in choosing the best route, and I consider him to be the finest climbers, whether it be over snow, ice or rocks, that I know, and quite unrivalled as the leader of a party."

On August 1st[1] we intended to cross the Wellenkuppe and Obergabelhorn to Zermatt, and at 3.30 left the Mountet with this object in view. Following the Triftjoch route to a height of about 10,500 feet, we turned sharp to the right and up into the much-crevassed glacier region at the north foot of the Obergabelhorn. After brief deliberation we decided upon a direct ascent from here to the summit of the Wellenkuppe, in order then to force a traverse to the Obergabelhorn by its north-east ridge.

A steep ice slop about 800 feet high required 2½ hours of vigorous step-cutting work. At 9.10 we set foot upon the snow ridge of the Wellenkuppe (12,829 ft.).

The crossing and ascent to the Obergabelhorn, which we began at 10 a.m., proved difficult only at the great tower. We had to turn this gendarme on the Zinal side by long, wearisome cutting on a very steep ice-wall. At 12.45 we stood on the summit of the Obergabelhorn (13,364 ft.). After an hour's halt we returned to the Wellenkuppe by the same way and made a comfortable descet by the usual route, getting back to Zermatt soon after 7.

Unfavourable weather confined us to Zermatt for six days, and not until August 8th were we able to make our way up to the Riffelberg. This day was chosen for telescopic observations of the north-east face of the Lyskamm[2] from the Hohthäligrat. In the course of the forenoon, while Norman-Neruda was doing some climbing with Dr. Tauscher and his wife on the Riffelhorn, I studied this Lyskamm north-east face minutely. By noon the three Riffelhorn climbers turned up on the Gornergrat, and after the meal it was agreed that we two, with the addtion of Joseph Reinstadler, should attack the Lyskamm on the following day direct from the Grenz Glacier.

On August 9th this very difficult ascent of the Lyskamm (14,889 ft.) was accomplished. We left the Riffelberg at 1.30 a.m., reached the top at 2.30 p.m. and were back at the Riffelberg at 10 p.m.

There is no doubt in my mind that we did not undertake

---

1 Not July 30th, as stated on page 389 of Studer's *Über Eis und Schnee*.
2 See also Appendix I.

this bold climb up one of the mightiest of ice-walls entirely for the reasons given by Norman-Neruda,[1] and that a good many things happened differently from what he relates. We were spurred on, above all, by the attempt made shortly before 1890 by the excellent Viennese mountaineer, Moriz von Kuffner, with the guides Alexander Burgener and the two Kalbermatten. Nothing but the peril of avalanches had driven these brave men back. With the study of a possible ascent over the rib, which falls abruptly from the highest peak to the Grenz Glacier, my *Herr* troubled himself but little, leaving this and other matters entirely to me. I convinced him that this rib was feasible and free from any special avalanche danger. And he believed me.

When Norman-Neruda retired for the night at the Riffel Hotel, I reported to him that Emile Rey and Bich had appeared with Miss Richardson, with the idea of climbing the Lyskamm. I knew the outstanding ability of Rey and wanted to conceal our plan from him. My counsel was therefore to allow Rey to start before us, even though this would involve some loss of time. This was done.

We left the hotel at 1.30. The weather was not reassuring, for clouds were appearing and disappearing over Monte Rosa and the Lyskamm. By the Obere Plattje we caught up with Rey, as he was halting there. He inquired about our destination. When we told him it was the Lyskamm he remarked: "We shall meet up there," and went his way. As soon as he and his party were out of sight we also departed, but in haste. Turning off the Lysjoch track to the right we crossed the difficult glacier and before 7 reached the bergschrund below the direct Lyskamm rib.

Before us stood the norht-east wall. And what a wall it was! Joseph Reinstadler (whose qualities as a guide I fully appreciate) as well as our *Herr*, began suddenly to feel – or

---

1 In the Österreichische Alpenzeitung, 1891. I questioned Norman-Neruda on this point in the summer of 1892, and he could not deny the force of my objections in any way. He merely remarked that he had written his article with a regard for certain well-known persons and that a correction would be difficult for him.

had for some time been feeling – a loss of appetite for this wall. I soon saw that I should have to decide. "The rib it must be," I said. And it was.

At 7.30 we took the bergschrund. After that I began to cut steps in the steep hard snow.[1] Reinstadler relieved me after an hour. Soon we set foot upon the rib. It is not only very steep but also difficult, sometimes very difficult to scale. Snow with ice underneath made it all the more ticklish. For safety's sake, only one moved at a time. The angle I estimated at about 60°.

Up on the left, far above our heads, appeared Rey, shouting jubilantly. His way was certainly the more comfortable. Reinstadler was much excited and wanted again and again to turn to the left from the glazed rib on to the snow. I was absolutely against this, because high above us I saw the most dangerous, great ice-cliffs with wall-like sides, which might break off. Resolutely I took the lead and stayed on the rib. However steep it was, it protected us at least from falling ice. After 11 a.m. we took a short halt.

Mist and clouds appeared, and it soon began to snow – a pleasant treat on this gigantic wall. But the rib led me safe. Suddenly the rock disappeared and I trod upon snow; so the top could not be very far away. I felt a joy that does not come every day in the mountains. The snow was good, and I had no steps tocut, since on leaving the rock-rib the incline decreased markedly. At 2.30 we set foot upon the small snowy crest of the east peak (14,889 ft). It was a grim but gratifying victory, if one can so describe an act of folly.

1 Contrast Klucker's letter of February 12th 1928 to the *Alpine Journal*; see Appendix.

AFTERWORD
The Pleasures and Penalties of Mountaineering

A. F. Mummery

The British climber Albert Mummery was arguably the founder of modern Alpinism. Certainly he was the foremost mountaineer of the late-nineteenth century, counting among his first ascents the West Face of the Plan and Col des Courtes, these achieved despite myopia and congenital physical deformity. His book My Climbs in the Alps and Caucasus *published in 1894 became an instant classic of mountaineering literature, its ultimate chapter: "The Pleasures and Penalties of Mountaineering" being the most eloquent "defence" of mountaineering ever penned. Mummery died on an 1895 expedition to Nanga Parbat in Kashmir.*

Well-known climbers, whose opinions necessarily carry the greatest weight, have recently declared their belief that the dangers of mountaineering no longer exist. Skill, knowledge and textbooks have hurled them to the limbo of exploded bogies. I would fain agree with this optimistic conclusion, but I cannot forget that the first guide to whom I was ever roped, and one who possessed – may I say it? – more knowledge of mountains than is to be found even in the Badminton library, was none the less killed on the Brouillard Mont Blanc, and his son, more recently, on Koshtantau. The memory of two rollicking parties, comprising seven men, who one day in 1879 were climbing on the west face of the Matterhorn, passes with ghost-like admonition before my mind and bids me remember that of these seven, Mr Penhall was killed on the Wetterhorn, Ferdinand Imseng on the Macugnaga Monte Rosa, and Johann Petrus on the Fresnay Mont Blanc. To say that any single one of these men was less careful and competent, or had less knowledge of all that pertains to the climber's craft, than we who yet survive, is obviously and patently absurd. Our best efforts must sometimes be seconded by the great goddess of Luck; to her should the Alpine Club offer its vows and thanksgivings.

Indeed, if we consider for a moment the essence of the sport of mountaineering, it is obvious that it consists, and consists exclusively, in pitting the climber's skill against the difficulties opposed by the mountain. Any increase in skill involves, *pari passu*, an increase in the difficulties grappled with. From the Breuil ridge of the Matterhorn we pass on to the Dru, and from the Dru to the Aiguille de Grépon: or to take a yet wider range, from the Chamonix Mont Blanc to the same mountain by way of the Brenva Glacier and the Aiguille Blanche de Péteret. It can scarcely be argued that Bennen and Walter were less fit to grapple with the cliff above the "Linceul" than we moderns to climb the Grépon "crack"; or that Jacques Balmat was less able to lead up the "Ancien passage" than Emile Rey to storm the ghastly precipices of the Brenva Péteret. But if it be admitted that the skill of the climber has not increased relatively to the difficulties grappled with, it would appear to follow necessarily that climbing is neither more nor less dangerous than formerly.

It is true that extraordinary progress has been made in the art of rock climbing, and that, consequently, any given rock climb is much easier now than thirty years since, but the essence of the sport lies, not in ascending a peak, but in struggling with and overcoming difficulties. The happy climber, like the aged Ulysses, is one who has "drunk delight of battle with his peers", and this delight is only attainable by assaulting cliffs which tax to their utmost limits the powers of the mountaineers engaged. This struggle involves the same risk, whether early climbers attacked what we now call easy rock, or whether we moderns attack formidable rock, or whether the ideal climber of the future assaults cliffs which we now regard as hopelessly inaccessible. Doubtless my difference with the great authorities referred to above is, in the main, due to a totally different view of the *raison d'être* of mountaineering. Regarded as a sport, some danger is, and always must be, inherent in it; regarded as a means of exercise amongst noble scenery, for quasi-scientific pursuits, as the raw material for interesting papers, or for the purposes of brag and bounce, it has become as safe as the ascent of the Rigi or Pilatus was to the climbers of thirty years since. But these pursuits are not mountaineering in the sense in which the founders of the Alpine Club used the term, and they are not mountaineering in the sense in which the elect – a small, perchance even a dwindling body – use it now. To set one's utmost faculties, physical and mental, to fight some grim precipice, or force some gaunt, ice-clad gully, is work worthy of men; to toil up long slopes of screes behind a guide who can "lie in bed and picture every step of the way up with all the places for hand and foot", is work worthy of the fibreless contents of fashionable clothes, dumped with all their scents and ointments, starched linen and shiny boots, at Zermatt by the railway.

The true mountaineer is a wanderer, and by a wanderer I do not mean a man who expends his whole time in travelling to and fro in the mountains on the exact tracks of his predecessors – much as a bicyclist rushes along the turnpike roads of England – but I mean a man who loves to be where no human being has been before, who delights in gripping rocks that have previously never felt the touch of human fingers, or in hewing his way up ice-filled gullies whose grim shadows have been sacred to the mists and avalanches since "earth rose out of chaos". In other words, the true mountaineer is the man who attempts new ascents. Equally, whether he succeeds or fails, he delights in the fun and jollity of the struggle. The gaunt, bare slabs, the square, precipitous steps in the ridge, and the black, bulging ice of the gully, are the very breath of life to his being. I do not pretend to be able to analyze this feeling, still less to be able to make it clear to unbelievers. It must be felt to be understood, but it is potent to happiness and sends the blood tingling through the veins, destroying every trace of cynicism and striking at the very roots of pessimistic philosophy.

Our critics, curiously enough, repeat in substance Mr Ruskin's original taunt that we regard the mountains as greased poles. I must confess that a natural and incurable denseness of understanding does not enable me to feel the sting of this taunt. Putting aside the question of grease, which is offensive and too horrible for contemplation in its effects on knickerbockers – worse even than the structure-destroying edges and splinters of the Grépon ridge – I do not perceive the enormity or sin of climbing poles. At one time, I will confess, I took great delight in the art, and, so far as my experience extends, the taste is still widespread amongst English youth. It is possible, nay even probable, that much of the pleasure of mountaineering is derived from the actual physical effort and from the perfect state of health to which this effort brings its votaries, and, to this extent, may plausibly be alleged to be the mere sequence and development of the pole and tree climbing of our youth. The sting of the taunt is presumably meant to lurk in the implication that the climber is incapable of enjoying noble scenery; that, in the jargon of certain modern writers, he is a "*mere* gymnast". But why should a man be assumed incapable of enjoying aesthetic pleasures because he is also capable of the physical and non-aesthetic pleasures of rock climbing?

A well-known mountaineer asserts that the fathers of the craft did not regard "the overcoming of physical obstacles by means of muscular exertion and skill" as "the chief pleasure of mountaineering". But is this so? Can anyone read the great classic of mountaineering literature, *The Playground of Europe*, without feeling that the overcoming of these obstacles was a main factor of its author's joy? Can anyone read *Peaks, Passes and Glaciers* and the earlier numbers of the *Alpine Journal* without feeling that the various writers gloried in the technique of their craft? Of course the skilful interpolation of "chief" gives an opening for much effective dialectic, but after all, what does it mean? How can a pleasure which is seated in health and jollity and the "spin of the blood" be measured and compared with a purely aesthetic feeling? It would appear difficult to argue that as a man cultivates and acquires muscular skill and knowledge of the mountains, he correspondingly dwarfs and impairs the aesthetic side of his nature. If so, we magnify the weak-kneed and the impotent, the lame, the halt, and the blind, and brand as false the Greek ideal of the perfect man. Doubtless a tendency in this direction may be detected in some modern thought, but, like much else similarly enshrined, it has no ring of true metal. Those who are so completely masters of their environment that they can laugh and rollick on the ridges, free from all constraint of ropes or fear of danger, are far more able to appreciate the glories of the "eternal hills" than those who can only move in constant terror of their lives, amidst the endless chatter and rank tobacco smoke of unwashed guides.

The fact that a man enjoys scrambling up a steep rock in no way makes him insensible of all that is beautiful in Nature. The two sets of feelings are indeed wholly unconnected. A man may love climbing and care naught for mountain scenery; he may love the scenery and hate climbing; or he may be equally devoted to both. The presumption obviously is that those who are most attracted by the mountains and most constantly return to their fastnesses, are those who to the fullest extent possess both these sources of enjoyment – those who can combine the fun and frolic of a splendid sport with that indefinable delight which is induced by the lovely form, tone and colouring of the great ranges.

I am free to confess that I myself should still climb, even though there were no scenery to look at, even if the only climbing attainable were the dark and gruesome pot-holes of the York-shire dales. On the other hand, I should still wander among the upper snows, lured by the silent mists and the red blaze of the setting sun, even though physical or other infirmity, even though in after aeons the sprouting of wings and other angelic appendages may have sunk all thought of climbing and cragsmanship in the whelming past.

It is frequently assumed, even by those who ought to know better, that if mountaineering involves danger of any sort, it should never be indulged in – at all events by such precious individuals as the members of the English Alpine

Club. Before considering this most pernicious doctrine, it is well to remember, that though the perils of mountaineering may not have been wholly dissipated into space by the lightning-like flashes of the Badminton and All England series, yet, nevertheless, these perils are not very great. With a single exception, the foregoing pages contain an account of every difficulty I have experienced which has seemed to render disaster a possible contingency. As my devotion to the sport began in 1871, and has continued with unabated vigour ever since, it will be evident that the climber's perils – in so far as a modest individual may regard himself as typical of the class – are extremely few and very rarely encountered. Such, however, as they have been, I would on no account have missed them. There is an educative and purifying power in danger that is to be found in no other school, and it is worth much for a man to know that he is not "clean gone to flesh pots and effeminacy". It may be admitted that the mountains occasionally push things a trifle too far, and bring before their votaries a vision of the imminence of dissolution that the hangman himself with all his paraphernalia of scaffold, gallows and drop could hardly hope to excel. But grim and hopeless as the cliffs may sometimes look when ebbing twilight is chased by shrieking wind and snow and the furies are in mad hunt along the ridges, there is ever the feeling that brave companions and a constant spirit will cut the gathering web of peril, *forsan et hæc olim meminisse juvabit.*

The sense of independence and self-confidence induced by the great precipices and vast silent fields of snow is something wholly delightful. Every step is health, fun and frolic. The troubles and cares of life, together with the essential vulgarity of a plutocratic society, are left far below – foul miasmas that cling to the lowest bottoms of reeking valleys. Above, in the clear air and searching sunlight, we are afoot with the quiet gods, and men can know each other and themselves for what they are. No feeling can be more glorious than advancing to attack some gaunt precipitous wall with "comrades staunch as the founders of our race". Nothing is more exhilarating than to know that the fingers of one hand can still be trusted with the lives of a party, and that the lower limbs are free from all trace of "knee-dissolving fear", even though the friction of one hobnail on an outward shelving ledge alone checks the hurtling of the body through thin air, and of the soul (let us hope) to the realms above.

I am of course aware that it is an age which cares little for the more manly virtues, and which looks askance at any form of sport that can, by any stretch of extremest imagination, be regarded as dangerous: yet since we cannot all, for most obvious reasons, take our delight "wallowing in slimy spawn of lucre", something may surely be urged in favour of a sport that teaches, as no other teaches, endurance and mutual trust, and forces men occasionally to look death in its grimmest aspect frankly and squarely in the face. For though mountaineering is not, perhaps, more dangerous than other sports, it undoubtedly brings home to the mind a more stimulating sense of peril; a sense, indeed, that is out of all proportion to the actual risk. It is, for instance, quite impossible to look down the tremendous precipices of the Little Dru without feeling in each individual nerve the utter disintegration of everything human which a fall must involve; and the contingency of such a fall is frequently brought before the mind – indeed, throughout the ascent, constant and strenuous efforts are needed to avoid it. The love of wager, our religious teachers notwithstanding, is still inherent in the race, and one cannot find a higher stake – at all events in these materialistic days, when Old Nick will no longer lay sterling coin against the gamester's soul – than the continuity of the cervical vertebrae; and this is the stake that the mountaineer habitually and constantly wagers. It is true the odds are all on his side, but the off-chance excites honesty of thought and tests how far decay has penetrated the inner fibre. That mountaineering has a high educational value, few, who have the requisite knowledge to form a fair judgment, would deny. That it has its evil side I frankly admit. None can look down its gloomy death-roll without feeling that our sport demands a fearful price.

Acknowledgments & Sources

The editor has made every effort to locate all persons having any rights in the selections appearing in this anthology and to secure permission from the holders of such rights. The editor apologises in advance for any errors or omissions inadvertently made. Queries regarding the use of material should be addressed to the editor c/o the publishers.

'Ladder Down the Sky' is an extract from *K2: The Savage Mountain* by Charles S Houston and Robert H Bates, McGraw-Hill Book Company, Inc., 1954. Copyright © 1954, 1979, 1997 by Charles S Houston and Robert Bates.

'The Upper Tower' by Peter Boardman is an extract from *The Boardman Tasker Omnibus* by Peter Boardman and Joe Tasker, Hodder & Stoughton, 1995. Extract copyright © Peter Boardman 1978. Reprinted by permission of Hodder Headline.

'The Death Zone' is an extract from *On the Heights*, Walter Bonatti, Rupert Hart-Davis, 1964.

'The Loneliest Place on Earth' by Hermann Buhl is an extract from *Nanga Parbat*, Karl M. Herrligkoffer, Elek Books, 1954.

'Act of Folly' is an extract from *Adventures of an Alpine Guide*, Christian Klucker, John Murray, 1932.

'The Air' is an extract from *Thin Air: Encounters in the Himalayas* by Greg Child, Patrick Stephens Ltd, 1988. Copyright © Greg Child 1988.

'The Climb' is an extract from *Total Alpinism* by Rene Desmaison, Granada Publishing, 1982. Copyright © 1973 Flammarion. Translation © 1982 Granada Publishing.

'The Gods Giveth, The Gods Take Away' is an extract from *Summits and Secrets* by Kurt Diemberger, George Allen & Unwin Ltd, 1971. English translation © 1971 George Allen & Unwin Ltd. Reprinted by permission of The Mountaineers, Seattle.

'Mirror, Mirror' by Ed Drummond is reprinted from *Ascent*, 1973. All rights reserved. Copyright © Ed Drummond and Sierra Club Books.

'The Void' is an extract from *The Untrodden Andes* by CG Egeler, Faber, 1955.

'White Spider' is an extract from *The White Spider* by Heinrich Harrer, Rupert Hart-Davis, 1959. Copyright © 1958 Ullstein AG Berlin. Translation copyright © 1959 Rupert Hart-Davis.

'Annapurna, Mon Amour' is an extract from *Annapurna* by Maurice Herzog, Jonathan Cape, 1952. Copyright © 1952, 1997 Maurice Herzog.

'The Long Grind' is an extract from *High Adventure* by Edmund Hillary, Hodder & Stoughton, 1957. Copyright © 1957 Edmund Hillary.

'The Ridge' is an extract from *Everest: The West Ridge*, Thomas F Hornbein, Sierra Club, 1965. Copyright © 1965, 1980 Thomas F Hornbein.

'The Devil's Thumb', is an extract from 'The Devil's Thumb', *Eiger Dreams: Ventures Among Men and Mountains* by Jon Krakauer, Dell Publishing, 1990. Copyright © 1990 Jon Krakauer.

'Avalanche' by George Leigh Mallory is an extract from *The Assault on Mount Everest* by Brigadier-General Hon. C.G. Bruce CB, MVO, and other members of the expedition, Edward Arnold, 1923.

'Above and Beyond' by Reinhold Messner is reprinted from *Mountain*, No 65, 1979. Copyright © 1979 Reinhold Messner.

'The Pleasures and Principles of Mountaineering' is an extract from *My Climbs in the Alps and Caucasus*, AF Mummery, Basil Blackwell, 1936.

'The Storm' is an extract from *Cho Oyu* by Herbert Tichy, Methuen, 1957.

'The Hard Way' by Doug Scott and Dougal Haston is an extract from *Everest – The Hard Way*, Chris Bonnington, Hodder & Stoughton, 1976, Copyright © 1975, British Everest Expedition.

'Attack on Kangchenjunga' is an extract from *The Kanchenjunga Adventure* by FS Smythe, Gollancz, 1930.

'King of the Equator' by Sebastian Snow is reprinted from *Explorers' and Travellers' Tales*, ed O. Tcherine, The Adventurers Club, 1963. Copyright © Sebastian Snow, 1958. Originally published as 'Kings of the Equator'.

'The Ascent of Nanda Devi' is an extract from *The Ascent of Nanda Devi* by HW Tilman, Cambridge University Press, 1937. Reprinted by permission of Bafon Wicks Publications, Joan A. Mullins and Pamela Davis.

'Aurora' by Jonathan Waterman is reprinted from *Ascent*, 1983.

'Triumph and Tragedy on The Matterhorn' is an extract from *The Ascent of the Matterhorn* by Edward Whymper, John Murray, 1880.

'Mischabel' is an extract from *On High Hills*, Geoffrey Winthrop Young, Methuen, 1927.